"Counsel's quick thinking on his feet,
the skilled probing for an opening,
the swift lethal thrust—
all this Nizer brings out
most effectively."

—John Barkham
Saturday Review Syndicate

"Go get it yourself and go sleepless a couple of nights!"

—Robert Travers
author of *Anatomy of Murder*

"Leaves the reader limp...
wonderfully gripping accounts
are both exciting and memorable.
They have heart as well as mind."

—Boston Herald

"Fascinating...Nizer is first-rate
in detailing courtroom drama...and
the four big cases he covers here
are fascinating."

—Roy Newquist
Chicago's American

THE JURY RETURNS
was originally published by Doubleday & Co., Inc.

Louis Nizer

THE JURY RETURNS

PUBLISHED BY POCKET BOOKS NEW YORK

THE JURY RETURNS

Doubleday edition published November, 1966

A *Pocket Book* edition
1st printing........February, 1968

This *Pocket Book* edition includes every word
contained in the original, higher-priced edition. It is printed
from brand-new plates made from completely reset, clear, easy-to-read
type. *Pocket Book* editions are published by Pocket Books, a division
of Simon & Schuster, Inc., 630 Fifth Avenue, New York, N.Y. 10020.
Trademarks registered in the United States and other countries.

L

Contents

TO DONALD

THE JURY
RETURNS

Chapter One

PAUL CRUMP

PART ONE: MURDER

Paul Crump was the youngest man ever to be placed in a solitary death cell in Cook County Jail, Illinois. The trail which led him there began almost at birth.

He was one of 13 children born to Byron and Leona Crump, who married in Alabama in 1910. Only seven children survived. His brother "B.J." was shot and killed when he was twenty-five years old. Another brother Maurice died of tuberculosis in 1935; a sister Shelly died in the influenza epidemic of 1919 (another sister, Surelia, suffers from tuberculosis); Guy was killed in France in 1944. Winifred died of measles and pneumonia when four months old. Raymond died of pneumonia when he was three years old. His brother, John, is an inmate of the Illinois State Penitentiary at Joliet.

When Paul Crump was five years old, his father (a coal worker and storefront minister belonging to no denomination) deserted the family in Chicago and returned to Jasper, Alabama. He went on to Gary, Indiana, but never rejoined his family or sent any financial support. Paul's intense love for his father was transferred to his mother, but he continued for a while to wear a silver earring inset with a zircon, in his right ear lobe, which his father had placed there at birth. It reminded him, he once said, to hate his father for abandoning their family.

The mother, Lonie Crump, worked as a maid by day and laundress at night, to support her brood. When Paul was ten he was arrested for stealing a bicycle. The next year he was sent to live with his maternal aunt in Guin, Alabama. After ten months he returned. In his own words, "When I was twelve, I lay under prostitutes' beds, clippin' wallets from their customers." When he was thirteen, he ran away from home and hitchhiked to Michigan, Wisconsin, and Ohio. At the age of fourteen he was sent to live with a relative in Augusta, Kansas.

Nevertheless, Paul managed in the meantime to "finish" Schoop Elementary School in Chicago. He participated in wrestling, swimming, and basketball. From the age of fifteen he worked, first as a dock hand at Cartage Company, then as a press operator at Ingalls Steel Mills.

He developed well physically and this only added to his problems. Sloping shoulders and lithe muscles, the mark of hitting power, were responsible for his prowess with his fists, as we shall see later. He might have vented his anger with life in the prize ring and perhaps become a middleweight champion; or, in view of his intelligence and qualities of leadership, he might have risen to achievement in worthier enterprises. Resentment often drives a man to superiority, but there is no precise way of determining why the road for some is for good and others for evil.

At the age of thirteen Paul took the next step from bicycle theft. He stole a car. He did not need it in the Southwest Side Area of Morgan Park where he lived and where there were still lumpy dirt roads, cobble-stoned streets, and weed-strewn lots. He was restlessly reaching out but not for a career of character.

By the time he was sixteen his rebellion against society was full-fledged. He had obtained an Army .45 revolver. With four others, at two-thirty in the morning of November 14, 1946, he drove a Ford car alongside one Fred Koch standing at 75th Street, Chicago. One of the men pointed a gun out of the rear window and took from Koch $8.00 in cash and his watch valued at $57. They then drove to 90th Street and held up Gregory Duerr, forcing him to surrender his wallet, his ring, and his watch for a total value of $126.00. At 3:45 A.M. they pointed a gun out of the front window at John J. Turchan, and took his wallet which had $2.00 and a check for $36.18 made by the Pullman Company. They also took Turchan's hat, valued at $5.00. Turchan later testified that while he was being searched by one of the boys the others in the car urged the holder of the gun, Edwards, to shoot his victim.

After another such foray, yielding no greater haul, the bandits parked the car and started home. Two officers on duty saw Crump and one of his associates, Delaney, walking at 4:55 A.M. Crump was wearing a hat but carrying the stolen one in his hand (another hat was to play a more decisive role in his life years later). They stopped them for questioning. Delaney had a knife. "Crump went for his gun in his belt, and we took from him a loaded Army .45."

Even though Crump was only sixteen years old, the fact that he was armed with a gun removed him from the shelter of the Juvenile Court. He was indicted, convicted, and sentenced to three concurrent terms of three to six years in the Illinois State Penitentiary at Pontiac.

We segregate criminals from society to protect the innocent, but we have not learned how to segregate the newly initiated criminals from the hardened criminals within prison walls. Youngsters are thrown into a postgraduate school of crime. They associate with experienced criminals whose regret is only that they are confined, and whose dream is freedom to prey again on the society which has punished them. The standard of conduct is depravity, from homosexuality to hatred of laws and their enforcers. Crump received his indoctrination in a career of crime from the hardened inmates of the Illinois State Penitentiary. There was one kind of segregation which was bestowed upon Crump in jail—the wrong kind. He was separated from the white men. This racial injustice, even among criminals, inflamed his mind against society. His target for vengeance became larger and clearer.

By the time Crump emerged from the penitentiary he had grown to full manhood physically. His broad shoulders, blacksmith's forearms, and trim waist made him appear shorter than his five feet ten. But power was evident in every movement. He had a high forehead worthy of better plans than he was making. He sported a thin mustache over a thick upper lip and at times a goatee, which accentuated the dazzling white of his teeth when he smiled. Sometimes he affected a bandana, pirate style. His eyes were fierce brown softened by a liquid quality which made his face seem more handsome than it was. His sullenness combined with strength and recklessness had a special appeal for girls. He was not unresponsive. He needed money and his deformed standards left no doubt about the right way to get it.

In May 1952 he and three others broke into a home and stole a shotgun worth twenty dollars. They were apprehended and indicted for burglary and larceny. He was released on bond and returned to Chicago, but he was never brought to trial on this charge because, within a month, he was indicted for the crime of murder.

After Crump left the penitentiary, he found it more difficult to obtain work under his right name. The fact that a man has "paid his debt to society" by serving a jail term does not mean that the defects in his character have been removed. It would be otherwise if we could believe that he had been reformed. It is not punishment but rehabilitation which gives society security against the criminal. Destiny had decreed that Paul Crump, a most unlikely subject, should be the instrumentality through which an attempted breakthrough of penology should be made. This recital in depth is necessary in order that the profound issue involved may be later fully understood.

Whether it served his purposes in getting temporary employment, or whether he had a penchant for aliases, which persons of questionable activities usually have (as if they would shed their past by adopting another name), Crump occasionally used the name Byron Fox. After a number of jobs of short duration, he obtained work under that name at Libby, McNeill & Libby in Chicago. At first he trucked potatoes from the preparation department to the cooler. Then he asked to be transferred to the night shift, where he operated a food homogenizing machine. Again his stay was short-lived. He got off on a "medical" but didn't send in his medical report, and so he was let out.

He had observed, however, that every Friday morning, precisely at five minutes after eleven, the paymasters came through a certain passage with a black satchel and green box. The designing mind finds temptation of which the innocent one is not even aware.

According to a confession later signed by Crump and his confederates (and which they vehemently repudiated), he needed money to "beat the rap" of the indictment outstanding against him.

One night at a bar Crump outlined a plan to his friend, Eugene Taylor, who was his age, twenty-two, to seize the payroll of Libby, McNeill & Libby. Taylor's brother Dave had been working at that plant for seven years and was still there. Since Crump had been fired five months before, Dave Taylor could augment his past knowledge with current information on the movements of the money carriers and the guards. Taylor eagerly joined in the venture. He thought "it was a cinch. He could stay in the building two or three days without being found."

Crump then approached Hudson Tillman, whom he had known since childhood. Tillman had a .32 gun though he was only nineteen years old. Crump asked him if he wanted "to make some money, about fifteen thousand dollars." Tillman was to provide his father's automobile and act as driver.

More guns were needed. They sought out Harold Riggins, who supplied two .38 pistols and a shotgun which he had stolen by breaking "into some place at Kankakee." Riggins was to receive five hundred dollars for his contribution to the arsenal.

The rifle's length made it too conspicuous. They bought two hacksaw blades in the local hardware store, put rags on the ends, and Crump patiently cut off the barrel so that it became a sawed-off shotgun. However, as in the stockyards, no by-product was to be wasted. The severed barrel was a potent weapon too. They would wrap black tape around the cut off pipe so that it could be used as an iron club.

No detail was too small in their preparation. They bought 3-In-One Oil and wiped the fingerprints off the guns with cloth. They "alled" ("when I say alled I mean o-i-l-e-d") the pistols.

Crump bought dark blue cloth for face masks. He and Gene Taylor cut eye slits into the masks and carefully sewed the openings. Crump also bought several pairs of rubber gloves at Walgreen's Drug Store. One set was red and he wore them himself. While such gloves were used by workers at the Libby plant, could his attraction to the bright color have been an unconscious desire to stand out even in the very effort at disguise?

They planned to wear ordinary fedora hats, to hold the

masks in place, and the entire ensemble left not an inch of skin exposed, so that no one could even give the generic description that the robbers were Negroes or white men.

They bought appropriate-sized bullets and shells for each of the guns. At the last moment they added another automobile for get-away purposes. This was Hal Riggins' Buick. In addition to supplying guns, he was to act as the driver of the second car.

One of the cars, the Buick, was to be stationed across the tracks from the stockyard. The red Oldsmobile was to be in the yard itself and would carry the fleeing bandits with their loot to the car across the tracks. They would transfer to the parked car and drive off, thus creating a decoy car for any possible identifier.

Now preparation and plan were complete. The next day would be payroll day, Friday, March 20, 1953.

At eight o'clock in the morning Hudson Tillman arrived in a tomato red Oldsmobile with white wall tires at David Taylor's home. They rode to Eugene Taylor's home, picked him up, and returned to await Paul Crump and Hal Riggins, who arrived in a blue, cream-topped Buick.

All the guns, masks, and rubber gloves had been hidden in an ordinary shopping bag in David Taylor's home. He went upstairs "to sneak the bag by my wife, while she was in bed. I know if she saw the bag, what she would say." Then they drove off in two cars to the Libby yards, to keep a rendezvous with a payroll.

Despite the meticulous planning, unforeseen contingencies arose from the very first moment. Riggins' car was to park within the yards next to the exit from which they were to emerge after the robbery. But that day a welder, Steven Tess, had been hired to repair a fire escape on the building. A fireman, Joseph Taunke, had been assigned to that spot to see that the sparks did not set fire to the small trucks, laden with food which came to the Libby yards. When Riggins attempted to park his auto there, the welder and fireman waved him away because it was a dangerous area. Riggins pretended that his car was stalled, and lifted the hood several times, to give veracity to his plight and gain permission to remain there. All he got for his pains was to be identified by these two witnesses, who got a good look at him. He had to move to 50th and Ashland across the tracks, and some distance from the building. Now Riggins and Tillman were both parked out of immediate range.

Nevertheless Crump and both Taylors entered the rear door of the building, as if they were employees; they proceeded up the stairs to the fifth floor, and entered the cooler room, which because of its forty-four-degree temperature was isolated. It had a door leading to a staircase where the payroll executives and guard would pass at about five minutes after eleven.

In the safety of the cooler room, the three donned their hooded masks and rubber gloves. Dave Taylor took the sawed-off shotgun, Gene Taylor a .38 pistol, and Paul Crump a .32 pistol and also the taped-up barrel. They were ready but nothing happened: "We waited and waited and waited."

Suddenly a man and woman entered the cooler. They were Gerhard Henriksen, a custodian who had gone to Building F to check some records in the vault, and Marie Zutko, a file clerk. On their way back to the office in Building E, they took the shortcut through the cooler. They were startled by two figures with hoods over their faces, and guns in their hands. One of them said, "Stick 'em up, make no noise or I'll kill you." They raised their arms. "Turn around and walk over to the wall." They were told to get on their knees, hands held high.

Crump had acted decisively in this unexpected crisis, but the moment the couple entered the room, Dave Taylor, according to his confession, said: "I broke and ran, see what I mean?"

Richard B. Austin, First Assistant State's Attorney of Cook County, then asked:

Q. Why did you break and run?

A. Inferiority complex.

To what strange uses Freud's theories have been put, even by illiterates! With a gun in his hand, he had fled from two defenseless employees, but his synonym for cowardice was psychiatric jargon. He returned to find "the intruders" facing the wall on their knees, and recovered his confidence.

There was quiet for a while and then Dave Taylor asked, "What time is it?" Crump answered, "11:02, it won't be long now." Another long silence. Then a number of men were heard approaching. They were Charles Baker, Assistant in

Personnel for Libby, McNeill & Libby, for which he had worked thirty-one years. Baker was carrying a black leather bag containing $17,000.00 in bills and $168.00 in silver. He was on his way to the plant cafeteria, where, as was the custom on payday, they cashed paychecks for employees.

Behind him was Martin Carlson, an employee for forty-one years, and Treasurer of the Libby Employees Credit Union. He had a green tin box, containing $3,150.33 belonging to the Employees Union.

Accompanying them was Theodore Rusch, a plant guard, dressed in blue uniform, with brass buttons, a silver star over his left breast, and insignia on his left arm representing Red Cross, First Aid. He had been on Libby's private police force for twenty-five years.

As these three passed the cooler door, Crump threw it open. He smashed Rusch's head above the left ear with the taped barrel, and yelled, "Give me your gun." Before he could comply, Crump brought the iron pipe down on his head again, and dragged him into the cooler. He forced him to his knees next to Henriksen and Miss Zutko. He kept demanding, "Give me your gun." Rusch said, "Don't shoot. Here, take the damn thing." Crump finally took it, a .38 Special Coating loaded with six bullets. Now Crump had Rusch's .38 in one hand, his own .32 in the other, and the taped "club" under his arm.

In the meantime, Dave Taylor had performed his function as planned. The guard having been removed from the scene, he stepped boldly out of the shadows, pointing his sawed-off shotgun at Baker, and demanding the black money bag. It was surrendered to him at once. Gene Taylor confronted Carlson with a pistol and a demand for the green box. He got it. Dave Taylor turned and fled. Crump then appeared at the top of the stairs and ordered Baker and Carlson into the cooler. They were placed on their knees, facing the wall alongside the others.

Now there was quite a collection of hostages: Henriksen, Miss Zutko, Rusch, Baker, and Carlson, all kneeling and facing the wall. Fearing that they might sound an alarm too soon, Crump decided to knock them all unconscious.

Miss Zutko was resting her hands over her head. He smashed her knuckles with a blow of the taped barrel, and then struck her head. She toppled over. Next to her was

Henriksen. He brought the pipe down on his head and he fell over. Before losing consciousness he felt blood running down his face.

Baker was next in line. At the trial he testified:

"I could hear him strike the people who were kneeling on my left, and hear bodies falling over. I was struck at my turn across the back of the scalp. I blacked out and fell over on my right side. I could hear him still striking people and I threw my arm up involuntarily to protect my head and the second time I was struck across the wrist."

Carlson glanced sideways and saw Baker hit twice. Then, as he waited in helplessness and terror, the blow fell on the top and back of his head. "I could feel the blood run down the back of my neck." Then he was unconscious.

Rusch, the guard, had already been struck twice. Now he saw the other victims lying in grotesque positions on the floor, and he knew he was to be disposed of next. He placed his arms over his head to protect his scalp. The blows descended on his hands, and then his head, and their force was so great they slipped off the top of his head and "struck me on the eye."

Crump, having concluded his task with methodical callousness, turned to run out the specified exit to join the Taylors, who he expected were waiting in Tillman's car.

At this moment, the most unexpected incident of all occurred. An office worker, Walter Schilbe, had walked through the vestibule a few moments before and thought he saw two men with "black shawls around their heads" in the cooler room. He was unobserved. Like the fishing trawler which accidentally came across the Dieppe invading fleet and sounded the alarm, which turned that surprise raid into a disaster, he reported what he saw to the Personnel Manager, Harry Larson. Larson went to investigate this unlikely story. "Looking around the edge of one door, I noted in front of me a dark silhouette. He had a hat on and some kind of hood on his face and head." He dashed down the steps in such haste that "I stumbled, cutting my lip." He actually passed Eugene Taylor, who demanded that he stop. He was literally flying with fear, and his terror made him twice as fast as his pursuers. Taylor stumbled, and his gun accidentally went off, hitting a blank wall. The shot alarmed everybody. Larson fled through a door and ran into Theodore (Ted) Zukowski, chief of the Libby plant guards, who was making his customary rounds from the men's dressing room through the various buildings. Larson's panic was message enough. Zukowski headed straight up the stairs.

So it was that as Crump emerged from his brutal disposition of his prisoners in the cooler room, he was confronted by the two-hundred-pound Chief Guard Theodore Zukowski, who had not been counted among the obstacles to be overcome.

Crump recognized "Ted," whom he had known when he worked at the plant. Furthermore, the uniform of authority and the gleaming star on his chest were warning enough.

He met the charging Zukowski with a shot from his .32 which hit Zukowski in the chest, passed through his right lung, and came out of his back. As the guard lurched forward, Crump blazed away with the .38 in his other hand. One bullet penetrated Zukowski's right ear through the temple bone and skull and lodged in the brain. The second bullet hit him in the nose and penetrated the base of the brain. Before the sharp cracks of the shots were ended, Zukowski fell dead on his back. The only movement was a flood of blood from his ear which formed a circle, as if his head cast a dark red shadow.

Crump stood frozen for a brief moment, as if death had enveloped him too in immobility. Then panic stirred him to violent flight. He threw off his dark blue mask and with it his gray fedora hat, and bounded down the stairs. He came out of another exit door than planned, and sped across the yard toward the tracks, where Hudson Tillman or Hal Riggins should have been waiting in a car.

He soon realized that his hysterical speed registered desperation and that he was being observed. He summoned all his force to slow down and achieve some semblance of casualness.

Like a walker in a race, whose eagerness violates the heel and toe touch, he ran, though he strove to walk. In tearing off his hood, he had pushed his hair straight up in the air. It looked as if fright might have made it stand on end. He had a goatee which did not aid his need to be inconspicuous. Also he was barely conscious of the fact that he was tearing at his rubber gloves in an effort to get them off his hands.

Their bright red color, plus his frantic motion in removing them, attracted attention as if they were a flag.

Three women, Mrs. Estelle Ballik, Miss Margaret Morrisey, and Miss Ann Civetko, were walking across the yard at that time. They worked at Swift & Company, and were on their way to lunch at Libby, McNeill & Libby at about 11:10 A.M. (their day having begun at 7:30 A.M.). Each saw Crump distinctly. He almost collided with them. Their attention was drawn to him because "First his hair was standing up, and he had on red rubber gloves, and he was walking like, as though he were dazed. I don't know how to express that." They described his clothes, a blue topcoat, dark blue pants, and blue suede shoes, but above all, those incongruous red rubber gloves. They saw him tear one of the gloves to shreds in an effort to remove it, and then throw both gloves under a boxcar.

When Crump got to 50th and Ashland, neither Tillman nor Riggins was there to pick him up. They had left, because they could not understand "Paul's delay," and they reasoned that the imminent and inevitable alarm would bring a horde of policemen. They were not going to be found sitting there alongside the incriminating black satchel filled with money.

Finding himself isolated, Crump decided to take a taxi to Dave Taylor's home. To his dismay and despite his thorough preparation, he had not one cent on his person. He did not even have the twenty cents necessary to take a streetcar. He accosted a stranger and begged him for twenty cents. He got a dime. The donor might have complied with the request, had he known that the beggar had only a few moments before engaged in one of the most daring robberies in Chicago's history, and had left behind him one man dead and a number of others slugged unconscious. Crump begged again and again and finally got his second dime. He went straight to David Taylor's home.

In the meantime, what had happened to Eugene Taylor? After he snatched the green tin box from Carlson, he ran to the cooler to join Crump and his brother. Dave had already fled with the black satchel. Suddenly, someone (it was Larson) passed him on the steps. He yelled at him to stop, but he turned the corner and up a short flight and disappeared through a door. Gene Taylor pursued him, stumbled clumsily, and his gun went off. The noise alarmed him more than anyone else. In his confession, he said:

"I ran all the way downstairs, put my gun in my pocket, taken off my mask at the same time. I still had my gloves on. I ran in one room and there was nothing but cases in there and I hollered, David, not too loud. I didn't want anybody to hear me holler the name. There was no David. I ran out of that room. I was trying to get my gloves off. I ran into two fellows and I tried to hide the tin box behind me. I asked them, how do you get out of here, just like that, and so he said, go straight through there, and that is how I got out of the plant."

Despite all the planning, Eugene Taylor had sounded an alarm by accidentally firing his gun, and then didn't even know how to get out of the building without asking advice from two potential witnesses.

Of course he exited through a wrong door. However, a green panel truck was parked there. The key was obligingly in it. He threw his tin box on the seat and drove off, careening wildly. He headed for 74th and Wabash, because he "knew a girl there." She was Lorraine Yarbro. Though he had been seeing her once a week, she denied that "we were sweethearts." Gene's regular employment was that of a conductor on a streetcar (C.T.A.), and he told her the tin box contained change collected by him, and that he had lost the key. He asked for a hammer, and with it he smashed the lock open. He asked for her father's coat, and when he took off his own, she found it heavy and discovered a pistol in it. It also had extra bullets in the pocket. At his request, she placed the money, gun, and bullets in her own brown box for safekeeping.

He didn't know how much money was turned over: "I started to count it, but I was so nervous and I wanted to get back to see what happened to my brother; I didn't know whether he got back."

He ordered a liveried service Cadillac to take him to his brother's house. David was not there. Gene put on his C.T.A. uniform and waited. David had been there but was still in the grip of the momentum of the morning:

"I took a walk on the street. I went over to my sister's house and she said, 'What's the matter with you, you are nervous'; she said my left eye had been jumping all day. She is pregnant, you know what I mean. I didn't want to upset her. She said, 'You didn't work today, you are still sick.' I said, 'Yes.' Later on I came back home. I came around the side, come up the back steps and he was there with his C.T.A. uniform on and I thought he was a policeman and I started to run and then he said, 'What is the matter with you?' I said, 'Man, I didn't know it was you. I didn't even know you got away.' So I grabbed my brother and hugged him."

They exchanged information of their escape from the hold-up scene. Then they rode together in the Cadillac, which had waited, to Lorraine's house. She told them that she had heard on the radio of a robbery at the stockyards and that a man had been killed. "We were just stunned, and I told David, you couldn't have done it, and I couldn't have done it."

Now the need for precaution had become more intense. They cut up Eugene's plaid, hunter's-type jacket, which he had worn that morning, poured lighter fluid on it, and burned it. The zipper, which remained like a guilty skeleton, was put in a garbage can.

But their loyalty to their comrades did not increase in the face of increased danger. They decided to keep the loot in the tin box for themselves.

EUGENE TAYLOR: Me and my brother and Lorraine are the only souls that knew about it, about that money.

Q. That is you weren't going to cut anybody in on that?

DAVID TAYLOR: Nobody on that but us.

EUGENE TAYLOR: We weren't going to cut them in on it. I probably would have given Crump something out of it, but we didn't tell them we had it.

Crump, who had conceived and led the expedition, and who had assigned to himself the doughty role of disarming the guard, and who had killed to protect the mission, while the Taylors simply snatched the money, was to be deprived of even his aliquot share of the loot.

Before David met his brother, he, Hal Riggins, and Hudson Tillman had fled the scene of the robbery in their two cars without waiting for Crump or Gene Taylor. They gathered in David Taylor's living room, sat on the floor, and turned the black satchel "upside down." $17,236.00 fell out in separate wrappers, each of which contained one thousand dollars in twenty-dollar bills, or one hundred dollars in one-dollar bills, and three hundred dollars in change, half dollars, quarters, and dimes.

Hal Riggins said, "Come on, let's divide up this money, I am not going to wait for Paul and Eugene. I am going to get out of town."

Hudson Tillman said, "Me, too, give me my money."

In the absence of Crump, David Taylor, his inferiority complex soothed by the fortune strewn at his feet, took charge.

He gave Hal Riggins five thousand dollars, to be divided with Hudson Tillman. Riggins gave Tillman one thousand dollars, keeping four thousand for himself. Taylor, in a gesture of equity, gave Tillman an additional five hundred dollars from the general pile and the "small" change to Riggins. They left immediately in the Buick parked a half-block away.

Dave Taylor kept the remaining sum of about $11,700 to be divided in three equal parts among Crump, Gene Taylor, and himself. He placed the money in a paper bag and hid it temporarily in the basement "behind the furnace."

Then he changed his suit, and burned the clothes he had worn during the robbery. He had "taken a walk" and returned to find a man in uniform, which turned out to be the harmless C.T.A. attire of his brother.

After an affectionate reunion, they went to Lorraine's house, but were startled to find a crowd a half-block away and police swarming over the place. The green truck which he had stolen at the stockyard and parked near his girl's house had been found. The police did not know that in the crowd were two anxious onlookers who were the men they were seeking. The Taylors dashed home, and by this time Paul Crump had arrived by streetcar.

There was no joyous reunion with him. Recrimination rather than honor is the rule among thieves. They demanded to know why he had turned the "cinch" robbery into a murder case.

DAVE TAYLOR: I said, Paul, I said, why did you do that? I said, when I heard the news on the radio I was shocked. That is what I told him. He told me like this, he said, Dave, I had to do it. He said, Dave, I tried to avoid it but I had to do it . . . it was either me or him.

So I asked him what happened. He said he told Ted to back up and Ted grabbed him and said, "Give me that gun." Then Paul said he tried to take his mask off at the same time and Paul said, "Turn me loose." That is when he shot him with the .32.

And the .32 didn't do him no good, he still tried to take the mask off, Paul said, "Turn me loose, turn me loose." And Ted said, "Give me that gun," and then he shot him again, that is when he shot him again.

Q. With the .38?

A. Yes . . . He shot him twice and he ran down and he threw his mask away.

Q. Now at this point Gene indicates he wants to say something, is that right?

EUGENE TAYLOR: No, I want some water, that's all.

This was Crump's description of the killing as related by Dave Taylor in his confession. But Crump had signed it too in these fatal words, "As far as this statement relates to me it's true. Paul Crump."

They all contended that these confessions were false and extracted by inhuman cruelty. This issue of duress resulted in a trial within a trial.

However, the confessions supplied clues to objective evidence, which gave the prosecutor an enormous advantage.

After their greetings and regretful description of how the unplanned events had overwhelmed the planned ones, Dave Taylor reported to Crump that he had given fifty-five hundred dollars to Riggins and Tillman. He advised him that Crump's share of the remaining twelve thousand dollars (in round figures) was four thousand dollars (not revealing to him the sum of thirty-nine hundred dollars in the tin box). Crump was surprised that the haul was so small. Actually he did not receive even this sum. That night Taylor took the money from behind the furnace and brought it to his mother-in-law, Mildred Malushame, who in turn delivered the money for safekeeping to her relatives in Birmingham, Alabama.

Before the money was thus hidden, Dave Taylor related:

"Paul got two hundred dollars that night because he wanted to buy some shoes and he wanted to buy his wife some clothes, something like that and I spent a few dollars myself and I gave my mother-in-law one hundred and fifty dollars."

Dave "used up about seven or eight hundred dollars" that day.

Thieves usually strive mightily to dispose of the weapons,

burn their clothes, and destroy all possible clues. Most frustrating, however, is the fact that the very prize for which all was risked, the money, cannot be used. The money is the "hottest" clue of all, and yet it cannot be destroyed. It is too dangerous to keep or use, and difficult to hide. Crump was reduced to begging for carfare to get home from the robbery. He was not much better off when the money was available to him.

Out of the two hundred dollars he received, he bought a pair of shoes and a hat. This was the only tangible profit he ever derived from the entire venture. He could have been an appropriate lecturer on the time-worn subject, "Crime doesn't pay."

But his responsibilities to the venture continued, even though only hazards and not rewards were in the offing. The red Oldsmobile was still on the block, and the sawed-off shotgun was in it. The car was locked. Tillman had ridden off with Riggins in his Buick, and had taken the keys with him.

Crump hailed a cab and went looking for Tillman in the parks. He could not find him. He returned in the grip of new desperation. He told Dave Taylor that under no circumstances could they permit the shotgun to remain in the car. For that matter, the car itself would have to be moved. He anticipated that its owner (it turned out to be Theodis Williams), from whom Tillman had borrowed it, would report it as stolen.

At great risk they approached the Oldsmobile, smashed the window, opened the door, and removed the gun. Then Gene borrowed his brother-in-law's auto and used it to push the Oldsmobile "around on Bowers Avenue up in the alley and parked it in some sandlot . . . it was dark during the time that we taken the car around there." Thus within eight hours after the robbery, the bandits had to break into their own getaway vehicle to retrieve their own incriminating gun. How ironic it would have been had they been caught under these circumstances. But a worse fate awaited them.

Crump, carrying the retrieved shotgun in a paper bag, went to a hardware store, and bought a saw and a frame to go with it. He and Gene Taylor sawed the shotgun to bits, and drove toward Jackson Park. Every other block Crump "would throw a piece out of the car." When they got to the lake at 63rd, they stopped "by a little lagoon . . . you can walk out on a little ramp like, it is just in the middle of the water, practically, and that is where Crump threw the shell parts of the gun."

David Taylor was working just as assiduously to dispose of the other weapons. He took the .32 and .38 (with which Crump had blazed away at Zukowski) to the lake at 43rd and threw them and the bullets and cartridges which he emptied from them "right under the bridge."

By ten o'clock that Friday evening they had destroyed the incriminating evidence, hidden the money, and "corrected" the errors which had been committed in the hectic rush of events. It had been a long day, having started at eight in the morning when they gathered for the mission. A killing, many bloodlettings, and numerous unexpected events had intervened. They must have been physically exhausted, and even more spent emotionally.

One other precaution, however, had to be taken. They had to find Tillman. He was only nineteen years old. He was also a drug addict and therefore unpredictable as well as irresponsible. They better take him in hand.

So they went to Tillman's home. A remarkable reception awaited them there.

Hudson Tillman had borrowed the tomato red Oldsmobile from Theodis Williams. It was to be returned Friday afternoon, by which time the job at Libby, McNeill & Libby would have been finished. Williams had been offered fifteen hundred dollars for the use of the car, though he ultimately received nothing. When the car was not delivered to him, he called Tillman. His mother answered and suggested he come over to talk to her. She advised him to report the car stolen. He so informed the police, giving them the car number 960-880. The description of the car and its vivid color matched that of several witnesses at the stockyards. A little more pressure on Williams and they had Hudson Tillman's name and address. They dashed to his house, but he and Riggins were in another state by then. The police were instructed by headquarters to occupy the apartment in force and in silence, and arrest anyone who entered.

Unaware of these circumstances, Crump and Gene Taylor approached Tillman's home in a final precautionary measure.

Crump later testified:

"We knocked on his door and someone seemed to have difficulty opening the door. I asked if Hudson was there, but got no answer. I walked down to the bottom step, believing no one to be home. When I turned around the door was opened and a blind flash and I heard a series of shots as I hit the ground and someone jumped over me and snatched me by the collar and lifted me bodily and dragged me across the street a distance of about a hundred yards. . . .

"My tie was taken off and my hands tied behind my back. I was taken back to Tillman's house. His sister about nineteen, a younger sister and a boy ten or twelve years old were all hysterical and she was hollering, 'Oh lieutenant.'

"The house was full with police with guns drawn. One was in the kitchen, two in the dining room and one sitting in the back part of the house. I was shoved and lay on the floor. A girl asked the officer if she could put a pillow or something under my head and he said I didn't need a pillow.

"They asked me who my buddy was and I told them Eugene Taylor. Then Eugene Taylor was brought into the dining room with his hands behind his back. . . . There were about eight officers there. One of them made a telephone call and said he got two fellows, what should they do with them. One asked me my name. . . .

"I gave him my name and he asked Eugene his name and then I asked him, 'Would you kindly tell me what I am being treated this way for.' He said, 'We don't know, kid, we were just told to come here and to wait and apprehend anybody that comes to this house.'

"And so I said I hadn't done anything and I wanted to get in contact with my mother to let her know."

Actually the police had no idea who their captives were, or whether they had any connection with the crime. They merely went on the assumption that under the prevailing circumstances, any friend of Tillman's was an enemy of theirs.

The neckties which bound Crump's and Taylor's hands behind their backs were removed in favor of handcuffs. They were taken to the 18th District Station.

At both his trials Crump testified to instances of police brutality, but his testimony failed to convince either judge or jury. In addition this contention was rejected in both of his appeals to the Supreme Court of Illinois.

According to Crump's testimony, plainclothes detectives entered their cell at midnight and ordered them to strip and stand "spread eagle like" on the bench. Every stitch of their clothes was inventoried and they were asked what articles were new and were paid for in cash. Crump's new shoes, purchased that day, came in for unusual attention. His tiepin and cuff links had to be explained. "I was told I must be a black millionaire in order to afford such expensive clothing."

Eugene Taylor had to provide information of the place and time he had purchased his ring, watch, and other possessions. Both denied with open-eyed innocence that they had used the robbery money to buy things, or that they knew anything about it.

Crump continued that later that night a policeman came to Crump's cell with "a blue-gray short-haired beaver hat." He "crushed it on my head." When Crump said he had never seen it before, the policeman did not believe him and "I became mad and tusseled with him. The turnkey grabbed me and pinned my arms. He asked me if I had a [criminal] record, I told him yes and he said I was a good suspect." Crump was also shown a "piece of pipe taped up, and when I said I never saw it before, he called me a lying dog." Later a representative of Libby, McNeill & Libby asked him whether he knew anything about the robbery or murder and he denied any knowledge of it.

After midnight, the light in Crump's cell went out. He testified that he was lying "on a piece of steel they have there," when three men entered in the darkness. They questioned him and when he said he was not anywhere near Libby's that morning when the robbery took place, "one of them took a swing at me and knocked me off the bench. I didn't give him any cause. I screamed and the other officer grabbed me. The lockup man told them that was enough. The captain might hear them."

But the next day, Crump and Gene Taylor, according to their testimony, were taken "to 11th Street," and after fingerprinting, each was placed in a cell, his hands cuffed behind his back.

Then the lights went out again, and some men, silhouetted beyond recognition in the darkness, entered. Crump testified that they blindfolded him, and led him away, turning him in circles to be unaware of his destination, and that his handcuffs were removed "and a strap was placed on my wrist to the elbow and cord tightened to point where circulation was cut off, behind me." He was taken to another room and told he would be made to talk and confess to the Libby robbery.

When he protested his innocence, he was, so he stated, lifted bodily from the floor, "with just my toes touching the floor, my hands up behind my back affixed to something. . . . After fifteen or twenty minutes my arms started getting dead and I asked them to cut me down. They said I would hang until I told them where the money was.

". . . Well, I took it until all my shoulders, the back of my neck was becoming numb. All feeling was leaving the upper part of my body. And I fainted."

When he regained consciousness, he was asked whether he was ready to talk. He testified that a policeman entered and demanded to know where Hudson Tillman was. Crump asserted that when he said that he did not know, he was hung again on his arms.

Crump remained steadfast in his assertions that he had no knowledge whatsoever of the Libby, McNeill & Libby robbery and murder.

The police had no evidence against either Crump or Taylor. Even the police were convinced by the suspects' sincere denials, and their inability to supply facts, which had they been involved in the crime should have poured out of them in the painful prodding to which they were subjected. Also, no money or other objective evidence could be found.

Mrs. Leona Crump had retained a lawyer, William P. Gerber, to discover what had happened to her son Paul, who had been swallowed up in the Police Department for forty-eight hours. Gerber demanded of the police, "If you have anything against Paul Crump, I want you to book him or charge him with a crime; or if you haven't got anything against him, I want him released."

The policeman replied, "I haven't got anything against him and he can go."

At ten twenty-five Monday morning, March 23, Crump and Eugene Taylor were released and went home. They had weathered the storm, and had every reason to believe the crisis had passed.

Due to the hue and cry in the community, the radio blaring spot announcements of the murder of Zukowski, and of the hospital reports of the five slugged employees, an exhaustive search for clues and witnesses had been made. Nothing had been found. The intense if not furious questioning by the police had not extracted a single admission. For the first time since the lurid occurrences at the Libby plant seventy-two hours earlier, the suspects breathed easier. In a certain sense Crump was more secure than if he had not been arrested at all. While he had suffered, he had learned that no incriminating evidence existed. The police had shown their fist, but their hand was empty.

However, within seventeen hours the heaviest blow of all fell upon Crump and his associates.

After Hudson Tillman and Hal Riggins had been handed their shares of the neatly packaged money which poured out of the black satchel, they rose from their squat positions on David Taylor's living room floor and took off. They had no concern for what had happened to Paul Crump or Eugene Taylor. As far as they were concerned, the camaraderie of joint adventure had been severed the moment the prize was in hand.

In Riggins' blue Buick they headed toward Kankakee. Tillman was more jittery than even the nerve-scraping events of the day justified. He insisted that they stop at the town of Robbins, Illinois. There Tillman directed Riggins to a certain house. He jumped out and disappeared in it for about "five or ten minutes." As Riggins later testified:

"He came out, entered the car and I sat and looked over and noticed him and he was pale, his face was pale, and he did not say nothing. He was talking foolish. I couldn't understand him, so I pulled from the spot and in the meantime I was trying to make sense to what his conversation was and I looked over again and he was like out on the seat with his eyes rolling around in his head. So I went to 137th Street and Western and stopped and got some ice from a vet, put a quarter there, and got this ice and in the meantime he was slobbering and what not over himself and I got scared, so I proceeded out toward Altgeld Gardens to a friend of mine's house I know."

Q. Where is that located, Harold?

A. 130th and I don't know. It's on the other side of Michigan Avenue.

Q. Why did you stop there?

A. Because I thought that he was passing out or dying on me, or something. I did not know exactly what was the matter with him.

Riggins' friend would not permit him to bring in Tillman "because of the small kids there." So he carried him to the back seat of the car "and packed ice around his head and under his arms, and over his chest, and then I proceeded toward Kankakee once more."

Had Riggins been as wry as his speech sometimes indicated, he might have thought that whatever Tillman took in that house, it was Riggins who was in a fix. Suppose Tillman died, what would he, seeking anonymity more than anything else, do?

But Tillman regained control of his eyes and muscles, and became absent-mindedly quiet.

He was soaking wet from the ice in which Riggins had generously packed him. They stopped at a clothing store and bought a pair of overalls, T-shirt, and a baseball cap. Tillman changed into these dry clothes in the back of the car. Riggins took advantage of the first opportunity to use his money. He also bought overalls and a T-shirt. Now, looking more like honest laborers than refugees from a hooded mask holdup, they arrived in Kankakee, and stopped for dinner in the train station restaurant. But perverse curiosity disturbed their peace and appetites. They bought the Chicago *Tribune* to read about the sensational twenty-one-thousand-dollar robbery which bannered the front page, and were horrified to learn for the first time that a guard had been slain.

Riggins announced to his associate, who was stunned in more ways than one, "I am leaving. I am not going to get trapped." He left the Buick behind him, because anything (except money) which connected him with that morning's events was to be shunned. He did not even want the encumbrance of Hudson Tillman on his hands. He, too, was abandoned, as Riggins took a Greyhound bus which left at six-thirty for Chicago. Arriving there, he checked the newspapers again, and the story was as grim as it was large in display. He approached his house with great caution. Police squad cars were swarming around it. Even more scared, he went to Altgeld Gardens at about midnight. It was now just about twelve hours after the robbery, but it appeared to him that he had lived a terrorized year in that short span. He shrewdly arranged for a woman to telephone his home. She reported that the police had been there. So he went to the Belmar Hotel on Washington Street, seeking the shelter of a room for "three or four hours." He left to take an aimless walk. When he returned, he saw squad cars in front of the hotel. He felt as if the police, like bloodhounds, were able to pick up his scent. He was mystified by their omniscience, which only later became clear to him. He ran to the Loop. Then he went to Gary. He took a train to Pittsburgh. The next day he boarded a train to St. Louis. He could get no feeling of safety from his travels. Distance did not diminish his anxiety. It only increased his loneliness. He yearned for the comfort of a relative or friend.

He was drawn back to his home in Chicago. After several days of flight, he boarded a bus to Chicago. He visited "my girl's sister's house" in Altgeld Gardens "and she told me the police had been there and stayed two or three days." He fled to Robbins, picked up a friend there by the name of Moore, bought a 1950 green Oldsmobile for $1295 in Moore's name (he could not even enjoy the luxury of owning a car which he wanted so much), intending to drive off to Florida.

While standing in front of his car with Moore, several police cars drove up suddenly. The police jumped out with pistols drawn. "One put a pistol in my stomach and told me not to move. He took three or four hundred dollars from my person and made me get into the car and lie on the floor." Riggins was taken to the police station. There he was asked where the loot of seventeen thousand or eighteen thousand dollars was. When he denied knowledge of the fund, two policemen "with large telephone books" struck him repeatedly on each side of his head. The blows made him deaf. They threw him into a cell. Fear made him cunning. He devised a plan to escape. The next morning he informed one of the policemen that the money was in Chicago, and that if he came with him alone, he would hand it over. So he was driven in police style from Robbins to Chicago. They parked the car a block away from his home:

"While we were walking I said he should go straight in front of the house, around the sidewalk toward the back to the garage. Instead of moving around, I broke toward the step."

He was going to run into the house, shaking off the policeman, and escape through a side door. He had the necessary lead. He bounded up the front step out of sight of the policeman. As he opened the front door two officers confronted him with drawn pistols. Another group appeared as if from nowhere behind him. It must have seemed to him that all day he was looking into the muzzles of threatening guns. He was handcuffed to one of his captors and taken to the police station. Fifteen police officers came to observe him. One of them asked him whether his name was Riggins.

"When I looked up he swung his topcoat and blinded me, and slapped me four or five times, up each side of the head and I doubled up."

Later, the mystery of the police's clairvoyance, which made it possible for them to dog his movements, was resolved when Riggins learned what Hudson Tillman had done several days before when he was left behind in Kankakee.

There is one satisfaction, of which no criminal can be deprived—the momentary splash of importance his ill deed confers upon him. Newspapers, which are the most important, if not the only history chronicles they know, record their deeds, giving them the illusion of achievement. So young Tillman found himself fascinated by the prominent stories of the robbery, in which he had participated, if only as a driver. His eyes eagerly devoured the big news in all the editions he could find. In one of them was the startling item that his mother, father, and wife had been taken into custody by the police. The authorities, being unable to find Tillman, who had that morning driven the tomato red Oldsmobile from the murder scene, visited the sins of the son on his parents. Perhaps his father or mother could inform them of the whereabouts of the only one clearly linked with the crime.

Tillman attempted to reach his mother by telephone and, unknown to him, the police facilitated his effort. She urged him to return and surrender. He was ready to do so. By arrangement, his uncle, Robert Hudson, who lived in Kankakee, drove him to Chicago. They were met at 115th Street and Vincennes by his mother and an attorney, Euclid Taylor. His own attorney put handcuffs on him, lent to him by the police, walked him to Lieutenant Olsen and said, "This is Hudson Tillman and I am surrendering him to you."

As befitted the great prize he constituted, he was immediately taken to headquarters. He was permitted to talk to his mother, his minister Rev. Keller, and his attorney Euclid Taylor. Then he was interviewed by the chief prosecutors and gave a statement. He revealed that he had hidden the fifteen hundred dollars he had received as his share of the theft, on his uncle's farm under some crates. All he had on his person was forty cents. These pennies and his overalls, T-shirt, and baseball cap with a long peak, were all he ever got out of the robbery.

He made a full confession of the entire misguided venture. Before the police would even take his statement, avid as they were to receive it, he was asked to write the names and whereabouts of all the participants in the robbery. He did so on a yellow piece of paper. If a hidden camera, such as is used in some banks, had photographed the robbers in the very act of gunplay, it would not have been more incriminating than that dishonor roll scribbled by Hudson Tillman. A veritable army of police was dispatched to bring in the culprits.

David Taylor, who up to that time had not been linked at all with the escapade, was asleep with his wife at 6:30 A.M. There was a loud knocking on the door. His brother Herbert opened it. Ten policemen rushed in, with pistols in their hands.

The policemen searched the closets and every nook and cranny of the house. They found nothing, but they had him, and he was carted off in a squad car, and his brother Herbert was taken along too, for good measure.

The Kankakee and Robbins police forces were advised about the undesirable wandering of Hal Riggins in their midst; and we have seen how they became shadows of his movements, and finally brought him in.

One can only imagine the reactions of the prosecutors and police when they saw the names of Paul Crump and Eugene Taylor on that yellow list. Theirs must have been mingled feelings of bitterness and elation. Acting on a mere hunch that any visitors of Hudson Tillman several hours after the robbery might be his confederates in crime, they had previously seized Crump and Eugene Taylor. They had them on their hands and had let them go. They had been talked out of holding them, by the criminals themselves. Suppose they had fled? With public anger at burning pitch, how would the police explain such bungling? They checked quickly. At 5:45 A.M. a policeman telephoned Eugene Taylor's number, and asked whether a girl by the name of Gene was there. Eugene Taylor replied sleepily that there was a Eugene Taylor there, but no girl. Within fifteen minutes there was a knock on his door. Taylor, quite disgusted by these dawn disturbances, opened it, and police officers swarmed in with pistols poised. He was ordered to dress and was unceremoniously hauled off, together with his roommate, Nelson.

Of all the men on the yellow list, Paul Crump was considered the most dangerous. The police did not know he had become sick. When he was released, the previous Monday, he had developed a high fever of 103.6. His mother Lonie Crump could not get a doctor to visit her home. His sister Maxine took him to the office of Dr. Isaac Rosen, who injected him with 200,000 units of penicillin, prescribed sulfa drugs and a cough medicine. This incident became crucial because despite Crump's description of how he had been maltreated prior to his release, he did not complain to Dr. Rosen about anything but his "cold," and the doctor's examination of his body stripped down to the waist revealed no signs of any bruises.

Crump was too weak to walk, and remained in bed for two days. At 4:30 A.M. on Thursday, March 26, his mother was changing, for the third time, his pajamas and bed sheets which were wet from perspiration. There was a crash of the windowpane of the front door. Simultaneously, windows in the rear of the house were smashed, making noises like a sequence of firecrackers. Crump asked, "What could that be?" A stampede of police was the answer. Treating him as a desperado, the police seized him by the throat and held him down on the bed with their knees, while putting a pistol to his head. One exclaimed, "Well, we got you now, you ————. You best come in. You are going to tell us the whole story. You are cooked this time. You won't get out from under."

In the meantime, other policemen, their guns ready for any emergency, rummaged through the entire house, turning over mattresses, cutting them open, emptying drawers and closets, all in search of money or other incriminating evidence. None was found. Crump was told to dress. His clothes were hastily donned over his wet pajamas. His hands were tied tight behind his back with a strap. The police pushed him toward the door. His mother pleaded that he was sick and too weak to walk. As they shoved him out of the door, he fell to his knees. The last words the police heard as they took him away were from Lonie Crump, "Please don't hurt him."

Richard B. Austin, First Assistant State's Attorney of Cook County, used Tillman's confession skillfully to unlock the doors of denial of Crump, Riggins, and the Taylor brothers.

The psychological factors in inducing men to turn on themselves and confess the most hideous crimes have been the subject of searching studies. Apparently even killers are not devoid of conscience, which is sometimes preserved against their will. It gives them some sensitivity which they would be the first to deny and scorn. Confession acts as a catharsis to relieve this deeply recessed pain. When they tell all, "a load is off their chest," but it should be observed that the "load" is a weight which has been created by guilt, and surviving conscience. So the whole process reveals that underneath the hard crust of callousness there is a soft area, like an aching nerve, which cannot be located, or identified, but signals pain and anguish. Confession stills this pain. Otherwise why would atheistic criminals, whose lives are a police blotter of nihilism, confess, in order to derive "peace of mind"?

Whatever the complex mechanism of confession may be, prosecutors have empirically concluded that confessions are best induced by demonstrating "that the jig is up anyhow." Futility will undermine resistance better than force. In noble or ignoble undertakings, the acceptance that defeat is inevitable paralyzes the will and induces surrender or assures defeat. If any "lesson" can be derived from the brutal sport of prizefighting it is that in this laboratory of man's will to win over pain, the fighter who will not accept his opponent's superiority, despite its evident demonstration, will often survive and win. A keen observer can almost pick the turning point in the contest, when not the blow, but its message of inevitable defeat is reflected in the eye, or in exclusively defensive movements of fear.

Criminals are sometimes equipped with great courage, and may suffer "third degree" cruelties without flinching. In some men, sadistic punishment only induces honest resentment and resistance. For them, the standards of conduct become reversed. Duress provides them with a "cause." The law enforcers cease to represent the public weal against its transgressors. They become lawbreakers, surreptitiously practicing inhuman methods, and the criminal sees himself as a martyr in his suffering.

So naked force may extract a confession, but it is seldom a complete and full one. It usually consists of grudging concessions as narrow as pain will permit. On the other hand, a confession obtained because facts which have already come to light make denial spurious has the completeness of authentic detail. Such a confessor gives because the more he gives, the more he gets inner peace.

The prosecutor used this most persuasive of all devices to convince Crump and his associates that all hope of deception was gone. He faced each of the suspects with the full admission of the previous one, thus obtaining ultimately a uniform chorus of loudly proclaimed self-guilt.

First, he advised Gene and David Taylor that Hudson Tillman had told all, and he related details of the participation of the Taylors which could only have come from an informed source. They then answered all questions put by him, while a stenographer recorded their words, which were like cords of guilt winding around them. How they struggled later to free themselves from their own created bonds!

Then prosecutor Austin brought Harold Riggins into the room. His very introduction of Riggins to the Taylors, in an off-hand friendly way, in itself extracted a subtle confession from him, as he testified:

"I said to David and Eugene Taylor who were sitting at the table 'Here is someone that you have not seen for a week, and perhaps did not anticipate seeing tonight.'"

Q. What, if anything, did they say?

A. They looked at Harold Riggins and said, "Hello, Harold," and Harold Riggins said to David and Eugene: "Hello Dave, Hello Gene." . . . I informed Riggins that David Taylor and Eugene Taylor had just completed a confession regarding their participating in the Libby, McNeill & Libby murder and robbery on the Friday before, and that while he had not ever seen me before and perhaps questioned my word, he might ask David and Eugene Taylor whether or not what I told him was true.

Q. Did he ask them then whether it was true?

A. Before he had a chance to ask them, Dave Taylor assured Harold Riggins that what I had said was true. That we had recovered the cash box, the money and gun, and some pellets and that in his opinion the jig was up. And that he and Gene felt that there was no further good to come of not telling of their participation in it and that they had told what had occurred at the Libby, McNeill plant, and he told Harold Riggins, "Since we have told all that we know about it, you might as well tell what you know about it."

Q. What did Harold Riggins say to that, if anything?

A. Well, he didn't say anything for a moment, and then he said, "All right."

Q. And then did you proceed to ask questions of Harold Riggins?

A. I did.

Q. And did he make answers?

A. He did.

Thereafter Paul Crump was invited into the room. He too was invited to greet his friends whom "you have not seen for a week." They all exchanged first-name greetings, a camaraderie which bode no good for any of them. Then Austin, like in the French children's song, repeated the prior verse, but added a new line, that Riggins too had joined the company and sung too. He increased the atmosphere of futility by pointing out "that three or four people had identified Crump when he appeared that morning 'in a show-up,'" that the hat found at the murder scene fitted Crump, and that Tillman, the Taylor boys, and Riggins had all told of his and their participation in the crime. David Taylor, he of the inferiority complex, was again most forward in assuring Crump that all this was true, and urged him to "tell his part of the crime." Crump agreed to do so.

One curious incident emerged from all these confessions. Apparently Eugene Taylor and Paul Crump had an opportunity to put their heads together before making their first statement. They did so, not to extricate themselves, but rather to involve Tillman more deeply. Even though he had only participated as a driver of the getaway vehicle, they both claimed that Hudson Tillman was in the cooler, and that he was the only one present when Chief Guard Zukowski charged up the stairs. By implication at least, they suggested that Tillman had fired the shots which killed Zukowski.

When the prosecutors took second statements from them, this theory collapsed. They then confessed that their confession was untrue:

Q. Now, Gene, to wind this up, yesterday afternoon you and Paul Crump told me a story that is entirely different from what you are telling me now, is that right?

EUGENE TAYLOR: That's right, sir.

Q. Was that story true?

A. Well, no, I told that story for one reason and one reason alone, to try to stick Tillman.

Q. You were mad at Tillman because he was the first one that squealed in the case, is that correct?

A. That's right. Paul and myself felt that he should be put in it up to his neck and that is why I tried to put him in it.

Q. And everything you told me now is the true story, is that right?

DAVID TAYLOR: That's right. I don't know how it could be enacted any better. It couldn't be changed any other way.

The result of their hatred for Hudson Tillman was that they made two confessions instead of one, and the corrections in the second served to emphasize its accuracy. Their venom toward the squealer had only involved them more deeply than before. There is a Chinese proverb which is morbidly analogous: "When you go to dig a grave for your enemy—dig two."

The prosecutor was now ready to try the case of the People of the State of Illinois against Paul Crump, Eugene Taylor, David Taylor, and Harold Riggins. The charge against all of them was first-degree murder. The law is that anyone who participates in a felony (like robbery), in the course of which someone is slain, is guilty of murder. There is no different degree of guilt for the driver of the car, who it was charged was Riggins, the robber who did not shoot, like Dave Taylor, or the one who fired the fatal shots, like Crump. All would be equally guilty in the eyes of the law although when punishment is meted out, discretion may be exercised on the basis of such factors.

Hudson Tillman had also been indicted for murder in the first degree, but the prosecutor moved to sever his trial from the others. The reason soon became evident when the list of witnesses was submitted to the defendants' counsel. Tillman appeared as witness for the State against his former confreres.

The crime had been committed on March 20. The trial was set to take place May 11, within two months. Crump's lawyer, William Gerber, had been engaged in a civil action until the end of April. He therefore insisted that he did not have adequate time to prepare his defense. He struggled to obtain an adjournment. His motion to have Crump examined by a doctor, to demonstrate that he was still too ill to undergo the ordeal of a trial, was denied. His pleas that the State's list of forty-five witnesses placed a great burden of investigation upon him, with insufficient time to perform it, also fell on deaf ears. The defendants' lawyers pointed out that there were cases a year old which had not yet come to trial. They asked, "What is the rush about this case? Why is the State so anxious on making this one particular case so important in their life?" The explanation was not merely the commendable desire to speed the processes of justice. Public clamor, ambition, and sense of duty all blended in immeasurable degrees to create a sense of immediacy. However, the ruling of the court denying an adjournment raised a constitutional question as to whether the guarantee of a fair trial had been violated by unreasonable haste. Even before the case had begun, the record contained the seed of an impressive appellate argument.

On May 21, 1953, Judge Frank R. Leonard mounted the bench in the Criminal Court of Cook County, Illinois, and announced, "Bring in the defendants, and the jury."

Crump, Riggins, and the Taylors were escorted into the room. They attempted to ignore the buzz of hostility and curiosity which rose from the crowded spectators' benches. The judge proceeded to conduct the *voir dire* examination of jurors to determine their impartiality.

It soon became evident that the sensational stories, in press, radio, and television of the brutally executed robbery and murder, and the lurid details of the capture of the perpetrators, conditioned many prospective jurors, and made them ineligible to serve.

When the jury system first developed in the thirteenth century, jurors were chosen from the neighborhood where the events occurred, because it was their knowledge of the dispute obtained prior to trial which was sought. Through evolution, rules of evidence were developed, and hearsay was excluded. Then a juror who knew anything in advance about the controversy was excluded, because the "facts" which he brought with him into the jury box had not passed through the processes of truth-finding. There could be no cross-examination to test the accuracy of the impressions such a juror had acquired. So it came about that a complete reversal took place in qualifying a juror. At one time, the more he knew about the controversy the more desirable he was as a juror. Now, if he has even read about the case and been influenced by external impressions, he is disqualified to sit.

In cases which have caused a public stir, and particularly since our newspapers and other news media are less inhibited than in England, it becomes extremely difficult to find qualified jurors at all.

The Crump trial ran into this problem with a vengeance. Day after day, the judge and lawyers struggled to find unbiased jurors, and failed. After weeks, four were accepted, and they sat by while a stream of prospective jurors were excused. One day the four jurors asked to see Judge Leonard in his chambers:

THE COURT (addressing the four selected jurors): The bailiff told me you wanted to say something.

MR. EUGENE J. GEHRIG: I feel like the spokesman. . . . The reason we are somewhat embittered is that we have to see how practically hundreds come and go . . . We can see that in two weeks four have been selected and if it's going on like this it will be another month. . . .

A JUROR: If they keep us caged up in that room like they have been doing, it's getting nerve-wracking. . . .

The Court attempted to appease the complaining jurors by promising to urge counsel to more speed. After three weeks a jury satisfactory to both sides was finally chosen and sworn in.

The question arose whether the jury should be permitted to go home every night or be kept in custody during the trial.

MR. BLOCH: As far as the State is concerned, they can go.

MR. CARLSON (attorney for Riggins): We don't want them locked up.

MR. GERBER: Lock them up.

(Mr. Gerber and Mr. Carlson confer.)

MR. GERBER: We will lock up the twelve.

(The two alternates may go home.)

The judge agreed. Humorist Harry Hershfield once observed that ours is the only system where the defendant if he is out on bail goes home and the jury is locked up.

The time had come for the prosecutor to present proof

which would convince the jury of guilt, not by mere preponderance of evidence, not by the clear weight of evidence, but beyond a reasonable doubt. This extreme test is the law's safeguard against depriving a citizen of his liberty or life unless the evidence is so overwhelming that reasonable doubt is excluded. The jury may be persuaded that the defendant is guilty as charged, but that is not enough. It must be persuaded "beyond a reasonable doubt" or he must go free.

The defence therefore always has this distinct advantage in a criminal case. It need not establish innocence. It is enough if it can create a reasonable doubt of guilt. The defendants in the Crump case had many surprises for the prosecutor, and the prosecutor had some for the defendants. There unknown factors give every trial unmatched suspense. The contending forces will clash, and the predominance of one over the other will only be revealed in the course of combat.

The State called as its first witness Rudolph Zukowski, the twenty-three-year-old son of the slain guard. He supplied only technical evidence:

"I last saw my father alive on the 19th day of March, on Thursday. He was forty-five years old and in good health. I saw him next on the 21st day at the Funeral Home at Leavitt and 20th Street. He was dead."

There was no cross-examination. More than formal proof of death had been presented. The specter of the dead man was in the courtroom, in the person of his son, and hovered over the proceedings, seeking retribution.

Dr. August C. Webb testified to the three bullet wounds, any of which would have been sufficient to kill Theodore Zukowski. One of the bullets, which he had removed from the brain, and which, except for the blood he had washed away, was in the original condition, was marked in evidence. The second bullet which entered the right side of the nose, had not been removed from the base of the brain "because it would have been necessary to mutilate the face to get it."

Those who had been forced by the bandits to get on their knees and face the wall in the cooler testified in succession. Each recital of how the bandit had struck from the rear with a taped metal pipe was shudderingly graphic. Cumulatively the impact was more horrible than even the killing of Zukowski, for at least he was armed and might have defended himself. But the deliberate, brutal, crushing of the skulls of helpless men and a woman on their knees, with their backs turned, was unimaginably inflammatory.

The incendiary effect was further heightened by their recital of the injuries suffered. Henriksen "had a hole up in my head, a three-inch gash," which required stitches and X-rays at Evangelical Hospital.

Marie Zutko was in Presbyterian Hospital and at home several weeks. Martin Carlson was treated for head wounds and bandaged. Charles Baker was taken in an ambulance to Presbyterian Hospital, where six stitches were put into his scalp. His wrists had to be X-rayed. The guard Theodore Rusch wound up in the same hospital and had six stitches taken in his scalp and two along his left eye. He was away from work ten days.

This parade of pitiful victims gave emotional momentum to the prosecutor's case, lighting up with deep feeling even the dull stretches of technical proof such as the drawings of the Libby buildings. It also seemed to give heat to the battle between the attorneys. As unexpected evidence entered the record, their bitter exchanges made the trial unruly. At one point the judge had to throw the weight of his authority at both lawyers. He told them to sit down and act with proper decorum.

The trial veered from the explosions of counsel set off by growing tension, to cold impersonal evidence of the scientific laboratory. Crump's red rubber gloves which he had worn to eliminate the risk of fingerprint marks, themselves provided an internal fingerprint. Raymond Heimbuch, in charge of photography at the Crime Detection Laboratory of the Chicago Police Department, testified that he was able to bring out traces of a fingerprint inside the third finger of the red rubber glove. Enlargements were made and turned over to Oscar Behnke, fingerprint technician employed by the Chicago Police Department for sixteen years. Behnke compared these photographs with the fingerprints taken of the same finger of Crump's hand and found them to be the same. He testified to the infallibility of fingerprint identification:

"The two fundamental principles—no two fingerprints from two different persons, or two different fingers from one person are identical; these characteristics do not change with age. We fingerprint authorities agree to twelve points of comparison."

Enlarged photographs of the two prints were submitted to each juror, and they followed each line in the skin, learning the descriptive technique as they went along:

"No. 2 ink print points up to single line that breaks and becomes double line, bifurcations."

Nature abhors identical sameness in its creations. Of the billions of faces, no two are alike. The variety of coloring in each flower of the same species is infinitely different. Each design of trillions of snow crystals is different. Nature's variety, even in fingerprints, appears to promulgate its insistence on imaginative creativity, as if God would be bored by repetition. Individuality is a precious rule of life which man in his perversity strives to eliminate for the gloss of uniformity.

Even in the mechanical realm, that which seems the same on the surface is entirely different when our senses are enlarged. This explains typewriter identification, for example. The imprint of two words, made by two machines, appears indistinguishable. But enlarge those imprints five feet high, and a child can select the word made by one machine from a thousand others. A triangular break, for example at the top of a letter as if someone had cut a telltale hole into the metal with a knife, or an enormous space between two letters whenever they appear next to each other, or a false alignment, so that a particular vowel always seems to be a quarter of an inch higher than its companion letters; these and other differences, particularly when combined, give each typewriter in the world a different face, easily recognizable from any other.

A shining wood table appears to be perfectly smooth, but when truly seen after photographic enlargement, it has innumerable hills and ridges. It is only our inadequate eyes which make the world simple; and it is only our inadequate insights which permit us to categorize man by race or color, ignoring the infinite variety of more significant differences, which are the mysterious glory of creation.

There was another form of identification, which the defense had not anticipated. After the arrests, the defendants and others were exhibited in a "show-up." Theodore Rusch, the guard who had been clubbed into submission with the taped barrel, had an idea. He asked Chief O'Malley to have each suspect exclaim "Give me your gun, give me your gun." When they repeated this phrase, he immediately identified Paul Crump as the one who had yelled these words at him on the murder day. So, although the robbers had taken great care to hide their faces, they had forgotten to disguise their voices. Here, too, nature is resourceful in its coloration. No two voices in the world are the same. Particularly under excitement, Crump's voice was as identifying as a photograph of his face or fingerprint.

The prosecutor offered numerous objects in evidence, ranging from recovered money to recovered bullets. They were marked by the clerk, and handed to the jury, which fingered them with excitement. Though inanimate and mute, these exhibits reconstructed the fatal events, as if time had been moved back and the jurors could peer at them as they were happening.

Lorraine Yarbro, Eugene Taylor's friend, had been put in jail, charged with being an accessory after the fact. This must have sharpened her realization that good citizens should cooperate with the police. She testified for the State about Gene Taylor's visit to her immediately after the robbery. She identified the green box, filled with thirty-nine hundred dollars, which he smashed open in her presence. She also identified a "Minute Maid orange juice bottle," to which she had transferred the money; she admitted providing safe-keeping for the gun, bullets, and shells which she found in Taylor's jacket. All these objects were accepted in evidence. She described the burning of his jacket, after it was "ignited with lighter fluid." It was obvious that she was reluctantly sending her lover to his death.

The prosecutor then sprang another surprise. Officer Lorne Ellenbeck testified that he had visited Dave Taylor's mother-in-law Mildred Malushame, with whom part of the proceeds of the robbery had been left. She was taken into custody. With the aid of her husband Dewey Malushame, the money, hidden in a suitcase in a closet, was retrieved. The brown paper bag and the bills it contained were offered in evidence.

Although the written confessions might still never be accepted in evidence, the prosecutor continued to avail himself of the objective proof which spoke more eloquently than even the words of self-condemnation.

So Officer Ellenbeck described how he, Chief Olsen, and

three other police officials took off in two autos with Gene and Dave Taylor at 2 A.M. on March 28, to find the guns and bullets disposed of by them. Dave Taylor directed them to 43rd and Lake and said, "Just a minute I threw some discharged cartridge cases around here." He was quite accurate. The police picked up "two large ones .38." Dave Taylor thought there ought to be another one, a .32. They looked further and found it. All were marked in evidence.

The next witness was even more of a shock to the defendants and their counsel. He was James Bodor, a commercial diver of twelve years' experience, who had once performed underwater operations for the Coast Guard. He had been engaged by the Chicago Scientific Crime Laboratory to descend into the lake at 43rd Street, and search for the two pistols which Dave Taylor said he had thrown there. In his deep-sea diving rig, Bodor stayed underwater a total of four hours over a period of five days. One day, while thirty-five feet from the shore in water ten feet deep where the visibility was only one inch, he found a .32 pistol. It was lying in a crevice between two rocks:

"I came to the surface and handed the gun out, and then I returned to the bottom to search for the other gun, but it was pretty late then, and the sea was kicking up pretty much, and we had to come out."

Q. Did you ever recover anything else?

A. No. . . . The way the rocks were lying, it is very possible the gun got in between where I could not get in with my hands.

The next witness testified to another remarkable salvage operation. He was Joseph Price, a technician with the Chicago Scientific Crime Detection Laboratory. With a group of others, he conducted a magnetic search at the bottom of the lagoon. The technique is to attach permanent magnets twelve inches by eight inches in size to a rope.

"You dip them down into the water and try to recover iron objects that might be down there."

Q. Did you recover any iron objects?

A. No, I did not.

Q. What happened with the magnet?

A. I lost one magnet. It became entangled in some rocks below and I couldn't pull it out.

So they never recovered the .38 pistol. But they moved on

to 63rd Street, where Crump had thrown the assembly parts of the shotgun into the lake after he had disposed of the other sawed-off pieces, one by one, while driving.

The magnetic search brought up "a lot of debris, tin cans, bolts, and rods."

Then persistence was rewarded. As they were dragging the water fifty feet north of the casting pier, one of the magnets came up with the trigger from the shotgun. The entire crew scratched their initials on it to identify it for the court. It was received in evidence.

Now the foundation had been constructed for the testimony of a ballistics expert. It was up to him to demonstrate that the bullets which entered Zukowski's body were fired by the recovered .32 pistol, and also matched the cartridges picked up at the lakefront.

The expert, John G. Sojat, gave a lecture to the jury on forensic ballistics, that is, firearms identification as distinguished from projectiles.

He had received the .32 pistol, recovered from its wet grave in an oily condition filled with grime and dirt.

"I removed the cylinder and pin, opened the action by cocking the trigger and I washed out the grime with hot water, drained it quickly with compressed air and then washed it with ethyl alcohol. I then oiled the parts and assembled the weapon."

Then he made tests by firing the revolver into a bullet recovery box, filled with absorbent cotton. The bullets were salvaged from the box. The cartridges which remained in the cylinder of the gun were also removed.

Thereafter a comparison microscope was used. It consisted of two scopes mounted side by side with matched optics, connected by a bridge, so that there was one common eyepiece for both instruments. There are stages permitting a composite image under special illumination. The bullets were rotated, and when similar markings were found, their striations were studied to determine whether they passed from one microscope to the other where the field was divided.

As in the case of fingerprints, or the face of typewriter letters, enlargement of vision reveals unerring identification marks. When the firing pin of a revolver strikes the primer, even an infinitesimal unevenness in the metal leaves a special mark on the cartridge, which is different from that made by any other gun in the world. So the cartridge, or shell as it is sometimes called, will reveal the gun which fired it, as if a photograph of the firing pin had been engraved on its surface.

In a similar way, the bullet which is ejected from the cartridge bears its own identifying marks, imparted on it by imperfections in the muzzle as it speeds through it at a velocity of eight hundred feet per second. These scratches form striations, which can be matched up with the inside of the bore, and will not coincide with the imperfection in any other gun.

By such scientific routes, the expert reached his destination. The .32 bullet which killed Zukowski was fired by Crump's .32 pistol thrown into the lake by Dave Taylor.

Although this gun testimony was impressive, the prosecutor was saving his oral howitzer for the real climax of this case. He was Hudson Tillman. No matter what would later happen to the defendants' written confessions, whether they would be accepted in evidence or barred as having been obtained by duress, no one could prevent Tillman from confessing to the deed on the witness stand and involving his confederates. What could be more deadly than the internal revelations by one of the participants as to the planning and execution of the crime? The prosecutor had some trepidation about young Hudson Tillman as a witness. If the defendants could destroy or even discredit him in part, they might fall within the shelter of the "beyond a reasonable doubt" rule. The defendants and their counsel knew this too. They were better prepared to face Tillman than any other witness in the case. Indeed, they had a number of startling surprises for him.

So, when the prosecutor announced that Hudson Tillman was his next witness, and he emerged from a caged door to enter the courtroom for the first time, and confront his erstwhile friends from the witness stand, everyone knew that a decisive struggle was at hand.

Events can never be reconstructed by generalities. The truth is composed of infinite details. At first glance, a telegraphed newspaper picture reveals a recognizable face and nothing more. When we look closely, we see myriad dots out of which the likeness is constructed. So the recital of happenings in real life becomes believable only as we perceive the innumerable incidents, often trivial, of which they are composed.

Hudson Tillman's testimony of the planning of the robbery, its execution and ultimate division of the spoils, was filled with such minute detail that it virtually ruled out the suspicion that he was inventing the story. At times its veracity was heightened by incidents which were embarrassing to him, but which flowed from the sequential recital as if he could not break the momentum of truth. So, for example, he told how Crump and he, finding David Taylor not at home during the early planning stages, visited "a friend at 42nd Street. There were girls there." Since he was married, this escapade, not necessary to the general description, could only have spilled from him, because he was traveling the path of recollection and could not stop to be selective. He told how Riggins' pistols were obtained and how the masks were sewn. It was he who was given a dollar to buy oil to wipe the guns clean of fingerprints, and black tape to wind around the barrel. He gave the address of the hardware store where he made the purchase. He specified another store where David Taylor bought extra bullets. He described the gathering of the robbers and the precise route the two autos traveled to the stockyard. Every detail of the parking difficulties was provided by him. Finally the hysterical departure from the scene with Dave Taylor hugging the black bag, and the circle of greedy-eyed men squatting on the floor, warmed by the sight of thousands of dollars lying in the center like a glowing fire, was told by him in words which were vivid despite their simplicity.

As if to plant a pole of truth at certain junctures of the story, the prosecutor, Mr. Bloch, would interrupt, to show him the object he had just talked about, and then mark it in evidence. So he recognized "a red rubber glove and a torn piece" of its mate as looking "like the gloves Crump wore." So, also, he identified the black tape on the barrel, the shopping bag in which the sawed-off gun was carried, and the gun itself to which he added the detail that it "had bolt action, had to pull back and let down."

He had not only described the clothes of each of his confederates in minute detail, which matched other witnesses' descriptions, but he said that on the day of the robbery, Crump had a goatee. Thus, the prosecutor anticipated Crump's defense, supported by his barber, that he was clean-shaven at that time.

The atmosphere got heated from the friction of the recital and the defendants' resentment. Hudson Tillman, their "friend," was transporting them on a stretcher of words into the electric chair. Crump's counsel exploded. He demanded that the jury leave the room so that he could make a statement to the judge. Reluctantly, the Court complied.

MR. GERBER: On behalf of the defendants, Paul Crump, David Taylor, Eugene Taylor and Mr. Carlson's client, Mr. Riggins, I am seriously objecting to the First Assistant State's Attorney remaining directly in front of this witness and staring him straight in the face. If Mr. Austin wants to remain in this courtroom, let him get over on the other side.

THE COURT: He can have a seat on the bench.

MR. GERBER: I know, but I know what he is doing . . .

MR. BLOCH: I am objecting to Mr. Gerber's remark and I want the record to show Mr. Austin is sitting among a large group of other people and I am standing right in the path of this witness.

THE COURT: Objection overruled.

MR. BLOCH: And the witness has been looking at me and answering questions to me.

MR. GERBER: I want to show where Mr. Bloch is standing and where Mr. Austin is observing that witness from . . .

THE COURT: Objection overruled. Bring in the jury.

There was only one exception to Tillman's stream of truth. When he told of his flight with Riggins, and even the purchase of overalls, T-shirt, and baseball cap, he carefully omitted his stopping at a certain house in the town of Robbins, and emerging incoherent and eyes rolling, so that Riggins had to pack him in ice. The cross-examiner did not intend to permit this lapse of memory.

Tillman had to face a triple barrage on cross-examination. First, why was he not seated among the defendants with whom he had collaborated in the very crime he charged against them? Why had his trial been severed from theirs? What promise had been made to him for establishing a case for the prosecution?

It appeared that Tillman had been previously indicted for

another crime of robbery, but the charge against him had been dropped (or as the law puts it, "nolle prossed," not prosecuted). The defense struggled to establish this fact before the jury, but the Court blocked it. The legal point was interesting. One can discredit a witness by asking whether he had ever been convicted of a crime. This affects his credibility. But the law does not permit a question as to whether the witness had ever been arrested or even indicted, because a man is presumed to be innocent, unless he is actually convicted. The defense argued that this rule did not apply to a "nolle pros" because the evidence was offered not to discredit Tillman's credibility, but to show a deal between the prosecutor and him. The jury might conclude that Tillman was induced to tell a falsehood by receiving personal consideration:

THE COURT: But it is not a conviction.

MR. GERBER: How could it be a conviction when they make a deal?

MR. CARLSON: Did the State make an offer of aid and help to this man in order to get him to testify here?

THE COURT: That is a matter of defense.

However, other evidence of special treatment of Hudson Tillman did get into the record. He was not kept in a jail cell, but rather in a witness room. Then he was released on bail, and remarkably enough who had signed his bond for one hundred thousand dollars?

A. Lieutenant Olsen.

Q. Isn't he Chief of the State Attorney's police?

A. Yes.

Q. Didn't he sign your bond?

A. Yes, sir.

When Olsen later took the stand, he was forced to admit that "if Tillman absconded, I don't know where I would get the hundred thousand dollars." To say the least, the prosecutor had not acted consistently with his representations to the court and jury, that Tillman were merely one of the criminals, and no consideration whatsoever had been given or promised to him for his testimony.

Tillman stuck to this version, despite the verbal volleys fired at him:

Q. You knew you had participated in a robbery which culminated in murder, didn't you?

A. Yes sir, I did. . . .

Q. Did you know that the possibilities of your getting the death penalty were quite possible, then?

A. Yes.

MR. GERBER: Now, Mr. Tillman, who promised you that if you testified for the State that you would not be given the extreme penalty?

A. Haven't anyone promised me anything, Mr. Gerber.

Q. You are just doing this voluntarily?

A. Yes sir, I am.

Q. And no one made a deal with you or your lawyer?

A. No sir. No one.

The second attack was to establish a personal motive for injuring Crump; the reverse of Crump and Taylor's abortive effort to involve Tillman more deeply in the murder:

Q. Do you know Paul Crump's brother?

A. Yes.

Q. He used to go with your wife?

A. Not my wife, not that I know of. He could have. . . . That would be something. . . .

Q. He went with your sister, didn't he?

A. Yes.

Q. He made her pregnant, didn't he?

MR. BLOCH: Objection. Move that the jury be instructed to disregard it.

THE COURT: The jury will disregard it.

MR. GERBER: Let me ask you, didn't Paul Crump's brother and your sister have intercourse without marriage?

THE COURT: Now, Mr. Gerber.

A. I just couldn't answer that.

THE COURT: Just a minute. The jury will disregard the question and answer.

MR. GERBER: Did your sister have a baby?

THE COURT: Sustained. Now, Mr. Gerber, please don't ask any more questions along that line.

MR. GERBER: Did you ever pull a gun on John Crump when he was going with your wife?

THE COURT: Objection sustained and the jury is instructed to disregard it.

A. There was never any bad blood between me and Paul Crump.

The third cross-examination sally involved Tillman's personal habits which might make his testimony untrustworthy:

Q. Are you a narcotic addict?

MR. BLOCH: Objection.

THE COURT: Sustained.

Q. Do you take the stuff?

MR. BLOCH: Objection.

THE COURT: Sustained.

Q. Didn't you buy some narcotics in Robbins, Illinois, and pay seventeen dollars for it? . . .

MR. BLOCH: Objection.

THE COURT: Sustained.

In the lengthy trial, in which thousands of questions were put and answered, these three rulings by the Court, rejecting any inquiry into Tillman's possible drug addiction, and its effect on his credibility, raised the most serious possibilities of reversing the judgment of conviction, if one were obtained.

The prosecutor had confessions signed by Crump, Dave and Eugene Taylor, but they could not be shown or read to the jury, or even referred to, until a legal question was settled. Had they been obtained by duress or were they voluntarily given? If they had been extracted from the defendants by force, whether subtle in the form of dire threats to their family or themselves, or by torture, whether in the form of enforced sleeplessness, hunger, or physical beatings, then they would be excluded from evidence. This would be so, even if the confessions were true. Why? Because one of the safeguards against tyrannical prosecution is that no one may be compelled to testify against himself. A confession is testimony against oneself. It must be completely voluntary to meet the constitutional test. The presumption of innocence carries with it certain corollaries. One of them is that the burden is upon the State to prove guilt by external evidence—and beyond a reasonable doubt. If a citizen can be subjected to the ordeal of demonstrating his innocence, then he is no longer protected by the presumption of innocence.

Therefore, the philosophy of the law is not merely that involuntary confessions are defective because having been extracted to avoid pain, they may be untrue. It is not their unreliability alone which concerns us. Rather, that even their accuracy cannot be taken advantage of because third-degree measures violate a person's dignity and rights, and might be applied to innocent men who are unfortunate enough to fall under suspicion. Does this rule permit some criminals to escape? Of course it does, but as Mr. Justice William O. Douglas of the United State Supreme Court once wrote in an opinion:

"Wiretapping, it is said, is essential in the detection of crime. The use of torture is also helpful in catching criminals who might otherwise escape, but a degree of inefficiency is a price we necessarily pay for a civilized decent society."

Consequently, before Crump's and the Taylors' confessions could be admitted in evidence, their contentions that those documents were crowbarred from them by legal methods had to be decided first. A hearing was held on this issue not in the presence of the jury. The judge ruled that the confessions would be received in evidence, but he did not deprive the defendants of their right to give their version of the facts when they presented their defense. If the jury then found that the confessions were bludgeoned out of the defendants against their will, it would be instructed by the judge to disregard them.

Dave Taylor was the first to try to invalidate his own confession. When he was first arrested, he claimed an officer was told to push him so he could shoot Taylor in the head. When Taylor denied Tillman's story, he asserted he was told that they would hang him by his thumbs. Later:

"They blindfolded me . . . and sat me on a revolving stool. I stated I was not involved in the robbery, one called me a 'black SOB' and hit me on the head, another hit me in the side with elbow and stepped on my foot, another grabbed me by my strudles, my private. When I started to holler some fellow came out and said they couldn't tolerate this and told them to take me back where I belonged."

He testified also that a threat had been made to lock up his wife:

". . . [F]or the rest of her life and my children in a home. I said my wife had not committed any crime . . ."

Before turning him over to cross-examination his lawyer asked him why he had signed the confession.

A. Because I knew I was under police supervision. They could kill me and tell people anything and they would believe it, and that is why I signed it.

Q. Is there any other reason why you signed it?

A. Well, they had my wife involved and family and I didn't want to see anything happen to them.

Q. Were you innocent of this charge?

A. I am.

MR. GERBER: Your witness.

He met the first attack of the prosecutor, that his confessions described the robbery in minutest detail by claiming that he had been coached by the police to tell such a story and "I remembered it by heart." Lorraine Yarbro's testimony he claimed was false, but he went along with it in his statement "to get rest." His information to Mr. Austin that his mother-in-law had the stolen money, was false. "That was money accumulated from friendly poker games."

Eugene Taylor was the second defendant to grapple with his own signed confession. He claimed he was kicked alternately from each side. He stood up in the witness chair and demonstrated how they attacked him with their feet.

He said he was terrorized when one policeman offered to flip a coin with another "copper" as to who should have the privilege of killing him.

It was true that he had signed a confession given him by Mr. Austin, in the presence of witnesses.

"The statement was not true, but . . . if I didn't sign, I would wish to Christ I had."

Then it was Paul Crump's turn.

"I was subject to elbows in the stomach. One of the officers had a small leather strap in his hand and he pulled my chin up to the front seat of the car. When one officer hit me on one side, I would fall over on the other, couldn't keep my balance, and he would curse me and tell me get off him and hit me in my side with his elbow, from one side to the other."

When he arrived at the police station four officers formed a circle and "took turns kicking me in the stomach and side." He testified that they subjected him to an ingenious form of torture, one officer standing on the handcuffs which bound his hands, the other pounding his knees. He screamed and kicked so hard, he fell over the chair on his head.

"The officer [from the State's Attorney's Office] heard me holler and came in and said we don't have any of that up here."

All the defendants drew a distinction between the State's Attorney's Office, which eschewed strong-arm methods, and

the police, which engaged in them. This was their explanation
for the devastating answer they made in the presence of witnesses, as they signed their statements, that they had been
treated "royally" in the office of the State's Attorney.

Crump's attack on his confession was not limited to his
claim that he had been subjected to violence. He said he was
told that if he would make a clean breast of the whole affair,
his family would get a five thousand dollar reward [given by
Libby, McNeill & Libby].

On cross-examination, he even added the charge that when
he was brought together with Eugene and Dave Taylor, they
"informed" him:

"That our lawyer [Mr. Gerber] had been arrested . . . was
in jail and that we didn't have anyone representing us."

It was a fact that when they signed their confessions, their
attorney was not present. Indeed, Harold Riggins had refused
to sign any statement without his lawyer. He, too, claimed
he had been beaten, and that he was about to be punished for
not signing when he was saved by a telephone call, apparently from the State's Attorney's Office, which feared that
third-degree tactics might undo the great gains achieved by
the self-incriminating recitals of all the other defendants.

From long experience as a prosecutor, Mr. Austin knew
that the psychological atmosphere in which the confessions
were obtained would not last long. The defendants had fallen
into a mood of resignation, a mood nurtured with continuous
reminders of evidence in hand, which made resistance futile,
and watered by surface kindliness (sandwiches, coffee, and
cigarettes were courteously offered). Indeed, the criminals'
egos began to assert themselves, and they vied with each other
to supply facts which the others had forgotten. Their pride of
recollection, their satisfaction at being the center of attention,
their pleasure at having government officials hanging eagerly
on every word, caused them to offer "corrections" of their
typewritten statements which filled in more detail. These
were insignificant to the point of triviality, but they demonstrated the scrutiny which they had given to the documents.
It was as if they were underlining certain words to assure
their own doom. Their initials alongside these minor changes
confirmed their approval of the entire confessions even more
than the signatures at the end.

But Austin knew that the euphoria resulting from confession would wear off. Later, the defendants would be consulting with their lawyers, who would find it necessary to attack these signed documents, if their lives were to be saved. In anticipation of the bitter struggle for survival which would some day come, he closed as many escape exits as possible. Although the confessions were dictated between eight at night and six in the morning, he telephoned distinguished friends of Chief Prosecutor Gutknecht and himself to attend the signing "ceremony." So it was now possible for him to put on the witness stand Dr. William A. Brams, a physician of forty-one years' standing, who saw the defendants follow the copies in their hands as Austin read their confessions, and later add his signature as a witness underneath theirs. For good measure, Dr. Brams also examined the defendants physically immediately after the signing, and swore that they had no bruises on their bodies, and that they had not complained of any injury.

Others who attended the signing formalities and signed as witnesses were Graydon Megan, Secretary of the Inland Steel Company in Chicago; John Edward Owens, a lawyer of thirty-one years' standing; Mrs. L. Robert Mellin, a member of the Board of Education of Chicago, and Jeremiah Buckley, a professor of law at DePaul University for thirty years.

Lieutenant Frank Pape took the stand to deny all accusations:

"I did not say push him and let the so and so run so I can hit him in the head, nor threaten to hang him by thumbs or squeeze his privates."

On cross-examination he was asked:

Q. You are a pretty good master at the art of third degree, aren't you?

THE COURT: . . . Objection sustained.

Q. You can hit a fellow pretty well without even leaving marks on him? . . .

THE COURT: Objection sustained.

Q. In your twenty years as a police officer, how many people have you killed?

MR. BLOCH: Object to that.

THE COURT: Sustained.

The greatest surprise was that Austin himself took the witness stand. At the beginning of the trial, he had been listed as a witness for the prosecution. The defendant's counsel had therefore requested that he be removed from the courtroom. This was on the theory, followed in many trials, particularly criminal cases, that prospective witnesses should not hear other testimony to which they may later accommodate themselves. So witnesses for both parties are excluded from the room, until they are called to testify.

MR. GERBER: If the Court please, I would like to ask that Mr. Austin be requested to leave this courtroom. He is a witness.

MR. BLOCH: If he is called he may be called as a rebuttal witness, and I don't believe there should be any rule on rebuttal witness.

MR. GERBER: I am requesting that Mr. Austin leave this courtroom. He is listed as a witness.

MR. AUSTIN: If the Court please, I have been informed that I would not be called as a witness, regardless of the fact my name is on the list of witnesses in the State's case.

MR. BLOCH: That's correct, Judge . . .

THE COURT: I will take Mr. Austin's assurance.

MR. GERBER: Does the State wish to cross Mr. Austin's name off the list, sir?

MR. BLOCH: At this time we can.

THE COURT: Cross it off the list.

Yet Austin now took the stand as a rebuttal witness. Since I was to encounter him much later in cross-examination, I was interested in this development as revealed in the record. He described the question-and-answer sessions conducted by him, stressing the voluntary cooperation of the defendants; the opportunities given to each defendant to correct his statement, which was read aloud in the presence of distinguished witnesses, how each availed himself of the privilege of correction, and confirmed that he had been treated "excellently" or "royally" by the State's Attorney.

After his first arrest, Crump said he had become ill with pneumonia and had visited Dr. Rosen. Since he had testified to severe mistreatment by the police immediately prior to this medical examination, it was obvious that Dr. Rosen was an important witness. But neither side called him. Judge Leonard made a surprising announcement:

THE COURT: I ordered a subpoena for Dr. Rosen. . . . I am going to hear your views, whatever you gentlemen have, but I am calling Dr. Rosen as a court's witness.

The judge then examined him as if he were a lawyer in the case.

    Q. Did you make a full and complete examination [of Paul Crump]?

    A. I examined him down to the waist.

    Q. Will you tell me what the condition of his body was, his arms, and his legs?

    A. It was clear. He had a cold. That is all.

    Q. There were no marks or bruises of any kind?

    A. No, sir.

    THE COURT: Gentlemen, either side can cross-examine this witness. Who wants to cross-examine him first?

Crump's lawyer chose to do so. Dr. Rosen asserted that Crump's temperature of 103.6 was not serious, but he did tell him to stay in bed. He injected him twice with penicillin.

The prosecutor elicited the fact that the doctor was interested in Crump's lungs, not in pathology, but there was no attempt to becloud his conclusion that Crump's body from the waist up was unmarked.

When Crump testified, he denied ever being at the Libby plant on the day of the robbery. Where was he at 11 A.M.? He chose the oldest and most masculine alibi. He said he was holed up with a girl in her room. Men in deep trouble have never minded confessing to immoral trysts to explain their whereabouts. There are not many better ways to make isolation plausible, and there is a sort of cynical reliance upon such an explanation being believable, while any other would sound like a tall story. So, although the prosecutor announced,

"May the record show that the wife of Paul Crump is also in the courtroom at this time,"
Crump testified that he spent the night preceding the robbery with a girl and remained at her apartment until three o'clock in the afternoon of the next day, during the very hours that money was being seized and a life snuffed out at the Libby plant.

Furthermore, his lawyer produced the girl on the witness stand. Her name was Fay Henton. She testified:

"I saw Paul Crump at six-thirty on the evening of March 19th at 23rd and Berkeley. We had some drinks and he came home with me. We played records, drank some beer, and then went to bed. He stayed all next day until two-thirty to three o'clock with me all that time and did not leave for any purpose."

The prosecutor proceeded to tear down her character: "I seen him about twice a week. He started spending nights with me around November or December. . . ."

Q. Did you know Paul Crump was married at the time that you were spending the nights with him?

A. Yes, I did.

But this was an instance in which the looser her morals, the more credible the alibi. Indeed, it was her loyalty to him, whether because of their relationship or money, which should have been stressed. This would tend to discredit the truth of her story, as she was ready to commit sacrificial perjury to save him. The jury had to weigh this interested testimony against that of numerous witnesses who had seen Crump fleeing through the stockyards, Tillman's confession, buttressed by those of the Taylors and Riggins, and Crump's own words, which he was now attempting indigestibly to eat.

To sharpen the contrast, another woman, a good one, tried to corroborate Fay Henton. She was Crump's mother, who testified that her son did not sleep at home on the night before the robbery, even though his wife was there.

Also when she returned home from work the next day, Paul was there, preparing to go out to a dance. He had no goatee at that time, nor had he worn one for several weeks prior to that day.

In answer to the only question put to her on cross-examination, she said simply that it was true, "I would like to help my son."

Crump's barber for two years, Harry Wood, swore that he had shaved off his goatee several weeks before the robbery date, because "he was too young a man to be wearing a goatee, made him look too old."

David Taylor also produced a woman to testify that he could not have been at the Libby plant at the time of the robbery. She was Emily Stokes. Hers was not an erotic explanation. Her activity was at the other end of the spectrum: "On Friday, March 20, 1953, about 10 A.M., I went to Mrs. Taylor's house to make choir robes. David was in bed. I was with his wife until around twelve-thirty. Dave Taylor did not leave while I was there."

Hal Riggins produced his alibi witnesses. One was James

Lewis McGrew, who saw Riggins drive away "about twenty minutes or quarter to eleven" on the crucial morning. The other was his father, Rev. Frank McGrew, who saw his son talking to Riggins before the latter left in a car "between ten-thirty and eleven o'clock." The obvious defect of this testimony was that it didn't exclude Riggins getting to the Libby plant in time for the robbery at 11:05 A.M. The minister's words might have been impressive, but the time element was so tissue paper thin that it seemed a few minutes were the difference between life and death.

There are as many styles of summation as there are variations in the personality of lawyers.

The art of persuasion permits of infinite approaches, from the wooing of the mind with irresistible logic to the shock treatment which stuns it into agreement. In between there are the variants of reaching the heart through the brain, or the brain through the heart. All are designed to press that inner lever which causes the head to nod in assent. The roads to persuasion are different in each case.

One of the most unpleasant is used more frequently in criminal cases than in any others. It is a road paved with good inventions, such as the chicanery of the district attorney, his ambition to become governor, and the "fixing" of the case against the defendant, who because he has a prior criminal record is a tempting prospect for police conspiracy.

It has been said that the stronger the words the weaker the argument. Such a summation was made on behalf of Paul Crump. The bitterness and recrimination of the trial exploded on both sides during the final arguments. The reason of course was that the law restricts counsel from making comments or expressing opinions during the trial. Such privileges are reserved for summation, although here too they must be based on the evidence and not wild assertions. There is only one extenuating circumstance for extremism (which is usually self-defeating), and that is the zeal of counsel. No matter how ill-conceived or ineffective the effort, there is something noble in an advocate pouring out his heart to save his client.

Although there were many reasoned and logical arguments made on behalf of Crump, there was also the following, which the jury obviously rejected:

"I don't mind the State making a murderer out of Tillman.

. . . I do mind, however, fabricating the story on these boys here, and they pick this yokel [Crump] . . . he's the pigeon. He has a past record. He was in the Pontiac Reformatory for armed robbery with a gun. He fits in with the plan. . . .

"This is the pigeon. He's the boy. And the State really fixed it good. They made the story. . . . From the No. 1 actor, Mr. Tillman. . . .

"Here is the most important case since Judge [then Chief Prosecutor] Gutknecht took office, and he knew the newspapers would be ramming it down his throat unless he got an early solution, and, brother, when Tillman came in with his story he got his boys working fast.

"That's why, less than two months after the occurrence of this particular crime, we are on trial. That's fast."

The prosecutor was so provoked by these attacks that he poured out his own vitriol. He resented Gerber's reference to him as "a merchant of justice" prosecuting the case for the dollar:

"Certainly if he knew the salary of an assistant district attorney, I doubt he would have made that statement.

"He asked, 'Who got the money in this case?' We didn't recover nine thousand dollars. How are they paid? They have the nerve to refer to us as merchants of justice."

This brought a motion for a mistrial from Riggins' attorney, Carlson, who offered to testify what his fee was. Gerber was also incensed and demanded a mistrial. The Court, sorely beset by these tangential outbursts, instructed the jury:

"You will disregard the question of merchants in this case. There is no evidence to show that they got any of this money."

There were long stretches of cogent, closely reasoned argument. The prosecutor pointed out that the confessions were not merely subjective:

"Each tells what the other did. There wasn't one inconsistency out of about 150 pages of statements taken from the three. And do you know why there wasn't any inconsistency? Because these confessions were true and the truth is not inconsistent. . . .

"Crump killed Zukowski because he knew Ted would know him and when his hat and mask were pulled off, that's when he gave it to him, because it was necessary to kill Ted Zukowski. . . .

"Why should you show them any mercy? Have they showed

any mercy to Zukowski? Did they show any mercy to those five people [on their knees]? . . . They stand on the mountain of fabricated lies and . . ."

    MR. GERBER: I am objecting to "the fabricated lies."

    THE COURT: Overruled.

The prosecutor demanded the death penalty for all defendants.

Judge Leonard instructed the jury concerning the rules of law which governed their determination. This is called "charging the jury." Under our judicial system, the jurors are the sole judges of facts. They decide which of the opposing versions testified to is correct. The judge may not interfere in this process. We leave it to the jury's common sense, based on its observation of those who testify, whom to believe. But the judge is the sole authority on the law which they must apply to the facts as they find them. If they disagree with his instructions of the law, they must nevertheless follow his views, not theirs. The reason for this is not only his superior learning in law, but rather that if he is mistaken, an appellate court can correct him. If however the jurors have adjusted the law to suit their own theories, then there is no way for the appellate court to know whether an erroneous statement of the law by the judge has affected the result.

So there are in reality two judges in every courtroom. The jury acts as one, with exclusive power to decide the facts. The judge acts as the other, with exclusive power to decide the law.

The lawyers submit to the judge "requests to charge" the jury on the law. He may comply or reject the request. The disapproved requests can then be reviewed by an appellate court.

When all these procedures, designed to protect the individual, and assure a fair trial under law, had been completed, the jury filed out to decide the fate of Paul Crump and the other defendants.

There followed that long wait when the heart, rather than a clock, ticks off the seconds. The agonizing suspension of uncertainty is tormenting because hope and despair alternately fill its vacuum. It is as if the body were wracked by high fever and low temperature in succeeding cycles. A decision, even if adverse, can be a relief after such torture.

Hours later it came. The jury filed back into their seats, looking solemn, while the noise of anticipation sounded like a continuing gasp in the courtroom.

The clerk read their verdict:

"We the jury find the defendant David Taylor, guilty of murder in manner and form as charged in the indictment and we fix his punishment at imprisonment in the penitentiary for a term of 199 years. And we further find from the evidence that the said David Taylor is now about the age of twenty-seven years."

Signed by the foreman and eleven other jurors.

The same verdict was rendered against his brother Eugene Taylor, twenty-two years old, and against Harold Riggins, also twenty-two years old.

The verdict was different in the case of Crump.

It read:

"We the jury find the defendant Paul Crump guilty of murder in manner and form as charged in the indictment and we fix his punishment at death."

It is customary for losing counsel to ask that each juror confirm his vote openly in the courtroom. This procedure avoids any error, or duress upon a juror which might occur if his fellow jurors overwhelmed him in the jury room. He has a last chance to state his real vote. I have never known a juror to reverse himself while in the jury box, although I have experienced on several occasions a juror giving a contrary answer because he misunderstood the question or was so rattled that he misspoke himself. The excitement occasioned by such an error is explosive, and the letdown after its correction correspondingly depressing.

The lawyers for the defendants made this last-gasp request.

Counsel for the defendants requested the Court to have the jury polled, and the Court so directed the clerk to poll the jury.

And the clerk inquired of each and every juror:

"Was this and is this now your verdict?"

And each and every juror so responded:

"It was and is."

Thereupon the jury was excused by the Court.

The judge set a date a month away for the completing

ritual of motions to set aside the verdicts (necessary to lay the foundation for an appeal to a higher court), and sentencing.

On August 10, 1953 the formal motions were made, and were denied by the Court.

Then the judge asked each defendant whether he had anything to say before he pronounced sentence on him. This privilege of a final statement has roots tracing back to ancient days, when it was wrested from tyrants, as another safeguard against oppressive prosecution. Even at the last moment the prisoner ought to be heard, for he might reveal corruption or abuse of process, which would be heard by the populace. Furthermore, the defendant, relying on the presumption of innocence, might not have testified at the trial. Even though convicted, he should be heard, for he may present some extenuating, unrevealed circumstance, which might affect the degree of punishment meted out to him. This is but another illustration of the magnificent precautions taken by the law to protect even the most wretched criminal.

Eugene Taylor declined the opportunity to speak.

THE COURT: The defendant, Eugene Taylor, will be sentenced to the Illinois State Penitentiary for a term of 199 years.

The judge turned to his brother:

"Have you anything to say, Mr. Taylor?"

THE DEFENDANT DAVID TAYLOR: Not necessarily. But I will say this: I think it was a very prejudicial situation.

The Court's reply was to sentence him to a 199-year prison term. Harold Riggins refused to speak and drew the same sentence.

"Paul Crump, have you anything to say before I pronounce sentence?"

THE DEFENDANT PAUL CRUMP: Yes, sir. I believe the wide publicity there was and prejudice on the part of the prosecution didn't give me the value of my testimony. The jury didn't have to deliberate on a verdict; they knew what verdict they were going to bring back when they went into the room, because of that. That's all.

THE COURT: In the People of the State of Illinois versus Paul Crump, indictment for murder, this day come the People, by John Gutknecht, State's Attorney, and the defendant, as well in his own proper person as by his counsel, also comes.

And now neither the defendant nor his counsel saying anything further why the judgment of the Court should not now be pronounced against him on the verdict of the jury heretofore entered and the finding of the Court rendered to the indictment in this cause:

Therefore it is considered, ordered and adjudged by the Court that the said Paul Crump is guilty of said crime of murder in manner and form as charged in the indictment in this cause on the said verdict of guilty and finding of guilty and that he be taken from the bar of this Court to the common jail of Cook County, from whence he came, and be confined in said jail in safe and secure custody until the fourteenth day of November, A.D. 1953, and that on that day the said defendant, Paul Crump, be by the Sheriff of Cook County, according to law, within the walls of said jail or in a yard or enclosure adjoining the same, there be put to death, by having caused to pass through the body of said defendant, Paul Crump, a current of electricity of sufficient intensity to cause death and the application and continuance of such current through the body of said defendant, Paul Crump, until such defendant is dead.

And may God have mercy on your soul.

The defendants were led back to their cells. As the doors clanged shut behind them, Riggins and the Taylors knew that for the rest of their dying days and nights, this would be their caged abode. Crump did not even have this gruesome solace.

There began within him the subconscious countdown on his life.

One often hears it said that the death sentence is preferable to life-long imprisonment. There is at least one touching animal story to support this view, that of a hummingbird which finds its young, captured and caged, and brings them poisoned berries to release them from their imprisoned life. I have never shared this view about human beings. I know that thousands of people each year, who are free, commit suicide because they cannot bear the restraint of their own skins. But these are necessarily sick people whose will to survive, so strongly implanted by nature, has been overcome by extreme neuroses or psychotic states. Otherwise, even pain is an intense form of consciousness, and there is some joy in breathing, eating, functioning, thinking, yes and suffering.

Leaving the possibility of the survival of the soul aside, we will all be unconscious as human beings for millions of years. Our span of consciousness is relatively as brief as the insect whose whole life cycle from birth to great grand parenthood, old age and death is twelve hours. The termination of this precious brief period of consciousness is more painful to a normal human being than any pain which the process of living may ordain. If one doubts the clear choice between life imprisonment and execution, let him observe the desperate struggle of almost every condemned man to obtain the privilege of continued breathing and consciousness even in the sordidly confined atmosphere of a jail.

Paul Crump began such a struggle. The ensuing events are unprecedented in the history of penology.

Harold Riggins and the Taylor brothers did not appeal from their convictions and lifelong sentences. As if relieved that they had escaped death, they accepted their punishment with long-lasting resignation.

Hudson Tillman was tried separately and sentenced to seventeen years in jail. Obviously, his cooperation with the prosecutor had resulted in merciful consideration. He did not appeal.

Crump stood alone in his plea to the upper court to reverse his conviction. Through new counsel, Edmund H. Grant, he pressed his appeal. The stenographic minutes of the trial and of all exhibits had to be printed, and submitted to the appellate court. This took considerable time, because both counsel had to proofread the record and agree on certain stipulations. So Crump's execution was delayed. Stay after stay was granted by the Court to permit preparation of his appellate papers. The mere effort to review elongated his life.

Then legal briefs and reply briefs had to be prepared and printed. Again this took time. Again there were stays of execution. Each time the warden brought word that Crump's date with the electric chair had been postponed.

An appeal is argued solely by the lawyers. No witnesses are heard. No new exhibits may be offered. The upper court decides on the record of the trial which took place before the jury. If litigants were permitted to present additional evidence on the appeal, the appellate court could not determine whether the jury was right, since such evidence was not before it.

Also, such practice would encourage litigants to hoard some testimony for the appeal. The appellate court is not set up to conduct a trial. In Illinois it is composed of three judges, who merely review the decision below. Therefore, the rule is that nothing outside the printed record may be brought before the appellate judges or considered by them. Indeed, even that record cannot afford the judges the opportunity to observe the witnesses, a privilege the jury had in deciding their credibility. That is why a jury verdict is rarely reversed on the facts. Even if the appellate court is inclined to disagree, it will accept the judgment of the jury strengthened as it was by observation and consequent evaluation of the witness, visually and orally. Reversals are based, almost always, upon errors of law rather than fact.

After lengthy consideration of the oral arguments and briefs, Chief Justice Bristow handed down a written opinion on March 24, 1955, almost about nineteen months after the verdict was rendered.

The standard by which the Court tested the validity of the verdict bode no good for Paul Crump:

"The record before us is voluminous, the defendant was aggressively represented, and the trial was a bitter one. No trial judge can be expected to sit as an arbiter in such a contest without the intervention of error. Too many rulings must be promptly made in the hurried process of trial for there to be a perfect record. Were the mistakes made of such a character that they constituted reversible error?"

In other words, the test is not whether a mistake was made, but whether it was of such consequence that it must have affected the result. Sometimes evidence is excluded which should have been admitted, but it merely corroborates other evidence already before the jury. Such an error will not cause a reversal. Or sometimes, evidence is permitted which should have been excluded, but its weight is inconsequential, and could not have altered the verdict. The law does not expect perfection in legal rulings during a complicated case. Justice is administered by human beings, and the most learned of them are subject to frailties. If affirmance on appeal depended on the infallibility of the judge who presided at the trial, judicial history would be filled with reversals. Because of a more tolerant rule of reason, the opposite is the fact. Reversals are rare.

Crump's lawyer set forth fourteeen major errors to justify upsetting his conviction. He had to run the gamut of demonstrating not only incorrect legal rulings but that they were so substantial as to constitute reversible error.

Crump succeeded. How?

His chief argument was that Judge Leonard did not permit the following cross-examination questions to be asked of Hudson Tillman:

"Are you a narcotics addict? Do you take the stuff? Did you ever take heroin? Didn't you on March 20th buy some narcotics and pay seventeen dollars for it?"

Tillman, who was shielded from answering these questions, was an accomplice in the crime. Said the Court:

"It is universally recognized that the testimony of an accomplice is fraught with weaknesses, due to the effect of motives, hope of leniency or benefits, or the effect of fears, threats, hostility, etc. . . . If Tillman's testimony was fully believed by the jury, it would have had a substantial bearing on the jury's findings and conclusions, both as to guilt and recommendations as to penalty."

Riggins had testified to Tillman's mysterious visit to a house in the town of Robbins, and his extraordinary, disoriented behavior when he emerged. Yet, said the appellate court, Tillman, who was under the control of the prosecutor, was never put on the stand to rebut this testimony.

The question thus arose whether Crump's lawyer should have been permitted to impeach the credibility of Tillman by cross-examining him concerning his drug addiction.

This matter had never before been directly decided in the State of Illinois. It was, as the Court said, "a clear-cut question of first impression." There had been holdings that a witness could be cross-examined to show that she was the keeper of a house of ill fame because:

"If a witness is engaged in an unlawful and disreputable occupation, in justice and fairness she should not be permitted to appear before the jury as a person of high character who is engaged in a lawful and reputable occupation."

However, the general rule concerning narcotics followed in most states, is that evidence of its use may not be shown to discredit the witness unless it is proved that the witness was under its influence at the time of the occurrence, or at the time he testified, or that his mind or memory or powers of observation were affected by the habit.

This rule is gradually yielding to the logic that "any disease impairment of the testimonial powers . . . ought to be considered." A court in Idaho held that:

"Habitual users of opium or other like narcotics become notorious liars. The chronic morphinomaniac is often a confirmed liar—the truth is not in him."

Chief Justice Bristow aligned Illinois with this rule:

"In our opinion, the jury was entitled to know whether Tillman, the accomplice witness, was or had been a drug addict, or had used narcotics on the day of the alleged crime, it being a very important factor going to the general reliability of his testimony."

There remained one other question to be answered before Crump could reach the minerva of a new trial. Legal error had been committed, but was it substantial enough to have mattered in the final result?

The prosecutor put his entire emphasis on this point. He demonstrated that Judge Leonard had charged the jury to examine Tillman's testimony with great scrutiny:

"The Court instructs the jury that while the testimony of an accomplice is competent evidence, such testimony is liable to grave suspicion, and should be acted upon with great caution."

Therefore, he argued, the error was not vital. The impact of Tillman's testimony had been blunted, even though he had not been queried on narcotics addiction. Furthermore, the People claimed that the other evidence of guilt was overwhelming, and the result would have been the same, whether Tillman had admitted using drugs or not.

This argument would undoubtedly have carried the day in a civil suit, or even in a criminal trial had the punishment not been death. The appellate court quoted from another of its decisions:

"Since the jury in this case had a wide discretion in fixing punishment and did by its verdict fix the maximum punishment—death by electrocution, it is not a case where this Court could affirm the judgment . . . even if it could say that the proof of guilt were clear."

In other words, had Tillman's credibility been further impeached, the jury might still have found Crump guilty, but would it have isolated him from the other defendants to sentence him to death? After all it was Tillman who demonstrated that Crump was the initiator as well as the executioner of the entire venture. Had his testimony been discredited, the jury might have sentenced Crump to 199 years. It was this imponderable factor of degree of punishment which made the error substantial. The appellate judge concluded with these life-saving words:

"The refusal of the Court in this case to permit cross-examination [of Tillman's use of narcotics] was prejudicial and reversible error."

This is another illustration of how the law, despite its disavowal of interference from sentiment, creates special merciful standards to avoid the finality of death. It has been observed that juries, which might be convinced of guilt, will find a lesser degree of murder to avoid the death penalty; whenever the punishment appears extreme, the jury may shy away from a finding which would compel its application. This is the leavening process of justice, which jurors, more than judges, bring into the courtroom.

Although the appellate court had reached a decision, it continued to rule upon other legal points raised on behalf of Crump, in order to guide the presiding judge at the second trial. So it ruled that the questions put to Tillman about Crump's brother having wronged Tillman's sister should not have been excluded:

"It was an area of proper inquiry . . . to determine if there was ill will engendered in Tillman because his sister had become an unwed mother as a result of defendant's brother's illicit relation with her."

Although it was no longer applicable to the Crump case, the appellate court questioned the presiding judge's refusal to adjourn the case and rushing Mr. Gerber to trial:

"On a charge of murder, where the prosecution is seeking the death penalty, every reasonable opportunity should be given the defendant to investigate witnesses against him and to prepare his defense.

"It is our opinion the Court abused its discretion in denying the defendant adequate time to prepare his defense in this case. Ten or eleven days to investigate forty-eight State witnesses and prepare for cross-examination thereof . . . can hardly be deemed reasonable."

Thus a warning was given that despite the ubiquitous criticism of the law's tardiness, our judicial system is more concerned with the full protection of the individual. A man's liberty is too precious to be sacrificed even on so noble an altar as that called "Prompt Enforcement." Anyone who is impatient with the law's delay (right as he is in many areas) would be more tolerant on this subject if ever he was unfortunate enough to be accused of violating one of the tens of thousands of statutes, and suddenly found his business undermined, his family distressed, his lifelong associations broken, and his entire life crumbling under the pressure of accusation. Such a man would not consider any safeguard provided by law too extreme or too time-consuming. He would understand that the concern of the law for his reputation and liberty is balm in a desperate hour.

Guiding the judge who might preside at the second trial, the appellate court then severely criticized the incident in which the First Assistant State's Attorney, Richard Austin, was permitted to testify in rebuttal, although he had announced that he was not going to be a witness, and was therefore not excluded from the courtroom like other witnesses:

". . . such a situation should not be permitted to recur on a new trial."

Judge Leonard's action in subpoenaing Dr. Rosen as the court's witness was not held improper in itself, but since the doctor's testimony was not given in the presence of the jury, the subsequent reference to it by the prosecutor, particularly since the jury must have been impressed by the mysterious reference to Dr. Rosen as "the Court's witness," was prejudicial error. It might have contributed to the infliction of the extreme penalty of death.

Finally, the Court reviewed the "requests to charge" which had been refused by Judge Leonard. It upheld him on all but one. That was a request that the Court charge the jury to consider the case as if Crump were a white man, and that there ought not to be any distinction in principle in respect to color:

"Although it is true that today, under our legal and social system, it should not be necessary to ask for, seek or expect to receive any special instructions because of race, color or creed, yet we must recognize that our American system of justice and equality before the law is still administered by human beings and is therefore necessarily subject and exposed to the imperfections of human frailties and prejudices."

The request to charge should therefore have been granted. Whatever precaution the judge could take against prejudice where all the defendants were Negroes, and the entire jury and prosecuting staff were white, should have been taken. The legalism that equality is assumed under law, and that such an instruction demeaned justice, was too esoteric. Necessary or not, the precaution was realistic, and should not have been rejected in favor of ideological theory.

Some day we will look back upon discrimination on account of skin color with the same mystification as we wonder how anybody could have argued that it was right for human beings to be slave chattels, bought and sold on the auction block. There are some problems in human affairs, whose existence takes on size because of the earnestness of discussion. The glare of debate creates the illusion of semi-validity. When the light of passion is turned off, and with it raucous contentiousness, the stage is empty. There was never a real issue in the first place.

If we must indulge in fantasy, there is a healthy one contained in a Chinese superstition to the effect that man was created in an oven, and the difference in color among the peoples of the world is due to the different degrees of baking. Isn't it silly to hate one another, because some of us are better done than others?

One of the grounds urged for reversal was "the improper and prejudicial remarks by the prosecution." The appellate court observed with some acidity that:

"An examination of the record discloses numerous instances of remarks and conduct by counsel for both the People and the defendant made during the heat, tension and strain of a strenuously and bitterly tried capital case which in the interest of a fair and impartial trial before a jury would have been better left unsaid and undone."

The opinion of the appellate court concluded with a statement which sounded not as if it had been written, but as if it were a trumpet sound from on high, and announced freedom:

"The extreme penalty having been imposed in the case prompts us to attach increased importance to the errors herein discussed, and to reach the conclusion that defendant's conviction did not result from a trial free of substantial and prejudicial error. A new trial is ordered. Reversed and remanded."

So while David and Eugene Taylor and Harold Riggins were doomed for life, and Tillman was incarcerated for seventeen years, Paul Crump was once more a free man, facing a trial.

The electric chair no longer stood athwart his last walk. Indeed, all punishment had been lifted from his head. He was once more the beneficiary of a presumption of innocence. The State would have to prove him guilty beyond a reasonable doubt all over again. He faced his coming ordeal with new hope.

There is a psychological game which offers you the opportunity to relive your life exactly as you did originally with all its joys and pains, and without adding any knowledge gained by experience, and thereafter continuing with the rest of your destined life; or foregoing the privilege of re-experiencing the past and continuing life to the end. Which would you prefer? Almost everybody chooses the latter. It is an indication of the balance of unhappiness which marks most lives.

I belong to the fortunate few who would eagerly repeat all his prior years including their pain and sorrow. Not only my avidity for life, but my general good health and overall happiness make the choice easy.

This is an imaginative exercise. We are not afforded such a privilege in real life. But in a second trial after the reversal, both sides have not only the invaluable opportunity to relive their prior experience, but also to modify and change their presentation as new wisdom dictates.

This was done. Each side was represented by new counsel: Crump by Stephen Lee, the People of the State of Illinois by Robert Cooney and Joseph V. McGovern. There was a new presiding judge, Elmer H. Holmgren, who had the benefit of the appellate court's rulings on troublesome matters which had taxed Judge Leonard. The case was tried without vituperation and with great skill. The dignity of the proceedings did not interfere with the intensity of effort to convict and to defend.

The strategy differed too. The prosecutor didn't put Hudson

Tillman on the stand at all. Thus, one of the key figures in the prior trial, whose confession against his accomplices had made their protestations of innocence seem as hollow as they were desperate, did not even appear. The reasons must have been the prosecutor's concern with the evidence of Tillman's drug addiction which would come into the record, and also the overwhelming independent evidence, including Crump's confession, which made it unnecessary to rely on a witness who had been chiefly responsible for the reversal.

The defense too changed its strategy. The alibi that Crump spent the night and the subsequent morning (on which the murder occurred) with Fay Henton was abandoned. She was not put on the stand. Instead Crump stressed the fact that one of the chief reasons for his "false" confession was his concern for his wife.

"Mr. Austin said my wife was involved . . . that she had made the masks, and that she purchased the gloves, and the— I don't know what else—but they had her involved in this . . .

"I told him it wasn't so, . . . he told me . . . David Taylor's wife was upstairs, they had her in jail, and my wife, under the physical condition she was in. . . . And the onliest way I could . . . keep her from being involved, was to make the statements."

Apparently, the benefit derived from the alibi was weighed against the prejudice it created against Crump. In the presence of his wife, who sat in the courtroom, it was doubtful that a confession of adultery would throw a sufficient cloud over his confession of robbery and murder. It was deemed wiser to rely on Crump's loyalty to his wife rather than on his betrayal of her even if it did establish an alibi.

These are the difficult decisions lawyers must make in presenting testimony. The winning of the jury involves imponderable factors of sympathy or resentment which can cause it to reject an otherwise credible piece of evidence. The lawyer never knows with certainty whether he has made the right decision in sacrificing some valuable testimony for a greater goal in the persuasive effort. This is what gives him anguish during the silent hours of the night when he should be sleeping. Judge Benjamin N. Cardozo once revealed that he suffered the same anxiety in his judicial work. A judge may write an opinion in which he sets forth the grounds of his decision with stentorian finality, but later may toss in his bed with the pangs of uncertainty. Indeed, I have sometimes found a witness's emphatic assertiveness a signal of his inner doubt. Usually it is his eyes which deny the sureness of his voice.

The State again presented prosecutor Richard Austin as a witness. But by now, almost three years after the murder, he had become a judge of the Superior Court of Cook County. This gave him additional prestige, and made his testimony of the voluntary nature of Crump's confession even more impressive.

William P. Gerber, Crump's lawyer in the first case, also took the witness stand, but his testimony was limited to his demand that Lieutenant Pape free his client unless he had a charge against him, and the fact that he was released; and the way he looked after his subsequent arrest—"he had a three-day growth. His hair was unruly." There was virtually no cross-examination of him, because he had not testified to the many charges which he had made when he was the lawyer in the case.

It was Paul Crump who bore the chief burden of his own defense. He testified eloquently concerning the ordeal of pain he had suffered at the hands of the police. He even made a drawing of himself strung up by the arms, to demonstrate the extraordinary torture device which the police used, but the judge would not admit this "visual aid" in evidence, confining Crump to oral description.

On the separate issue of whether Crump's confession had been obtained by duress, the prosecutor presented fifty witnesses, who denied any impropriety and saw him read the confession carefully and sign it. On the issue of the robbery and murder, the prosecutor presented thirty-seven witnesses against the defense's six. While the Court always instructs the jury that it isn't the number of witnesses, but the quality of the testimony which must guide them, the State's edifice of detailed description loomed high in the courtroom. It was a structure of many colors, from the description of Zukowski "lying on his back, his face covered with blood, and a pool of blood accumulated on the side of his head" to the statements of witnesses who saw Crump running from the scene of the murder—"he walked across right in front of us and he pulled off the red rubber glove, we would have bumped right into him if we did not slow down or stop"; from the finding of the bullets and the gun under the confessed guidance of Dave

Taylor, to the expert testimony that they were shot from Crump's gun; from Lorraine Yarbro's admissions that Gene Taylor had brought the payroll box to her home and emptied its contents on her floor, to a stenographer's testimony that Crump and Taylor had admitted in his presence their involvement in the crime and identified the bullets and gun. To cap the entire incriminating structure, the typewritten confessions were received in evidence, thus spilling out of the mouth of Paul Crump himself the detailed planning and execution of the crime.

Yet Crump's chances were not hopeless. His denial that he had even been at the Libby, McNeill plant on the day of the robbery raised an issue of mistaken identity, no matter how thin. His far more impressive testimony that his confession had been improperly wrung from him raised still another issue of its possible rejection, and beyond all that, would the jury find that there was not even a reasonable doubt about his guilt?

The law had created a steep protective embankment which the prosecutor would have to scale. If the prosecutor could not eliminate any reasonable doubt which might linger in the jury's mind, then Crump might still go free. At least his chance of escaping the extreme penalty of death seemed real.

In this atmosphere, both sides summed up before the jury. Crump actually asked for permission to add to his lawyer's address. He made an emotional appeal. Unfortunately, the printed record only contains his concluding statement:

> PAUL CRUMP: I don't have anything else to say, but I just want you people to know that I have no argument with the law. I never have. I have did some wrong. I did it in 1946. I paid for it. All I am asking you people—
>
> MR. MC GOVERN: We are going to ask if this defendant wants to talk about the wrong he did in 1946—
>
> PAUL CRUMP: I am referring to the record.
>
> THE COURT: Sustained.

Thereupon Mr. Lee resumed his argument to the jury.

The prosecutor's summation depicted the care and cunning of Crump's preparation for the crime, reaching crescendo with the final statement:

"When Crump knocked them all unconscious, lying there with blood running over their bodies and faces, he did not have enough; he has two guns and now he turns to the man who isn't here, Mr. Zukowski. . . . You saw his son and he looks like a decent fellow.

"Zukowski can't speak but his body speaks to us. You will never see a man more vicious or rotten than Paul Crump who sits right there, . . . and you have to give him the death penalty, otherwise we might just as well let these robbers run wild."

It is not accidental timing that the judge's charge to the jury follows the summations of both sides. The law recognizes the stormy emotions which skilled advocates may stir, and contrives to have the calm and objective instructions of the judge precede the jury's retirement for deliberation. It is as if the law in its wisdom sought to neutralize passion with reason.

Among the numerous instructions, defining murder, intention, etc., the Court instructed the jury that Crump's confession had been introduced in evidence, and it "must be considered by you." However, in determining its truth or falsity, if the jury found that "such confession was made because the defendant was influenced by threats of violence of any kind, then you may wholly disregard such confession."

Of course, the Court followed the appellate court's direction on the color issue:

"It is the duty of the jury to consider the prisoner's case as if he were a white man, for the law is the same as to both white and colored men, there being no distinction in principles in respect to color."

The jury filed out. Once more Crump lived through the excruciating hours of uncertainty as to whether he would walk out of the building free to live, love, and labor, or be caged in a cell for the rest of his dreary days, or be strapped in a hideous black chair until electric bolts burned his brain and shut off his heart.

The jury returned. It gave its answer:

"We, the jury, find the defendant, Paul Crump, guilty of murder, in manner and form as charged in the indictment, and we fix his punishment at death."

Few men have twice heard themselves condemned to die. Once again Crump heard the ritualistic words of doom:

". . . on the sixteenth day of March, A.D. 1956, the said defendant, Paul Crump, be by the Sheriff, according to law, within the walls of said jail . . . there be put to death, by having caused to pass through the body of said defendant, Paul Crump, a current of electricity of sufficient intensity to cause death and the application and continuance of such current through the body of said defendant until such defendant is dead.

"And, Paul Crump, may God have mercy on your soul."

Through his new counsel, George N. Leighton, Crump appealed from his second conviction, to the highest court of Illinois. Time and again the electrocution was postponed, because the printing of the record and preparation of briefs consumed almost two years. This time the chief contention for reversal was that Crump's confession was improperly admitted into evidence. After lengthy consideration of oral and printed arguments, the appellate court handed down its decision. The Court recited in detail the testimony on both sides, calling attention to the "four civic leaders" who had witnessed the signing of the confession and their statement that Crump and his confederates had been asked "if he had been mistreated or abused" and replied, "absolutely not, that they had wonderful treatment. Those were their words."

The appellate court also commented on the fact that fifty witnesses testified on behalf of the State, denying any duress or mistreatment, and that

"his own doctor and the doctor who witnessed the signing of the confession . . . could not find a bruise, welt or mark of physical violence or injury in their . . . examination of the defendant."

The Court observed that in summation Crump

"was permitted to argue in his own behalf. It was a splendid effort to evoke sympathy and humane consideration. But for the overwhelming proof of guilt, the result could have been different."

There was almost a note of reluctance and regret in the Court's words as it reached its conclusion, and they only emphasized the thoroughness and fairness of its consideration of the case:

"Two juries with the approval of two judges have found defendant guilty and decreed the extreme penalty. We have examined the long record critically and considered all claims of alleged mistakes in the trial. We find not one of a substantial or reversible character.

"The judgment . . . is affirmed."

The Court fixed the date of execution as Friday, January 31, 1958. An application was made by Crump's lawyer for a rehearing. It was denied on January 15, 1958. Crump was scheduled to die sixteen days later, which was almost five years after the murder. An application to the United States Supreme Court to review the decision of the Illinois court was denied. Application for rehearing was also denied.

There were no other proceedings which could be taken in the state courts of Illinois. But a new attorney, Donald Page Moore, took up the fight for Crump, by attempting to obtain jurisdiction in the lower federal courts. His theory was that Crump had been denied proper access to his own attorney when he signed his confession, and that this posed a constitutional question. He brought a habeas corpus proceeding, that is, to free the body of Crump on the ground that he was illegally detained in jail.

The lower Federal Court dismissed the petition without hearing. Moore appealed to the Court of Appeals. It reversed. The case went back to the District Court for a full hearing. It found that Crump's confession was voluntary. Another appeal to the Court of Appeals resulted in a unanimous opinion in November 1961 by Hastings, Chief Judge and Duffy and Schnackenberg, Circuit Judges, affirming the lower court.

Still Crump and his attorney Donald Moore did not quit. They tested the Court of Appeals decision by filing a petition for a writ of certiorari to the Supreme Court of the United States seeking a review. The Supreme Court denied the writ although Mr. Justice Douglas and Mr. Justice Brennan dissented.

Now all legal proceedings, State and Federal, had been exhausted. Crump's life had been extended almost nine years by the heroically determined effort on his behalf. Every resourceful and imaginative device to test the validity of his conviction had been employed. There was nothing left.

Crump was moved from his regular cell to the isolation cell near the execution chamber. Warden Jack Johnson began the tests and rehearsals with electricians, guards, and prison doctors, which precede electrocution. Crump would die on Friday at twelve midnight, on August 3, 1962. This date was final. It could not be and never was postponed.

It was at this point that I entered the case.

PART TWO: REHABILITATION

Power is a far greater lure than money. Its exercise is the ultimate gratification, because man needs to prove himself, and nothing feeds his sense of self-importance as much as his dominion over others. The bookkeeper who will forego a raise if he receives a corporate title, or the man who seeks public office to wield power on behalf of its citizens, share the same trait, the bolstering of ego. The pursuit of power probably more than any other factor has molded human history: patricides to seize kingdoms; decimating wars to rule millions of conquered; business warfare to build industrial dynasties; and lust for authority which affects all relationships, personal, social, and political.

There is a price, however. Not always does the exercise of power provide inner satisfactions. One such instance in which the responsibility which accompanies power is a harrowing experience, is an appeal for clemency in a criminal case. The Governor must face a heartbroken mother, who knows that only he has the Godlike power to prevent her son from dying at an appointed hour. He must listen to the wail of a shattered wife, who pleads that her children be not made orphans by executive fiat. He must weigh the priest's, minister's, or rabbi's appeal for divine compassion.

On the other hand, he must listen to the district attorney's reminder of the majesty of the law, which he has sworn to uphold, and the public interest, which requires that the jury's verdict after full and fair trial and numerous appeals be not nullified capriciously. Indeed, these warnings of his duty to reject anguished considerations, which were never extended to the victim of the crime, are often supported by the judge who presided at the trial, the wife and family of the murdered man, and above all by public clamor against interference with the judicial process. Such public concern has been known to unseat an otherwise popular Governor. It is not easy for a political figure, no matter how susceptible to emotional appeal, to ignore his duty.

Every President and Governor has attested to the ordeal which applications for clemency constitute. It is one power which any executive would gladly surrender.

This has led to certain procedures to relieve the Governor of hysterical, sentimental pressures, and make the application for clemency a more orderly and quasi-legal procedure.

So, in Illinois, for example, the Governor may convene a special session of the Illinois Parole and Pardon Board, composed of five commissioners, to hear testimony and make recommendations to the Governor whether the case is a proper one for the exercise of clemency. The hearing is in the nature of a full-fledged trial. Witnesses may be called by both sides and be cross-examined. The hearing is held in a courtroom presided over by the five commissioners, who act as judges.

Crump's lawyer, Donald Moore, requested such a proceeding, and notice of it was served on Judge Frank R. Leonard and Judge Elmer H. Holmgren, who had presided at Crump's trials, Warden Johnson of the jail where Crump was to be executed, the State's Attorney Daniel P. Ward, Mrs. Veronica Zukowski, wife of the murdered man, and Raymond Zukowski, his son.

Three weeks before the hearing, overtures were made to me by prominent citizens of Chicago to join with Moore in arguing Crump's plea for clemency before the specially convened Parole and Pardon Board.

I was legally engaged at the time—indeed, there were several simultaneous engagements. Each profession has its special hardships. In business enterprises one often hears of seasonal rushes, which create inordinate problems. The lawyer faces a not dissimilar dilemma when cases pending for a long time come to judgment day at the same time, or an emergency representation competes for immediate attention with an old case which has finally reached fruition. Nothing is more enervating to me than tearing my mind from its exclusive, rooted concentration in one matter, to transplant attention in other soil. It is not the hours of work which matter, since all the time available, even to sleeplessness, would be bestowed upon the original case anyhow. What is painful is the diversion of attention from a case which is all-absorbing at the moment. There is a continuation between the conscious effort and the subconscious search for solution. This quiet permanence of mental effort, even while one is eating, conversing, or sleeping, is an invaluable aid to the thinking process. It is the mysterious source from which ideas bubble up to the conscious mind. It requires, however, a full dedication to the subject matter—all else being excluded or the process stops. That is why creative artists in all fields are notoriously absentminded. Truly analyzed, they are extraordinarily presentminded, but only with their creative effort. Their minds, like their bodies, cannot be at two places at the same time.

It so happened that when this first call came to me to enter the Crump case, I represented Darryl F. Zanuck. This, in addition to the fact that I knew nothing at the time about Paul Crump, resulted in my unequivocal declination to represent him.

Thursday night, preceding the clemency hearing on Monday, July 30, 1962, I received the following telegrams:
I am facing execution in electric chair of Cook County Jail at 12:01 AM August 3, 1962. . . . My attorney believes that assistance of co-counsel will be required in order adequately to cope with critically important issues of public policy raised by my petition for executive clemency. For this reason, I earnestly beseech you to come to Chicago to assist in the presentation of my case. Since we have no funds, necessarily your appearance would be without fee. I hope that in the name of justice and humanity you will respond affirmatively.

Paul Crump

July 28, 2:07 AM
Urgently request you join with me as co-counsel in representing Paul Crump in proceeding for commutation of death sentence scheduled for hearing before Illinois Parole and Pardon Board in Chicago at 10 AM Monday, July 30th. Fundamental issues of justice and public policy presented by our petition based upon claim of petitioner's complete rehabilitation during his 9 year incarceration since arrest. Petitioner's execution set for August 3. Need older and wiser head to assist. Please respond as soon as possible.

Donald Page Moore
Attorney for Paul Crump

A telegram from a prominent citizens' committee of Chicago signed by David Wallerstein, President of a large chain of theaters, also arrived urging me to undertake the task.

As if it were military strategy to obtain the objective, this opening barrage of telegrams was followed by a telephone offensive. A series of calls came from Chicago and New York pressing acceptance upon me. While flattered and moved by these desperate calls, I saw no reason at first why I should respond.

To a friend in Chicago, Les Weinrott, whose plea was at least modified by reasoned consideration of my own problems, I explained that I had already obtained sailing accommodations for my wife and myself on the S.S. *Constitution;* that this was not only a vacation trip which (to use the puritanical approach to pleasure) I had earned; and that if I undertook the Crump representation, all this would have to be foregone. I explained that for several years I had canceled vacation trips because of emergency legal matters, and that (like the reporter in the stereotyped drama who gives up his honeymoon because the editor calls) I had given a solemn promise to my wife, Mildred, that this time we would sail.

He laughingly undercut my labored persuasive effort by saying, "You surely will sail, Lou. The Crump case can't stop you even if you argue it. Crump will either be dead Friday night, or his sentence will be commuted. You will be sailing Wednesday, in any event. There can be no delays here."

I had never experienced such a literal deadline before.

I turned to the principle involved. Crump, I was told, had been rehabilitated during the nine years he waited for execution. Never before had clemency been granted on such grounds. Indeed, six prior applications on behalf of other prisoners on the ground of rehabilitation had all been denied by the Parole and Pardon Board and by the Governor. A new precedent was therefore at stake, and one in which I believed. But where was the real evidence of Crump's rehabilitation?

I had opened the door. Within a half-hour, a messenger was dispatched by plane from Chicago with a valise full of documents.

When I received them, I turned at once to some two hundred pages of affidavits which had been prepared for submission to the Parole and Pardon Board. They were made by the warden, assistant warden, two nurses, twenty-eight guard officers, four chaplains, three physicians, in short everyone who had been in intimate contact with Paul Crump during those nine years. These affidavits differed in form from those usually drawn. It is customary for the attorney to dictate the substance of the witness's statement. While the witness approves its accuracy, he benefits from the improved grammar and syntax of his lawyer's dictation. But Moore had adopted a literal approach, and it heightened the effectiveness of the statements. The witness's words were taken down just as spoken in all their colloquialism, prison jargon, and American lingo. Sincerity came through the documents, which more polished language might have blocked out.

I had approached the reading of the documentation with calm curiosity and a suppressed sigh as if I wished I could turn to more worthwhile literature. But the words were flames which leaped from the paper and enveloped me with zeal. I never went to sleep. Before dawn broke I knew I would be in Chicago the next day fighting for Paul Crump.

When Warden Jack Johnson first assumed office in 1955, he found Crump "choked up with hatred, animalistic and belligerent."

Shortly thereafter Crump and twelve other condemned men on Death Row staged a riot. They smashed lights, ripped apart wooden benches, set fire to blankets and mattresses. The warden had to have six shells of tear gas thrown into the cells to flush out the insurrectionists. The guards did not carry brass knuckles, blackjacks, and miniature baseball bats. The warden had decided that "a single word of love was what was lacking in this jail." He installed two telephones outside the tier and told the inmates, "Any time you guys want to talk to me, call me up."

He arranged for groups of three and four to visit him and the new prison sociologist and psychologist.

The prisoners stated their gripes about food, inadequate reading matter, brutal guards, and dirty cells. But Crump, bitter and sulking, refused at first to attend any of these meetings. Later Crump recalled: "Finally I began to see that the Old Man was serious about his philosophy. There was a guard who beat up an inmate with a baseball bat. The next day I was sitting in the office next to the warden's and I heard him tell a bunch of guards: 'If I hear of this happening again, I'll break your goddamned leg.'"

It began to dawn on Crump that law officials were not

deliberate tormentors, and that the society they represented was not his enemy. Was it possible that he was its enemy?

During the many years that the courts were passing on Crump's case, he sat alone, caged with his own thoughts and feelings. A great struggle began within him. While judges were reviewing the law, he was reviewing himself. He carried on his own appeals to reverse the ignorance, cupidity, and hatred which beset his soul. He strove to release and develop the goodness within him.

The very first affidavit revealed the mysterious beginnings of rehabilitation. It was made by Hans W. Mattick, the assistant warden. He was not merely a prison official. His horizon of understanding derived from a remarkable background as an administrator of prison war camps, a graduate of the University of Chicago with a master's degree, a lecturer at that university on criminology and at Indiana University on sociology, President of the Illinois Academy of Criminology, and the author of several books on juvenile delinquency. These qualifications gave special impact to his story.

He had not taken any special note of Paul Crump, but one day Crump asked to see him. He was working on a manuscript and inquired whether there were any books which would improve his writing. Mattick advised him that the better way was to learn how to read analytically. Then he might write better. He assigned Melville's *Moby Dick* to him and asked him to write an essay of about fifteen pages about it. He did so. Then Mattick related,

"I asked him to read the entire book over again from cover to cover. But that he should read it as a lover would read a letter from a loved one when the status of the relationship was in doubt. Then he should write another essay. . . . I was interested to see if he was sensitive to symbolic messages in the book."

Crump perceived that the essence of the book was that though evil might seem to triumph, the spirit of man would rise again.

"Paul then did an analysis which would have done credit to an English literature major in college."

The man who in his confession had used such phrases as "I taken a walk," "the onliest way I could keep my wife out of it," and "I know I have did some wrong," devoured book after book, and particularly mystic poetry like Blake's. He became articulate and thoughtful. He rewrote his novel *Burn, Killer, Burn!*, which has since been published.

The thirst for learning was only one facet of the rebirth of a man.

Mattick went on:

"From this intimate contact with Paul, I was able to really get to know him. I have seen all types of prisoners sentenced to death—at least twenty. Some of them become immersed in self-pity; some go to pieces; some fill themselves with a sense of injustice. But Paul seemed to rise above these self-centered concerns."

Crump's interest in others resulted in his becoming tier clerk. He could have played favorites, or settled personal scores. Instead he applied himself conscientiously to his responsibility as internal administrative head.

One of the prisoners was a manic-depressive who would go through a twenty-four-hour cycle of alternate depression and elation. By the twelfth hour he was screaming and banging his head on the bars. Then he would calm down, and ultimately retreat under his blanket in a sort of coma.

"Paul would see that his needs, such as cleanliness and food, were taken care of. This guy was a great big man, six feet four inches. He was a Jamaican Negro. When he was aggravated, it took more than three men to handle him. Paul would look after him."

There was a young prisoner who was a self-mutilator.

"Paul would keep an eye on him and see that he did not hurt himself. When the kid was shaving, Paul would make sure that he gave back the safety razor with the razor still there."

Another prisoner charged with murder was a policeman named Dawson. A former "cop" is in constant jeopardy from the inmates, and is usually placed in the maximum security tier.

"Paul saw to it that the policeman got his food and that nothing happened to him."

In a prison, the same door which locks a man in also locks the guards out. If any disorder occurs inside the community of inmates, it is invaluable to have a trusted prisoner who has the respect of his fellow prisoners, but can exercise his will even at personal risk to preserve order.

"Out of Paul's natural leadership quality, he gained the respect not only of the inmates but also of the guards.

"He wrote letters for those who could not write. He was a kind of charismatic type. . . . Though he worked along with the administration, he was not a stool pigeon. He kept his personal integrity, and therefore he was accepted by the inmates who needed a mediator and a leader."

The chief nurse of the Cook County Jail, Elizabeth Wesseling, a graduate of Loyola University of Chicago, testified that Crump was put in charge of a tier for the chronically ill, such as ulcer patients, diabetics, and alcoholics. He guarded and protected them against their own ignorance.

"He knew how to handle a person with the d.t.'s. One such prisoner would have died, were it not for Paul. He saved this man's life. It is a fact."

It was prison procedure for the chief doctor and chief nurse to make the rounds in the prison hospital among the sick.

"Never before had a woman been on the tier. Paul always knew when we were coming and would have everything under control. By that I mean he made sure there was no cursing and that everyone was decently dressed and that everyone was in his cell.

"I feel very strongly about Paul, a feeling which I didn't develop toward any of the other men. It's just that Paul is so very, very exceptional."

An affidavit by Patrick Roark, a fellow prisoner, revealed that Crump sorted out the malingerers from those really ill.

"An inmate, Richard Clemmenson, had been complaining that his broken leg was still continuing to bother him, and Crump decided that Clemmenson was really experiencing more pain than he should. Crump then went out of his way to see that Clemmenson received a special examination and it was determined that the leg in fact had not been properly set."

Another inmate, "Shaky" Maloney, had palsy. He was unmercifully ridiculed by other prisoners, who derived satisfaction from finding weaknesses in others. Maloney continuously responded by fighting his tormentors. Crump not only taught the prisoners that their jests were cruel, but was able to win over Maloney to the subtleties of being above such crude taunts. Crump's conduct ranged from such psychological discipline to physical service.

He would himself bathe the old and infirm men and see to it that they had clean clothing.

Crump's character impressed itself even on the most undisciplined. Hardened "punks and wise kids," leaders of juvenile gangs, who defied the most professional approaches of prison and religious authorities, yielded to Crump and respected him. He lectured them in their own terms, "Why don't you get smart. Do you want to end up in this place the rest of your life?"

Dozens of guards asserted that Crump actually reformed young criminals and set them on the right road.

"His relationship with them was like an older brother or father. If something bothered them, they would take it to Crump. None of them ever gave Crump 'any lip.'"

Whenever a psychopath or particularly difficult case taxed the disciplinary skills of the authorities, he was transferred to Crump's tier. Invariably Paul succeeded, even using force at the risk of his life, when he needed to do so.

One such prisoner, by the name of Nix, secured the lid of a sardine can and sharpened it into a knife blade. He threatened Crump with it, but Crump personally disarmed him, forbade the use of sardine cans on the tier, and reduced this dangerous inmate to submissive obedience.

Another prisoner had an uncontrollable suicidal drive. He repeatedly cut his wrists. As a final resort the warden placed him in Crump's tier, in the hope of saving his life. Crump organized shifts of inmates to watch this man so that he could not pull the stitches out and bleed to death. He finally obtained control over the man's will, sufficiently to abandon his wrist-slashing, if on no other basis than that it was a futile exercise against Paul's alertness.

Another prisoner, Robinson, went on a hunger strike. Crump knew he was diabetic and might go into a coma. He used persuasion and the threat that he would transfer him to another tier, and deprive him of Crump's supervision, to get him to eat. Indeed, his influence was so great that often the mere threat of transfer to another tier would bring an unruly prisoner into line.

Captain Ray Schumacher, a guard officer of Cook County Jail for sixteen years, testified that Crump

"settles disputes which come up between the men. He's a combined judge and orderly among the men. He prevents fights. He's capable of doing it. He really does."

It is not a coincidence that violent epileptics are often

found among criminals. Crump always carried a spoon, so that he could press down the victim's tongue and prevent him from swallowing it and thus strangling himself. He fought powerful men during their fits, and many prison guards attested to the fact that time and again he saved epileptics' lives.

Captain Schumacher related Crump's solicitude for the blind and crippled. Woe befell those prisoners who stole food or other objects from them.

"Paul sometimes goes without eating to make sure that everyone else gets a fair deal. . . . I've seen Paul work with the men; you know, there's more to it than that. He has some sort of special magic."

Joseph Touhy, a guard officer for seven years, told of an incident in which a prisoner, jealous of Crump's influence, hurled epithets at him.

"The guy was saying, 'Do I have to listen to this nigger just because he's going to the chair?'"

The other inmates, white and colored, were so incensed that harm might have come to the prejudiced perpetrator, were it not that Crump, to save him, locked him in his cell.

"We completely approved of Paul's action in this case, and therefore for his own protection we kept the guy locked up in his cell."

In the course of freeing himself from the corrosion of hate, Crump succeeded in eradicating his innermost bitterness [ingrained in childhood] against the injustice he had been subjected to because he was a Negro. One guard, Sergeant Charles Snead, observed that

"Color does not mean anything to Paul. All you have to do is go down and take a look. You see him picking up a white guy and giving him a shower. He is therefore as effective with both Negroes and whites."

He rose above retaliation, understandable as that would be. It was Crump who was "tolerant" about color.

The guard officer in charge of the jail laundry, Morris Goldstein, attested that:

"Whenever any laundry was missing, as when a prisoner did not return something because they had forgotten or held back, I would ask Paul to go get the sheets or the blanket. He'd speak to the other prisoners, and get them all back.

"We hate to see him go. He always gives the guards a smile, and says hello. He cooperates in every way he can."

One of the guard officers, Peter DeStito, had a little cousin who was born with "a hole in his heart." Substantial quantities of blood were necessary if the child's life was to be saved. DeStito appealed to the warden to ask the prisoners to be blood donors. He was informed that it was up to the prisoners, and of course he turned to Crump. The affidavit continued: "In, oh, fifteen or twenty minutes Paul had about fifty signatures of men who were willing to donate blood. Paul got all of them to volunteer. And all those that signed gave blood, too . . .

"I've never seen any other condemned man, so, oh, changed, so willing to work, so good natured. You know what they say about an exception to a rule; well Paul's the exception."

In 1957, there were thirteen condemned men in one of the tiers, and they planned a desperate escape through one of the air vents. They had accumulated broomsticks, and turned them into sharp lances by breaking them. The guard to be disposed of was John Maraldo, stationed on the catwalk. Crump discovered the plot at the last moment. At the risk of his life, he got to Maraldo and warned him in time to escape to the control room. To cover up the break for freedom, the prisoners' plan called for a diversionary riot. Mattresses were burned. Sinks and bowls were broken and thrown as weapons; but Maraldo, whose capture and keys were to make escape possible, was out of reach. Crump single-handedly fought the rioters until an emergency squad brought the insurrection to an end.

Crump knew the inexorable rules by which criminals lived in jail, and that the pent-up hatred against him for thwarting an escape would make him a marked man for injury or death. He never hesitated, however, to do what was right. He had already elevated himself above the criminal code, which required loyalty to the lawless, even to one's own attempted assassin. He recognized only the moral code, thus achieving freedom for his conscience, while his body was still imprisoned. His standing with the great majority of prisoners was so high that he must have been shielded by them, just as he had shielded so many of them. It was difficult even for hardened prison guards to understand the phenomenon of his rehabilitation. As one guard officer said in his affidavit, "It's sort of bewildering."

The extraordinary fact was that in this chorus of praise for Crump, there was not a single dissent. Everyone in the jail who had any contact with him had been interviewed. The result was a unanimous paean of glory. It was almost too much when I read guard officer Thomas Harris's comment that Crump sat up all night with the sick and that, "He's a sort of St. Paul on the spot"; or the affidavit of Joseph Rifka, a guard officer for six years, of how Paul had spread the Christmas spirit and inspired the prisoners to decorate their cells with imaginative ingenuity; or Inspector Sergeant Leon Kozloff's affidavit of how Crump cared for an old Orthodox Jew who was in his seventies and set in his ways.

"The man had a skullcap and a prayer shawl. He read the Hebrew Bible every day. He would eat only kosher food. In the jail, this is a very difficult desire to satisfy. Paul would give the man his own eggs."

Crump provided a quiet corner where the old man could pray aloud every day, and prevented others from ridiculing him. Guard Simon Clark revealed that Crump sang ballads well "and was very good at playing the harp"—(the harp!). I yearned to read of some fall from grace. My rule of probability told me that perfection, even if true, was incredible. I later discovered two retrogressions in Crump's amazing ascendancy and I took pains to have testimony at length about them. I wanted Crump to be a dimensional human being, not a saint, for saints do not need clemency or commutation of sentence.

Warden Jack Johnson was so moved by Crump's rehabilitation that he wrote to the Federal judge pleading in favor of his petition for a habeas corpus writ. Although the warden's intervention was unsuccessful, Crump, who was trying desperately at the time to stave off his execution, was so grateful that, clutching the letter, he fell down on his knees and wept for nearly an hour. "I have a father," Crump said, "a white father." The warden observed:

"I think it was the first time in his life, Paul ever completely let himself go. And for the first time, he really believed in another person."

Paradoxically, it was because of this relationship that Crump asked the warden to pull the switch on the night of the execution. He wanted his friend to perform the act, so that he would not think of it as an act of personal venom. Warden Johnson understood and promised he would do so.

Was Crump feigning? Were his good deeds calculated to evoke mercy? One of the guard officers, Fred Defourneau, who saw Crump about four times a week for two years, and thereafter daily, described his own background in order to support his judgment:

"I served as a sergeant in the Engineers Battalion of the United States Army. I was in charge of a squad of thirteen men who were specially trained for disarming and dismantling explosive shells and mines.

"In this sort of work, it was an absolute necessity to form good, precise, and intelligent estimates of the men under my direction. A bad guess about a man might lead to everyone in our unit being blown up."

Defourneau related that Crump had become proficient in reading and interpreting the Bible; had arranged radio silence for reading periods; had pulled down several prisoners who had attempted to hang themselves and "gave them a good talking to with kindness not harsh words"; had persuaded prisoners about to be released to follow a decent life. "He is more of a leader than an inmate," the affidavit concluded. "I do believe we now have a first-class citizen in Paul Crump."

Charles Thornton Sweeny, the administrator of the Northwest Illinois Community Hospital, and at one time an assistant administrator of Methodist Hospital in Gary, Indiana, had worked as a law clerk at the Cook County Jail. One of his thankless jobs was to distribute copies of indictments to prisoners as well as postal cards with which they would notify their families. He also was mail censor and he read everything which came into or out of the prison. When he first met Paul in 1955,

"he was a very hostile, aggressive, egotistical individual. He had a chip on his shoulder. In the course of delivering indictments, Crump would subject me to verbal abuse and profanity."

Crump's library at the time consisted of cheap paperback novels.

"There was no sudden metamorphosis with Paul Crump. There was no bright flash of light striking him down on the road to Damascus, but rather a slow evolution of his personality. This change was also reflected in the content of his mail which I censored—no longer the typical sex-starved prisoner, writing to unattached females, hoping eventually to get out and establish a liaison."

Sweeny admitted that at first he was afraid of Crump, that he was "menacing," and that this emotion was replaced "with a feeling of warm friendship and regard for the man as an intelligent, warm, friendly human being.
"I think it's a great pity that a man of the intellectual caliber and understanding of Paul Crump does not have an opportunity for further education, and to become a teacher or a social worker."

The affidavits were a shrewd mixture of statements by guards, who talked like "screws," and approached the behavior of prisoners with cynical experience, and statements by sociologists who evaluated the phenomenon of Crump's rehabilitation with psychiatric insights. Yet their conclusions were identical. Their enthusiasm for Crump was steeped in sentiment, uncommon to both.

So, for another example, was the affidavit of the administrative assistant of the sheriff in charge of correction at Cook County Jail. He was John H. Gagnon, a research associate and trustee of the Institute of Research at Indiana University, who had written his Ph.D. thesis in sociology. He had observed Crump from his early "embittered, anti-administration" attitude to his belief that "though condemned to death, he could still have a meaningful life."

Then followed the statement of Sergeant William Heyer, a guard officer, that the prison was spic and span as never before, because Paul assigned the inmates to clean and mop, and "he works along too."

Officer James McGinnes described Paul's unobtrusive dedication not only to the mentally deformed, but to the physically maimed:
"I saw him assist one of those guys who had an operation, the type where the guy no longer had a rectum. Paul assisted the guy in taking a bath. He does not have to do things like that, but Paul does. He goes out of his way to help the other inmates."

One of the extraordinary facts about Crump's new view of life was that the change within him didn't set him off, as it might, as a reformed purist, to become the butt of ridicule by hardened convicts. He activated his goodness, and unwittingly, gave it a missionary impact.

"By setting the proper example and by, oh, having that something, he is able to get through to some of the hard eggs. . . . After Paul's worked on them, he's cracked the shell, and many of them turn out to be pretty good inmates. For example, one of those guys who recently tried to break out of Bridewell was sent in here. He was very boasting when they brought him in here. They put him in there with Paul. After being there, I could see that he had changed. Paul had gotten to him."

Tributes followed from Dr. Michael I. Gererrieri, prison dentist; Walter Makowski, chief security officer, and from personnel assistant to the warden, John H. Stroger, Jr.

Like a symphony whose upper theme is finely spun in esoteric tones and is followed for contrast by the clamor of drums, I found on the very next page the statement of guard officer John Este:

"If an inmate is having any trouble he will get in touch with Paul, even if he is not in Paul's tier. . . .

"When a prisoner in another tier has been fighting, we will lock him up in a tier where Paul is. . . . Paul will make a model prisoner out of him; he'll straighten the guy out. Paul's a natural leader."

Dr. George Shropshear, medical superintendent at Cook County Jail, sang Crump's praises for tending to ill prisoners: "Paul is able to detect hypo-glycemic, i.e., an insulin reaction."

He warned the medical department at once whenever adrenalin was not aiding an asthmatic:

"There is a grapevine that no one has access to other than the prisoners. Many prisoners are kept in line because of Paul's control of the grapevine."

Dr. M. Charhewicz, who had served in the Twenty-eighth Field Hospital in Germany and later was assigned to the Cook County Jail Hospital, observed that Crump aided prisoners seventy or eighty years old.

"He serves them their food; helps them to the washroom, helps them clean their cells, and even themselves. . . ."

Father Cronan Murphy, chaplain at Cook County Jail, attested that Crump, one of his "parishioners," not only practiced his religion faithfully, but also exerted a wholesome influence upon his fellow prisoners. "It is always a source of wonderment to me how any man could possibly maintain sanity under the conditions to which Paul was subjected by the mere fact of incarceration while awaiting death. No human being could assess the price Paul has already paid many times over for any guilt he may have had."

I read on through the night. The affidavits were like irregular, haphazard pieces of marble of varied colors. But when one stepped back to get an over-all impression, there emerged a mosaic of reconstructed personality, of rebuilt character.

When I had concluded my first reading of the affidavits I reread the following sentence from the People's brief, submitted in opposition to clemency:

"As we have said, rehabilitation, whether real or honestly imagined, or falsely posed, should not govern the recommendation of this Board. It is not a basis for clemency."

This was a correct statement of the law, but it infuriated me. It reduced punishment to mere vengeance, or warning for the future. It ignored, no, worse than that, it rejected what seemed to me to be the only conscionable ground for ever inflicting pain—the hope of reform and redemption. Had we not in the twentieth century emerged from the darkness of death by retaliation? Was there no higher purpose for the brutalizing exaction of ending life, than that we had sated ourselves with revenge? Where rehabilitation has occurred, the total objective of punishment, it seemed to me, had been achieved. Yet the law said rehabilitation was "not a basis for clemency." It was a law which had to be reformed, and I was burning to make the attempt.

While I was caught up in the circle of Crump's rehabilitation, which personalized the issue, I knew that the principle which was involved extended beyond him to hundreds of others, still unknown, and indeed to a more enlightened concept of penology. That Crump succeeded, under the handicap of prison darkness, constituted an unbelievable saga of man's power of redemption. He seemed to me to be the symbol for all mankind struggling to emerge from centuries of murder to the enlightenment of brotherhood.

As I dozed off, I thought of the words of Nathaniel Hawthorne:

"The best of us being unfit to die, what an unexpressible absurdity it is to put the worst to death."

In the morning, as early as I dared wake my friends in Chicago, I telephoned my decision to fly there immediately. Curiously, my acceptance tempered their elation with caution. Now they felt it their duty to warn me that defeat, if not inevitable, was strongly indicated. While an article in *Life* Magazine, setting forth Crump's rehabilitation, and columnist Irving Kupcinet's telecast, as well as other printed comments, had created sympathetic public opinion in some quarters, the general view was that a brutal murderer, convicted twice, and the recipient of every conceivable legal resource, ought to pay the penalty provided by law in a crime-infested city. Furthermore, the political overtones were ominous. Governor Otto Kerner would be risking his career if he yielded to entreaties for clemency in so shocking a case. He would have to be courageous beyond the call of duty to commute the sentence. He was being asked to create a new precedent, six times previously denied by other Governors and himself.

The worst news of all was that Warden Jack Johnson, Crump's "white father," and his dedicated friend, might not be permitted to testify. No one knew what had happened, but the warden, who had talked freely to the press in support of Crump, might have been subjected to discipline. Also the hope of a favorable statement by Richard Cardinal Cushing himself, which had been a real probability, had suddenly vanished. Apparently as the hour drew near, the factors needed for a precedent-shattering decision were melting away.

I thanked them for their solicitude about me, but did not everything they said indicate that Crump needed more help, not less? What did the probability of defeat for a lawyer have to do with it? Victory and loss percentages are appropriate for baseball box scores, not for an advocate for justice. Indeed, now the challenge was greater. The cause appeared more noble because no moral issue should be hopeless. It would have taken a sledgehammer to keep me away.

My friends almost supplied it. After emotional acceptance of my determination to plead for Crump, they called back to say that they had arranged a television program and press interview upon my arrival, to help create favorable public opinion. I threatened to withdraw at once, unless all this was canceled. We were engaged in a quasi-judicial proceeding before the Parole and Pardon Board. Any attempt to try the

case on the television screen and in the newspapers was
bound to prejudice the five Parole and Pardon Board commissioners against us. Indeed, as we shall see, the district
attorney, in the argument before the Parole and Pardon
Board, castigated the prior publicity on behalf of Crump.
Furthermore, a man's life was at stake. Any conduct by
counsel (even though sincerely planned to create public
sympathy) which might be distorted as creating a carnival
atmosphere, could endanger our cause. I insisted, on pain of
withdrawal, that there be no preliminary announcement of
my appearance in the case.

Mr. Weinrott called back to say that although the newspapers knew of the developments, he had obtained their
voluntary withholding of the item, until I actually appeared
at the hearing Monday morning. "I cannot guarantee this,"
he said, "because it would be the first time, to my knowledge,
that such a pact had been made, but I hope it will work." It
did, chiefly because most of the newspapermen knew the
inside story of Crump's remarkable conversion to rectitude,
and wanted to assist him, and besides the announcement of
additional counsel was hardly an invaluable bit of news.

I had apparently impressed Crump's counsel and friends
deeply with the need for anonymity, because when I arrived
in Chicago, I found that my reservation at the Sheraton-
Chicago Hotel had been made in cloak-and-dagger style in
the fictional name of Mr. Louis Doubleday.

It was Saturday. We had less than forty-eight hours before
the hearing would begin. Not a precious second could be
wasted. I immersed myself in the two huge printed volumes
(more than fifteen hundred pages) of Crump's prior trials,
and all the briefs and opinions on appeal, as well as the excellent brief prepared by Moore for the instant hearing, and
the opposing brief. This reading, like some of my writing, had
to be conducted while eating a snack on the plane, riding in
cabs, talking on the telephone, and even shaving and bathing.
How I wished we had two months instead of less than two
days. While there is no ameliorating substitute for thorough
preparation, it is true that working at feverish pitch against
the ticking of a clock intensifies the concentration so that
absorption is accelerated. Thus time is artificially stretched.
Also the body is adrenalized by crisis, making sleep unnecessary. There is no universal rule for all in these matters. Every

person must learn the preconditions for effective functioning, suitable to his or her unique physical and emotional mechanism. But I find that increased energy from stimulation can be put to best use only if serenity pervades the whole effort. Unless the speeded-up motor is controlled by self-disciplined inner brakes, it can only cause runaway confusion. Efficiency cannot be obtained by hyperthyroidial haste, or gritted-teeth determination. A conscious effort must be made to relax so that true speed and power can emanate. A famous surgeon once instructed his class that the rupture of a certain artery will cause death unless it is sewed together within 2½ minutes. "You can do it in two minutes, provided you don't hurry."

So, paradoxically, one must train himself to be calm at the very moment when elation or desperation causes emotional momentum. It is a deceptive calm, and I can understand how observers of a lawyer in the midst of trial are deceived into believing that he is unconcerned and disinterested almost to the point of listlessness. They will be safe in assuming that beneath the surface there is raw-edged concentration.

Serenity is more contagious than humor or good spirits. It tends to settle down the jittery. It breeds confidence, just as hysteria undermines it. We soon learned that we needed all the calm we could muster.

I had formed a most favorable impression of Donald Page Moore from our telephone conversations. While he was given to uninhibited expressions of admiration, they were embarrassing, not cloying, because their sincerity, no matter how misguided, was genuine and one knew that he would be just as sharp and critical, if honesty so required. He was the kind of man who wore his inner thoughts, as well as his heart, on his sleeve. When I met him, our rapport quickly ripened to friendship. His heavy-set body, rotund face, in which his blue eyes were aged by old-fashioned unrimmed glasses, and his intense earnestness, made him look much older than his mere twenty-eight years.

He was very emotional, chuckling gleefully, or clouding up with tears in his eyes, whenever good or ill fortune hit us. His dedication to Crump's cause was so complete that I feared the consequences to his health if Crump were executed. He represented that Midwestern type of lawyer, epitomized by

Clarence Darrow, who hid his profundity and learning behind homespun philosophy and careless attire. He even affected a slight stutter, as if he weren't sure of his thoughts, or was handicapped by inarticulateness, while weaving a spell of eloquence. Despite genuine modesty ("I hope I didn't spoil anything, Mr. Nizer, by what I said to the court"), he was a legal scholar and his research was of the highest order. Of course, the chief bond between us was that we were both committed to save Paul Crump and crash through an archaic concept of penology.

We reviewed the list of witnesses and planned the hearing procedure. Scheduled to testify was a psychiatrist, Dr. Jordan Scher. I feared being immersed in complicated and disputable jargon of a brilliant but uncertain science. If we had some evenings to spare, in which to elicit privately all of Dr. Scher's views, and to subject him to cross-examination drills on controversial subject matter, I would have reserved judgment. But our preparation time at this point was more limited than Crump's life span, and I preferred to rely on the earthy, realistic, impressive evidence in the more than two hundred pages of affidavits, as well as a group of effective live witnesses. So I recommended that we eliminate Dr. Scher from our witness list. Moore instantly agreed. When Moore notified Dr. Scher that we would not call him, despite prior conferences with him, he became offended at what he thought was a discourtesy. I should have taken the precaution of calling him personally, explaining the reason for my decision, and expressing our gratitude. In the rush of events, I failed to do the considerate thing. The lesson was not lost on me, for the practice of law is not a disembodied application of rules to people. It is contact with human beings, and the winning or losing of a witness often equates with the winning or losing of a case. That is one of the reasons why the law is more of an art than a science, an art not only in imaginative interpretation, but in human relations; in the use of infinite psychological insights to win the mind of a witness, a juror, or a judge.

The time had come to meet Paul Crump. Aside from the need to give him solace as he faced the last forty-eight hours before decision, there was a delicately critical question which I wanted to put to him.

The prison authorities arranged to have him brought from

his isolation death cell to the visiting room for a final meeting with his lawyers.

When Moore and I arrived at the Cook County Jail, the guards peered at us through a small window set in a huge metal door. The wired glass in that window revealed its bulletproof character by exhibiting five or six bullet scars. There were enormous noises as keys were turned, heavy levers lifted, and the huge iron door clanged open. After we entered, the ominous door shut, repeating the sounds as if they were delayed echoes. My eye quickly took in the surroundings. On the right were metal bars from ceiling to floor, with another heavy door requiring a different guard's enormous key. Behind these bars, a corridor led to the conference table where prisoners met their visitor.

On the left was a solid wall, from which a quadrangular steel turret jutted out. It looked like a huge, stationary military tank with guns pointing in all directions. There were several small bulletproof windows, which permitted the guards, sitting in safety behind the armor, to spray their shots in any direction. Even if by some ingenious means a large number of the prisoners could escape from the labyrinths beneath, they would have to approach this final exit, and here they would be open targets for guards sheltered by an impenetrable steel fort. All this gave meaning to an otherwise incongruous sign which hung at one of the entrances to the cellblocks, and which read, "THINK."

While waiting for Crump to be brought from the cell at the far end of the building, next to the electric chair, I continued to utilize every second by reading and underlining passages in the printed record. How strange they seemed, in this setting, which physically revealed the ultimate futility of his struggle to escape the law's exactions.

Finally Crump arrived. He looked immaculately clean in a gleaming white T-shirt and dark prison-gray pants. His face was shiny from a fresh shave. His hair was neatly barbered. (I observed with relief it was not yet shaved.) His mustache made a very thin, low line on his thick lip. He looked in perfect trim, from his powerful neck, tapering down to sloping shoulders, to his flat stomach. His arms, extending from the short sleeves, revealed huge biceps and gave veracity to the athlete's chest dimly outlined beneath the shirt. His good health made the imminence of death seem more outrageous.

One could detect immediately his good relationship with the guards. They were at ease with him, as if indeed he was one of them, and they nodded him toward us in a friendly manner. He approached, solemn-faced, only his eyes revealing the unrest which must have been stirring within him. As we sat down across an open table, and greeted each other, I could see that he was appraising me as I was him.

Moore made a lavish introduction of me, which I welcomed because I knew its purpose was to give Crump confidence. I brushed aside the amenities in an effort to break the tension. "Let's save the compliments and congratulations until we have won. Right?" He smiled broadly, his white teeth shining happiness. For some reason this momentary display of gaiety gave me a more poignant jolt than his first solemn appearance. I attempted immediately to diminish the quiet fear which seemed to come from his eyes. "Mr. Crump, I do not want to buoy up your spirits with false promises. But I must tell you that your conduct, while here, has brought forth such a volume of impressive tributes to your rehabilitation that we are confident the Board will recommend commutation of sentence to the Governor, and that he will act favorably. Let me assure you that every ounce of strength, thought, and skill that I possess will be applied to win commutation for you. Warden Clinton T. Duffy of San Quentin is here. We have carefully interviewed him. He will be a wonderful witness for you. Religious ministers of all faiths will testify on your behalf. Every guard and prison official is with you. I am confident you will win. Please keep up your courage and your faith. We will not fail you."

He thanked us unemotionally, in low, vibrant tones, but he inhaled his cigarette smoke so deeply that it seemed to disappear within him for a long time, finally jetting from his nostrils in a fierce stream.

I wanted him to talk and loosen up. What better way was there than to change the subject to one of his own cherished activities?

"I understand you are finishing a novel," I said. "Writing is really hard work, isn't it? How are you getting on?"

His eyes banished the harrowed look that was in them, replacing it with excitement. He began slowly to talk of his difficulty in creating characters, and became more articulate, as I engaged him in a discussion of the problems which faced a novelist, the struggle between authenticity and imagination, and the need to fuse the two. He lost himself in reverie for a moment and talked about himself. "When I first arrived here, I learned that I was the youngest prisoner ever to occupy a death cell in this jail. I asked myself, how did this happen to me? It couldn't all be the fates. Not everyone else could be to blame but me. There must be something awfully wrong with my attitude toward the world. I hated society. I hated my father. I hated the law. It seemed to be my special enemy. Now I was going to die, and I had hardly lived. The least I could do was to be useful for as many days as I had to live. I determined not to waste another hour with bitterness and hate. If I had a little more time, I would try to educate myself, so that I could be of greater usefulness. As I went on, my eyes were opened to the beauty of living helpfully, of the joys of doing good for a change. I had done so much harm to people, I wanted to make up for it, in whatever small way I could—even while in jail."

After a while he seemed thoroughly thawed out. He was talking easily. Even the lazy curling from his cigarette was a smoke signal of repose. This was the moment to broach the highly sensitive subject which was the real purpose of my visit.

"Paul, may I call you Paul? I am going to ask you a question. You don't have to answer it, but I feel it is our duty to bring the matter to your attention, so that you can act on it if you wish. It is the kind of decision which we as lawyers have no right to make for you. Only you can make it. But let me assure you in advance that no matter what your decision is, it will not affect our effort on your behalf. We will pour our hearts out for your cause irrespective of your answer. So don't let your judgment be based in the slightest on the effect it will have on us. In other words, we are not using any pressure on you to make the decision one way or the other.

"There is one vulnerable point in our case. We contend you are rehabilitated, a man who has seen the right way and changed. This, of course, is the truth. We know, however, that the district attorney will argue that there can be no rehabilitation without repentance, and that there can be no repentance without full confession.

"In other words, Paul, we are going to be confronted with

the argument that contrition can only follow confession, and that to this day you have never admitted committing the crime for which you were convicted; to this day you haven't said, 'I'm sorry for what I did in the Libby, McNeill & Libby robbery and murder.' The district attorney in his printed brief has already made much of this point. He argues that there really has been no rehabilitation, because you still stand by (what he characterized as) your perjured testimony, that you weren't even at the scene of the robbery and had nothing to do with it. You may be sure that at the hearing, tomorrow, we will hear plenty about this. He will ask, 'Why doesn't Crump, even at this last moment, tell the truth? Why doesn't he admit that his original written confession was the truth? How can we believe that he is rehabilitated when he still stands by a story which two juries and six appellate judges declared was a lie?'

"Now, Paul, even if we go into the trial without any confession by you, we believe the evidence of your rehabilitation is overwhelming. But, if you wish to discuss with us a possible statement of confession and repentance, which we would present to the Board tomorrow, we are ready to do so."

I had finished, but he continued to look me in the eye as if he were still listening to the echoes of what I had said. Then he lowered his eyes, and sat still endlessly in thought. Finally, he looked at me again and said, "Mr. Nizer, when I progressed to a certain point in my education, and began to have better understanding of my relationship to the world, even the limited world of a jail, I still felt frustrated by lack of faith. I wanted to learn to believe. I never had any religion. So I decided to adopt one. I studied the different religions, and liked what they taught, but I chose the Catholic religion because it had the greatest discipline, and I figured that's what I needed.

"At first, I was like all converts, pretty fanatical about my new religion. Then, with greater maturity, I recognized that being devout doesn't relieve one of the duty to translate his belief in daily conduct—in doing good, no matter how trivial. So I spent less time in prayer and devotion and more time in helping the terribly sick people, in body and soul, who inhabit a prison. Still I am dedicated to my religion. I attend Mass. I go to confession, and I have given much thought to the subject you have discussed with me. So, some time ago, I decided to find out what my religion requires of me concerning such a matter. I inquired of my monsignor, and I intended to be guided by his advice, because to me this is a religious question. He asked high authorities and I was informed that my religion expects me to confess my sins in private communication. It does not require me to make any public statement. So, Mr. Nizer, this is my answer: I consider confession a matter between my God and myself. I have cleansed my soul and I am ready to meet my Maker. I will not make any public statement."

I was so moved as well as impressed by his reflective manner, the maturity of his thinking, and the beauty of his expression, that every word he uttered was engraved in my mind in accordance with a lawyer's habit of concentrated memorization. I have therefore set forth his reply literally— for it showed the growth of the man. I also accepted his answer as final, since it grew out of profound religious conviction. We would simply have to overcome the obstacle of his silence, like all other obstacles in the case. It also confirmed our view not to call him as a witness in his own behalf. He would be subjected to severe cross-examination on the very subject which he considered sacrosanct between God and himself.

We stayed longer in order to ease the atmosphere again before leaving. I did not want him to feel he had let us down. However, he sensed that we had more important things to do on his behalf outside of the jail, and by a subtle gesture of slowly pushing away from the table, as if he were about to rise, he indicated we need not linger to give him solace. Once more we cheered him with expressions of our confidence, supported by assurances of our fullest effort, and with promises of our resourceful dedication, designed to give him hope.

Then we shook hands warmly. His hand clung to mine for an extra moment, as if in prayer, and then we left. Moore had tears in his eyes. I tried to be casual, as I looked back and smiled, but the same thought raced through my mind as when I leave a hospital bed of one fatally stricken, "I wonder if I will ever see you alive again?"

My strategy was to concede that Crump, at the time of the crime, was an animalistic killer. I knew that the district attorney would revel in the gory details of the slugging administered by Crump to a helpless woman and men on their knees, and then the cold-blooded shooting down of Zukowski. The People's brief had a special section devoted to the historical recital of these brutal events, and the words virtually dripped with blood. They were designed, of course, to revive the memory of the dark deeds, and to inflame the mind, so that any consideration of mercy would be burned out.

I, therefore, proposed that I should open the proceedings by relating the horror of the murder in vivid terms. I would castigate Paul Crump as a vicious killer, and then point out that if the district attorney wished to repeat the shattering details, he was simply building our case, because the more vile Crump was painted, the greater the miracle of his rehabilitation!

Moore screamed with delight at this gambit. Pounding his hands on his knees he yelled, "That's it!" I made our approach clear to our witnesses. "Do not try to mollify or skirt any accusation that Crump had committed one of the most dastardly crimes in Chicago's history. Our point is that he has changed. The bloodthirsty animal has become a fine human being. If the State executes Paul Crump, it is killing a different man from the one who committed the crime."

In this way, I hoped to take the wind out of the sails of the district attorney when he arose to deliver a prepared speech describing the crime. His words might then be more boring than shocking. Also they would be recognized as tangential to the real issue—Crump's rehabilitation. They would be exposed as an attempt to prejudice the Board, rather than to discuss the redemption of a man who at one time was concededly evil.

Sunday night was long and oppressively hot. The morning seemed choked by lack of air. We drove to the courtroom where the hearing would take place, still studying the papers on our knees.

Though it was fifteen minutes before ten o'clock, the long room was packed with several hundred spectators crowded closely on the wooden benches. Outside the courtroom dozens of curious persons milled about aimlessly in disappointment at not being admitted. Inside it was stiflingly hot, and noisy fans on the walls strove to disguise the heat by driving it in patternless waves. Underneath an impressive judicial bench with seats for five commissioners were large tables for counsel. But they were pre-empted at both ends by television cameras. Photographers, perched precariously on the ledges, had only cameras where their faces should have been, and their hands were forever clicking their mechanical ears. Occasionally a light would flash as if a Cyclops had opened a white eye.

Counsel's chairs were so tightly pressed against the tables by reporters and photographers squatting behind them and in front of the first row of spectators that each time I arose to examine or cross-examine, there was no freedom from the press. A chair placed in the aisle, parallel with counsel table, constituted the witness stand.

The windows had to be open, though it wasn't clear whether to let the stifling heat in or out. Brake screeches, differently pitched auto horns, and general hubbub of street noises, topped by an occasional identifiable shout, streamed into the room. All this, augmented by buzzing fans, whirling cameras, swishing noises of newspapers used as fans, and the hum of restless talk added to the din. For any of us to be heard, it was necessary at all times to shout. The subtleties and shading of tone, so necessary for emphasis and clarity, were impossible. Very early in the proceedings our clothes and hair gave signs of wilting, and as the long day proceeded, the participants in the hearing all acquired the same bedraggled look.

In the fourth row, on the aisle, sat Paul's mother, Lonie Crump. Her eyes were closed at all times, and her hands tightly clasped in her lap. Next to her sat a white woman, her hand resting, in a comforting gesture, over Mrs. Crump's hands. The picture of a white hand over clenched black hands made an independent composition as if a circle were drawn around it, and registered on my mind indelibly.

The district attorney, James Thompson, took his seat alongside of us. He was very tall, and his blond hair was closely cropped. He was young enough for his bespectacled face not yet to register the sternness and cynicism of his professional work. On the contrary, he had a pleasing look. Moore had told me of his reputation as a skilled advocate. It was not easy to detect whether supreme confidence or poise accounted for his manner. Donald Moore introduced us, and we shook hands amiably. There is always respect among men who know that they are doing their duty. Our process of justice operates on an adversary system, and without able opponents, confronting each other, truth would be much harder to come by.

While we were trying to find room to spread our papers on the table, which had shrunken from the invasion of microphones and other equipment, there were three traditional knocks on the door alongside the judge's bench, and the commissioners (Wise, Craven, Jones, Lerner, and Kinney) filed in behind each other and took their chairs. That breathless moment of beginning had come.

Chairman Kinney gaveled for silence and made an opening statement. He had a no-nonsense manner, but it was combined with judicial dignity and courtesy. He was one of those judges who commanded a courtroom without effort. He had clean-cut features and he made a handsome figure. The other commissioners were likewise keen and earnest, as their questions later indicated, and devoid of pomposity. The tone of the hearing, despite the handicap of the heat and noise, was of the highest order.

Chairman Kinney anounced that Governor Kerner had called this extraordinary session of the Parole and Pardon Board to consider any petition Paul Crump desired to present. Notice had been served on the judges who had presided at Crump's trials, the various district attorneys, the warden, and the relatives of the murdered man. Then he defined the Board's limited function as described by statute:

"The Pardon Board shall in no case act as a Court of Review to pass upon the correctness, regularity or legality of the proceedings in the Trial Court which resulted in conviction, but shall confine itself to a hearing in consideration of those matters only which properly bear upon the propriety of extending clemency by the Governor.

"After this session, the Pardon Board, without publicity, shall make a report upon the case to the Governor with their conclusions and recommendations. The report to the Governor shall be advisory to him in his constitutional action upon the case.

"Are you ready, gentlemen? You may proceed."

MR. MOORE: May it please your honors, I would like to introduce co-counsel in this case, who has come here at my request and also at the request of Mr. Crump and the Committee of prominent citizens here in Chicago, who, like myself, is serving without fee in this matter, Mr. Louis Nizer, of the Bar of New York, who is sitting at my left, and I would like to ask leave of the Chairman and the Board for Mr. Nizer to make an opening statement on behalf of the petitioner, Paul Crump.

As I arose to begin our plea, I was conscious of the special significance of Chairman Kinney's statement that the Board would not review "the correctness, regularity or legality" of Crump's trials and convictions. This did not exclude consideration of some lingering doubt of guilt, no matter how tiny. Clemency was really the exercise of caution not to make error irrevocable; to provide an opportunity for ultimate correction which death would foreclose. Despite the fact that a criminal had been found guilty beyond a reasonable doubt, any doubt (if the Board and Governor wished) might be sufficient for commuting a death sentence. So, for example, a conviction affirmed by an appellate court in which the judges divided sharply could give rise to a typical argument for mercy. While the verdict could not be challenged, the infallibility of man could be, and life imprisonment would be assurance against any unforgivable miscarriage of justice.

But in the Crump case we were deprived of this approach. His very success in reversing the first conviction, on technical evidentiary grounds, and the fact that in a second trial he had again been condemned, with unanimous approval of the appellate court, and that his legal remedies had extended over nine years, precluded the argument that perhaps an innocent man was being walked to the death chamber. No, we had to break new ground. So we announced boldly in the opening statement:

"Our application here is not based upon any claim that the previous judicial procedure is defective and gives rise to overtones for clemency.

"We commend the police authorities for their apprehension of Mr. Crump and the others who committed this dastardly crime, for their diligence in bringing the culprits to justice. We admire the thoroughness of the judicial procedure which determined guilt.

"It has been customary in applications of this kind to express some doubt of the proceedings, some challenge which might appeal to the Board. We do not do so. As reasonable counsel, we feel this man has received two trials, and has had appeals to the highest court of the land. We do not challenge these proceedings."

We even surrendered the customary arguments that Crump's

background made society partly responsible for his lawlessness.

"We think that crime, unfortunately, is not limited to slum areas, and fine men have come from slum areas. Nor do we argue that society is responsible for what happened here. That is for the sociologist and psychiatrist."

The real issue is "that we have here a rehabilitated man, a newborn man, a transformed personality." I gave a general description of the contents in the more than two hundred pages of affidavits, presenting a long-range view of the entire landscape of Crump's new character. I left the close-up view of vivid details to the end of the hearing, when the judges' eyes would be keener because of emotional involvement.

I strove to make the issue clear and clean-cut. Where it is discretionary to grant relief or not, confusion operates against affirmative action. The tendency of the mind is to be relieved of heavy responsibility and to take advantage of complexity to justify a negative decision. Therefore, I quoted the People's brief that "rehabilitation is not a basis for clemency," and made it the simple issue of the hearing. "If rehabilitation is not a basis for clemency, what is? Is not the entire objective of all punishment, if not the hope of the world, to rehabilitate the criminal? This is the only civilized objective. It is the vital issue for this board and the Governor."

We feared that the Board would be loath to set a new precedent, because the consequences might be unforeseeable. This frequently presents an obstruction to persuasion. "Perhaps," thinks the judge, "I should grant the extraordinary relief in this case, but where will it lead in hundreds of other situations? Must I not resist the temptation to tinker with a rule, which might be unfair in this case, but which is salutary as a general proposition?"

There is an old saying, "Hard cases make bad law." It means that adjusting the law to fit a special circumstance makes bad law generally. It is part of the persuasive art to remove the fear from the judge's mind. So I continued:

"Crump's rehabilitation is unique. Granting him clemency will not commute the death sentence of every murderer. We wish there were other instances in which rehabilitation was as miraculous, as the evidence in this case will demonstrate. Unfortunately there are not, and it will be helpful to the penologists to keep Crump alive and find out, why not."

There was one final preliminary task to be achieved in the

opening statement. The notion had to be removed that clemency would be an interference with the judicial process. Even if the trial was fair and guilt certain, clemency was not ruled out. The Illinois Constitution created the power in the Governor, solely in the exercise of his conscience. At the time this provision was written into the Constitution in 1870, one of the delegates said:

"Pardons are sometimes given as a reward to furnish a new and better life. . . . The whole scheme of salvation is based upon the idea."

There were presidential precedents for clemency even where guilt was undeniable. President Grover Cleveland had commuted sentence for the hanging of Robert Boutwell, on the ground that his partners in the crime had been sentenced only to life imprisonment. The analogy was not perfect because there the district attorney and the presiding judge had recommended clemency. We were not that fortunate.

President Benjamin Harrison had saved a murderer, Frank Capel, from hanging, because there was no premeditation "and the good conduct of the convict in prison, together with the evidence he furnishes of penitence and a desire to redeem himself, has impressed me."

President Abraham Lincoln commuted the capital sentence of José Bento de Deas of Massachusetts, "Because of his old age, long term of imprisonment and friendless condition." Lincoln once said:

"When a man is sincerely penitent for his misdeeds, and gives satisfactory evidence of the same, he can safely be pardoned, and there is no exception to the rule."

Lincoln often disregarded opposition to clemency from prosecuting authorities. Sandburg, in *The War Years*, describes a sobbing old man pleading for his son's life after he had been sentenced by court-martial to be shot. General Butler protested against Executive interference with Army courts-martial, but Lincoln signed a presidential order that the boy was "not to be shot until further orders from me." The old man was still desperate, not knowing when the presidential mercy would terminate. Lincoln assured him, "If your son never looks on death till further orders come from me to shoot him, he will live to be a great deal older than Methuselah."

Lincoln evaluated very highly exemplary conduct after conviction. In 1864, he wrote to Secretary of War Stanton that a soldier sentenced to death for desertion "had since fought at Gettysburg and in several other battles." There was a recommendation of pardon. "Let it be done," commanded the President.

General George Washington had taken similar action in a desertion case, pardoning a soldier sentenced to death. "The Commander-in-Chief expecting, that by his future good behaviour, he will atone for his past crimes, and show himself worthy of this act of clemency."

We contended that there were no hard and fast rules for the showing of mercy. The only inhibition on the Executive was his conscience, and any fact which appealed to the noblest instinct for justice tempered with mercy, could properly be weighed by him. In the phrase of Bracton, "The King ought to be not only wise, but merciful, and with wisdom mercifully just." Therefore, we sharpened the issue again. The People's position that rehabilitation was no ground for clemency was wrong:

"We will conclude our opening statement with this summary. We are not here to challenge the judicial process. We are not here to condone what happened. We believe Crump was a vicious animal at the time he was convicted and the more Mr. Thompson wants to stress that, the more it contrasts with the great change in this man. The only thing we ask is that his life be not snuffed out and that he be confined to jail for the rest of his life."

We opened our testimony with statements of three religious leaders of different faiths. This set a profound moral tone, as if trumpets from on high ushered in the proceedings.

Rabbi Marx, regional Director of American Hebrew congregations, a graduate of Yale University and the University of Cincinnati, pleaded for clemency and concluded with a story told by Hebrew scholars:

"A man sinned and the King asked him to seek repentance. 'Return as far as you can, and I will come to you the rest of the way.'

"Society must also say, 'Come halfway, we will come the rest of the way.' God says, 'My hands are stretched out to the penitent. I reject no creature who gives me his heart in penitence.' "

There was no cross-examination.

Before the next witness could take the stand, it became

evident that no one could compete with the noise of the cameras, and the turning fans which seemed by their motion to be signaling "No." Chairman Kinney held a brief conference with his fellow commissioners, and announced that unless more silence could be maintained by "the press and photographers, we will retire to our own chambers. This is the last we will see of this." The tumult subsided somewhat.

Rev. Wesley M. Westerberg then took the stand. He was an ordained clergyman of the Methodist Church. He had been educated at Northwestern University and at Yale, and was President of Kendall Junior College in Evanston, Illinois, "a college limited to the giving of a second chance." He professed to speak for a prevalent view among churchmen, though not for the entire Protestant community. He argued that every human being lives in two orders, one of grace and one of law:

"In the case of Crump, where we have good reason to believe that the destructive process is at an end, and the creative process has begun, . . . the death sentence makes a mockery of the values that our society and our religious heritage espouses. Here it seems even the State can act with grace.

"If, as Crump says, one ought to be ashamed to die until he has contributed something in justification of his living, we the People of the State of Illinois ought to be ashamed to execute one who is in the midst of making his restitution and his contribution."

Once more, Thompson announced he had no cross-examination.

Then Very Reverend Monsignor Daniel M. Cantwell took the witness seat. He was Chaplain of the Catholic Council on Working Life, and also a member of the Illinois Committee for Employment trying to help men released from jail to secure employment.

He asserted that "the reform in Paul actually happened," and that he was not "faking rehabilitation." As to whether this was sufficient to commute the death penalty, he believed strongly that it was, and cited a lengthy treatise on crime and punishment made by Pope Pius XII. It held that in the application of penal power, there must be considered not only strict law and justice, but also equity, goodness, and mercy.

"Otherwise, there is danger that the *summumius* (the highest law) be converted into *summa iniuria* (the highest injury). . . . A remission of the punishment should be taken under consideration whenever there is moral certainty that the inherent purpose of the penalty has been obtained, that is, the true interior conversion of the guilty person."

After this quotation, he urged the Board to recommend commutation and Executive clemency because of the "compelling evidence of rehabilitation in Paul Crump."

We had determined to steer clear of the general issue of capital punishment. If being opposed to the death penalty was to be the basis of commutation, it would inspire opposition from the apparent majority who espoused it. Furthermore, the valid argument could be made that as long as capital punishment was the law of the State, as it was, it ought not be sabotaged by indirection. For this reason, we chose instead to accept capital punishment as the prevailing law (without being drawn into a debate as to whether it should be repealed) and urged that even under this law, rehabilitation was ground for clemency.

However, the brilliant monsignor could not resist the temptation to engage the district attorney in a philosophical point on this issue. He did so with such logical charm that I could not help but be amused, even though it violated our strategy concept. He said,

"I would not want this Board of the Governor to miss a subtle point in the State's Attorney's position, when he says that those of us arguing clemency are really arguing from a position against capital punishment. I think it can, with equal merit, be said that he is arguing from a position of not just enforcing capital punishment because it is the law, but of keeping it because he favors it."

Still, there was no cross-examination.

We moved on to our next witness, Clinton T. Duffy, the former Warden of San Quentin Prison. He had been born at San Quentin, and had worked in the institution for thirty-two years, so that he had spent virtually his entire life from birth to retirement in that famous prison center. One felt that he had been a prisoner of his own chosen profession. While warden, he had also served on California's Advisory Pardon Board, by appointment of Governor Earl Warren.

His patrician, sensitive features and refined diction gave no trace of a quarter of a century of association with a criminal community. He was soft-spoken and hardheaded, like a kind but firm father.

Several days before he had talked with Crump for two hours in Warden Johnson's office, and thereafter during a tour of the prison, observed Crump when he didn't know he was being watched. He saw him help an old man in the convalescent ward distribute blankets and do other chores.

"There was a young boy fourteen years old, a situation that would scare any warden, to have a youngster in a ward like that with a group of grown-ups, and the youngster told me that Paul Crump was his friend and that he was all right. And then Crump came over, put his hand on this lad's shoulder and said, 'This boy is going to be all right. He is here, we hope, for a short stay, and when he goes out, he will be a better person for it.' He said, 'Don't worry about him while he is here. Nothing will happen.'"

Warden Duffy asserted that Crump was not acting "because I can tell it after all the years of experience that I have had in prison work."

To protect that young boy was "to stick his neck out. . . . I sincerely recommend to you, gentlemen, having been a member of a parole and pardon board myself, that if I had a recommendation to make, sitting on this case, I would recommend to the Governor that his case be commuted to life imprisonment."

MR. NIZER: What is your view concerning rehabilitation as a basis for the exercise of clemency?

MR. DUFFY: . . . Precedent has never been this way. Some day it should start, and I say it is the right thing to do. Let us change the precedent, let us go along with the man who has made good . . . on the grounds of a changed person, or rehabilitation.

Chairman Kinney, rather than the district attorney, asked some cross-examination questions. He inquired whether Duffy wasn't the author of a recent book of memoirs, entitled *88 Men and 2 Women*, all of whom were executed while he was warden. He replied that they were, but some others were commuted to life imprisonment for various reasons. I immediately attempted by redirect examination to counteract any impression that while execution was the rule in his own prison in California, he was applying another standard to Illinois.

After establishing that the executions referred to in the title of his book had taken place over a twelve-year period, I asked:

Q. Would you accept the principle that in any consideration of the commutation of sentence the factors must be based upon the individual circumstances of the particular man? I think that's a fair implication of the Chairman's question to you.

A. I don't think there is any other answer, other than the way the individual faces up . . .

We took advantage of the opening to drive home another point.

Q. Have you found in your experience that a person like Crump has an effect upon other inmates in their rehabilitation?

A. Oh yes, very definitely. Should Paul Crump be commuted to life, I can see where he would be a very valuable person in the institution working with other men.

I say he should be put through a diagnostic clinic, and then transferred to an institution where he could work with men on morale programs . . .

I elicited by another question that Crump would be invaluable to maintain discipline in prison administration, which was always plagued by understaffing.

For the first time, the district attorney requested the privilege of cross-examination, and we were particularly alert to learn what awaited us in later crucial exchanges with him.

MR. THOMPSON: Warden Duffy, in your experience as the Warden of San Quentin, and as a member of the Parole Board, have you had occasion to see in California men under death sentence who have shown evidence of what you call rehabilitation, or repentance for their crimes?

A. Very few, if any . . . Cook County Jail is a very unusual situation. Throughout most States in the nation where they do have capital punishment, the inmates are kept behind bars at least twenty-two hours a day, and the other two hours they are under heavy guard in an exercise area just outside their cells . . .

Q. Then, are you telling us that of all the persons under death sentence in California with which you have come into contact, there has not been one who in his years or months on Death Row has made any significant change?

A. . . . They may have gotten a little closer to religion, yes, . . . but as far as doing a great deal for themselves, the opportunity has never been there for them.

Q. Of these very few, can you tell us, sir, how many have applied for Executive clemency to the Governor of California on the grounds of rehabilitation or repentance, or whatever you care to call it, and how many times the Governor of California has responded with clemency on that ground?

A. There have been none that have applied . . . on the grounds of rehabilitation. There have been none that have been granted clemency on the basis of rehabilitation, because they have not been rehabilitated. They haven't had that opportunity to be rehabilitated as Paul Crump has had and as he has done.

Member Jones of the Board asked Duffy whether Caryl Chessman had been rehabilitated before execution. Duffy replied that Chessman had been at San Quentin on a sentence of five years to life for first-degree robbery, was let out, and returned under sentence of death. He knew him well during the three years when stay after stay delayed his execution.

"He was a very arrogant, mean, hating individual, resentful of authority, and he did not change during the years that I knew him. He was not rehabilitated."

When Warden Duffy left the stand, I felt that his references to Crump's sheer heroism in guarding young prisoners from homosexual attacks had not been sufficiently developed. After all, Duffy had only visited the prison for several hours.

We had begun our case with ministers of all faiths, who gave abstract religious recommendations; continued with an expert prison authority who had very limited personal experience with Crump; now we were fortunate in calling to the stand a man who combined religious and sociological insights with daily intimate contacts with Paul Crump. He was the most remarkable witness of the entire proceeding. He would be able to trace from daily observation Paul Crump's mysterious growth as a human being. He could tell the Board every step of his progression, yes, and the few retrogressions. He could give greater meaning to Paul's protective arm around the youngsters who would otherwise be prey to sexual predators.

The witness was Father James Garret Jones, priest of the Episcopal Diocese of Chicago, Director of the famous St. Leonard's·House, and Director of prison work for the Illinois diocese with an assistant staff of seven priests and six laymen.

He had a brilliant educational background, having graduated from Canterbury College, where he majored in Social Psychology. He had a Bachelor of Divinity degree from Nashotah House, where he majored in Moral Theology and Greek. He had also done graduate work at Butler University in Education, and at Yale and DePaul Universities and the University of Chicago in Philosophy, Sociology, and Psychology. He was full-time Chaplain in Cook County Jail during the years that Crump was in Death Row.

Father Jones' face was that of a young man of less than forty. His gray hair, shadowed slightly with black, did not add to his age. It only increased the handsome quality of his even, friendly features, framing them with unexpected maturity. He wore the black garb and turned-about white collar of his calling, but they failed abysmally to give him solemnity. His demeanor and speech eschewed either the holy attitude, or the forced humor which ministers sometimes adopt to achieve the common touch. His zeal was not touched with a sense of superiority due to the nobility of his work. Nor was it humble, either. He had a healthy, inoffensive ego, and his recital was filled with such psychological acuity that one felt he was entitled to the immense satisfactions from his achievements, for they were real, and obtained under the most difficult and at times dangerous circumstances. This was no ordinary chaplain moving among the prisoners with an aloof spirit of grace. This was a man who was fascinated by human nature, understood its torments, and entered into the fray. When, as he recited, he took off his coat literally and symbolically and forced his way into the hostile death cells, and then into the hearts of the condemned, he was carrying the fight to the enemy (hatred and contempt of him and for what he stood) by treating the prisoners as equals, not sinners. He won them on their terms, not his, and the victory was more real and lasting for that reason.

I shall let him tell his extraordinary story in his own way. He was present in the bullpen on the Saturday afternoon when Crump entered Cook County Jail, and undressed, bathed, dusted, and his clothes fumigated. Crump was sullen and would not talk or "participate in eye contact." He was so hostile that he was placed in an isolation cell in Death Row. Nevertheless, he was one of the ringleaders of a riot which was so serious that the State Police, the sheriff, and firemen had to be summoned. The sheriff suffered a coronary attack and was carried out on a stretcher. Father Jones and another chaplain who attempted to disperse the rioters were injured by broken crockery thrown in their faces.

There was a pact among the condemned prisoners not to talk to any chaplain. This was due to an incident involving a chaplain during the execution of Emanuel Scott. Tension is always high after an electrocution, and in this instance it took the form of a boycott against chaplains.

Father Jones obtained permission to invade Death Row. He took off his coat and announced that if they could not communicate on a religious basis, he would challenge them to a bridge game, at which some of them professed to be expert. He learned to his dismay that they had their own rules, and the first glimmer he had of acceptance was when much later Crump asked for a copy of the rules so that they could change from "delinquent to conventional bridge. In all honesty there were a couple of things I still would like them to adhere to, but they don't."

The wall of silence having been broken, Paul began to talk to guards occasionally. "A guard's wife died and Paul felt human compassion for the authority figures."

Father Jones traced Crump's emergence from his hardened shell, step by step. He described Assistant Warden Mattick's instruction to Paul, and his essays on *Moby Dick;* then his immersion in religion:

"It was one of those gushing things, Mass, three, four times a week; confession once or twice a week; communion three times a week, to the point where at one time very early in this religious stage he was reading part of the priestly divine offering in a Latin-English abridgment. . . .

"Later he returned to what I would term his third stage of religious development, where he is right now, and I would describe him as a normal, average, practicing Roman Catholic layman . . . It is not overpiousity; there isn't an extreme amount of religious talk. It is simply sort of accepted and understood. This is my faith. This what I live."

Just as there is preventive medicine, there is preventive testimony. Its purpose is to render an opposition argument ineffectual before it is made. Knowing that the district attorney would attack Crump for failure to confess, we savored Father Jones' description of Crump receiving communion, because this meant "that he must have made his confession to God in the presence of a priest regularly." The witness drove home the point by explaining his own philosophy of true repentance:

"I go to God in the secrecy and privacy of the confessional, and when I am repentant, I receive holy communion. These are the same rules of the Roman Catholic Church.

"I would suggest to you that I am not bound to publicly . . . express my repentance, and I would suggest to you that I don't see why Paul should be expected to make any more of a repentive action than that which he had done, the normal practicing way of his faith."

Surely Mr. Thompson's inevitable arguments on this point would sound more feeble, because it would be flying into the gale of Father Jones' anticipatory rebuttal.

Chairman Kinney had already received in evidence the more than two hundred pages of affidavits, crammed with glowing testimonials to Crump's conduct. But they lay silently on the judge's bench, until summation when I intended to bring them to pulsating oral life. In the meantime, Father Jones, drawing from his personal experience, sculpted an incident here, etched an insight into character there, and generally painted a picture of evil vanquished by moral awakening—all with artistic insight.

So he told how potential suicides would be transferred to Paul's wing and put under his surveillance. Out of an average of about twenty thousand inmates a year in Cook County Jail, there were a good many such cases, some "phony and others real . . . and we have some every year who succeed. Only once did he ever fail in talking a man out of suicide."

Crump's growth was visible above the surface, but also had deep roots of psychological understanding. Father Jones testified:

"One of the little things he taught me was, I used to go

through these tier blocks, loaded with cigarettes, candy stickers, and so forth, a charitable man of God, you know, and pass them out. It was Paul who told me that I was making a very bad mistake; that inmates had very little to give, and that if I wanted as chaplain to give that which I thought my God had, I had to in some way make it reciprocal, that I could ask for a toothpick, ask the inmate for a puff of his cigarette. I learned early that this would establish a very quick relationship—and this was taught me by Paul Crump."

Father Jones saw Crump struggle with epileptics, psychotics, and alcoholics. He was never asked by the prison authorities to undertake these tasks or others more dangerous but

"he understood the . . . Godly authority to protect the extreme youth and the helpless from tier predators. I know you all know that these predators exist both homosexually and in taking inmates' property, meager as it is.

"Paul was always known as a stand-up person. You did not sexually or property-wise assault another person if he was on that tier. He would not stand for it. A couple of times this resulted in a fight. Paul, I don't think ever lost one in his life, although when a fight occurred, he used such force as was necessary to stop the predator. I never saw him go beyond and kick a person when he was down, or beat him beyond simple submission."

Father Jones illustrated his point by referring to a twelve-year-old boy charged with murder. The State's Attorney had chosen to prosecute him as a felon, and not as a juvenile before the Youth Commission.

He was so tiny that the handcuffs put on him kept slipping off, and the child had to hold his hands up to remain handcuffed. He was of foreign descent and could not speak English. Ordinarily, such a youngster would be prey to the wolves, as they are called, in the jail, who might fight to the death over him. He was deliberately put in Paul's tier.

"This child was never in any way assaulted or harmed. He was later bound over to the Commission, and is now, by the way, a healthy member of society."

Was Crump's progress ever marred by revolt and wrongdoing? Indeed it was. From Jones' experience with fourteen hundred inmates at St. Leonard's House, if the rehabilitation process after prison, "is a continual climb, like a car going up a mountain. . . . You can pretty well guess that you have got yourself a guy who is a phony, who is not really meeting his problems. . . .

"We don't mind a bit if a man has done solitary confinement while he has been in prison . . . if he has never regressed or revolted . . . we feel we have a vegetable, and there is nothing left to rehabilitate, or he is a warden's man."

He then related two incidents where Crump's temper flared against the rules of the prison. A parakeet flew over the wall and into the window of a cell. The prisoners somehow got birdseed and fed it. The administration decided that this was against the rules:

"Well, Paul revolted. He absolutely said he was not going to let that bird go from his cell. A phony would have smiled sweetly, 'Yes, of course, you must live up to the rules, no birds in this institution,' and so forth. He revolted. He was real. He wasn't playing a game with these rules at all. Later, by the way, he learned the rewards of being real because the bird was permitted to be kept."

On another occasion, a cartoon appeared in a Chicago newspaper of a condemned man being dragged to the electric chair, as he resisted hysterically. The prisoners in Death Row cut out the picture, and with paste made from mashed potatoes and water put it on a central post with a sign "Man's Inhumanity to Man." The administration did not consider this picture to be either appropriate art or educational pronouncement for visitors of the jail. The cartoon was ordered taken down. Crump sided with other condemned prisoners in their refusal to do so.

On other occasions, too, he had "sullen days." Nevertheless, when St. Leonard's House had its frustrating failures because released prisoners, whom it had re-educated, returned to jail convicted of new crimes, they were placed in Crump's tier for his evaluation of what had gone wrong:

"We were given some very healthy advice by Paul Crump as to some of the mistakes we had made."

Life grants immunity to no one. The healer gets sick. The psychiatrist cannot live with his wife's neuroses. The lawyer needs advice. And a minister is sorely troubled and requires solace. Father Jones fell upon such a desperate hour. His wife was about to deliver a child *placenta previa.* She was rushed as an emergency case to Mount Sinai Hospital in

Chicago. Her condition was deemed critical. She was taken to the operating room. Father Jones was informed that she would be there four hours.

"There was nothing I could do. I didn't know what to do with myself."

The hospital is not far from Cook County Jail. In desperation, he walked the streets aimlessly, but some inner, undefined feeling took him toward the jail. He entered it, and as if directed by the radar of a profound urge, he wandered into Paul Crump's cell:

"Paul knew something was wrong. He asked me what was wrong, and I was able now to begin to see why he could minister to some of the problems I had sent him, because he certainly, in my personal crisis, admirably ministered to me."

The minister had come to the condemned man for advice and solace!

Father Jones added a scientific touch to his religious and emotional appeal.

"All I can say in terms of not knowing why he changed . . . that by their fruits you shall know them. . . . I see the result. . . . In the interest of nothing other than criminological science you should wish to keep this man alive in order to have a reference person."

He argued that if anyone had discovered that something in Crump's blood, in conjunction with blood of others cured cancer, and no scientist could tell why,

"there wouldn't be any question in the world that we would keep this guinea pig reference person alive, and study that blood to the end of time to find out how we can stop cancer."

He contended that the criminal delinquent cancer of our society "is far more serious than physical cancer, and that we have every reason on that scientific basis alone to spare his life."

His conclusion was the cry of one mired in the dark struggle of making man a social animal, and seeing a tiny light which he did not want snuffed out:

"It seems to me when you have a positive person like Paul Crump who can work with other inmates . . . that we will have established another step in the *bonne commune,* in the goodness and safety of our community."

His final words were abrasively persuasive:

"I cannot for the life of me see if we walk that man to

that chair at 12:01 Friday morning, that we have committed anything else but social suicide in terms of the goodness of our community and of this man."

The district attorney put no questions at all to Father Jones, but if we had any notion that this was acquiescence, we were to be shocked rudely by later developments in which our case, even according to the most optimistic view among us, was brought to the brink of ruin. Thompson's failure to cross-examine was simply good strategy. One doesn't tangle with an overpowering witness. He chose to have him leave the stand as quickly as possible so that the recollection of his testimony would recede. Vigorous countertestimony, which was in the offing, would aid in the dimming of the impression just made. In the battle of persuasion, intervening time tends to act as solvent of words previously spoken.

On the other hand, Father Jones received from the Board the highest compliment which can be paid to a witness, and that is, to be asked for more advice, rather than to be cross-examined.

Member Craven wanted to know whether Father Jones would be able to follow the "guinea pig" developments of Crump if he were "incarcerated in Stateville, or Pontiac, or Menard, or wherever." The reply was, "If it's any institution in the State of Illinois, we have a staff member there."

We were unexpectedly led into a discussion of miracles. Member Lerner asked:

Q. Are you sure that Crump is not an actor and conned you . . . that he is rehabilitated?

A. I have no absolute certitude. In terms of all my professional training and the years that I have known Paul Crump, I am as sure as I can be . . .

Q. You heard Mr. Nizer refer to this matter as a miracle.

A. Mr. Nizer and I should today theologically sit down and talk about all the miracles.

MR. NIZER: Father, I referred merely as a figure of speech to the miraculous change that has taken place. And I am willing to accept that there is some divine providence in it.

FATHER JONES: There is divine providence in every breath we have taken.

What I am hoping, that this is not just a special divine

miraculous act but the result of a marvelous team of scientific approach that we can . . . copy in a thousand cases, and not one.

As in all court dramas, there was the customary note of humor:

MEMBER LERNER: Speaking of the regression, did Crump ever trump your ace?

FATHER JONES: His rules in the beginning were fantastic. Wild cards. Imagine playing bridge with wild cards.

There are some problems so lurid and difficult that we seek to avoid the responsibility of solution by turning our heads away. Ignoring them may lull our consciences for a while, but ultimately they compel attention, and they are more grievous because we did not have the courage to act sooner. For a long time "look the other way" was the American attitude toward juvenile delinquency. It still is to the prevalence of dope addiction.

The frightful sex problems in our jails is another.

The Crump case can serve an additional useful purpose if it brings attention to degrading conditions which exist in "corrective" institutions. That Crump should have to engage in dangerous fights to protect young prisoners from older ones ought to point not only to his rehabilitation, but to the desperate state of affairs in prison institutions. The sex problem is greatly responsible for the tensions, belligerence, and discipline difficulties which prevail there. Far worse, it ought to open our eyes to the fact that our prisons are centers of corruption, sending out thousands of men deformed for life by the sex practices forced upon them while incarcerated. This is equally true of women's prisons.

Such studies as have been made show that homosexual practices in long-term institutions range from 60 per cent to over 90 per cent of the male inmates. Haywood Patterson, one of the nine Negro victims of race prejudice in a rape case in Alabama, who was sentenced to prison for sevety-five years on a rape charge, wrote a book called *Scottsboro Boy*, in which he revealed that a fifteen-year-old Negro boy was beaten by an old wolf unmercifully. Other prisoners just looked on. "They knew a young woman was being born."

In *New Horizons in Criminology*, the authors, Barnes and Teeters, describe the struggle of inmates who go foraging for "a girl friend," using knives, fashioned from any stray bit of metal, like spoons. It was in such a brawl that Richard (Dicky) Loeb of the infamous Leopold-Loeb murder case was slashed to death by another inmate of the Joliet, Illinois penitentiary.

In many countries this problem is solved by permitting conjugal visits either in jail, or under certain circumstances, by brief furloughs of the prisoner to his family.

In Sweden, the prison cells are closed rooms which afford privacy, and the wife is permitted to visit her prisoner-husband each Sunday.

Also, since 1945, a Swedish statute permits a prisoner to leave the institution to visit his home for forty-eight to seventy-two hours. In 1952, 2527 home leaves were granted. In 1954, 3805.

In England and Wales since 1951 these home visits are permitted to enable the prisoner to renew his contacts with his family and prepare for freedom. Similar statutes exist in Northern Ireland, Denmark (where visit privileges are granted only to inmates of open prison camps), Greece (which permits visits of five days each six months of the year), and others.

In South America, many countries provide for supervised visits of the spouse to the prisoner within the prison. This is the practice in Chile, Argentina, Colombia, and Mexico. In 1957, a new open prison was instituted in Mexico called Fábrica de Hombres Nuovos, where the rehabilitation program was aided by a wing which was a twenty-room "hotel" for private conjugal visits.

Indeed, some countries permit women to visit the unmarried prisoners.

Puerto Rico allows male prisoners to visit their homes for forty-eight hours once every two months. Women prisoners, however, are limited to supervised visits within the prison.

In 1951, Buenos Aires prisons permitted private visits of husbands and wives in prison every fifteen days and for a two-hour period. In 1956, Argentina instituted the privilege of home leaves once a month for twelve to twenty-four hours for male or female prisoners.

In Brazil, small rooms in the prisons, specifically set aside for the purpose, are used by the inmates to receive their wives. However, no prostitutes are permitted in the Brazilian prisons.

Russia provides for prisoners' families in its penal colonies, particularly where the agricultural colonies are part of the prison system.

In all of these countries, where the prison sex problem is not ignored as it is in the United States, conjugal visits are conditioned at different ways upon good behavior, or length of imprisonment, etc. The disciplinary problems, which arise from caging men in cells, and which cannot be overstated, are tremendously relieved by such visits or furloughs. But far more important, particularly in cases of short-term imprisonment, is the preservation of the marriage and family relationship, the removal of suspicion and jealousy, and the avoidance of degenerate habits, which may continue after prison release.

I have referred thus briefly to this problem because if the goal of punishment is rehabilitation, ought we not recognize a counterforce to rehabilitation, which results from sexual deprivation?

We announced that we would present no more live witnesses. The formal term is "We rest," but it really means we come to a temporary halt, ready to spring to action when our adversary advances. There is no resting on one's oars in legal combat.

The Board declared a recess of half an hour. The spectators filed out, dragging some of the noise and heat with them. As the five members of the Board left the bench to disappear through an adjoining door, Moore observed that the psychiatrist, Dr. Scher, who was to have testified for us, followed them into the chamber behind the courtroom. He was surprised to see Dr. Scher in the courtroom at all. He was given to alarm, and so I shrugged off his excited whisper to me, although I too was somewhat mystified by the incident.

To obtain seats, some of the spectators sauntered in before the expiration of the recess, and their presence was like an inhalation which pulled the rest of the crowd into the room, with increasing speed. The commissioners entered again. The chairman's gavel could be seen banging, although it seemed silent against the noise. Then Thompson arose and announced:

"The State has, as such, no witnesses to call. However, there is a man who is familiar with this case and has been since its inception. . . .

"This man was one of the ablest prosecutors in the history

of Cook County. He later served a distinguished career on the local Bench and now serves with distinction as Federal District Judge. . . .

"I call on the State's behalf of the case, to the stand, Federal Judge Richard B. Austin."

Suddenly an inanimate name which I had repeatedly seen in several volumes of Crump's prior trials, materialized into a breathing human being. Richard Austin, who had called his distinguished friends to his office in the early hours of the morning to hear him read the confessions of Crump and his confederates; Richard Austin, the name which bespoke the majesty of the law, was again on the scene to support the State's position. A short man, whose head against the light seemed particularly aggressive, took his seat in the witness chair. He had a sharply angled broken line for a nose, a lower protruding lip, and a chin which was forceful even though it receded somewhat. His hair was crew cut, which struck me as being incongruous. He spoke emotionally, but he did not sound like an advocate, rather he was like a Federal judge pronouncing a terrible judgment from on high. His passion and brilliant marshaling of arguments against Crump made us feel as if the garden of rehabilitation, which we had carefully planted and nurtured, was being swept away by a gale. Any attempt to select from his testimony would do injustice to its force. I will set it forth virtually in its entirety:

"JUDGE AUSTIN: I first met Crump . . . within three or four days of the killing . . . in order to determine whether there has been any rehabilitation, you should first know something about him at the time he is alleged to have been unrehabilitated. And then ascertain whether or not there has been any change during that nine-year period. I suggest to you that there are two Crumps. One who, when armed with sawed-off shotguns and revolvers, holds up stores and citizens. Kills his friend, Ted, an unarmed guard. Smashes the skulls of unarmed men and women, who are his former fellow employees.

"And another Crump who was, and apparently is, to all appearances, when he's unarmed and in custody, a meek, mild, cunning, clever and intelligent man, doing whatever is necessary, at all times, to avoid the consequences of his conduct. That, in my opinion, is what he's been doing for the past seven years and is currently doing today. . . .

"You have available to you your psychiatrists, your psychologists, your penologists. Those who have been in contact with him and who are better able to give you an opinion, than the evidence which you have, or will hear today.

"And in the face of that, what is your batting average? . . . I do know that throughout the country the batting average is that those released on parole let the Parole Board down. And in their judgment that they will no longer be a menace to society . . . they are wrong 66 to 70 per cent of the time.

"Who has Crump fooled, misled and deceived in the past? Well, for one he deceived the Illinois Parole and Pardon Board. None of you gentlemen were on it at the time he did this, but when they released him prior to the time of his max [maximum period of confinement] [for an old robbery charge], they must have believed that he was rehabilitated; that he would no longer return to crime. Who else did he mislead? The day of the murder, gentlemen, Crump was picked up by the Chicago Police Department for questioning . . . and he was so persuasive and so convincing of his innocence . . . that they released him without booking him.

"Of course, there could be no show-up of his victims, one of whom was in the morgue and the other five were in the hospital getting their smashed skulls and scalps rehabilitated. What was the unarmed Crump like? A day or two after the murder, I had him before me for hours. He was meek. He was mild. He was polite. He was intelligent, and he feigned cooperation.

"He was permitted, prior to his last confession, private conferences with his lawyers. At the time of the signing of his confession, according to one of the several civic leaders who were present . . . and who testified at the trial [he said] that he said he had absolutely not been mistreated or abused, and had received wonderful treatment at the hands of the State's Attorney's office.

"According to his own doctor and other doctors, who examined him immediately, within five minutes of the time he signed the confession, examined him in the nude, and there were no bruises. There were no welts. There was no mark of any physical violence on his body. And that's in the record. And that's in the Supreme Court reports. And that's in the trial records.

"What was Crump like at the time of his second trial? He

was an eloquent, persuasive, intelligent man, making a closing argument on his own behalf.

"I suggest to you, and the Governor, that this evidence does not justify any finding of rehabilitation.

"Has there been any evidence of remorse? Has there been any evidence of repentance? Has there been any evidence of contrition? Has he said to Mrs. Zukowski, 'I'm sorry that I killed my friend, Ted?'

"Has he said to the five victims whose skulls were bashed in, 'I'm sorry I treated you, my former fellow employees, that way?'

"Has he said to the civic leaders, whom he did in effect call liars at the time of the trial, 'I'm sorry that I perjured myself when I said that I never made a confession. And that you weren't present when I signed the confession?'

"Has he said to his own doctor, whom he, in effect, called a liar at his trial, 'I'm sorry, Doc, I still maintain, as far as the record is concerned here, that I was beaten and harassed and covered with lumps, and bruises and abrasions. And you were lying when you said that you didn't find a mark on my body?'

"I say, that unless there is repentance, unless there is remorse, unless there is some contrition, there is, in my opinion, no, no evidence of rehabilitation.

"What witnesses have testified here, and what witnesses have filed affidavits?

"Wardens and ex-wardens, who are noted throughout the country for being opposed to capital punishment, clergymen, none of whom I have ever met who are not opposed to capital punishment. . . .

"There would be, on my part, at least more evidence of their sincerity, if they had started an investigation of the three codefendants of Crump, who are now serving 199 years' sentence in the penitentiary.

"No effort has been made to see whether these men are rehabilitated. And isn't it more likely that those who didn't fire the shots from the revolver and shotgun, more likely might be rehabilitated, than the man whose conduct you are aware of, as a result of your study of this case?

"What is being done, gentlemen, is an effort to circumvent the law; to circumvent the death penalty, provided by the statutes of this State.

"Two juries, not one, have invoked this punishment. Two trial judges approved those verdicts. The Illinois Supreme Court approved it. The United States Supreme Court, by failing to review it, approved it.

"For more than six years an effort has been made by certain members of the legislature to abolish the death penalty in Illinois. . . . I wish those who are in favor of this legislation would be as tolerant of my opinions as I am of theirs . . . why by the fact of legal maneuvers, eight years have elapsed, resulting in a bonus to this defendant?

"He and his counsel are solely responsible for that delay. I say that if the purpose of this hearing is what I believe it to be, an effort to avoid the imposition of the laws of the State of Illinois, that it not be done this way.

"I suggest that whether there should be a death penalty in Illinois, should be left to the legislature. . . .

"In conclusion, may I say this. If you and the Governor believe, on this evidence, that rehabilitation has taken place, and that is the ground for granting Executive clemency, you must do more than commute the death penalty. If you believe that, you should release this man immediately. It would be unconscionable, it would be intolerable to further confine a rehabilitated man. . . .

"Thank you for this opportunity, gentlemen."

MR. NIZER: May we ask the Judge a few questions, sir?

CHAIRMAN KINNEY: Proceed, Mr. Nizer.

It is difficult to imagine what a cross-examiner feels when he rises to combat a witness who has injured his cause, perhaps fatally. Probably the gladiator who went into the arena knowing that he or his opponent would die, experienced a similar emotion of fatalism. Here, it was someone else's life, Crump's, that hung in the balance, but that made the responsibility even more awesome.

The only weapon the lawyer has is words. With these I had to discredit or dislodge Judge Austin from his position, or we were lost. He was a sincere, doughty adversary and would fight back. Our position might be worsened. How far could one gamble with him? All the skills acquired over a lifetime had to be employed to hold the witness in check, to compel him to answer questions, without going off on argumentative excursions, which would enable him to score by repeating his original testimony. Yet, caution was also ruled out. Judge Austin had done too much damage to permit of the safe approach.

Truth has many shells. Each is the truth, but each presents a different aspect, depending on the bias, self-interest, or other psychological coloration which remains on the surface. As one after another shell is removed the picture of truth changes. Only if one can reach the core, hidden beneath the protective covering, does one feel he knows the bare truth. The task of cross-examination is to remove these outer shells, leaving the witness and the truth exposed.

The lawyer's ordeal is even more forbidding, because he has only moments to decide on a campaign. We had not expected Richard Austin to appear. Indeed, District Attorney Thompson, whether guilefully or not, had announced that the State "has, as such, no witnesses to call." Our strategy had to be improvised on the moment. The risks could not be assessed by reflection.

So, as I got to my feet, I was filled with turbulent emotions, chiefly a desperate concern for Paul Crump's life, now hanging in the balance on every question.

I decided to throw Judge Austin off balance, if I could, before opening a full-scale attack.

MR. NIZER: Judge, were you requested to come here by the State Prosecutor to testify?

A. I was.

Q. As a witness for the State?

A. I was asked by them, and I stated to the press that I was available for either side to come here and relate any knowledge of Crump's background that extended for nearly 9½ years. I have been available for either side.

Q. I did not ask you whether you were available, Your Honor.

A. They did ask me to come.

Q. When was that, sir?

A. Well, let's see, they sounded me out about a week ago. And I then indicated that I would come.

Q. Who was it that requested you on behalf of the State to testify, sir?

A. No one asked me. They asked me if I might be available, and I gave them an answer.

Q. Did anyone, specifically on behalf of the prosecutor, ask you to come here as a witness, sir, or did you—

A. Perhaps Mr. Thompson asked me to come here as a witness.

Q. When was that?

A. The latter part of last week.

Q. Did he state to you that he asked you to be a witness in this proceeding, or did he merely ask you whether you would be available if necessary?

A. Well, I don't know how he specifically told it. I know that I told him that I would be available if he wanted me. And, I think, perhaps, I got definite word over the weekend that they wanted me.

Q. And who gave you that definite word?

A. Mr. Thompson.

Q. Do you know that Mr. Thompson announced that he had not called you as a witness to this proceeding?

A. He hadn't called me originally. And I don't know what he announced. I wasn't here this morning.

We had already fared better than I had hoped. From "No one asked me. They asked me if I might be available" to "Perhaps Mr. Thompson asked me" to "Mr. Thompson gave me definite word to come" to "He hadn't called me originally. And I don't know what he announced," there was none of the certainty of his original testimony, which had sounded more like a lecture by an expert to the uninformed.

It is a curious phenomenon in cross-examination that the effect upon the witness and judges of uncertainty dragged from him, may be out of all proportion to the importance of the subject matter. A witness who flounders about, whether he was subpoenaed or appeared voluntarily, may cast a shadow on his most impressive recital of important facts. Reliability is a continuous string. It depends on complete consistency. To be partly reliable is to be unreliable.

I stepped up the attack:

MR. NIZER: You have given a recital of some of the events at the time that you were a prosecutor in this very case.

A. That's right.

Q. And a very able and conscientious prosecutor. Have you read the transcript of that trial, which lies in front of the prosecutor?

A. I have not read the transcript. I have not.

I faced him with the records which revealed that "immediately" after the confession Crump had been examined not by his own doctor, as Judge Austin had just said, but by Dr. Brams, who was Judge Austin's doctor and friend. I could not pin him down on this error, because he had recalled that other doctors had examined Crump. Of course one of them was Dr. Rosen, whom Crump had visited long before the confession night. Thompson and Moore later skirmished over this point. However, Judge Austin had been further shaken by our quick resort to specific passages from the trial testimony.

I attacked from another direction:

MR. NIZER: You also, in referring to the original circumstances of this terrible crime, said that Mr. Crump knew that Ted, the victim of the crime, who was killed, was his friend.

Was that not an inadvertent error on your part? Can you point to any place in the testimony of either trial which indicates that the man who was killed was his friend?

A. I can't point to it in the testimony, but I can refer you to the widow, who said that Crump used to call her deceased husband, 'Ted.'

I was sharp with him for avoiding the question and trying to prejudice the Board with a statement of supposed knowledge outside of the record.

MR. NIZER: Is there anything in the testimony that indicated that he was his friend; is there to your knowledge, or is there not to your knowledge?

A. Nothing in the record. Nothing in the record.

He had yielded under pressure. I took a deliberate pause. The time had come for the main attack.

Q. Now, Judge, you have recited in rather vivid terms some of your descriptions of this terrible crime. Have you read the 220 pages of affidavits submitted by fifty-seven witnesses for Paul Crump in this clemency proceeding?

A. I have not.

Q. You have never seen them?

A. Never seen them.

Q. You knew that they were in the hands of the prosecuting attorney before you came here?

A. That's right.

Q. Do you know who those fifty-seven affiants were?

A. I understand a great number of them were guards at the Cook County Jail.

Q. Do you know who the others were?

A. No I don't.

Q. You referred to the kind of testimony that has been given here. Were you present this morning when any of the testimony was given?

A. I was not here. I had it summarized for me during the noon hour.

Q. You had the testimony this morning summarized for you, by whom?

A. By Mr. Thompson.

Q. So you are going on a summary of the prosecuting attorney within a half hour, or an hour, during your lunch hour . . . is that what you referred to as the testimony that was presented here, in characterizing it?

A. That's right.

Q. And telling this Honorable Board that that testimony is inadequate on that basis, is that correct?

A. That is correct.

Q. Do you recognize, or do you not, sir, that if there is a case of genuine rehabilitation—a man who has changed his outlook on life to be a social instead of an anti-social creature—that that is a proper element in the exercise of the conscience of the Governor for commuting a death sentence to 199 years in prison, is that a factor, is my question?

A. That is something that only the Governor and this Honorable Board can determine. I'm not going to determine it for them.

Q. I'm not asking you to determine it, Judge. I'm asking you whether you consider it a vital factor in the considerations that face this Board and the Governor?

A. I say the point involved in this case is whether there is any reliable evidence of rehabilitation.

Q. I am asking you, sir, not to pass on whether it is reliable. I say, if there is, assume, sir, that there is genuine rehabilitation . . . is this a proper vital consideration for this Board in making its recommendation to the Governor to commute sentence?

A. I have no opinion on that.

Q. You do not wish to express an opinion on that. Do you agree with the following sentence here:

"Rehabilitation, whether real or honestly imagined should not govern a recommendation of this Board. It is not a basis for clemency."

A. I believe . . . in this case, that that is my feeling on the matter. I believe that there are unrehabilitable people. And this defendant has heretofore deceived and misled this Parole Board when he convinced—not this Parole Board—

Q. Judge, you have told us that. I do not want you to make any repetitious remarks, so as to prejudice the court. My question is, and would you be good enough to answer it: Do you agree with the philosophy that rehabilitation is not a basis for clemency?

A. And I believe that.

Q. You do believe that?

A. Yes. In regard to this particular case, as I have heretofore said.

Q. No, I didn't ask you with regard to this particular case. I distinctly asked for a direct answer. I thought you gave one, but I will give you a further opportunity to elaborate. Do you believe in the principle as state—

CHAIRMAN KINNEY: Just a moment.

As I drew close to eliciting an answer which would contradict the entire theory of the prosecutor "that rehabilitation is not a basis for clemency," Thompson arose and signaled that he wanted to interrupt.

MR. THOMPSON: Mr. Chairman, Mr. Nizer is asking Judge Austin if he agrees with a quoted statement he is reading.

Judge Austin has stated that he agrees with that statement as it relates to this case.

Now in fairness to the Judge, I think it should be made clear the statement Mr. Nizer is reading, is a statement from the answer [brief] of the State's Attorney in this case.

So that the answer of Judge Austin is responsive to his question. And that Mr. Nizer not be allowed to go beyond that.

MR. NIZER: I do not think that it is well taken, Your

Honor. The statement obviously is a general statement of philosophy. And I didn't say in this case.

MR. THOMPSON: It's a statement in response to the petitioner in this case, which is a capital case.

MR. NIZER: I do not think it is necessary for me to argue with counsel.

I turned to another attack.

Q. Judge, do you recognize that there are objective tests of whether a man is rehabilitated; objective in the sense of his conduct over a period of years . . . confirmed by third persons, such as inmates, guards . . . would you recognize that objective evidence as a proper weight of consideration on the subject of rehabilitation?

THE WITNESS: I would like to answer it in my own way, if I might.

Q. If you will answer the question first, and then elaborate on it, I do not care. But give me an answer. Do you consider that a proper subject for rehabilitation?

A. I would think that there would be some evidence of rehabilitation.

Q. Thank you, sir.

A. But I would say that it's to the advantage of a certain person, under certain circumstances to appear to be rehabilitated. And I'm aware of perfectly sane men malingering to the extent that two of the outstanding psychiatrists in this city rendered an opinion that he was insane, and only after intercepting a letter written by this defendant, awaiting trial in a capital case, in which he instructed the witnesses how to testify. And stated that he fooled the psychiatrists into writing an opinion that he was insane.

I'd say you can feign rehabilitation, just as you can feign insanity. And it's must less difficult.

Q. Judge, there is no doubt that it is possible to feign some posture in any circumstances in human experience. It is just as possible for there to be genuine rehabilitation, isn't there?

A. It's possible.

Q. And you have not read the 220 pages of affidavits, which in this case indicate a genuine rehabilitation . . . you have not read those, have you?

A. I have not read them.

Q. How many times since March 28, 1953 [a period of nine years] have you had a personal conversation with Paul Crump?

A. Never.

Q. How many times since 1953 have you visited Cook County Jail where Paul Crump was confined?

A. Well, on many occasions, but on none of which did I see Paul Crump.

Q. So that what you are giving us, as your characterization of his non-rehabilitation, is based, as I think you have stated, upon your observations of him during the time that you were the prosecutor . . . when he was concededly a savage and desperate criminal. That is the basis upon which you have given your testimony here?

A. Mr. Nizer, you don't put words into my mouth.

Q. I'm not attempting to, sir. Let me ask it another way.

A. Let me answer the question that you have asked.

Q. All right, fine.

A. My opinion is based upon the feigning at rehabilitation that he used to get out on parole from the—by the predecessors of these gentlemen. The eloquence and persuasion with which he talked himself out of the Stock Yards Police Station, that he had nothing to do with this killing.

And in addition to my observations of him during the time he was in the custody of the State's Attorney. And during the time he was on trial in the Criminal Court Building.

Q. And that was all before 1953, right?

A. That's right, sir.

Q. And most of it in 1953 and 1954?

A. That's right. The second trial, I think, was in 1955.

Q. Would you consider the opinion and testimony under oath of the guards, many inmates, the chaplain, the head of the medical department, the head of the linen department, the chief nurse, and many others who have dealt in daily contact with Mr. Crump over a period of nine years, as having some significance on that subject of rehabilitation?

A. Not as to genuine rehabilitation. I would consider

it in regard to whether he was acting purportedly re-habilitated.

Q. You are assuming in that answer, Judge, as a basis for your answer that he is feigning, and therefore all this testimony is the victimization opinions of those against whom he has feigned, is that right?

A. His background indicates that to me.

Q. On the basis of his background.

Now sir, with respect to capital punishment, do you recognize any case at all . . . in which clemency by the Governor . . . may be exercised without necessarily being in derogation of capital punishment; do you recognize that?

A. Let me say that the last commutation of the death penalty that I'm aware of in the State of Illinois, I thoroughly approved of. It was granted by Governor Henry Horner to a man by the name of Henry Burdick, who was a seventeen-year-old lad. And I thoroughly approved of that.

Q. You still feel good about that, don't you?

A. I do.

Q. Now, my question, which I don't think you answered, Your Honor, is this: Is it necessarily an abrogation of the principle of capital punishment, if a Governor, in an appropriate case, commutes sentence from death to life imprisonment? Is this necessarily an interference with the judicial process?

A. Not in an appropriate case.

Q. So, therefore, since you hope the opponents of capital punishment give you the same tolerance as you give to them, that tolerance implies that if the case is genuine, you do not accuse those who are for clemency of necessarily undermining capital punishment in a subterranean way. That's right, isn't it?

A. That's right.

MR. NIZER: No further questions.

There is an infallible sign as to how effective a witness has been. If the judge examines him, one can tell whether the questions are designed to aid the witness in establishing a point more clearly, or to finish the cross-examiner's task of drawing admissions from him. Unless the judge remains inscrutably silent, he will psychologically reveal himself, no matter how carefully he phrases his questions to appear unbiased. Not only the direction of the inquiry, but the tone and manner of the judge can be read by the discerning observer as if the judge unfurled a plaque saying "I agree" or "I disagree with this witness." We soon had such an acid test of Judge Austin's final impact on the members of the Board. One of them put a series of questions to him, and I could almost see the strings of cross-examination being picked up and drawn in tighter.

Member Craven wanted to know whether the Governor's power to commute "was part of the judicial process, or do you consider that when he exercises his executive power to grant clemency, that this is an interference with judicial power?"

Judge Austin conceded that "it's perfectly legal for the Governor to commute for any reason that may come to his mind."

Member Craven pressed on. "Under what circumstances do you believe a Governor in good conscience could commute a death sentence?"

Judge Austin specified two circumstances, "when there is reasonable doubt as to guilt, or where the penalty appeared too severe."

Craven pursued him. Would subsequent insanity be another circumstance for commuting? Judge Austin agreed. Then he put the ultimate question:

"Now where there is a death penalty, no reasonable doubt as to guilt, and no question as to the penalty being too severe for the crime, would a Governor, in your opinion, in good conscience, be properly exercising his executive power to pardon, in the event that the defendant is in fact rehabilitated?

A. Well, in my opinion, no.

Craven had used the word pardon. I wanted to make sure the Board understood the difference between the words pardon and commute.

MR. NIZER: "Or to commute."

MEMBER CRAVEN: I'm using the word "pardon" as to reducing something from a death sentence to a lesser sentence.

Judge Austin did not answer again, he was excused.

Because Judge Austin had admitted not knowing Crump

during the critical period of rehabilitation, and, also, that he had not even read the affidavits that attested to that change, we felt that his testimony was seriously undermined.

As frequently happens in court struggles, where the inexorable rules of drama are always at play, triumph is immediately followed by disaster. We were suddenly struck the greatest blow of all. It came in a most unexpected way. We heard the voice of one of the commissioners calling a witness to the stand, whom neither we nor the prosecutor had summoned.

MEMBER CRAVEN: I understand that Dr. Scher is in the audience. I have some questions to ask you, if you will assume the stand.

Dr. Jordan Scher, called as a witness by the Board, was examined by Member Craven.

He gave his impressive qualifications, which included being a director of the Chicago Psychiatric Foundation, consultant at Cook County Jail and at Northwestern University, editor of books on schizophrenia, and director of narcotics at Cook County Jail.

He had come in contact with Crump repeatedly since 1957 because there were a number of epileptics and psychiatric patient in the tier of which Paul was "barn boss." Dr. Scher had also examined Crump twice a week during the past four weeks.

Moore and I strained eagerly to hear the first question, which would tell us how he was going to testify.

Member Craven put a technical question to him. "What classification would you put him in, Group 1, 2, 2B, 3, or 3B, which one?"

"Classification-wise, he could very easily pass for a sociopathic. For a normal person, a psychopath," replied Dr. Scher. "The person of intelligence can present the appearance of a person he wishes, if he has control of what he wishes to say. Therefore, it is difficult to make any comparison or fair assessment."

Moore was pressing forward so hard I thought counsel table, cameras and all, would give way. Then came the blow.

Q. Are you of the opinion that Paul Crump is selling something?

A. I don't know.

Q. Do you have an opinion?

A. No clear opinion, although I could understand that he could be selling something under these circumstances. Moore seized my arm to the bone.

The excitement within us made it even more difficult to hear the continued questioning.

Q. Would you classify Paul Crump as a person who is feigning rehabilitation, or one who is rehabilitated?

A. I think it is impossible to determine.

Q. You say he could fit into one of those categories?

A. That's right.

Q. But you have no opinion of which.

A. I think I can see points in both directions and can't come to a clear conclusion to that.

Q. Have you seen any institutional record on his incarceration?

A. No, I have asked to see other material, but I haven't had them made available.

Q. Your consultation with him has been on an academic basis.

A. Yes.

MEMBER CRAVEN: I have no further questions.

MR. NIZER: May we have the privilege of a few questions?

CHAIRMAN KINNEY: Yes.

Should we attack the witness? We could cross-examine him concerning Moore's conferences with him and the testimony we had hoped he would give on Crump's behalf. But it would then appear that we were struggling against a distinguished medical authority. We needed affirmative help to sustain the heavy, precedent-shattering burden upon us. To assault the witness was the last resort, only if everything else failed.

What alternative was there? To demonstrate to the witness that his testimony was not inconsistent with our desire to obtain a recommendation of commutation. There was an escape hatch. It was the difference between the kind of rehabilitation required to set a man free, subjecting the public to the risk of its genuineness, and the kind of rehabilitation required to keep a man in jail for life, where the risk of error would be inconsequential to society. Could we turn Dr. Scher's uncertainty into this channel? Could we justify his opinion on the ground that public safety required that there be no commutation to freedom, and yet get him to agree that Crump's performance over a period of nine years warranted keeping him alive, provided he was not freed?

Even while he was testifying, I decided on this approach. This had to be a very uncross-examination if it was to succeed. I wanted him to feel that there was no basic disagreement between us, and I smiled reassuringly at him. My tone and manner were likewise courteous to the point of being deferential.

Q. There is a distinction, Doctor, is there not, in determining whether a man is rehabilitated enough to leave prison environment, or whether he is rehabilitated enough to avoid death but remain in prison?

A. There might or might not be. I think there is the question of capital punishment.

Q. Assume that rehabilitation is genuine enough for the purpose of commuting death sentence, and keeping him in prison for life. That test of rehabilitation need not be as severe as if we were to send him out in society, isn't that right?

A. Yes.

Q. From that viewpoint, Doctor, you have not only examined Mr. Paul Crump, but you have also obtained the general information, I take it, from the prison authorities, guards, and inmates, have you not?

A. Yes.

Q. Would you be good enough at this time to state what the opinion was of all those who dealt with him, as to his conduct?

A. The thing that struck me most in all the time I have been associated with the jail was the incredible capacity of this individual to enlist the sympathy and interest and affections of all people around him in the jail. This trait is found in a gifted person and also in a very gifted psychopath, so it would not determine that correctly.

Until the last part of this answer, I thought he was coming along with us. Suddenly the reel had let out again.

I smiled broadly, and in a light manner, asked:

Q. With your background and skill, surely you would

have some opinion if he were a psychopath, wouldn't you?

A. No, a psychopath is noted for cleverness. Even a psychiatrist can be fooled. We can't tell.

He laughed amiably at his own vulnerability.

"I accept that. I accept that," I said good-naturedly, and laughed.

Q. In evaluating the genuineness of a person or what he says would you give special attention to conduct rather than talk?

A. I think that would be stronger.

Q. And we wouldn't have to delve into the realm of psychiatric examination . . . you have heard about this man's conduct . . . in aiding the sick, how he has given insulin to diabetics, used a tongue depressor to save epileptics from swallowing their tongues—he does this over a period of nine years. Would you say that is significant conduct?

A. Yes.

Q. Would you not, therefore, Doctor, recommend to this Board . . . on that record of conduct, the exercise of clemency, keeping him within the jail, rather than taking his life?

A. I see no reason why it should not be from a psychiatric point to preserve his existence, that he represents a most unique human being, whether he is a psychopath, sincere or repentant, I don't know. I don't know if it's rehabilitation that has created some phase of a new life over nine years, but this is a remarkable factor. How completely sincere it is underneath I don't know but there is the surface evidence.

So he recommended that Crump's "existence be preserved!" Our relationship was cordial. We were nodding our heads at each other approvingly. We proceeded to buttress the case for rehabilitation.

Q. May I ask you this, Doctor, does not Crump's good conduct have an effect on the rehabilitation of other inmates with whom he comes in contact?

A. There is no doubt Paul has distinguished himself as some inspired individual.

Q. Does not this take some strain off the disciplinary problems of the administration?

A. Yes, he can take the strain off, say the tough guy that would come in, he would keep the others in line.

Q. And every time Crump has stood out by his actions it has been to keep order and prevent rebellious conduct?

A. That is right.

Q. Thank you.

Thompson, now hearing the good doctor testify that Crump was an "inspired individual," valuable in rehabilitating other prisoners, in maintaining discipline and worthy of having his life preserved, decided to take a hand in the matter. He asked whether Crump had the "capacity to feign rehabilitation" and drew the admission "I think he has. He is no different from anyone else." But when he asked whether Crump "is the only man who fits your description in Illinois" as being rehabilitated, the answer was devastating:

A. I am sure he isn't. If he is rehabilitated I think this is the result of his own efforts. He is a remarkable person.

MR. THOMPSON: I have no further question.

MR. NIZER: I have no further question.

(Witness excused.)

One of the commissioners recalled Father Jones to the stand. How glad we were to see him again. He seemed like a haven of dry land, after the stormy seas through which we had passed.

Member Jones asked him to explain the function of a barn boss. Father Jones traced the origin of the title. It was dangerous to admit guards into the jail. "They are outside the bars, looking in. Food comes up in an elevator and is delivered to the cell block. There are no guards in contact with the inmates." So it is a prisoner who is barn boss; who delivers the food to the inmates locked in the cell. At first, the prisoners designated the barn boss, but later the administration selected him. Unless the State assigned a hundred more guards to the jail, the barn boss system is the only one which protects the guards. The difference between Crump and the other thirty-two barn bosses out of a prison population of thirty-two hundred was that:

"The majority would carry out their duties, for a personal

gain, in some cases sexually. Paul differed from them in that I never knew him to use his authority in a personal way."

With Father Jones unexpectedly on the stand again, we had on opportunity to close the testimony on an ascendant note:

MR. NIZER: I have one question. Are you familiar with the course of conduct by Mr. Crump through the years his good deeds have come to the attention of the warden and the authorities?

A. I would say most of his good deeds were not brought to the attention of many people, but rather quietly and silently done.

Q. And is it your conclusion that the man is not feigning but is sincere?

A. I don't think he is feigning. I think he is sincere.

Q. That is all.

(Witness excused.)

Summation is a painting in words which re-creates the scenes of a trial. Like true art, it should by its composition, selection of detail, and faithful coloration reveal the truth, perhaps as we have never recognized it before. Profusion of incident, unevaluated, can be confusion. The artist knows that no two scenes are ever alike. Each requires a different approach for true revelation. Indeed, even the same scene is never the same from one instant to the next. Matisse found that the change of light altered the subject, and he therefore returned each day at precisely the same time, so that the Vence Chapel would not become a different building under his very eyes.

A lawyer, too, must fashion his summation for each case differently. Otherwise the symmetry of truth will not emerge from the mélange of testimony and argument. But he has one additional task. He must persuade the resistant mind. Beauty, for the lawyer, is not an abstract ideal. It is the beauty of logic moving on irresistible emotion, to the conquest of the mind.

In each case, I seek to find that particular mode of expression, that oral structural device for summation, which will create the greatest emotive power toward persuasion. I knew that the 220 pages of affidavits were overwhelming. I remembered that night when I first read them and became inflamed with the rightness and bigness of Crump's cause. I intended to read excerpted passages from each affidavit, so that their cumulative weight would crush any concept of feigning.

But this was not enough. These were the brilliant colors filled with light and hope. Contrast was needed to heighten their effect and to give them full meaning.

An idea struck me. Why not describe an electrocution in its most horrible detail? No generalities. No feelings spared. A description so vivid that the commissioners would feel the same revulsion as witnesses of an execution who faint when they try to live through another's death.

From prior debates on capital punishment, I was familiar with the physiological aspects of death in the electric chair. The electric current causes instantaneous contraction of all muscles in the body, resulting in severe contortions of the limbs, fingers, toes, face, and protrusion of the eyes. Usually there is a star fracture on the lens of the eye, and in some cases the heart is contracted and in tetanized condition, or even fractured. After death, the temperature of the body rises to a high point; at the site of the leg electrode, a temperature of more than 128 degrees F. has been registered within fifteen minutes. The blood is altered biochemically, becoming very dark and coagulated. There are scientists who claim that electrocution does not kill instantly, and that in some cases it is the autopsy which finally executes the law's edict. Man's inhumanity to man had to be translated into a rhetorical question, "Could the Board, or Governor, permit such inhumanity to Crump, who now lived a humane life?"

I wanted to personalize the issue even more. I wanted an accurate description of how the macabre ceremony of electrocution would be conducted in Cook County Jail on Friday at 12:01 midnight when Crump would be strapped into the electric chair. So my friends in Chicago must have been startled by my request that they obtain from actual witnesses an account of the last killing in that very chair. They secured an authentic detailed description of the preceding execution from Dr. George Shropshear, chief physician at the Cook County Jail, Father Aidan Potter, Catholic chaplain at the jail, and Ray Brennan, reporter for the Chicago *Sun-Times*. Francis Mitchell, a writer, prepared the material for me.

Now the time had come for summation. I revealed part of

my plan immediately. The best way to be helpful to the Board, faced with the awesome responsibility of recommending life or death, was to read from the fifty-seven affidavits, made by almost every person who came in touch with Crump during his confinement in jail. Then I began to free the imprisoned words from the affidavits, and they re-created the scenes of Crump's transformation. Here he obtains fifty pints of blood for a guard's niece; there he pushes a depressor into the mouth of a violent epileptic; now he goes hungry to give eggs to an old Jew, who must have kosher food; later he protects a bigot who has insulted his race.

Suddenly I stop the march of words and address the Board. "Will it help society if this Friday at 11:45 P.M. a barber shaves Crump's head, so that his brain can more easily be fried by the electric current which will be shot into him? Shall we at 11:50 P.M. dress him in an antique suit of underwear, open at the chest and substitute for his prison pants khaki shorts cut Bermuda length, so that the electrodes can be placed on his bare skin, and shall we put socks and tennis shoes on his feet, in the event that he is able to walk the twenty feet to the green steel door behind which is man's ingenious chair for death?"

The Board members seem startled by this intervention. But in a moment I am back to the affidavits, and the words conveying man's goodness are jumping out again from the pages. Paul is seen struggling with an alcoholic in the throes of delirium tremens; then he massages a heart patient through an attack; now he is giving a young "punk" advice about the joys of living free; he is having a friendly quarrel with a diabetic who has not taken his insulin; "Shut off your radios everyone, this is reading time"; he is pulling down a prisoner for the third time, who is intent on hanging himself.

The words stop. Instead I speak, "Will it not ennoble us to save such a life, or shall we be vengeful? Shall we drop a mask over Crump's head at 11:48 P.M. Friday and while a chaplain intones words he cannot hear in his roaring head, walk him, supported by four guards, through that green door? Shall we sit him in a monstrosity of steel and leather under a glaring yellow electric light and while witnesses look on through a one-way window, place metal bands around his ankles, and near his groin, straps over his arms, and then lower the metal headpiece with a huge visor over his head?"

Once more I return to the pastel colors of man's regeneration. The words tell how Crump prevents narcotics addicts from stealing the phenobarbital needed by the epileptics; how he half-carries old, sick inmates to the shower and washes them; how he acts as a tourniquet to prevent a severed artery from causing death. The words sparkle and light up a scene:

"When the riot began, the condemned men trying to escape came up the stairs. Paul hit the ringleader. That was Sherwood. Paul knocked him out with the first blow.

"Then Desoney jumped Paul, and Paul was able to throw him down. Desoney just didn't bother to get up again.

"Then Paul scuffled with De Goto. De Goto was a real big strong guy. He grabbed Paul. Paul finally got him down to the floor and subdued him. At this time the warden arrived and then everything was put in order."

The words spell out gentleness as well as strength; Paul's solace to troubled prisoners, yes, even to the chaplain when he desperately awaits his own verdict, whether his wife will survive the surgery she is undergoing.

Then the fierce dark shade again: "Will it be of service to society or humanity if at 12:01 Friday night, the electrician, on signal, pulls the switch which sends nineteen hundred volts through Crump's body, throwing it violently against the straps; turning him blue, and sending the smell of burning flesh through the room? Will public safety be improved if after twenty seconds a thin wisp of smoke rises from the top of Crump's head, and the voltage is reduced, so that the body will not smoulder too much; or when he falls back from the straps, as the chaplain touches the chest with holy oil, too distressed to notice how hot it is?"

So I continued the summation in two streams of arguments, the stream of Crump's miraculous regeneration and the ugly stream of licensed murder.

In Ocho Rios, Jamaica, there is a remarkable phenomenon of nature. A stream, appropriately called Roaring River, cascades down a steep, rock mountainside and flows directly into the sea. The thunderous fall of icy water dislodges those who climb onto the rocks and attempt to withstand its freezing force. They are pushed directly into the sea which because of shallowness and a burning sun, is actually warm. Lying in the pleasant water one observes the soft play of iridescent lights formed by the pink sand bottom and the nearby roaring falls, while sunlight squirms brightly in the water like headless golden fish.

I intended the summation to buffet the judges emotionally from the fierce icy ugliness of execution, to the beautiful warmth of man's return to humanity. I continued to create shock upon shock, from cold to hot, from foaming blackness to azure blue and green mixed with sunlight. When I had completed the excerpts from the affidavits and also the final act of the guards carrying off Crump's charred body in a cart, I turned to a concluding plea:

"The opinions in these affidavits are not those of some do-gooders, of some unsophisticated people who believe that everybody is good. These are hardened people accustomed to viciousness and incorrigibility.

"We can't control the length of our lives, but we can control the depth and width. And Crump, even within prison walls, has demonstrated a growth of the width and depth of his life.

"I am going to conclude by reading to you a statement which Paul Crump penned personally. He wrote it longhand. Nobody assisted him. He sent it to the Governor. This statement, entirely apart from its own meaning is a good indication of how this man has grown intellectually, in his articulateness, and also gives an insight into the fact that this is no longer the same man who committed those brutal crimes.

"Paul Crump wrote this, and the original in his handwriting is in the Governor's hand."

" 'As I stand here on the threshold of eternity, with malice toward no one, and fully recognizing the contempt God has for the sin of deceit; and desiring not to tempt His wrath and loss of that heavenly balm of salvation, I am completely devoid of all human motives, except the desire to live so that I may justify my life and the faith of those who have done so much for me.

" 'I humbly pray that the dictates of your inner convictions will justify your mercy toward me, as I prayerfully wait, with my life in your hands, and the faith that God will guide your judgment.

" 'Paul Crump' "

"Here is a man who is worth preserving and we place his life in your hands."

The terrain is never low unless one looks from the top. A lawyer who limits his view to his own case will neither see the strength of his adversary nor his own weakness. There was one argument against commutation which bothered me more than any other. In the middle of the night, when silence permits thought to enter an opponent's camp, I saw this argument as the strongest in his arsenal. I pondered the answer to it, swerving from one view to another. I even thought of raising the question myself to diminish its force by anticipation. Also I feared its lying fallow in the commissioners' minds, and defeating us without even an opportunity to answer. Still, I waited. Perhaps it would not be raised at all. We could bide our time to the very end of the hearing. Neither Thompson, nor Judge Austin, nor Dr. Scher had said a word about what I thought was their best argument.

Suddenly it came. When I had finished summation, one of the members of the Board addressed me. Unerringly, he put his finger on the point which had perplexed me:

MEMBER JONES: Mr. Nizer, I have a question I would like to ask you, but I ask it because in your opening statement you mention that there was a principle involved here, the principle of rehabilitation as a cause for commutation—a view of the case which is being taken throughout the nation.

It has been established that Crump's rehabilitation did not begin to appear until two years after his incarceration. According to Father Jones it did not become conclusive until after five years.

Would you then contend that in a state, like Illinois, where there is capital punishment, the imposition of the death penalty should be delayed until there is opportunity for a show of rehabilitation?

Once again, I was conscious of the fact that if our answer was not satisfactory, Crump's life might be forfeited.

MR. NIZER: Mr. Jones, I get the full impact of your question and I owe it to you to make a very candid answer.

I do not so contend. I do not claim that in a state that provides for capital punishment there should be automatic delays in order to give opportunity for observation with respect to rehabilitation, because that would change the law under which we live.

If that law is to be changed it should be by eliminating capital punishment. But so long as the statute is here, when a man is convicted and sentenced, unless there are appeals and natural delays of judicial process I would not say, let's have an automatic cessation of capital punishment, until we find out whether the man has reformed.

But as a practical matter, sir, in almost all death sentences, anyplace in the land, there are several years which intervene, because where a man's life is at stake, irrespective of his being able to afford counsel, there are always public-spirited lawyers, such as my able confrere, Mr. Moore, who dedicate themselves to seeing that all the processes of justice are exhausted.

Consequently, as a practical matter, there are several years of observation which usually are available, whether one chooses to give that time or not. . . .

One other observation, which I think is implied in your question which I wish to answer fully.

A prison society is hardly the place to find out whether a man is rehabilitated. . . . When in such a case as this, which I think is unique, a man blossoms forth . . . I hate to use the word "miracle" any longer, since I have been, in jest, I hope, reprimanded. But when such an extraordinary change of character takes place in soil where there is no sunlight, all the more reason why we should save that human being to find out what the potential is of the human being.

If this were merely a scientific exercise, as Father Jones, a religionist, puts it, commutation would be warranted. But I should like to feel, and it is always so, the lawyer becomes the religionist and the religionist becomes the lawyer. I should like to feel that it is something more than a scientific experiment.

It is an expression of mercy, inherent in the word, "clemency." This would be a breakthrough in penology; fulfill our hopes that we can change the system for the better. It would be a stimulus to all prisoners to behave and reduce the needs for discipline. Social good would be done by commutation, whereas inflicting death on Crump will do no one any good.

If I thought it would in some way make up for the

pain and anguish of a family for the senseless killing of
one of its members, I would withdraw in a moment. It
would do no good.

Member Jones pursued the matter with one more question.
Ought the judicial process therefore not be swift? I replied
that the delays caused by crowded court calendars must be
diminished, for justice delayed is justice denied; but that
particularly in a capital case involving the punishment of
death, we ought not slow up, or speed up, but in the classic
Anglo-Saxon tradition provide a thorough and exhaustive
procedure to assure a fair trial.

I hoped that the questioner's nod, smile, and silence indicated that we had hurdled another obstacle in our desperate
effort to make midnight on Friday an uneventful hour at
Cook County Jail.

Thompson's summation attacked our position point by
point.

"Mr. Nizer says that the Police Authorities did an excellent
job. . . . I suppose that is a final bow to the men who have
been stigmatized for the last nine years with the charge of
brutality.

"Mr. Nizer said the courts show no mercy . . . only the
Governor can show mercy. I challenge that . . . the jury
in this very case showed mercy to Crump's codefendants when
they did not return a sentence of death as to them.

"We are told Crump's background is no longer significant.
. . . The one trouble with this case, gentlemen, is that it's been
conducted on two levels. One campaign in the public press
to win public sympathy, to force a decision from the Board
and Governor, and another campaign before this Board."

He then cited the *Life* Magazine article about Crump, and
his interviews in the press.

He pointed out that in his childhood Crump had not lived
"in a Negro ghetto but in a home which his mother owned."
Society had given him more chance "than the average person
in his circumstances would have received."

"Mr. Nizer said in his opening remarks . . . that he gloried
in the judicial procedure that was employed in this case.

"Well, Mr. Nizer, I do not glory in it. I think it's tragic, all
over the country, that we must take seven and nine years to
re-examine what we do in criminal trial. I could not lay that

blame at the door of Paul Crump. . . . It is the system which needs changing."

He quoted the religious leaders who "detected a growth of Crump's soul."

"And yet, not once have I heard from the lips of Paul Crump, or from anyone who speaks upon his behalf, that he is contrite for the crime he committed. . . . There has been no contrition on the part of the witness . . . none at all and I think that is a very significant factor in determining whether or not there has been rehabilitation."

He quoted Dr. Scher as saying that it is extremely difficult in examining a man in such an artificial society as a prison, to determine whether or not he has been rehabilitated.

Then Thompson charged that "there were passages in the affidavits that Mr. Nizer did not quote." He proceeded to do so.

"Let me read three sentences from three affidavits. Page 119:

" 'I say any conscientious person would act in the same capacity as Paul tries to do.'

" 'I can't especially describe what Paul does. Most of the sick prisoners can do what they have to do for themselves. No, there is no exceptional action on Paul's part that I can think of. Though I do know that Paul would tell kids to go straight.'

"The affidavit of James Coleman, which was partly read. Mr. Coleman is talking about Crump's effort to educate himself.

" 'He's done a wonderful job at this. He could easily be mistaken for an individual who has had a couple of years of college training. This has greatly impressed me. In fact, this has impressed me more than his rehabilitation.'

"And on page 151 from the affidavit of Charles Thornton Sweeny:

" 'I know of one instance, where he, single-handed, broke up an escape attempt, not out of any altruistic motive, but it was a selfish one. It was just before the time of his second appeal, and he didn't want anything to interfere with it, so he broke it up.'

"Now I commend counsel for putting those things in."

Thompson turned to my answer to Member Jones, that I would not automatically delay death sentences to afford the opportunity for rehabilitation. He found this unconscionable. If a man's legal rights were exhausted in a year, without time for rehabilitation,

"Mr. Nizer would say put him to death. Some people have never read *Moby Dick*, or written essays. Some ordinary men cannot do that. Is Mr. Nizer saying put them to death, also?"

His closing comment was that only the Governor must exercise his conscience in determining the question.

"You gentlemen, do not do it. You have no conscience job to perform here. That awesome power is left . . . as it should be, to the Governor of this State. . . .

"You gentlemen are no more than the ministers to the Governor's conscience. I hope and I know that you will perform that ministry in good faith. Thank you, gentlemen."

As a lawyer listens to his adversary's summation, he can tell its effectiveness by the degree of his own discomfort. If his eye is drawn to the clock, in the hope that little time is left for his opponent; if he must restrain himself from squirming in his seat, or crying out an answer, or even shaking his head in negation, then his opponent is scoring. If he can sit by in dignified boredom, he is not being hurt. I felt no anguish during Thompson's oration. He was eloquent and articulate, but he was more concerned with me than with the issue. It is an old device of an experienced debater to lure the opposition into an attack on his skill or errors, and thus divert him from establishing his case. Whenever I hear my name mentioned in every second sentence, I know that my adversary has become more fascinated with the personal duel than with his client's cause.

I hoped we had sufficiently anticipated the State's arguments about lack of repentance, the long delay in the Crump case (though this was greatly offset by the cruelty of thirteen stays of execution which constituted suffering only next to death itself) so that the keen members of the Board would supply the answers to these contentions.

The great philosophical issues involved—whether rehabilitation was a basis for clemency, the potential of the human being to change for good, and its portent for a new approach to penology, indeed, for all mankind steeped in murder for centuries, had virtually been ignored by the prosecutor. We stood practically unopposed on the real issue, which transcended even Paul Crump.

Moore and I had agreed that he would address the Board in rebuttal. He did so, answering Thompson in detail. The charge of a publicity campaign to force the Board and Governor to give relief was

"not true. . . . The last four months this town has been full of rumors and conjecture. They're going to attack the courts, the prosecutor, the police. . . . Reporters put questions to me. . . . We had to tell our story."

He attacked Thompson's statement that the procedure in the Crump case "was a disgrace." Step by step he indicated the appeals, reversals, and stays of execution, asking at each step: "Is that a disgrace?" He told of a case where all courts had condemned a man, but the United States Supreme Court voted 7 to 2 that his constitutional rights had been violated. The right of appeal is the law of the land. "How dare Mr. Thompson call it a disgrace."

As to Thompson's argument of lack of contrition, he replied that Crump's conduct rather than words constituted contrition. He criticized Thompson's reading three lines from a twelve-page affidavit and claiming that we had omitted significant passages. "Read it all," he urged. Concerning the State's claim that Crump was feigning rehabilitation, Moore read off the list of fifty-seven affiants and asked whether

"Every single one of them was fooled and bamboozled, not for a day, not for a week, not for a year, five years, six years."

He concluded that the Board, despite Thompson's contention to the contrary, did have a conscience problem.

It was a question by Chairman Kinney which gave Moore an opportunity to discuss the medical aspect of rehabilitation. The chairman asked:

"Would not your argument for rehabilitation have been a little bit deeper and more conclusive had you had more medical testimony here today?"

Moore replied:

"Some people believe that psychiatrists and sociologists hold the key to the universe. . . . Some of us believe that the detailed living of a man over seven years means far more than any expert opinion could. . . . If we had enough money, we could have paraded a flood of psychiatrists in here, who would have said just wonderful things about Paul. . . . Clinton Duffy with forty years' experience in dealing with these problems, provided wisdom worth much more than the opinions of an expensive expert. And Dr. Scher, who didn't charge me for his advice in this case, did say that Crump's record . . . in the last seven years had been extraordinary . . . and that all of the objective evidence is consistent with the proposition that he is rehabilitated."

Member Jones asked whether Crump's race had anything to do with the severe sentence. Moore replied that having no evidence to support such a theory he would have to say:

"No I do not think race had anything to do with it."

Before the hearing ended, Member Craven put a telling question to Thompson. In view of his stress on the lack of contrition, if Crump would make a statement of repentance on the record, "Would your position be any different?"

MR. THOMPSON: No, because my position . . . was twofold. No. 1, that there was no evidence of rehabilitation. But even if there were, that in this case, as in all criminal cases, that should not make a difference.

Thus the end, like the beginning, posed the vital question, Should rehabilitation, even if genuine, result in commutation of a death sentence? This was the moral question. If despite centuries of contrary rulings, the answer would be yes, a door would be opened not only for Crump's life, but for new concepts of dealing with the lawless, and beyond that endless new doors, not yet perceived, for the reconstruction of human personality.

The best summation was not made by any of the lawyers. It was made by Paul Crump. He wrote the following letter to the members of the Parole and Pardon Board which they received the day after the hearing.

"Gentlemen,

"My attorneys have asked me if I wanted to make a direct statement for your consideration. This may be my last opportunity to speak my thoughts; since it seems that my life perhaps has become important to others besides me, I take this opportunity to speak what is in my mind and heart.

"There is no way in which I can prove to you what I say is true; I can only say that I do not speak because I am trying to save my life—I say these words because, so close to death, I think my thoughts are honest and perhaps may be remembered in some future case where some other more deserving man, may be helped to life, to service, to meaningful atonement.

"I want once more to express my guilt and sorrow and anguish of conscience for the many and violent and inexcusable and tragically consequent wrongs that I have done in my life. In one sense I am fortunate because facing death I have looked squarely at my life and have seen myself, my past and my sins. When I came into the jail, I clutched to reasons or justifications or determinants for my past sins. I have learned that these were lies which I held to. These were craven excuses that I made to myself.

"Whether God has forgiven me is not for me to know. But I have gained a feeling that has freed me from constantly evoking the excuse for my wrongs and has allowed me to begin to live for the first time. My life in the jail has been full of errors and mistakes and my own misjudgments. But I have tried to be a man, and I have learned something of what it is to give, to do service, to do a kindness, to respect another, and thus, finally and at last to respect myself.

"I believe that the only way in which a man can atone for his past sins is through service to others. I have tried as best I could to make things better for those who have been near to me during these past years of my life in prison. I believe that I have been given the strength if I should be spared to help others in the future. I do not class myself with those who could make a great contribution. I do believe that my contribution could have meaning and could be helpful to other men.

"I cannot prove by anything I say that I have really changed. I do not think that men can ever prove the fundamental things of life by what they say. The only proof that I can offer to you that I have changed, is my actions over the last seven years.

"Some may think that being faced with death, a man will do anything to save his life. That is almost true. Seven years ago, if someone had told me that by saying something or doing something my life would be spared, I could have done it. But I have found in myself and by observing others, that while a man will try to do anything to save his life, he does not have the power to live a lie.

"I know that some believe that rehabilitation is not enough reason to spare a life. I do not know if rehabilitation is a meaningful word, but it seems that others have used it in talking about me. I do not know if those who think this word is meaningless are right or wrong, but I do believe that it is possible for a man to change. I have come to that conviction because unless I believe it is possible for a man to fundamentally change, there is no meaning in life. I do not believe that we are trapped by circumstance. I do believe that it can be a manifestation of God's mercy on Earth. I believe that man, so long as he has the will to live justly, can make himself and others better.

"I know that this process does not end when a man enters jail, even under sentence of death. Sometimes it can rather be the beginning, than the end.

Sincerely,
Paul Crump"

I returned to New York a day ahead of sailing time. It was not necessary, as in two previous years, to cancel the trip because of legal emergencies. My Chicago friends were right. I did not miss the boat. But what neither they nor I had realized was that my heart and mind would be left behind, and anxiety would substitute for them.

There was the usual departure ceremony on the ship, appropriately named *Constitution:* the commotion of friends threading their way to our stateroom through other seeking visitors; the champagne toasts, more hearty than meaningful; the canapes more decorative than edible, the flattery of flower baskets pre-empting sitting room, and the noisy gaiety of good will orchestrated by alternately shrill and hoarse bass toots from other boats. My wife and I joined in all this appreciatively, accepting good wishes laughingly as the spirit of festivity demanded. There were loudspeaker announcements that visitors must go ashore, repeated time and again, in recognition of a reluctance to obey. More urgent announcements pushed them off. The boat emptied and became silent, leaving a momentary impression of loneliness. Finally it moved out of the harbor, creating the illusion that the city, and a throng of waving populace, were drifting away from it. The symbol is clear. All cares are cut off and recede from a new world of serenity on which we now resided.

But my mind was wandering and wondering. It was in the room where the five commissioners were sitting up all night reading the testimony and fashioning a recommendation to the Governor. It was in the Governor's office, where he was receiving admonitions and entreaties from advisers. It was in the dark death cell, where Crump must have thought that every scraping sound was the approach of guards to prepare him for the jolt into eternity. Even when I took a constitutional around the deck I felt I was pacing the corridor of the courthouse waiting for the jury's return.

The night before, we had more bad news than good. Although the Board's deliberations were secret, reports were rife of disagreement on a recommendation of no mercy. One newspaper headline did predict that the Board would unanimously recommend commutation of the death sentence, but expressed doubt that the Governor would follow such advice. Speculation is a bent mirror, and one can see tall or short depending on the angle of sight. Editorials were in the main favorable, based on extensive coverage of the hearing. On the other hand, Judge Austin had appeared on television and repeated his condemnation of Crump as a wily deceiver who, after a nine-year delay, ought to receive the penalty meted out to him by two juries. Without benefit of cross-examination, we could imagine his impact on public opinion. And we knew that the Governor was bound to be sensitive to public indignation. So it went through a night filled with more gloom than darkness.

Crump, too, must have had forebodings. He wrote a poem, to be published posthumously, about his death in the chair. It was printed later in a magazine entitled *Renewal*. The title was "The Executed":

> *An empty cell*
> *Scattered clothes*
> *A letter half complete*
> *Moments of fiery hell*
> *For all of those who walk*

The lonely streets
In that dark before the dawn
The reason may elude
When the spark burns the spawn
With death we now conclude
Muttered prayer
Life is crust
The worst has come to pass
Soul is bare
Flesh is thrust
Society has been repaid
With vengeance wrest from
God's merciful hands
The barbarians were given sway
To produce the stench of after-death
And baked human clay.

No news is bad news when you are on a vacation. No one wishes to spoil your holiday by imparting the unpleasant truth. So as Thursday went by in silence, and the execution hour approached, I knew that the void represented the worst; that Crump's life was ebbing away. The clattering of the ship sounded like the traditional din which prisoners make on execution night, screaming and banging tin cups against the bars.

Then the phone rang. I picked it up eagerly. Would we accept a cocktail invitation. Later it rang again. Would I please come to the radio room! There was a long-distance telephone, and it would be clearer there. I sped to the top deck projected by hope. It was my friend, Ben Bodne, calling from New York. He had been driving home from his golf course when he heard the car radio announce Governor Kerner's decision. He stopped at the nearest gas station to telephone the news. Maddeningly, static intervened.

"I didn't hear you, did he commute or not?" I screamed. Now he couldn't hear me.

"Hello, hello," we both shouted.

The whistling noises which faded and grew louder seemed devilishly intent on keeping me in suspense. Finally we broke through in communication, and he was congratulating me. I needed no more. The rest of the wheezing noises sounded like symphonic music. Within an hour there were three cables from Moore, the Chicago committee, and one from Miriam L. Rumwell on behalf of Paul Crump himself. The Board had unanimously recommended commutation of the death sentence to 199 years' imprisonment, and Governor Otto Kerner had followed the recommendation in a written opinion which read:

"I have today commuted the sentence imposed upon Paul Crump from death to imprisonment for a term of 199 years, without parole.

"In doing so, I am fully aware of the responsibility of my action. It is admitted in the petition for executive clemency that Paul Crump was fairly tried and convicted, having received the full process of law accorded by our judicial system. Yet the Constitution of Illinois grants to the Governor the power of executive clemency to be exercised in exceptional cases. This is such a case.

"In any capital case, there can be no easy decision. Every possible factor must be evaluated before a final decision is made.

"I am personally opposed to capital punishment. My personal convictions, however, will not predetermine my actions in a request for commutation in a capital case.

"It does not follow, however, that every request for clemency must be denied. To take that position would be to abrogate the power which was consciously and deliberately invested in the Governor.

"The most significant goal of a system of penology in a civilized society is the rehabilitation of one of its members who, for a variety of complex reasons, has violated the laws of the society. If that premise were to be denied, solely because it is a capital case, a great disservice would be done to what we hopefully embrace as the ultimate goal of this system.

"What has troubled me is how the concept of rehabilitation can be judged and evaluated in a case where the process of law, after the extensive review permitted every defendant by our concern for justice, has determined that a man committed a crime so repugnant as to merit a sentence of death.

"I do not suggest that by my decision in this case I have totally resolved this dilemma, nor that I can set forth standards so universal as to lead to an inevitable conclusion in the next case.

"We must, however, be able to hold forth to others the hope that they can look forward to a useful life—to life itself—if they will make the necessary effort to face squarely their past actions and alternatives.

"Before me is a voluminous record of testimony and affidavits from almost all of the people who have had any association with Paul Crump since his imprisonment nine years ago. This record is virtually unanimous that the embittered, distorted man who committed a vicious murder no longer exists. Rather, the record speaks eloquently of the degree of introspection, the maturity of judgment and of values he has achieved, and of the genuine contribution he has made, and can continue to make, as a human being even in this restricted environment. Within this framework, Paul Crump must be accepted as rehabilitated.

"Under these circumstances it would serve no useful purpose to society to take this man's life. The power of clemency entrusted to the Governor permits giving effect to this judgment.

"This consideration, however, can never be entirely free of doubt, for the real test for Paul Crump lies ahead. The years he must face in prison will serve as a true test of his willingness and ability to be of service to his fellow man."

I later saw film scenes of Warden Johnson advising Crump that his life had been spared. Crump was asked to comment. His clenched jaw muscle moved. Then hands behind his back, and licking his lips nervously, he began by thanking "the Governor, the warden, and my lawyers—" His voice broke. He swallowed hard to regain control, quivered, and turned sideways to hide his emotion from the cameras. He started to walk out, and the photographers yelled, "Look this way, Paul. Give us a smile." He continued walking, but turned his head toward them and his smile looked like a silly grin as tears flowed from his eyes.

Is this the end, or is it the beginning of which the end is unknown? When I read Governor Kerner's opinion, the words of Judge Austin came back to me. In his testimony before the Board, he had said:

"In conclusion, may I say this. If you and the Governor believe on this evidence, that rehabilitation has taken place, and that is the ground for granting executive clemency, you must do more than commute the death penalty. If you believe that, you should release this man immediately. It would be un- conscionable, it would be intolerable to further confine a re- habilitated man.

"And with that statement, I believe that all of the lawyers, the witnesses who have testified, the affiants who have signed these affidavits would unanimously agree."

The opponents of clemency knew how much courage it would require of Governor Kerner to commute the death sen- tence to lifelong imprisonment. By suggesting that relief, if given at all, must be complete freedom, they intended to fore- close any relief. It is not uncommon strategy to frighten a jury into inaction by pointing out that a favorable verdict will lead to consequences beyond those intended. So, perhaps, it would be unfair to suggest that Judge Austin meant his proposal to be taken literally. But whether he did or not, is not the logic overwhelming?

Prison is a cage to restrain the morally deformed from prey- ing on innocent people. If rehabilitation has produced nor- malcy, what sense is there in restraint? One may as well keep a cured patient in a hospital for life, because he was originally considered incurable, or keep a man no longer insane in an asylum for life, because it was not originally expected that his mind could be restored. The only distinction is that there is a punishment factor in the case of a criminal, which is lack- ing in the case of the sick. But punishment of whom? The re- habilitated person is not the person we wish to punish. In effect he is another person, and therefore is not responsible for the prior transgression. The law does not yet fully accept this principle in the case of rehabilitation, but it does not hold a man responsible for a crime committed while insane.

The moral outrage of punishing a reformed man is akin to punishing a son for the sins of his father. For are we not all descendants of our changed inner selves?

Indeed it would be unconscionable to keep Crump locked up. Everyone ought to agree that Crump being rehabilitated should be released to society, subject to parole supervision which would assure his service in restoring others to similar grace. We need experienced reformers like Crump.

The reason our prison system is in disrepute is not that it fails to punish. It is because it fails to reform. Often it does the very opposite. It embitters the corrupt and corrupts the initiate. Listen to Crump, in another poem he wrote, called "The Cook County Jail":

> Steel and stone tomb of archaic tradition
> Wasting the vast potentialities of
>   repentant youth . . .
> For that suddenly exploded wrong . . .
> Detonated by that hair triggered mechanism
>   of monotony's total abjection . . .
> And the romantic illusion anticipated in
>   the distracting half-chance . . .
> Lurking behind the red door of suicide.
> Seekers of that glittering fools gold
> From yesterday's plundered rainbow
> In the empty pot just around the fatal
>   scientific bend
> Of to-morrow's "pre-death-stination"
> Old men
> Hoodlum-wise to the felonious craft of
>   the crowbar, the knife and the gun
> Teach the bloody perfection of their art
>   to rapt, bulging eyed beardless
> Punks, sitting cross legged at their feet
> Their rosy-cheeked, cherub faces already
>   criss-crossed with
> The premature shadows of death
>   house bars.

Our prisons too often are schools for crime, for young criminals learning to be proficient in their trade, "their faces criss-crossed with the premature shadows of death house bars" which will result from their ultimate deed. Are not our penological institutions a demonstrated failure? "At least 55 to 60 per cent of the prisoners leaving jail today will return within five years," reported Dr. James V. Bennett, Director of the Federal Bureau of Prisons. According to J. Edgar Hoover, 70 per cent of the persons arrested by the F.B.I. have records of previous arrests.

The average prisoner spends 15,840 hours in jail. Only thirty hours are spent on rehabilitation, writes Dr. Alfred C. Schnur of the University of Michigan and previously Assistant Warden of Minnesota State Prison. He reports that such rehabilitation as does take place during the prison term "must be largely the result of the prisoner's own do-it-yourself project."

Crump has written:

"You can't research rehabilitation in books. They say I am rehabilitated. I know I'm different. I am another Paul Crump. . . . My rehabilitation has not been a mechanical kind of thing. It's been a thing I've suffered.

"I can't say rehabilitation can be successfully applied to everyone. It's a struggle. It's not something you decide on an instant's notice. To want to be reconstructed you have to fight."

Who will give direction and aid to this fight? At a meeting of the American Correctional Association in 1962, the emphasis shifted from custodial problems to progressive correctional ideas. Significantly the newly elected president was the Professor of Sociology at the University of Maryland, Peter P. Lejuns. Instead of being limited to officials and staffs of prisons, there were in attendance many college professors, psychiatrists, and medical men. Concentration was on rehabilitation.

Expiation, while desirable, is a theological concept. Punishment is a vengeance concept. Even reliance on the "eye for eye—tooth for tooth" principle of the Mosaic Code should be read in the light of the prior practice of killing whole families for the death of one person. "Eye for an eye" was actually a limitation of the revenge principle rather than a proclamation of it. It was an attempt to humanize the principle of retribution. Furthermore it should not be read literally, but rather as a confirmation of an old principle that the punishment should fit the crime.

There is virtue in the principle of reparation—to force an offender, like Crump, to work and pay damages to Zukowski's family. But even this is made possible by rehabilitation. Yes, rehabilitation is the key, the lock, and the door, all at once. Having broken through to a new plateau, that rehabilitation will cancel out even a death sentence, must we not now pursue our enlightened course by restoring, under proper safeguard, such a "cured" prisoner to a useful role in society? We cannot afford to waste one human being, one soul.

Crump has offered himself as an extension of the scientific probing in which society is engaged. He recently wrote:

"Anyone who is rehabilitated behind bars is obligated to the perpetuation of the doctrine. . . . The men who are the first fruits of enlightened penology should go out and lecture . . . talk to youth groups . . . stand in their own unglorification and tell the whole story of crime and prisons."

Crump could be an excellent assistant to Father Jones at St. Leonard's House to guide men who have paid their prison penalty, but are struggling to free themselves from imprisonment by their own impulses and distorted views of society. He could be a missionary to prisons throughout the country, bringing his keen understanding of inmates and his demonstrated control and influence on them to the aid of sociologists. He could be both healer and patient for the continued observation by the new breed of penological scientists. He could set an inspirational example for all those who believe that when goodness has been replaced by wickedness it can be restored, and that redemption is possible in life as well as in death.

The rarest flower in India grows out of the filthiest slime. Nature, mysteriously, causes it to bloom under conditions totally unsuitable to seed or beauty. When in the slime of a prison, a miracle of rehabilitation occurs, we must nurture its growth not only out of scientific curiosity, not only for the opportunity to eliminate a foul condition which disgraces our social structure, but out of awe for man's potentiality to rise from degradation to the fulfillment of a better humanity.

I shall continue to plead for Paul Crump, because he has become the symbolic instrumentality of regeneration, even for the most evil.

When I contemplated the possibility of writing this chapter, I wrote to Paul Crump for his written permission to do so. Although the printed volumes of his two trials, and the hearing before the Parole and Pardon Board, are public records, available to anyone who wished to write about him, I would not do so without his approval. The reason is that ours was a client-attorney relationship, and this imposes a special duty on the lawyer, which transcends his rights as an author. As in every instance, in *My Life in Court,* and in this book, I would not write about a client without his blessing to do so.

By this time Crump had been transferred to Joliet, where at the age of sixteen he had served his first term. The circle of crime had completed itself.

On April 4, 1963 I received Crump's reply. It was on a prison form bearing his number 25,705, the initials of an approving officer, the relationship of the addressee, described as attorney, and a huge red stamp across the typewriting, which read "Special Letter." These face marks of censorship, and lack of privacy, made the contents even more striking.

After granting the permission which removed my professional inhibitions, he wrote "I have thought of you often since our hurried midnight conversation, and your name is uppermost on my long list of people to pray for." Then after expressing the hope that I would visit him, and wishing me success in my writing, he closed with the formal greeting "Respectfully yours" and his signature.

But underneath was another line. It was composed of only nine words. The first eight were pleasant. The ninth word left me stunned. I reread the line again and again. Each time the last word moved me more profoundly than anything I have ever read.

Words, like living things, are chemical. A word in one context will be soothingly unimportant. The same word in another context will have an explosive effect on the emotions. It is the sequence and mixture which turn the benign chemical into a volcanic force. In this instance, I felt not only deeply stirred, but the recipient through one word, extraordinarily placed, of the largest fee any lawyer ever got.

The sentence at the end of Crump's letter read:
"P.S. April 2, 1963 I celebrated my 33rd birthday. Thanks."

Chapter Two

DIVORCE

PRESIDENT KENNEDY once said that when he entered the White House he expected that his most difficult task would be making decisions between right and wrong. To his surprise this was not as challenging as he had imagined. What was far more perplexing and burdensome was the constant need to choose between two alternatives, neither of which was desirable.

In domestic and personal affairs too, the decision, whatever it is, may not be a satisfactory solution, but rather the lesser of two evils. Yet it must be made, for the realities of life are often too complex for the neat pattern of a choice between good and evil. That is why blueprints for a better society are more likely to please the theoretician than those for whom they were designed.

The corollary of the proposition that we are required to make the better of two unpleasant choices, is that we must frequently adjust conflicting ideals so that one is not sacrificed to the other. This is the constant preoccupation of law. That is why the law is so inexact and contentious a "science," or rather why it is an art rather than a science. The judge encounters this struggle between idealistic theories encroaching on one another wherever he looks; in civil law, the clash between the freedom of the press and the right of privacy; in criminal law, the freedom of the press and the defendant's right to a fair trial. Illustrations abound in thousands of in-

volved situations. I shall deal here with only one of them—
the divorce law.

The clash is between the sanctity of the marital contract,
and the need to provide an escape where the relationship
becomes intolerable; between the marriage institution which
is the foundation of the family, and, therefore, requires stability, and the instability which results from incompatibility;
between society's concern for children, the innocent victims
of the broken home, and the equally great injury which may
be done to them in a hostile parental environment; between
financial concern for the wife who is traditionally not a bread-
winner, and the imposition of alimony on the husband which
may thwart his future. These and infinite variations involving
emotional conflicts which defy simple solutions, mean that
justice is not absolute, not a clear choice between right and
wrong, but rather the best accommodation to the passions
and rights of the contestants. To make matters still more
frustrating, their offspring, who have become additional parties to the original marital arrangement, affect the rights of
all.

Of course, it would be ideal if all marriages prospered, but
one out of every four results in divorce, and this does not
mean that the others are all successful. In the large social
sense, it is as important to declare war on family disruption
as we have on poverty; to teach family reorganization in the
law schools as we do corporate reorganization. In the meantime, the law is compelled once more to make a choice between two or more unpleasant alternatives.

Fifty States of the Union have prescribed almost fifty different grounds for divorce. Many overlap, but their strictness
or looseness reflect the local mores of how best to discourage
the untying of the marital knot. Until recently New York was
the only State which permitted no other ground for divorce
than adultery. Since 1787, this severe standard had been
maintained. Recently, another attempt was made in the legislature to provide additional grounds, ranging from physical and
mental cruelty to separation for two years, and from conviction for a felony to homosexuality. The "reform" of the divorce
law finally succeeded. The struggle had been long and
circuitous.

Recently, in the Rosenstiel case, the highest court in New
York upheld a Mexican divorce where both parties had flown

for the express purpose of obtaining one. We argued that the jurisdictional requirements of Mexico had been met and, therefore, even though the grounds were crucially different from those in New York, its courts should honor Mexico's decree.

There is usually a moral compulsion behind a legal rule, and in this case it was the effect an adverse decision would have had on over two hundred thousand marriages in New York, where one of the parties had obtained a prior Mexican divorce (the other spouse appearing). Thus, the consequences of a harsh divorce law pyramided into a structure of relief whose façade was completely foreign to New York's concept of domicile.

The proponents of a more liberal divorce law pointed to these anomalies. They decried the need to shop for more favorable jurisdiction either in the United States or abroad. The wealthy could afford these trips. The poor either suffered along or engaged in the artifice of perjurious proof of adultery; or tried to obtain annulment on preposterous assertions that a marriage, years old, had not been consummated, or that there were fraudulent representations before marriage about wealth or the willingness to bear a child, or on other farfetched grounds. New York had the highest number of annulments of any State—proof that they were another form of evasion of the strict divorce statute. It was contended that more liberal grounds for divorce would not increase the number of divorces, but more realistically provide remedy where devious ones would be sought anyhow.

On the other hand, opponents of "reform" contended that marriage, like all other relationships, would run into crisis and unhappiness, but that its unique social status demands permanence. Anything short of adultery should not be permitted to terminate it. They insisted that time will often provide balm and a new perspective to so profound a relationship, made closer by the ties of maturing children. Delayed escape from marriage may permit wisdom to leaven the difficulties, to overcome "the tyranny of the trivial," and to adjust to a long and ever-changing process.

Distinguished advocates for both positions made their arguments to the legislative committee which recommended a new statute. The arguments on both sides were general. The conflict between the contending forces was expressed in wide-ranging rhetoric. I prefer to illustrate the evil of shopping for a divorce with a specific case tried in the courts. Where is there a better laboratory for exposition, or one which gives truer insights into the motivation, meanness, and nobility of men and women enmeshed in emotional strife?

In order to protect and not to involve our client's children I have disguised the names and identities, without other sacrifice of authenticity.

While still at Indiana State College, Theresa and Robert acquired the unexpected degree of Mr. and Mrs. Mallin. Their impulsive and young marriage was nevertheless a brilliant success. She was Titian-haired and her beauty was robust, more in the tradition of Lillian Russell than the frail style of her own day.

The Mallins were extremely charitable. Mrs. Mallin had done valuable volunteer medical work, and she and her husband gave freely of their time and money to aid sick and needy children. Their lives were filled with love, so plentiful that it overflowed to the community.

They decided to buy a larger house nearby. Thus began what Ibsen once described as "the thousand strands of the web of fate, so strangely entangled." They sold their old house to Mr. and Mrs. Browne, who became their closest friends. If there is anything to the theory that one never abandons a home lived in with love, the symbol was ominous, because the new occupant, Loretta, darkly pretty, vivaciously petite, was to take over not only physical possession of the premises but the love which had filled it.

The Mallins and Brownes saw each other virtually every night—a constancy which life in the suburbs encourages. They even extended their companionship to joint vacations. For a long time the dividing line between affection and love remained indistinct. Earl Browne's working hours were unusual. He was employed as an executive on the night shift in an aviation plant where he was required to go to work at midnight and return home at four in the afternoon. When he visited with his friends, he would excuse himself early to gain his sleep before departure for work. Loretta remained behind and was later escorted home by Robert. These ten-minute trips became inordinately long, so that even Theresa became alerted to them. In the last stages Robert would disappear from bed in the early hours of the morning, and when detected by his wife, who found her former peaceful slumber sensitive to the faintest noise, he would offer implausible excuses such as that he was looking for the dog, or that he thought he heard a burglar and searched the surrounding streets.

The most trivial incidents became inflammatory. One night the two couples were out together as usual. Theresa had a cold, but her formerly solicitous husband ignored her. Loretta sneezed, and Robert was gallant with handkerchief and concern. Even worse, although Robert was finicky about food and would not permit anyone to touch his plate or drink from his glass, on this occasion he offered Loretta the right to sip from his soda and presented the cherry to her. If he had written a love letter to her in public, it would not have been as significant to his wife, who had never achieved a similar concession.

On another occasion, when the two couples went to the beach together, Robert's attention was so tactlessly concentrated on Loretta that Theresa openly reprimanded both of them. He was in a fury and when he drove home, he rocketed at reckless speed as if he would crush the gas pedal with his foot, and he vented his anger against the red lights, disregarding them as if they were moral rather than traffic restraints. Finally, a car deliberately blocked them. It was a policeman off duty, and, therefore, out of uniform. Robert was in just the wrong mood for interference. He was insolent and defiant, even after the officer's badge was exhibited. The policeman threatened to arrest him. Theresa pleaded with her husband to quiet down, but he got out of the car and advanced on the officer threateningly. In the course of opening his coat to show his authority, she saw the policeman's gun. She became alarmed and tried to restrain Robert forcibly. He struck her across the face with his fist. The officer announced that he would also charge him with striking a woman, and was hardly impressed with Robert's retort that it was his wife. Patrol cars were called and while the officers were deciding whether to arrest immediately or issue summonses, Robert, in an uncontrollable rage, went back to the car and punched Theresa in the head. Later he appeared in court, was fined for speeding, and after he explained that he had struck his wife only to bring her out of hysteria, he escaped with a serious reprimand.

He demanded a divorce. She refused, saying that she loved

him, there were the children, and that he was sick, but she knew he would overcome his infatuation.

Conditions at home changed completely. Gone was the happy household with jest and laughter at the dinner table. His guilt, and the frustration of furtiveness, turned him surly and vicious. The mother had to warn the children to be silent lest their chatter, no matter how innocent, should irritate him and bring on tantrums of abuse and despotic orders. Even his love for his children did not survive his seething emotions. His son had to submit to serious surgery. Robert showed only casual interest, whereas formerly he had doted on the children.

His continuous bickering, vile language, and tyranny created a nervousness around their lives, until the very air was filled with jitters. He took elaborate pains to build a little wall of blankets each night between himself and his wife. Their former inability to stay away from each other, even if only to touch hands when in public, had turned to this.

Theresa was so upset that one evening she spilled hot coffee and scalded her forehead and arms badly. This was the occasion he chose to advise her that she better learn how to dress the wounds herself because he was leaving.

He packed and left, full of indignation at nothing, bursting with recrimination at no grievance, beside himself with anger over no injustice. So, as has been the case from time immemorial, sex can turn a man's head, while conscience inverts his feelings and makes him storm at the world.

When he also put economic screws on her by reducing the former payments for the household to an insufficient trickle, she turned desperately for advice and remedy. She engaged detectives to provide the facts, which she instinctively knew only too well. However, she wished to determine whether her husband's fever was temporary, or whether all hope for their marriage was lost.

Since Loretta was still married, Robert's trysts with her continued to be cunningly planned. The sleuths' reports, worded in the jargon of their trade about "subjects" and "operatives," spelled out their ingenious arrangements. They would drive their respective cars to a local railroad station where they signaled each other with blinking lights. He would park his station wagon and take over the wheel of her car. After kisses, inappropriately intense for mere greetings, they would drive off while she cuddled against him enveloped by his right arm.

Sometimes they would go to an empty apartment of a friend. Most of the time they would have dinner, then drive to an isolated parking section. The detectives primed themselves for the next rendezvous. Their prey almost didn't get to the parking space because their embraces and kisses caused the car to careen as dizzily as they must have felt. They finally arrived at their deserted destination, put out the car lights, and got into the back of the car. They removed their outer garments and carefully placed them along the rear and side windows to block out any view into the car.

After a while the three "operatives" and a photographer approached stealthily. They suddenly opened the front and rear doors and flash-bulbed the couple in the awkward dishevelment of passion. She screamed with fright and then, still unclad, sobbed that this would ruin her marriage. He offered large bribes for the photographic film. Since he was preoccupied at the same time with rearranging his clothes, his business proposal was not without its ludicrous aspect. After they had transformed their improvised bedroom back into a car and themselves into passengers, they drove away, she remaining in the rear crying quietly.

Now Theresa waited breathlessly for the denouement. It was possible that Loretta's fear of exposure would break up the relationship, and that the shock of detection and the impending scandal would restore Robert to his former sober self. Would he, though forlorn and ashamed, return home? She and the children were eager to welcome him back. She was determined to ease his way during the difficult transition, and by love, devoid of any recrimination, restore their tightly knit, happy family. These magnanimous intentions never had an opportunity to be exercised. She was in for a new shock.

Robert withdrew all the money from their joint bank account and took off permanently for another state. Loretta left her husband and joined him there. These were no impulsive acts. They were arranged with meticulous legal care. In order that his wife should not be able to attach his property in New York State, he "sold" his stock interest in his business to his mother. The consideration for this transfer was so inadequate, and spaced over such a long time, that it effectively put out of reach any practical remedy. His brothers arranged nevertheless to send him income, and expenses for the extensive legal fees which eventuated.

A curious aspect of this was that Robert's mother and brothers loved Theresa, disliked Loretta, disapproved of Robert's irrational behavior, and tried to bring him out of his sensuousness to his senses. Nevertheless, his fierce determination to leave his business, wife, and children, all to possess Loretta, and his physical decline, until he was virtually ready to explode into a nervous breakdown, made them cooperate with his scheme. Blood is thicker than justice.

After establishing residence in the new State, Robert instituted a divorce action there on grounds of his wife's cruelty and ungovernable temper. All he could summon up to charge her with was that she used vulgar language and thus embarrassed him.

We were then faced with a serious legal dilemma. If we ignored his suit, as would ordinarily be the right strategy, his unilateral divorce would not be recognized in New York. So, if he returned to this State to resume his business efforts with his brothers, we could proceed against him. Suppose, however, he really stayed on in the other State where Loretta had joined him? Suppose his domicile there was not temporary for divorce purposes, but a genuine settling down for an indefinite period? Then the divorce decree which he would obtain there, if we defaulted, would be valid in New York, because the husband's residence gave the court of that State jurisdiction of the case. All information was that this was his intention. Loretta obtained a one-day Mexican divorce, and joined him. Indeed, seven years have passed since then, and they are still living together out of New York.

He had cruelly cut off his wife from income, except occasionally a nominal check. We sued in New York and obtained an alimony award of four hundred dollars a week, but it was uncollectable. He had stripped himself of all property that might have been seized in this State. If we ignored his divorce action, he would obtain his freedom and marry Loretta.

Every rule has its exceptions. This was one instance where it was advisable to appear in a foreign State to defend the suit. True, we would thereby confer valid jurisdiction upon that court, but was there ever a matrimonial case where the husband's chance of success was less? We had photographic and other positive proof of his adultery. He had abandoned a loyal wife and his three children, pilfered funds from their joint account, and run off with his paramour to another State. He had engaged in a transfer of his property to leave his wife and children penniless. Loretta had tauntingly telephoned Theresa and told her she would not receive another cent from Robert. With this background of treachery and cruelty, all he could summon up, even now, to accuse his wife of, was that she used filthy words and humiliated him.

He had the audacity to ask the court to grant him relief. We would prevent this, put in a counterclaim for separation, based on his absconding and adultery, and seek alimony relief. So we decided. Little did we know that we were heading into one of the greatest judicial scandals in American history.

We retained a local law firm of the highest standing to represent Theresa. Robert countered by adding a young attorney of no particular experience to his counsel. We thought this a strange addition to Robert's law representation, but still had no reason to know of any relation between the judge and new counsel.

At the trial, Robert's brothers, two sisters-in-law, and his seventy-year-old mother testified that Theresa's cruelty consisted of vulgar speech and conduct. Theresa presented as witnesses a large number of mutual friends, all reputable, who denied that she ever behaved or spoke in any manner but "as a perfect lady." It turned out that Robert prided himself on being a storyteller, and was frequently goaded on by his friends to perform. Like most frustrated amateur entertainers, he needed very little encouragement to begin, no encouragement to continue, and a great deal of encouragement to stop. His repertoire included filthy stories. When he testified that he was humiliated by his wife's vulgar language, he forgot that she had in her possession two homemade motion picture prints of his pantomime performances which in color depicted the most off-color, smutty gestures. They were exhibited in court and rendered ridiculous his pretended sensitivity to his wife's language.

The law, ever alert to the ease with which spurious accusations can be made, protects the innocent by a salutary rule. In order that cruelty, which consists of vulgar language and violent temper, be sufficient grounds for divorce, the cases hold it must produce such continuous, intense mental pain and suffering as to endanger health, and force abnegation of the marital relation. Unaware of this, Robert readily admitted that despite the cruelty of vile language to which he was subjected, he continued throughout the years, and until a month before he abandoned Theresa, to cohabit with her. This in itself should have defeated his action for divorce, even if his testimony had been accepted as true.

Theresa's proof of Robert's adultery with Loretta constituted not only a counterclaim for separation in her favor, but a perfect defense to his action. Even if he could establish her cruelty, he could not obtain a divorce if he himself was guilty of infidelity. Five witnesses testified to their posture in the back of the car. The photographs made it impossible for Robert to deny the scene and setting. But he had the audacity to explain away the incident on the theory that he was stretched out on the back seat to "be a little more comfortable," because he was suffering from gas. He had unfastened his belt and trousers to "relieve the pressure against my stomach." Loretta was partly unclad because she was "warm" and "uncomfortable." He conceded that despite their mutual indisposition, "I brought her toward me and held her around the shoulders and I kissed her cheek and I believe I kissed her lips."

He admitted that he put his "coat and jacket on the rear seat of the car" and hung up Loretta's coat "on the little hook so that it would not get crumpled." The theory for shedding their clothes was the uncomfortable heat, but it was a December night, the five witnesses wore overcoats, and the official Weather Report put in evidence showed that the temperature was forty-five degrees. Furthermore, the windows of the car concededly were all tightly closed.

The court found "of all five of the raiders who testified, not one witness was able to definitely testify that he observed the parties in the commission of an act of intercourse." He ignored the overwhelming testimony of a reputable witness to the contrary.

The notion that their intertwined bodies, their kisses and embraces, represented an innocent search for relief from gas pains and warm temperature on that wintry night was nevertheless accepted as true by the judge. He also believed Robert's accusation that his wife had humiliated him by her use of unseemly language.

So the judge denied Theresa's request for a separation and granted Robert a divorce against her. He cut off her alimony except for a nominal sum for the three children, and they taxed her with half of the costs. The rule of probability never took a worse beating in any court.

In divorce actions it is not unknown for a desperate defendant, when caught *in flagrante*, to offer implausible explanations, but the courts do not abandon every vestige of common sense to accept them. The test of adultery is not actual evidence of intercourse, but "opportunity plus inclination." For example, in the Heath case, the wife was not found in the act of adultery, but was observed lying on her bed clothed in underwear and a bathrobe. The man accused of being her paramour was lying beside her with his shoes and coat removed. The court would not countenance the wife's explanation that this was a harmless interview with her husband's former employee for the purpose of discussing her writing for him a recommendation which would enable him to obtain future employment.

Nine days after the judge granted Robert a divorce, he married Loretta. This, despite his repeated testimony that he was not in love with her, nor she with him, and that they had never discussed the possibility of marriage. She had not been presented as a witness by Robert at the trial and when we examined her before trial, she continually refused to answer questions about her relationship with Robert, on the ground that to do so would tend to incriminate her.

We began a search for the explanation of the incredible decision. We learned that the judge was under investigation by the Bar Association for his conduct in a number of cases.

The judge sought an injunction against the Bar Association on the ground that only lawyers and not judges were subject to discipline by the Bar. He claimed that only the House of Representatives of the State had the constitutional power to determine whether a judge should be tried for misdemeanor in office. He was upheld on this legal point. The Bar's noble effort to pursue the matter was frustrated by an injunction.

A grand jury then took up the matter, and after investigation found that the judge was unfit, and recommended that he be impeached. These findings were expunged from the record in another attack based upon the ground that the grand jury exceeded its jurisdiction.

By now the newspapers were demanding that the matter

not be hushed up. This crusade, in the best tradition of the American press, helped to bring about such public indignation that the House of Representatives appointed a committee to conduct a "thorough investigation into the said charges of official misconduct" of the judge.

The committee conducted hearings. It was revealed that the young attorney, whom Robert had added as counsel, had given gifts to the judge. When the judge testified before the committee of the House of Representatives, he was asked:

> Q. So [as a lawyer] I could do the judge all the favors and give him all the gifts I wanted to, and it would not be within the purview of the ethica which says that I cannot curry favors with a judge and give him gifts, is that your interpretation?
>
> A. That's my interpretation of it.

The committee, on the basis of all the testimony before it, reported that the judge had committed "misdemeanor in office," and concluded its report by recommending his impeachment because "There have been flagrant violations of the Code of Ethics governing judges."

The House of Representatives voted 65 to 25 to impeach the judge, declaring that he "was and is guilty of misbehavior and misdemeanor in office."

The impeachment trial took place before the Senate of the State. The judge admitted that he had accepted favors and gifts from attorneys including Robert's young attorney, but contended that the Canon of Ethics, approved by the Supreme Court of his State, was never enacted into law and therefore did "not have the force of law."

The Senate voted 20 to 14 to impeach the judge, but this fell three votes short of the two-thirds required. Although eighty-five legislators had voted against him and only thirty-nine for him, in the two houses of the legislature, the judge had escaped removal, and went back to the bench, and continued to act as judge.

We retained outstanding appellate counsel to reverse the judge's decision against Theresa on grounds of the evidence of the improper relationships between Robert's counsel and the judge. All requests for review of the decision were denied without opinion. We then sought a review of the case by the United States Supreme Court, claiming that a Federal question was involved because newly discovered evidence disclosed for the first time during the legislative investigation of the judge and his impeachment trial before the Senate, that Theresa was deprived of "a fair and impartial trial, equal protection of the law, and due process of law contemplated by the Constitution of the United States of America." The United States Supreme Court also refused to review the case.

Why had all upper courts rejected the opportunity to correct this obvious miscarriage of justice? The answer lies in the philosophical principle that the law's objective is to achieve stability in the social order. It will even sacrifice an individual, if to protect him means to create general chaos. If every decision ever rendered by a judge whose integrity comes under suspicion were subject to review, the settled rights of hundreds of citizens would be cast in doubt. The confusion and injury would be limitless. Litigants who had relied on the court's decisions and disposed of property, or spent the judgments collected, or remarried and raised new families, would be subject to new trials in retrospect. The injustice from such a belated effort to correct a possible wrong might far exceed the injustice done to an aggrieved victim.

Furthermore, there are practical considerations requiring the same conclusion. Years may have passed since the possible corrupt decision. Evidence may have disappeared. Witnesses may have died. The revival of contests may constitute a new injustice to litigants, who must cope with stale issues which they had a right to think were determined forever.

Besides, who can be certain that even a corrupt judge was always corrupt? It is an unwarranted assumption that every decision he handed down was tainted. Yet if one case is opened, is not the door ajar for re-examination of all his cases?

If one balances the grievance of justice denied to a few individuals against the chaotic uncertainty and instability of a general reopening of all contests previously put to rest, the rule that finality of decision for all is more important than rectifying the possible grievances of a few, can be understood. Above all is the salient fact that judicial venality is uniquely rare, far rarer than absconding bank officials, corrupt public officials, or deceiving business executives. Another instance of a prominent judge being convicted for dishonesty and sent to jail is Judge Martin Manton of the Circuit Courts of Appeals of the Federal Judiciary in the Southern District of New

York. In that situation, too, the courts refused to engage in a general review of hundreds of decisions rendered by him, lest irreparable harm be done in exhuming the settled past. In a society where imperfection due to human failing must be reckoned with, the individual citizen must occasionally be sacrificed in the interest of the public good.

This explained the refusal of the courts to act, but we felt it did not relieve us, as attorneys for Theresa, from the responsibility we owed to her. There was another balance to be considered; the judicial system for the protection of the many, as against our duty as lawyers to protect our client. We simply could not resign ourselves to the idea that she had to be victimized in accordance with a salutary rule for the general good. We knew only that we could not rest while two burdens weighed on us; one the fact that even in a uniquely rare instance our judicial system can fail so miserably; and second that our client was unjustly defeated and left in a precarious position. Theresa was penniless. She was bewildered. She had lost faith in law and justice. Her faith in us made the dilemma worse. It served no purpose to explain to her why the highest courts refused to review her case, or that the United States Supreme Court does not entertain disputes in certain cases unless constitutional principles are involved. She, the betrayed and innocent party, had lost and even been taxed with costs.

The bitterness of the children was also a sorry consequence. They now hated their father. More subtle in its possible injury to them was a loss of faith in justice and decency. They had seen their mother pilloried and their father triumphant. When the good suffer and the wicked prosper, there is a tendency to atheism, not only against the moral order in heaven, but on earth too.

Finally, there was our pride—pride in the judicial system, which we consider the highest development of man's efforts for a rational order, and a lawyer's duty to see that it is not tarnished. It was no longer a matter solely of Theresa's rights. Important as they were, something else was at stake. We felt that we must restore our faith in a profession to which we had devoted our lives.

What could be done? The divorce granted to Robert could not be upset. We had pursued that matter to the highest court of that State and then leaped beyond to the United States

Supreme Court. There was no earthly place to which to appeal. Furthermore, that divorce decree would be recognized in every State of the Union. It had been obtained with both contending forces present, which, therefore, conferred jurisdiction on the court. Every other State was bound under the Constitution to give full faith and credit to the decree. So the divorce was final. It could never be upset.

We had to look in other directions for a remedy. Every conceivable attack against Robert, whether for the moneys he had seized from their joint bank account, or past indebtedness for the four-hundred-dollar weekly alimony awarded in New York, ran into the practical obstacle that he had divested himself of his property, and any judgment against him would be uncollectible. We could sue to set aside the transfer of his property from his own name to that of his mother on the ground that it was fraudulent, and compel its restoration to its rightful owner. But this was an involved, protracted proceeding in several States, and at the end of the journey we could collect judgments for only comparatively small sums of money on past, owed alimony, or 50 per cent of the moneys previously in their joint account. This would in no way make up for the real damage done her.

As in all complex probems, it is wise to reduce them, if possible, to the simplest syllogism. In Socratic manner, we asked some elementary questions. The answers cleared away the haze of perplexity and indicated the legal remedy with such clarity that no one could mistake its propriety.

Who had injured Theresa? The judge, but he had been held immune.

Who else? Robert's brothers, who had made it possible for him to transfer his stock to his mother and who had sent him moneys from New York. These very moneys had been used to finance counsel fees for the long litigation and appeals.

Who else had injured Theresa? Robert's mother, who had postured as the purchaser of Robert's stock.

Who else? The corporations in which Robert held stock and which his brothers controlled. It was likely that these companies had supplied the funds to Robert to carry out his divorce scheme in another State.

What had all these participants in the arrangement done? They had made it possible for Robert to abscond, financed his plan, placed his property out of reach of his wife, and finally helped to execute the scheme by testifying that Theresa had used vile language.

We instituted an action on behalf of Theresa, against Robert, his four brothers, the corporations which they controlled, and his mother for a conspiracy to deprive her of her marital rights, and requested $350,000 damages.

Robert's family must have been startled. They had probably considered the controversy closed when the United States Supreme Court had refused to intervene. They had undoubtedly been advised by their counsel that Robert's divorce and marriage with Loretta were beyond legal attack. This was true. But now they found themselves defendants in a suit which would unerringly probe into their contributions financially and otherwise to the triumph Robert had achieved. They would also be subject to full inquiry concerning how that triumph had been attained, because the complaint set forth the entire history of the controversy from a to z (adultery to zymogenic judiciary). They faced a jury trial in which the truth would be fully exposed. Who had advised Robert to leave New York State? Had there been any maneuvering of the case to the judge? Who had suggested that certain counsel be retained? Had Robert, as the complaint charged, telephoned Theresa before the decision came down and bragged "that the case had been 'fixed' and that he would be granted a divorce?" These and dozens of other questions would be posed in open court, and the answers to them dug out of the hides of the defendants and witnesses by cross-examination. If there was scandal here, it would not be hushed up. We would not permit it to be neatly interred with a final sigh of either regret or resignation. We had found the legal leverage to dig it up and subject it to the stimulating air and sunshine of a full and fair trial.

We knew what the counterattack would be. The legal sufficiency of our complaint would be tested to the hilt. A preliminary motion would be made to dismiss our action on the ground that it belabored defendants who could not be sued, and for grievances which were barred and could not be asserted. The danger of such a countermove was inherent in any proceeding which was off the beaten track. The unusual form of procedure subjected it to the challenge of orthodoxy and established law. We had girded for this inevitable legal contest. For weeks before we served our complaint, we had canvassed every legal authority and avenue to maintain our position. We knew that this might be the decisive test. The issue would most likely be fought out in advance on legal grounds, with appeals to upper courts. If our complaint could be upheld and a motion to dismiss defeated, the defendants might not dare to go to trial. If we lost, the last hope was gone.

As anticipated, the defendants retained able counsel and moved to dismiss our complaint on the ground that it was defective.

The first attack was that an action for alienation of affection is not permitted any longer under the State statutes. The defendants insisted that in realistic terms that is what our complaint really charged. It was quite true that the ancient action that permitted suit against anyone who had stolen "love" had been abolished. Public policy had shifted from concern over interference with a love relationship to concern over the abuse of the remedy. Such suits had opened the doors to too many irresponsible and fraudulent plaintiffs. Affection is such an intangible property that its theft is as difficult to disprove as to prove. The legislatures of many States found this cause of action a club too often wielded by fortune hunters and perjurers. So they wiped it out. Henceforth no one could sue for alienation of affection.

Our answer, however, was that our complaint did not assert such grievance. We claimed a conspiracy to deprive Theresa of her marital rights, not a deprivation of her love. None of the ingredients of an alienation of affection action were even pleaded in our papers. We would not permit the defendants to build a straw man so that they could knock him down. We would not permit them to distort the real thrust of our grievance and then tell us we were prohibited by statute from making it.

The second attack upon our complaint was more formidable. In essence, said the defendants' counsel, we were attacking the divorce obtained by Robert. We could not do so collaterally. The same charges of fraudulent procurement of divorce, including the history leading to the impeachment proceedings, had been made previously and in the United States Supreme Court. The divorce had survived all attacks. It was final. It must be accorded full faith and credit in all other States of the Union. Our conspiracy charges, argued the defendants, were only a guise to review the same issue. This was proven by the fact that without such a finding of a fraudulent divorce, we could not succeed in the New York court. They asked that our complaint be dismissed for asserting a cause of action precluded by the judgment of divorce.

Our answer was, that far from challenging the divorce decree, we accepted its finality. It was one of the links in the conspiratorial chain which had caused damage to Theresa and on which we relied. As Judge Charles Breitel had said in an Appellate Division decision in New York:

"On the one hand there is a profound and imbedded philosophy that decided issues remain decided and that litigation come to an end. On the other hand, there is the equally compelling policy that fraud be frustrated, and consequently that one who defrauds not gain sanctuary . . . by successful concealment of a larger and basically different scheme."

We were complaining of a larger scheme in which Robert and Loretta, with the aid of the defendants, fled from the jurisdiction in which they resided, arranged a dishonest "sale" of his assets to make him judgment proof, received secret financial support in the interim, and engaged in a fraudulent divorce proceeding resulting in a judgment which deprived Theresa of alimony and dower rights.

The oral argument on the motion to dismiss shifted back and forth among the sparse legal authorities. We attempted to lift the discussion above the plane of technical legal analysis.

It was plain that justice had collapsed. We conceded that a blank wall faced us, and that we were trying to break through. True enough, the divorce could not be upset. True enough, there was a public policy against reopening all cases decided by a judge who had been tried in an impeachment proceeding. But this did not prevent a suit which accepted the finality of his decision, and charged a scheme of which it was one of the successful steps.

There must be a remedy for every wrong. The judicial process was too noble to surrender to abased standards. If we had fashioned a vessel to retrieve a cause unjustly lost, it should be accepted with open arms, not cast aside because its shape was novel.

Our adversaries were making respectable legal arguments, but I believed their cause was unjust and argued with passion, which rose from innermost conviction of a just cause.

Weeks later came the decision. It was finely spun with legal argument, but it too could not hide the deep feeling which animated the judge.

For the purpose of testing the adequacy of a complaint, its allegations are deemed to be true. In reciting these allegations, the judge pointed out that a divorce had been granted in favor of Robert "even though he had been actually apprehended while committing an act of adultery with his paramour"; that the defendants had "aided in the plan to spirit Robert out of the State, to sojourn at his mother's apartment for the purpose of later bringing a matrimonial action"; that they had "aided him stripping and divesting himself of his property by spurious transfers . . . while he continued to live on the same high plane as he did before the conspiracy was concocted."

There followed a detailed description from the complaint of the judicial shenanigans of the judge and the proceedings against him resulting in a clear majority of the legislature to remove him as judge, but his escape by a few votes from the two-thirds majority required.

Then the judge addressed himself directly to the attack upon our complaint. We were not seeking by improper collateral attack to circumvent the divorce decree.

"Plaintiff concedes that the decree is final and binding upon her, but further says that it was only part of and one of the steps in a larger antecedent conspiracy to deprive her of her status. She therefore says that . . . it is one of the main props in the corrupt conspiracy which was successfully mounted against her by the defendants and constitutes one of her main items of damage."

As to the charge that our complaint set forth the now prohibited cause of action for alienation of affection, the judge held that "it does not charge the defendants with that," and added the incisive satirical observation:

"That seems to have been managed by the defendant husband pretty effectively on his own."

Then came the ringing conclusion which was an echo from time immemorial when injustice has sought to barricade itself against exposure:

"Somehow, somewhere, this case should have a thorough airing, and I think the matters alleged in this complaint urgently call for sustaining it against an attack on its insufficiency as a matter of law.

"Motion denied."

An appeal was immediately pressed, but the five judges of the Appellate Division unanimously affirmed.

Now that justice had raised her sword high ready to descend on the guilty at the trial, settlement conferences began. The former sympathies of Robert's family for Theresa were revived and bespoken with fervor. Pressing some people against the wall squeezed decency out of them. Theresa was offered a cash property settlement, and alimony. She accepted.

We had come a long route to obtain this financial justice for her. It was another illustration of giving something late which, if given earlier, would have caused less pain to the giver and constituted more to the receiver. Had Robert acknowledged his obligation in the beginning, he would not have had to travel subterranean paths. They ultimately led him into the open anyhow, and he did not even avoid the payment to ameliorate his journey of dishonor.

This case constituted an exercise of heart and mind which strengthened our conviction that although justice, being man's child, may falter occasionally, it usually reaches its destination. But what a sad commentary it constitutes upon the practice of shopping for a divorce in a jurisdiction where the grounds therefor are more lenient.

No one could have foreseen the involvements of this case, nor those which are bound to beset other migrations for marital freedom. Certain it is that if the necessity for flight to Minerva was not present, if the local law provided possible relief, the resort to extreme measures would be less likely to occur.

A divorce is not the death of a marriage; it is a death certificate for a marriage already dead. The courts merely provide a decent burial.

However, marriage, too, is often misunderstood. It is not a perpetuation of a romantic idyll. If it were it would fail as a marriage, because it would exclude unavoidable pain of growth and adjustment; anguish over the rearing of children, from illness to familial rebellion; and inevitable frictions and dissensions, which proximity produces.

Balzac wrote, "Marriage must continually vanquish a mon-

ster that devours everything; the monster of habit." He must
have had in mind the encroaching boredom of sameness, from
unrelieved mundane tasks and routine patterns of living to
the sexual relationship, particularly in view of the lack of
resourcefulness and imagination, often imposed by prudery.
Yet all these handicaps are overcome by blessings and joys
not obtainable in any other relationship. The very relaxation
of companionship, so contrary to ardent romantic intensity,
makes permanence possible. But unless these long-range ties
and their own kind of ecstasy are understood as the real rewards of marriage, it will be deemed a failure if only because
the goals set are illusory.

Prevention of divorce requires early education in these matters, and a better understanding of family living. Such courses
are now part of the curricula of many high schools and col-
leges. They should become universal. They are not merely
courses in sex education, but a preparation for those crises
which must be overcome in every marriage if it is to succeed.
New techniques have been developed to strengthen "inter-
personal competences" which create harmony through recognition that the romantic beginning is only the prelude to a far
deeper and meaningful relationship. Indeed, the romantic
notion of love is a Western concept, regarded as unreal in
vast areas of the world. While we are fortunate to adhere and
thrill to poetic concepts, they mislead us when they become
the exclusive standard by which we gauge a successful marriage. It has been said that the honeymoon is poetry and thereafter there is prose. But this does not exclude excitement or
beauty. It is no rejection of romanticism to recognize the
evolutionary realities of life in physical and psychological
union. Aside from the changes imposed by time and inner
growth, there is the miracle of children which transforms even
the romantic ideal of oneness into new and partially divided
loyalties.

The marriage structure changes constantly in profound ways
which baffle the most learned professionals, and it is, therefore, destructive oversimplification to test the marriage by
whether the courtship and honeymoon relationship have been
preserved. Nor can it be tested by the absence of quarrel (if
for no better reason than that tiredness produces a poison
causing ill temper), or whether there is retreat into self-in-
dulgence, or whether there is emergence of other frailties which

cannot forever be compressed by the posture of perfection which romanticized love imposes on us.

When husband and wife distressfully turn to the law for relief, the process of determining fault involves each in increased bitterness. Such contests ought to be avoided, because they add indignity to the tragedy of a lost love. The process of fault-finding is particularly hazardous in matrimonial disputes where the cause is circular, each wrong creating a retaliatory wrong. The assessment of guilt involves not only tracing the origin, but weighing the preponderance of responsibility. In some cases the villainy of one and the innocence of the other is clear, although even then the simplistic approach is bedeviled by psychiatric excavation for the unseen cause. In most cases the guilt is shared, and it is interesting that if both parties in a contest have been found guilty of violating established standards (for example, if both have committed adultery), the court will not grant relief to either. This hands-off attitude, as if to say "a plague on both your houses," not only favors the husband since the wife may be left without alimony relief, but still worse, neither can obtain a divorce. So in the very case where, even by the severest standard of adultery, the marriage ought to be terminated, they are both condemned to permanent marital bonds. Thus, we have another anomaly: one adultery warrants ending the marriage, two requires its preservation. The court cannot abandon its duty to resolve the controversy and more particularly to protect the children. But we can add to the judicial procedure, family counseling and psychiatric techniques which might heal the breach, or at the very least, contain the nasty belligerence of the contest.

Such experiments have already been conducted, and with considerable success. In California, a Conciliation Court is made available to husbands and wives before or after a divorce action has been begun. Eleven highly trained marriage counselors deal with thirty-five hundred cases a year. Judge Roger A. Pfaff of the Los Angeles Consolidated Domestic Relations and Conciliation Court reports that 60 per cent of these cases result in reconciliation.

Time is not wasted on hopeless cases, such as mental hospital patients, criminals sentenced to jail, deserters, and others where there is immovable resistance to salvaging the marriage. However, even though the cases treated are selected because of their better potential, the successes are still impressive. The resourcefulness of the procedure is indicated by the judge's unique power to stretch his jurisdiction beyond that of husband and wife. He can order the mother-in-law to stay away from the family household, when he learns confidentially from the parties that she is the cause of the dissent. Judge Pfaff has even directed the interfering woman to disappear permanently from the scene on pain of penalty for contempt of court, and he reports that he has received grateful letters from husbands, such as one thanking him for getting "the other woman off my back." If the power of the judge to extend his scepter of relief so widely is questioned on the basis of orthodox legal principles, some justification for it may be found in the old maxim that the State is the third party to every marriage contract, and should be enabled to fulfill its sociological function.

In Toledo, Ohio, conciliation attempts are mandatory in cases where children under fourteen are in the family.

In Ann Arbor, Michigan, similar conciliation efforts conducted under the court's direction have resulted in 40 per cent "apparent reconciliations."

Orthogamy is the science of straightening out a marriage which has gone wrong. The orthogamist must combine the skills of a marriage counselor, psychologist, psychiatrist, pastor, doctor, and lawyer, or at least he should have their talents available to him. It may be that a wise grandmother may be an effective orthogamist, but we can no more depend on the accident that experience and common sense will combine to create scientific competence, than that primitive herbs and wives' tales should substitute for modern medical knowledge.

We must fortify, in Keats' words, "the holiness of the heart's affections" with the pragmatic techniques of orthogamy if we are to preserve the marriage institution. Then at least we may diminish the necessity of choosing between two unsatisfactory alternatives. And if we must do so, the choice will be clearer and easier to make.

Chapter Three

FRUEHAUF

It seemed to be an ordinary day. The hour was approaching when Roy Fruehauf would take his mind off the largest trailer company in the world and engage in the loving domestic ritual, casually performed, of calling his wife to tell her he would be leaving in an hour, inquire about their three children, and avoid abruptness by engaging in chitchat about the plans for the evening. Before he could make the call, his secretary told him that the editor of the Detroit *News* was on the phone.

"Mr. Fruehauf, do you wish to make any statement?"

"About what?"

"Oh, I thought you knew. We got it over the wire some time ago. You have been indicted."

"What?"

"For giving Dave Beck two hundred thousand dollars."

The editor did not misunderstand the silence, nor the click which cut him off. Fruehauf descended to the street where his car had been waiting. As he walked through the lobby, he could see even from a distance on the newsstand, the headline, erect like a flagpole, and so large that it pushed most of the ordinary type off the front page: "U.S. Indicts Fruehauf." Then in somewhat less exclamatory size, as if the reason could only be anticlimactic, was the subheading: "Ex Teamster President Beck Also Indicted for Receiving $200,000 From Trailer Executive."

The remaining space on the front page was occupied chiefly

by a large picture of Roy Fruehauf, ironically taken on the occasion which he received an honorary degree from Tri-State College, of which he was a Trustee, as he was also of the Detroit Institute of Technology. The smile on the photograph gave a false impression of unconcern about the condemnatory news which surrounded it. Some readers would search the face for criminal characteristics.

He rode home in a state of shock, sweating profusely. When he staggered through the front door, his wife, Ruth, who had heard the news on the telephone, radio, and even special television bulletins, greeted him with meaningful embrace. He was too dazed to notice that her anxiety had already been drenched in tears. She had shut off all instruments which might desecrate the house with the ugly news, but the telephone continued to ring its alarms. Church dignitaries (for he was a Deacon of the Presbyterian Church), city and State officials (for he was Chairman of the city's charitable drive called "The White Feather"), corporate officials, directors and friends all were calling to commiserate, but causing only misery by the very expression of sympathy.

It wasn't only Fruehauf's world which had collapsed around him. Roy Fruehauf, himself, sturdy as his trailers in business adversity, could not stand the blow. He lay prostrate in bed, numb and uncommunicative. His doctors were greatly alarmed. It was not until months after I had been retained to defend him, that Roy Fruehauf recovered sufficiently to see me.

The blow fell more heavily on Fruehauf because the Fruehauf Trailer Company had also been indicted for the same transaction. He cherished the impeccable reputation of his family name, which was proudly displayed on trailers which could be seen on the roads of America wherever one went. Now his name and that on the trailer were besmirched. Although an indictment is not inconsistent with innocence, for it only means that a grand jury has had enough evidence presented to it to require the defendant to stand trial, the fact that the United States makes a formal criminal charge against one of its citizens is disgrace enough to one who had spent all his life to achieve honor in his community.

The impact of an accusation is in indirect ratio to the high standing of the accused. A criminal or sharpshooter can derive full solace from his presumed innocence until proven guilty.

A reputable citizen will suffer almost as much from the stigma of a criminal trial as from conviction itself. Fruehauf suffered also for his company, which would carry unexpected burdens while competing against its 150 competitors.

So it was that when his Washington attorney, the distinguished Clark Clifford, called me to undertake Fruehauf's defense in New York, where he had been indicted, I had to be educated to the facts not by the client, but by his attorneys, associates, his old friend and doctor and by his beautiful wife, who was as knowledgeable as any of the others. When Fruehauf used the phrase, "I want to talk things over with my wife," it was no mere gesture of domestic felicity.

Fruehauf had inherited a fine tradition from his parents, upon which he had built his own imposing structure of business advance and communal leadership.

His father, August, had been a blacksmith. Progress dictated the building of wagons as well as the selling of harness. His mother was chief assistant, buying supplies and painting the wagons. High quality was the key to success and to satisfaction. Even the reins looked like perfect strips of licorice. His parents finally built the finest brick blacksmith shop in the nation, with big bay windows in front and an interior so long that it could house sixty horses at one time.

But events were moving in far-off places which were to affect them vitally. In Springfield, Massachusetts, in 1886, Charles Duryea had invented the first successful automobile, and Dr. Rudolf Diesel had patented an engine in 1892. In 1896, Henry Ford put his first car into production, and the beginning of the end of August Fruehauf's hard-earned career was fated.

One day, Frederic M. Sibley, Sr., a Detroit lumber dealer, who had acquired a summer place on a lake in upper Michigan, wanted to ship his boat there. A horse and wagon would take many days. He asked August Fruehauf whether he could rig up a contraption to hook on to his Model-T Ford roadster to haul the boat. Fruehauf thought he could. Piece by piece, he beat out and bolted a sturdy two-wheeler which he hooked to the rear of Sibley's Model-T frame with a pole which acted both as tongue and brake. He called it a trailer.

Sibley was so impressed with the speedy shipment of his boat that he thought a similar rig with a platform would be efficient for running about his lumber yard, picking up orders and delivering them. It would save man-hours and horse feed. So August Fruehauf built a stronger trailer with a platform. It worked. Orders came with a rush. A fifth wheel was added and later automatic coupling. By 1918, August Fruehauf was doing $150,000 business a year in trailers. He incorporated, making himself president, his wife vice president, and his son Harvey, treasurer and sales manager. Roy was in school and too young, or he would have had a title too. Then, in accordance with American tradition, August obtained bank loans to make possible his growing manufacturing processes.

In 1925, Roy's mother died and he left school to work side by side with his brothers Harvey and Harry. By 1930, when August Fruehauf died, his company's sales had passed three and a quarter million dollars. Roy rose in the ranks until he became president. His creative imagination and drive lifted the company to heights of which even his father had not dreamed. The company created special trailers for milk, so that it could be poured out at the destination without the use of cans; for flour, molasses, glue, rice, wheat, liquid yeast, pickles, wine, sugar, ice cream mix, vinegar, alcohol, liquid oxygen, road oil, sulphuric acid, bulk cement, asphalt, bakelite, ink, salt water, penicillin, and 175 other products. Crating was expensive and now became unnecessary for many industries. Special refrigerated and air-conditioned trailers with smooth interior linings and non-skid floors were designed to ship live hogs, so that they would not be skinned or shrink in transit, with steam cleaning units to keep the vehicle clean. On return trips, refrigeration down to twenty degrees below zero, if required, made possible the shipment of perishable foods.

Instead of boxcars, railroads began to use modern trailers on flatcars, a technique which became known as piggyback operation. Boats too used trailers for fishyback shipment.

During World War II, the government became trailer-minded. It ordered trailerized equipment for gasoline, tank retrievers, launchers, radar and electronic units, gun mounts, laundry units, machine stops, and more than 125 other types. The new missile age finds the trailer an essential carrier.

So, due chiefly to Roy Fruehauf's dynamism, August Fruehauf's blacksmith and wagon establishment became an enterprise whose annual sales exceeded five hundred million dollars! Recognition for business achievement never provides complete gratification to the good man. He must fulfill himself with something more than financial success. Out of his abundant energies, Fruehauf rendered service to communal causes so that he became a director of organizations as varied as the Salvation Army, Detroit Grand Opera Association, Y.M.C.A., and Starr Commonwealth for Boys. He was decorated "Chevalier of the Legion of Honor" by France, for "outstanding contribution to the industrial development of France." Fruehauf, who had never finished high school, received an honorary degree of "Doctor of Commercial Science" from Tri-State College of Angola, Indiana, and numerous other recognitions.

Now, the indictment, like a sudden hurricane, threatened to destroy in one fierce blow the efforts of two generations of Fruehaufs. Roy might have to resign the presidency of his company even before trial. Indeed, it was uncertain whether such a sacrifice would save the corporate image, since it too had been indicted. The other world of prominence that he had created for himself, that of a leading citizen, lay in the debris of apparent hypocritical inconsistency. And then there was always the precious third world, that of intimate relations with wife, children, and close friends, and the pressures upon them. All would be lost, unless—unless he was acquitted and his good name restored. It mattered not in this instance that the statute provided for one year imprisonment if found guilty. It might as well be a hundred. A conviction would mean total destruction of everything he had achieved in the fifty years of his life. This is why Fruehauf, broad and powerfully built, with a handsome jovial face, which must have made him the most perfect Santa Claus at Christmastime, was forlorn and in collapse in the midst of the ruins of his life.

The purpose of the Taft-Hartley Statute (Section 186a) is a salutary one. It made it a crime for an employer to bribe a labor representative, so that he will betray the members of the union. From reading the indictment, one would think that is exactly what Fruehauf was charged with doing. It read that he and his corporation "did willfully and knowingly pay and deliver to Dave Beck, President, International Brotherhood of Teamsters . . . . $200,000." Actually, the money was a loan to Beck, repaid in full four years before the indictment, and long before any investigation was begun. Irrespective of the literal application of the criminal statute to such a situation, where was the moral reprehensibility? Had there been an evil purpose for the loan? Had Fruehauf or his company made it to receive advantages in labor negotiations? There were none. His company employed ninety-eight hundred workers, and of these, less than three hundred were represented by the Teamsters Union. The reason was that the corporation was not in the business of trucking. It merely manufactured trailers. It used a small number of drivers (less than 3 per cent of its employment force) to deliver empty trailers between plants and branches. The corporation, as a manufacturing enterprise, had 116 different labor agreements with a multiplicity of different unions, but there were only a relative handful of contracts with Teamster locals.

A careful analysis of these contracts showed not only that there were no advantages for Fruehauf over competitors, but that the hourly wage increases for drivers were larger than those given to other union employees. Finally, to clinch this analysis of lack of illegal motive, the International Brotherhood of Teamsters of which Beck was president had no relations with the Fruehauf Trailer Company at all. Neither had Beck. It was the locals, which are wholly autonomous, which negotiated the contracts in the twelve out of seventy-five branches and plants which used any drivers at all.

How different the facts were from the indictment. How wary a reader must be in scanning headlines. Would not anyone have concluded from reading them that Fruehauf had given Beck a "gift" of two hundred thousand dollars, and that the iniquity had now been uncovered?

At the time of the indictment, Dave Beck was languishing in jail. The notoriety of his fall from grace was widespread across the nation. The name of his successor, James Hoffa, certainly did not diminish the prejudice in the public mind against any leader of the Teamsters. Therefore, the mere coupling of Fruehauf's name with Beck's cast a shadow of prison bars across the sunlit reputation which Fruehauf had enjoyed. Yet at the time of the loan, and its repayment in full, Dave Beck had been a respected and powerful union leader welcomed at the White House by several Presidents. So we were confronted with a familiar problem in law and in life, the adjustment of time perspectives. We are inclined to evaluate the past in circumstances of the present, as if events and the time of their occurrence could be separated without distortion. The violation of this principle of relativity causes constant mischief. One of the reasons we do not learn from experience is that time is a floating thing which becomes blurred when we look back upon it. We knew that at the trial, the jury would have to be made conscious of this anachronism.

In the meantime, our search for complete innocence of the loan to Beck continued. The rule of probability told us that since labor advantage was not the reason for the loan, there must be some other cause for Fruehauf's gratitude to Beck, which made it natural for Beck to seek, and Fruehauf to provide the loan. Our questions were like a series of keys, until the right one unlocked the door of the mystery.

During the Korean War, transportation, as always, was the magic word which transformed paper logistics to reality. Our railroads, in run-down condition at best, were inadequate for the enormous new burdens placed upon them. The government turned to trucks and trailers. Between 1940 and 1955 the trucking fleet increased 111 per cent, to almost ten million vehicles. The trailer total had grown from 130,000 to 700,000. Here was an unexpected precious transportation asset. President Eisenhower, whose brilliance in logistics during war games had brought him to the attention of President Roosevelt, who lifted him over many superiors to Commanding General in Europe during World War II, surely knew the importance of the new transportation arm, which would get the military hardware, gasoline, and food to the Armed Forces in a distant land. He appointed an independent advisory committee of the trucking industry, called ACT, to keep the goods moving. On this committee, he designated Dave Beck, President of the Teamsters, Burge Seymour, President of Associated Transport, Inc., one of the largest trucking companies in the United States, and Roy Fruehauf, president of the largest trailer manufacturing company in the country. So it was that Fruehauf for the first time met Beck. The committee met regularly and also reported to President Eisenhower directly. We had a photograph of one of these meetings with the President, who was flanked on one side by Beck (whom Eisenhower called "Dave"), and on the other side by Fruehauf and Seymour. All three surrounding the President were now indicted for the two-hundred-thousand-dollar transaction with Beck.

At this very time, in 1953, Fruehauf ran into corporate trouble. It wasn't the decline of his business, but rather its huge success which threatened him. For it attracted "raiders," who sought to buy up the stock in the open market and obtain control of the great prize. Corporate democracy, like political democracy, is not without its hazards. Where the stock of a corporation is held by thousands of small stockholders, a concentrated block of stock, sometimes as little as 15 per cent, becomes working control. This is not too different from the phenomenon of a local political leader controlling the nominations for high executive and judicial posts because he commands the loyalty of his cohorts, who are a small minority, while the majority of citizens do not vote in primaries.

Fruehauf faced such an election campaign in his corporation—a proxy fight. George Kolowich was conducting a "raid" on Fruehauf stock. He was apparently backed by substantial financial interests, because the reports on stock trades revealed abnormal turnover and acquisition of Fruehauf stock. While the drive to buy control must be skillfully directed lest it push up the price and make the venture too costly, if it succeeded, Fruehauf and his administration would be voted out, and Kolowich and his group would take over the company's affairs. Such has been the fate of many a corporation. "Raiders" have become extremely skilled in proxy warfare. Sometimes they deliberately drive the price of the stock down, either by selling a large block at one time, or by other less scrupulous devices, in order that they might then buy the stock at the depressed price. The financial sections of the newspapers carried lively stories of the developing proxy war for control of the Fruehauf Trailer Company.

But for every offense there is a defense. Roy Fruehauf consulted his corporate counsel and friend, Alfons Landa, who bore honorable scars as well as victorious medals from similar battles. It was decided that the only way to hold off Kolowich was for Fruehauf to buy up more of the company stock. Since he started with a substantial nucleus of family ownership, if he could add to his holdings in proportion to Kolowich's purchases, working control would remain with him. Of course, every other orthodox device of soliciting the votes of the individual stockholders would be followed. This phase was likely to be successful because the Fruehauf tradition and corporate prosperity made support as inevitable as that for a candidate for President who had served an effective term. But Kolowich and his group were not leaving things to chance. They were buying stock to control votes. Force had to be met with force. In this case, the sinews of war were, to put it in Napoleon's words, three things, money, money, and money. Fruehauf begged and borrowed money from every available source to purchase Fruehauf company stock.

On one occasion, when the ACT Committee was meeting, Beck commented on the newspaper reports he had been reading about Fruehauf's struggle, and said to him, "Why don't you ask me to help?" Fruehauf was taken aback by this question and answered simply that it had not occurred to him. Beck then explained that the Teamsters Union had millions of dollars which it sought to invest in mortgages, or in secured loans at proper interest. Fruehauf appreciated the suggestion, and a few months later, when the battle of the buy took a turn, because Fruehauf stock plunged downward, and he was desperate to acquire the stock which he knew Kolowich was aiming for, he turned to Beck. It was arranged that the Teamsters' counsel, Simon Wampold, should meet with Fruehauf's attorneys. A contract was drawn for a million-and-a-half-dollar loan from the union to the Fruehauf Foundation, so that it could buy Fruehauf Trailer Company stock. The loan was fully secured. The newly acquired stock was placed in the union's possession for that purpose. A promissory note for the loan was personally endorsed by Roy Fruehauf and Alfons Landa, who was a wealthy businessman in his own right. Landa, too, had a large number of shares of Fruehauf stock, and the battle was his as well as Fruehauf's. The note bore interest at 4 per cent, which in 1953 was the going rate. The entire transaction was made in good faith, approved by the executive committee of the union, and announced in the public press.

This loan saved the Fruehauf corporation from the raiders. It preserved the Fruehauf ownership and the Fruehauf tradition and skill. When Kolowich was beaten off, most of the stock acquired with the million and a half dollars was sold to repay the union. It received its million and a half dollars in full together with 4 per cent interest which, at that time, was a high rate of interest. The union had made a satisfactory business deal. It had served another union purpose, that of providing more jobs for its members. This was due to the fact

that the Fruehauf Trailer Company had organized an investment company to make loans to small truckers so that they
could buy trailers. The more trailers on the road the more
Teamsters would have jobs. Kolowich had threatened to wipe
out this investment company, and in other ways liquidate
parts of the growing enterprise. Raiders often do this because
corporations own land, buildings, or factories which can be
sold at large profits, thus making possible a quick financial killing. A long-range program of continuance and service which
motivates the founders and their experienced successors is
often scoffed at by take-over managements who seek only to
capitalize on the prize they have captured, even if financial
rape and death are the means to it. So the Teamsters Union
had profited from its million-and-a-half-dollar loan to Fruehauf
in more ways than one. Nevertheless, Fruehauf felt greatly
indebted to Beck, as one does to a bank which had made
survival possible even though its loan was a sound investment
and repaid with interest.

This was the background when a telephone call came from
Beck to Fruehauf some six months later, stating that he personally needed a loan of two hundred thousand dollars. His
lawyer, Simon Wampold, would be traveling through Detroit
and would meet with Fruehauf. Wampold merely asked
whether Fruehauf could help obtain the two hundred thousand
dollars from a bank. Beck had large real estate assets, but did
not wish to dispose of them. Apparently he had used up his
bank credit in Seattle. Fruehauf explained that if he had two
hundred thousand dollars at that time, he would unhesitatingly
make the loan himself. However, he was still in a struggle with
Kolowich, and every cent he could scrape together went
toward the buying of Fruehauf stock. But he did not disguise
his emotional obligation to Beck, and undertook to place the
loan in some bank. Would he not have been an ingrate to do
otherwise? Neither Wampold nor Landa, outstanding lawyers,
thought even a direct loan to Beck was a violation of law,
or they would not have permitted it. Nor, of course, would
Fruehauf have touched an illegal transaction. Acting openly
and innocently, without the slightest intimation that he would
be charged with criminal conduct, Fruehauf got busy to re-
ciprocate in a much smaller way Beck's enormous gesture to
him. He called Burge Seymour, also a member of the ACT
Committee, to inquire whether he could help out Beck.

Seymour thought that in view of Beck's prominence (no one could have foreseen that he would plunge from the rarified peak he occupied then into the dungeon of a jail) that he ought to be able to place his loan with Manufacturers Trust Company in New York. The loan officer was not available and so there was delay. To accommodate Beck in the interim, Fruehauf advanced his company's funds in the amount of one hundred seventy-five thousand dollars and Seymour his company's funds for twenty-five thousand dollars. Beck gave his note for two hundred thousand dollars bearing 4 per cent interest. Within six months, Manufacturers Trust Company did make a loan to Beck for two hundred thousand dollars, receiving Beck's note with endorsements of Fruehauf and Landa. The Fruehauf Trailer Company and Seymour's company then were repaid in full. Four thousand dollars interest was paid by Beck. Subsequently, he paid back the loan to Manufacturers Trust Company together with interest.

There was no gift, no bribe, no labor motive involved. Everyone who advanced any money was repaid in full. Yet it was this interim loan of two hundred thousand dollars by Fruehauf's and Seymour's companies which resulted in the indictment of all of them, together with Dave Beck himself.

The government must have had its doubts about the criminality of this transaction, because it handed down its indictment at the very last moment of the five-year statute of limitations. This delay was all the more extraordinary since the true facts had been fully developed four years earlier at the Senate hearings of the Select Committee on Improper Activities (called the McClellan Committee). Fruehauf and Seymour had appeared voluntarily before that committee and answered all questions put to them without any hesitancy or objection. They did not plead the Fifth Amendment because they and their counsel earnestly believed that the truth would not tend to incriminate them. Counsel to that committee was Robert Kennedy, and one of the members who put keen questions to Fruehauf was Senator John F. Kennedy. Senator Barry Goldwater was also a member. When Fruehauf picked adversaries, he picked them!

Senator Kennedy, appropriately enough for a man destined for the heights, addressed himself to the moral issue. He asked Fruehauf:

"Do you think it is proper for Mr. Beck, because he was

the means by which you received this $1,500,000 of Teamsters' money . . . . I am asking you this as a general question, is it proper for a trade union leader in that position to ask . . . for special financial favors? Do you feel that that is good practice?"

Fruehauf replied:

"I don't see where the union was injured."

SENATOR KENNEDY: No, I will agree that the union was not injured.

Nor did Kennedy claim that Fruehauf had violated the law as it then stood. He was using the Senate hearing in its most proper sense, to devise new legislation. He was probing for an amendment, later adopted, which would prohibit loans, as well as outright gifts, to labor leaders. He asked Fruehauf directly:

". . . do you think this committee should consider recommending that there be a limitation placed on the rights of labor leaders to carry on financial dealings with companies [to] which their union has loaned money . . . ?"

FRUEHAUF: Well, I would have no opinion on that.

While questioning Dave Beck, Senator Kennedy conceded that "there is no law against" the loan which Beck had obtained from Fruehauf. But he pressed the moral question whether it was proper for a trustee of the union to obtain a favor personally because the union had invested funds previously with the lender. He was testing the wisdom of new legislation to outlaw such relationship. But here was a statement from a high source that what had happened was not illegal. Also while it raised the question of Beck's ethics in "capitalizing" on his union's act, it did not necessarily impugn Fruehauf for his responding act of gratitude. As Fruehauf said frankly in answer to a similar question from Kennedy, he knew that without Beck's original suggestion to him and recommendation to the union, he never would have received the million-and-a-half-dollar loan which saved his business. He, therefore, did not separate entirely the union's act from Beck's kindness to him.

At the McClellan hearings, Robert Kennedy as committee counsel had produced evidence of the entire transaction, presenting every check which had passed between the union and the Fruehauf Foundation and the later loan transaction— all voluntarily handed over to him by the participants. Furthermore, F.B.I. agents had asked for interviews and written statements from Seymour and Fruehauf. These had been freely given in minute detail, and all books and records of the transactions were also produced and photostated. The Department of Justice had even submitted questionnaires to Fruehauf concerning the number of his employees in the Teamsters Union, etc., and these had been fully answered years before the indictment. So the government had had full revelation of the facts, stated under oath by unsuspecting citizens. It had sat upon them for years, and now, virtually on the last day, indicted these men who had volunteered the information to them.

Is there anything more mysterious than human judgment? The logical processes by which one person decides that something is right, while another says it is wrong, have been the subject of centuries of philosophers' speculation. We have speeded up the calculations of the sciences such as mathematics, physics, and chemistry, by means of artificial machine brains. But there is no instrument, and there never will be, which can render moral or artistic judgments. The reason, of course, is that the standards by which they are evaluated depend on sensitive factors of conscience, religion, ethics, taste, and experience, all as variable as the individual. If we ever created such a judgment computer, it would serve no purpose, because it could provide no universal precept. Each machine would respond to values fed into it by the individual programmer.

That is why there are dissenting opinions in our highest courts. The interpretive view of one judge, necessarily conditioned by his lifetime's precedents, will differ from another's, in determining what is right or wrong. Often the scales are so closely balanced that one additional fact will tip them. It is the lawyer's function to recognize these determinative weights. They are the vocabulary of persuasion.

It is no mere rhetorical flourish to say that the law is a noble profession. It is just that because it reduces to some order, no matter how uncertain, mankind's hope that justice will prevail over the stronger fist, the heavier purse, and the distorted moral perspective. Yet all is at the mercy of refined judgment, which is as individual as a fingerprint.

Every case presents fascinating problems of selectivity. Which facts are unimportant or prejudicial? Which will turn the mind from disapproval to acceptance? We call it strategy. That is why lawyers like to discuss a case with their partners to bounce various alternatives off each other's minds. Discussion leads to unexpected bypaths, and sometimes one finds there the distinguishing fact with the special persuasive impact.

Such a problem was posed in the Fruehauf case. Should the prior $1,500,000 loan from the Teamsters Union to Fruehauf be put into evidence? Either side could very likely exclude it from consideration. The statute which forbade gifts to labor leaders did not depend on motive. Some courts had held that whether the purpose of the gift was to gain a labor advantage or not, it was illegal. Such transactions were simply forbidden—period.

Yet government counsel, discussing strategy among themselves, must have decided that they would like to put before the jury the fact that there was a prior $1,500,000 loan from the union to Fruehauf. They thought it would aid the prosecution. The reasoning behind this was discernible. Would it not be prejudicial to the defense to show that Beck had "used" union funds to aid Fruehauf—that they were trafficking with each other? Beck's later disgrace might rub off on Fruehauf if they were coupled with each other. "Birds of a feather flock together" is an axiom with just the right amount of homey wisdom to poison the jury against Fruehauf. So the government never objected to the assertion of the prior loan. Indeed, it projected the fact itself, with whatever prejudicial nuance could be derived from bandying around huge amounts.

But we, too, had a right to object, and limit the case to the two-hundred-thousand-dollar loan, which was the sole basis of the indictment. Should we? We decided not to, and to join with the prosecutor in presenting the former million-and-a-half-dollar transaction. So both sides came to the same conclusion, but for directly opposite reasons.

We evaluated the situation not in strict legal terms of statutory language, but rather in human terms which would justify our moral position. From this viewpoint, the fact that Beck had befriended Fruehauf and that his union had aided him in a legitimate transaction. provided an innocent motive for Fruehauf's subsequent loan to Beck. He was simply responding, as any decent man would, to a prior favor. The emotion was clean and, therefore, the act too was clean. The possibility that Fruehauf was undermining Beck's loyalty to his union; that he sought venally to gain a labor advantage—all this was eliminated if the full history of their relationship was explained. The clearer the truth became that Fruehauf had not the slightest intention of tampering with a union leader's loyalty to his workers, the safer he was. At least this was our concluding judgment after a struggle with the conflicting strategic elements involved.

Lawyers cannot conduct polls on such matters, but sometimes they are forced on us. At a private dinner party, the host, who knew about the Fruehauf situation, bantered about his guilt and that only guile would get him off. It was not seemly to discuss the case, but the situation developed in which the host pressed the matter on the ten guests around the table as an informal jury. How would they vote? When they were told that two hundred thousand dollars was "given" by Fruehauf to Beck, they thought it was dastardly. When they learned that it was a loan fully repaid, they were doubtful but still cynical about the purpose of such a favor. I broke my silence to reveal the prior history and how Fruehauf's company had been saved. All but one around the table shifted over at once. A lady put it succinctly, "I think Fruehauf would have been a heel not to help out Beck, after what he had done for him." That was the common voice expressing a moral judgment upon which all cases depend.

One hovering fact changed the entire picture, just as a shift of the clouds in the sky will change the vivid colors below. When the conformation so dictates, the foreboding gray of guilt will change to the bright cast of innocence.

In the meantime, the formal ritual of pleading not guilty, furnishing a bond, and setting a date for trial had to be endured by men unaccustomed to standing as accused criminals before the bar of justice.

It made me shudder to sit with Fruehauf on a front bench, while counterfeiters and unkempt narcotics peddlers with dilated eyes, and scraping gait, as if they were afraid to lose contact with the floor, struggled forward to croak through frozen vocal cords, "Guilty," or "Not Guilty." Many of them had been in jail for a long time, and as they emerged through a side door from the dimly lit cells in the basement of the courthouse, they blinked their eyes, dazzled by the light on the fine oak-paneled walls and on the black marble behind the judge's bench. Fruehauf and Seymour, escorted by their lawyers, sensed the indignity of following men accused of heinous crimes. They answered "not guilty" in varying degrees of inaudibility.

Worst of all was the fingerprinting. I asked permission of the judge to accompany Fruehauf into the basement cell. We descended in a wire caged elevator, so deep that the impression grew of a trip to purgatory. Then we curved our way past barred cells in which were silhouettes of men bent over in Van Gogh postures of despair, to a room where the air was fetid, and in which a gleaming white sink stole all attention. It reflected the light as if it were a milky bulb itself. On a metal table, attended by a clerk, whose non-sensitivity was born from repetition and handling (literally) of characters who were accustomed to this underworld, was a large ink pad and special cardboard forms with printed outlines to receive five separate finger impressions of each hand. The clerk unceremoniously pressed each finger on an ink pad and then in turn pressed the finger hard onto the form, leaving a smudge of concentric lines. He handled the fingers firmly, like a dexterous surgeon, expecting no cooperation. Then he gestured toward the sink and the purple-stained wet soap. They washed guiltily as if blood were being removed. Paper towels, frustratingly non-absorbent, failed to dry the hands completely. During all this, I chatted about the new plan to fingerprint all citizens, but my effort to divert attention from the sordid activity, by equating it with civic responsibility, was rather transparent. Finally, we rose from purgatory by means of the same caged elevator, but now it seemed to be a protection against the evil around us. When we finally emerged into the street, we were conscious as never before of the contact of air on our skins. It was a symbol of freedom, no longer to be taken casually.

Aside from nationally observed holidays, the calendar is marked for each of us by private events, such as birthdays or anniversaries. When the court sets a day for trial, that date become engraved on the minds of all those involved. Trial preparation accelerates, as worrisome announcements are made—"only six days remain." All business and social commitments yield to the date.

Nature protects us from consciousness of fleeting time.

Otherwise, we would live in anxiety, if not terror, of each approaching day of death. Any experience which makes us aware of the passing seconds is, therefore, a breach of nature's protective wall. Fortunately, the break-through ends with the trial and we go back to sublime unawareness that every moment carries us nearer to blank infinity. Once again, we can enjoy the frivolous hours spent on trivia. I can think of no more devilish punishment than that for the poor soul who is advised medically that he has three months to live. His effort to spend them fruitfully (even if there were no pain) is defeated by the very consciousness that time is running out. The profound isn't profound enough. The joyous isn't joyous enough. Patience, the currency with which we buy hope, disappears completely. The need to select immediately, among many alternatives, deprives him of the confidence to make any choice wisely. The anguish of perplexity and indecision is added to the race against doomsday.

These thoughts pass through my mind as the trial date approaches which will pronounce doom or triumph for a man entrusted to my professional care.

Finally, the intervening time has shrunk to nonexistence. The date is here. We come to court early. Fruehauf attempts to create a light atmosphere by exchanging pleasantries with Burge Seymour, but neither can hide his nervousness. The jests are forced and the laughter a little too gay. Ruth Fruehauf hovers near her husband just close enough to give him comfort while disguising the effort to do so. The clerk calls out the name of each defendant, who is placed at a side bar. This is the first wrench. Fruehauf must leave us to go behind the rail. Dave Beck is brought in by the marshal. He has been transported from a Seattle jail for the trial. The right section of the courtroom is then filled with a panel of prospective jurors. Twelve empty chairs face the bench as if they were wooden jurors at attention.

The defense counsel and government prosecutors exchange formal greetings as they take their places at two tables behind each other. Cyrus Vance (later Secretary of the Army) of Simpson, Thacher & Bartlett represents Burge Seymour, Mortimer Sullivan represents Seymour's corporations, Professor Charles Seligson represents the Fruehauf Trailer Company, Charles Burdell, Beck's Seattle attorney, has come East to represent him, and I represent Roy Fruehauf.

S. Hazard Gillespie, the United States Attorney for the Southern District of New York, has designated several of his ablest assistants to represent the government. They are John A. Guzzetta, Edward Brodsky, and John Mills, and they are flanked by F.B.I. investigators, who have assisted in the preparation of the case.

There is interesting psychological byplay even in seating arrangements for counsel. This occurs in every suit where there are many defendants, such as anti-trust litigation. Defense attorneys, except for lead counsel (who sits nearest the jury box, so that he has ready access to the aisle leading to the witness chair), usually wish to sit at the end of the table as far away from the jury box as possible. They wish to be as unseen and unheard as possible, to support their final plea that their particular client was hardly involved at all in the unfolded history of events. Each trial day that goes by without their client's name being mentioned is deemed a triumph. They strive to minimize whatever connecting links there are. This strategy of getting lost in a crowd requires that counsel refrain from making an impression on the jury. Anonymity is the protective cloak, and occasionally when such a lawyer, representing a "remote" defendant, must object, it is not unusual to hear him say, "I have been sitting here for days, Your Honor, although the testimony does not involve my client at all. . . ." So, in trials of multiple defendants, some lawyers find gallery seats far preferable to box seats.

When all is in readiness, the court clerk advises the judge, who is waiting in the chamber adjoining the courtroom, reviewing the briefs submitted by counsel. He then enters, and everyone jumps to his feet, as if to render an ovation, but silence indicates that it is only the custom of respect. Judge Sidney Sugarman is regarded as one of the ablest district court judges in the nation. He belongs to those who resist the pull of power toward arrogance. They are wise enough to recognize that dogmatism is inconsistent with the uncertainty of dogma, and they express their resultant humility by open-minded approach to all forms of thought. In professional terms, we call this judicial courtesy. However, tolerance has a tendency to thin the blood of conviction. If the intellectual process is of high order and thorough, it results in a strong and firm opinion. It is not debilitated by the fact that nothing is ever free from all doubt. If absolute certainty was the precondition for decision, the judicial process would be paralyzed. It is this bridge between tolerance of thought and ultimate action which every public official, whether President, judge, or executive, must cross. Indeed, isn't it a necessity for each of us in all personal decisions?

We are ready to pick a jury, but the judge surprises us by announcing that if there are any motions to dismiss the indictment he will hear them immediately. We are eager to make such an argument, but intend to do so after a jury has been selected and government counsel has made his opening statement. Then we will have his admission on the record that the two hundred thousand dollars was not a gift but a loan which was repaid. If our legal argument should prevail and the indictment is dismissed, there could be no appeal or retrial, because that would be subjecting Fruehauf and the other defendants to double jeopardy. Having once started the trial, they cannot be tried a second time for the same offense. Therefore, we believe a motion in advance of the prosecutor's admissions as to the true nature of the transaction, and before a jury is chosen, would be premature. I advise the court that we intend to withhold such motion until the prosecutor has completed his opening statement, or the government's case has ended. Judge Sugarman, however, advises us that the government's brief concedes that the transaction was a loan. He will, therefore, consider this a binding admission. He will entertain a motion immediately.

It is a hopeful sign for it portends the possibility that he has been persuaded by our briefs, and may dismiss the case. If so, he is deliberately preserving the government's right to appeal and test his decision. Since a jury has not been chosen, the trial has not begun and there can be no double jeopardy if the upper court should disagree with him.

So, I launch into a full-scale argument as to why the indictment must be dismissed. First, we establish the moral base of our defense, which is the innocence of the loan, it being a reciprocal favor having no labor connotation. This background gives a favorable glow to the legal contentions paraded in front of it. It is always thus. We resist "technicality" or "legalism" unless they lead us to a moral result. Then they are welcomed, because the mind leans toward the heart. Justice is an emotion attained through logical processes.

Our first contention is that a loan is not prohibited. The statute was designed to proscribe gifts, and only gifts, whether of money or property. "It shall be unlawful for any employer to pay or deliver money or other thing of value to any representative of any of his employees . . ." The word "lend" does not appear. The phrase "pay or deliver" does not cover a loan. One makes a loan. He doesn't "deliver" it. And one "pays" a loan only when he satisfies it by repayment, not when he makes it. Criminal statutes, according to decided cases, should be read so that the verbs have ordinary "marketplace" usage. They must not be given broader meaning, for we do not deprive citizens of their liberty by interpretation when the language is not explicit on its face. In others words, penal statutes must be strictly construed. This means they must be held tight, to their literal meaning. If there is any ambiguity, the doubt must be resolved in favor of the accused. The United States Supreme Court, for example, applied this rule most recently in a unanimous decision, in which it refused to extend the definition of "lottery" under the U. S. Criminal Code to radio and television giveaway programs. We cite Funk and Wagnall and Webster's International Dictionary for definitions of "pay" and "deliver." Not even the synonyms include "lend" or any derivative of it.

If Congress had intended to prohibit a loan, it would have said so, specifically in the statute. It knew how to do so when it wished. When, for example, in connection with "Elections and Political Activities," Congress defined in a criminal statute what constituted a "contribution" or "expenditure," it did not content itself with the words "gift" and "payment." It added the word "loan."

Also, when Congress, in the Federal Corrupt Practices Act prohibited certain election contributions by national banks and other federal corporations, it expressly defined the term "contribution" to include a "loan" as well as "gift." Only one year after Congress passed the Taft-Hartley Act under which Fruehauf was indicted, it enacted a similar statute which forbade financial benefits conferred by bank officers on examiners. Once again, the word "loan" appeared in the language. So the omission of the word "lend" in our case was meaningful. As the United States Supreme Court expressed it in one of its cases:

"About only one aspect of the problem can one be dogmatic.

When Congress has the will it has no difficulty in expressing it. . . ."

Whatever doubt there could be about all this was conclusively dispelled, we contend, by an amendment which Congress passed twelve years after the Taft-Hartley Act was originally passed. That amendment added the word "lend" to the statute. So now, for the first time, it reads that no employer should "pay, *lend*, or deliver, money" to a labor representative. This amendment did not exist at the time Fruehauf's loan was made to Beck. Was it not clear, therefore, that the statute as it originally stood, did not prohibit loans? Congress later decided to broaden it, and the new language gave notice to any citizen that he must not engage in such a transaction. But how were Fruehauf and Seymour to know that their interim loan to Beck was illegal, when Congress had not so considered it at the time, as witness its amendment?

The government sought to blunt the force of this attack by contending that the amendment was only intended to make doubly clear that which was forbidden anyhow. It urged that the amendment was a clarification, not a new proscription. This seemed to us to be sheer sophistry. But there is little persuasion in name-calling. As politicians have learned, "mud thrown is ground lost." So we set about to trace the legislative hearings which had brought about the amendment. Did those responsible for it consider it a new provision, or a more explicit restatement?

It appeared, as we have seen, that the McClellan Committee had delved into the very Fruehauf-Beck loan. In addition, testimony before it revealed loans by officials of a baking and candy company of Zion, Illinois, to James G. Cross, President of the Bakery and Confectionary Workers International Union of America. Furthermore, James Hoffa, Beck's successor, had borrowed money from the employers of Teamsters either directly or through labor relations advisers to such employers. Senator John F. Kennedy, who was co-author of the Labor-Management Reporting and Disclosure Act of 1959 and manager of the bill during its passage through the Senate, felt that loans, too, should be barred. He said, "The Becks and Hoffas will find future collusion with employers vastly restricted—*with no more loans* from employer groups." He had previously commented on the fact "that while there is no law against" making a loan, the committee should take cognizance of the new revelations. So it did. Clearly then the amendment *added* a new prohibition, which the original statute did not have.

Senator Barry Goldwater, who plumped for even stronger amendments, described the one passed as, "adding a prohibition on any loan as well." We quoted George Meany, President of the A.F.L.-C.I.O., to the same effect, and a letter sent by Robert F. Kennedy, counsel for the committee, to all Congressmen explaining that the amendment "Safeguards against secret conflict of interest transaction by . . . *loans* to union officers."

We argued that even the new statute did not intend to forbid such a loan as Fruehauf made, because there was no labor aspect to it. But in any event, the history of how the amendment came about showed that what Fruehauf and Seymour did was not prohibited at the time they did it. Therefore, we concluded, the indictment must be dismissed. What it charged was done, was not a violation of the then-existing law.

In reply, the government's counsel tried to pull away from the concession in its brief that the transaction was a loan.

MR. GUZZETTA: I will simply say that the position the government takes is that the government has called this a loan . . . . we say that this is not necessarily so, because . . . a loan is accompanied by certain attributes and those items were not present in this case.

For example, there was no collateral given by the recipient of this loan for two hundred thousand dollars. . . . Beck did not pay the 4 per cent interest.

MR. NIZER: I know of no rule of law, that in order for a loan to be a loan, it has to be collateralized, or that the debtor has to pay some interest, or that it has to be endorsed.

Far more cogent was the prosecutor's contention that the statute which forbade giving "money or other things of value," included a loan because it was "a thing of value." The judge asked whether this language did not refer to a tangible thing. Ordinary interpretation would give to "other things of value" a meaning distinguished from money, such as jewelry, bonds, real estate, etc. But did it mean a loan in the sense of "use of money"? Then why the phrase "pay or deliver"? Furthermore, the indictment itself rejected the prosecution's argument. It said that Fruehauf had paid or delivered "a thing of value, to wit, *money* in the sum of two hundred thousand dollars." In any event, we thought the government's finely spun argument was inconsistent with the clear and unambiguous warning which a criminal statute must give a citizen. The very fact that such involved reasoning had to be indulged in, to determine what the law forbade, in itself indicated the stretching of the statute beyond its simple intendment.

However, government counsel had refused to admit that its brief bound it to be admission of a loan. It had fudged the issue sufficiently to make the judge's reliance on its brief a daring undertaking.

The answer came immediately. The judge ruled:

"I am convinced that the language which I read into the record from the government's brief is a judicial admission that the transaction was a loan."

He then held that a loan was not a violation of the statute before that statute was amended to add the word "lend" to the prohibited acts. He pointed out that he had preserved the government's right to appeal, by acting on a motion in *advance* of the actual trial (thus avoiding double jeopardy). Then came the words wafted on wings of freedom.

"I am now granting the motion to dismiss the indictment . . ."

The victory was so sudden that the fires of elation had no time to build. We congratulated our clients almost prosaically, and carried out our briefcases laden with unused preparation notes. Perhaps our spirits were dampened by the gnawing realization that crucial tests were still to come on appeal. Obviously, the government would not take such a licking lying down. It was not the real issue of the case (whether a loan, as well as a gift was prohibited), which worried us. Rather it was the way we had won. A courageous judge had seized upon the government's admission in its pretrial brief that the transaction was a loan and had cut through a lengthy proceeding. But this raised a host of questions. Perhaps government counsel had the right to change his brief. Could he argue that the evidence then presented at a trial would wipe away his admission? Could he even go further and claim that the admission didn't exist? He had caviled about the language during the argument. It was a loan, but it wasn't a loan, because no collateral existed and full interest was not paid (or so he said and there was no proof at a trial to establish the fact one way or another). Irrespective of the real issue, had we not gotten ourselves involved in a procedural maze in which the government might win because of the harsh technique by which it was pinned down by the court which relied on a brief prepared possibly by a subordinate, who it might be argued had made an "inadvertent" concession?

Like the peasant who could not enjoy an unexpected feast because he was conscious of the lean days ahead, we did not savor the dismissal of the indictment because we feared the poverty of our position in the appellate courts.

We knew, however, that we would learn our fate even before the appeal was argued. This was due to a rule that the government had two choices in prosecuting appeals. It could appeal to the Federal Court of Appeals (before going to the U. S. Supreme Court) and raise all the questions which any litigant could; in this case, the procedural question as well as the substantive one. In that event, we would have to justify the way in which the case was thrown out—on a mere admission in a government brief. The second choice the government had was to skip over the Court of Appeals, and appeal directly to the Supreme Court of the United States. This could only be done if it limited the appeal to a legal question, in this case, "Is a loan of money a violation of Section 186 of the Taft-Hartley Law, as a gift would be?" The procedure of dismissal would be waived.

The reason for this privilege of direct appeal is that if no questions of fact have to be passed upon (such as was the loan a bona fide one, or a mere ruse to hide a gift), and if only a legal question exists involving, let us say, the constitutionality of the statute, or its interpretation, then the highest court will pass directly upon the pure legal question, without review by the lower appellate court. Which method would the prosecutor choose? If he chose the first, we would be subjected to a critical review of a dismissal which was granted before there was a stitch of proof. If he chose the second, we were out of the woods, for then he would have to limit himself to the simple legal question whether a loan was a violation of Section 186.

Suspense can be more exciting than the excitement it

anticipates. But writers of legal fiction usually depict legal suspense in stereotyped conflicts. Rarely do they envision the drama of intellectual alternatives as hair-raising. But so it can be, and was on that day when an associate burst into my office waving high the government's brief and exclaiming, "They're dropping all collateral matters. It's an appeal directly to the Supreme Court!"

Quickly, we opened the brief to the first page where the ground for the Supreme Court's jurisdiction must be stated, and were delighted with the words which we knew must be there, that the Court had jurisdiction because only a legal question was being presented, and it was

"whether a loan of money comes within the foregoing restrictions."

We advised Fruehauf immediately that we were going directly to the Supreme Court and that the issue of illegality would be tested, solely on the basis of statutory construction. He knew how pleased we were that the contest was bare and clean. It was the unanimous opinion of all counsel that we were fortunate to avoid discussing "judicial admissions made in a government brief," or how binding they should be, or whether the loan was a genuine one or not. Now the government would have to concede for the purpose of the appeal that there was a bona fide loan.

How unpredictable are human affairs, including the "certainties" of Supreme Court precedents. As we left for Washington, no one suspected the shock which awaited us at the argument, not even government counsel, who must have assumed, as we did, that he was there to argue a legal question and nothing else. So far as we could learn, for the first time in history, the Solicitor General of the United States, in an unprecedented series of letters which followed the oral presentation, caused the government to change its earlier position. The extraordinary development left the case in shambles.

The Supreme Court building is the most beautiful in Washington. It seems to be constructed from sheets of dazzling white sky. The architecture is ancient and conveys the idea of a temple. Dozens of shallow steps rise from a huge marble plaza, sacrificing modern design to the eye's pleasure. The profusion of horizontal lines formed by the steps, topped by vertical cylindrical pillars, provides an aesthetic contrast. Nor is emotion ignored. The sheer expanse of spotless marble gives nobility to the structure, enhanced no doubt by the engraved inscription on the façade, "Equal Justice Under Law," and the consciousness that this is the ultimate seat of justice in the land. The building is serene and aloof, as if it were a photograph of itself, and when from afar one sees dark figures moving up its immaculate steps, there is a feeling that its purity is being smudged by use.

As if the inside of the building aspired to its external beauty, the white marble grandeur continues underfoot on staircases, walls, and ceilings. But now it is compromised by the need for practical use.

The courtroom itself is a disappointment. Being defective acoustically (shouldn't the architects have thought of this as a chamber designed for argument?), it has been necessary to hang red drapes, and even add microphones to the lectern and bench for the dialogue which flows in a continuous two-way stream. The lighting is also inadequate and so special lights have been spotted. Like the electric blubs hung in Europe's cathedrals, which desecrate the darkness with an anachronistic light, these destroy the symmetry with accouterments.

The entrance to the courtroom is directly opposite the justices' bench, instead of unobtrusively from a side, and, therefore, a wooden screen has been placed in front of it. The justices' chairs are of different designs and sizes. The reason is that some justices have brought them from the old Supreme Court chamber. Intellectual size is not readily measurable and critics may differ about it, but one cannot quarrel with the fact that five-foot-four-inch Mr. Justice Frankfurter cannot use the same size chair as six-foot-one-inch Chief Justice Warren, without his feet dangling uncomfortably toward an unattainable floor.

These various improvisations to meet utilitarian requirements disrupt the intended design. The symbolic moral is that beauty for beauty's sake, though it requires inspiration and imagination, is one thing, but to make beauty enter life and become part of its pulsating existence is a rarer and more difficult art.

Despite the spaciousness which abounds in the building, the courtroom itself is cramped. This is due to the fact that the architects did not anticipate certain needs (it is not the only instance in which builders have not been on adequate speaking terms with occupants requiring special use). So, for example, a large section of the courtroom is occupied by desks for counsel whose cases have not yet been reached for argument, and who pore over their briefs and make notes up to the last moment of articulation. On both sides of the lectern, where the arguer stands in isolated grandeur or humiliation, depending on the discourse, are huge tables, where associates sit with mounds of books and exhibits. These eat up more space. Alongside the justices' bench are the large desks for court clerks and a coterie of library assistants who bring law books to any justice who may require them during the argument.

Since there is an assured large audience, composed of clients, lawyers, public officials, and their families who take the trek to the legal Mecca from all parts of the United States to hear the argument in which they are directly involved, as well as domestic and foreign visitors in the capital who wish to see our institutions in operation, the courtroom is too small to accommodate them all.

Except for the announcement, "The President of the United States," there is none more awesome in all the world than "The Justices of the Supreme Court of the United States." A red curtain parts and the nine men familiar in static pose on the photographs hung in thousands of law offices, appear in the flesh. First, Chief Justice Earl Warren, who strives to synthesize equity with the heart, steps to his center chair. Then in order of seniority of service on the Court, alternately to his right and left the veteran justices, who have served for more than twenty years, take their places: Mr. Justice Hugo L. Black, sharp-featured except for blue kindly eyes already a historic figure; Mr. Justice William O. Douglas, the youngest justice ever to be appointed to the Court, and now a Renaissance figure showing the furrowed face of a man of action, who has recorded his travels in many books, while writing dissertations on legal philosophy as well; Mr. Justice Felix Frankfurter, a legendary figure because of his legal knowledge, razor-edged mind, and felicitous tongue; and surrounding them Justices Tom C. Clark, William J. Brennan, Jr., John M. Harlan, Charles E. Whittaker, and Potter Stewart, who had written opinions which have helped sculpt the new face of the nation, but whose body of decisions is not yet large enough for a generally accepted evaluation of their ultimate place in the judicial firmament.

We sit impatiently through a preceding argument. Mr. Justice Black leans back in his low chair, so that his head is barely visible above the bench. His soft questions seem to emanate mysteriously from the background. Mr. Justice Frankfurter, on the other hand, leans forward intently until it appears that he consists of a disembodied head which like a machine gun is firing questions, supplying the answers, and commenting on them all at the same time, while counsel stands by trying to make his helplessness appear to be respectful silence. Mr. Justice Douglas has become taciturn with the years, as if he were saving his bolts for his written opinions, which crackle with vitality. Chief Justice Warren sits upright, broad and tall, his deference to counsel being exhibited by absolute, immovable attention. Only occasionally does he put a question. It is almost always addressed to the morals of the controversy, rather than to legal rules. The kindliness of the inquiry turns to cold disdain if he is evaded. Mr. Justice Clark listens and observes in repose, but suddenly his comment with an abrasive edge demonstrates the hidden fires within. Mr. Justice Brennan's questions seem generally to be ferrets to discover the balance between a rule of law and the social concern in the controversy. Mr. Justice Harlan and Mr. Justice Stewart's brilliance in treating law as a stable science is rooted in tradition.

Thus the Court is composed and always will be, of men of different backgrounds, philosophy, wisdom, perspective, temperament, and learning. Let those who are critical of the fact that the Court splits in reaching decisions reflect on how it could be otherwise. Let them also ponder whether the democratic process isn't best served by a melting-pot phenomenon even on the highest Court.

At last our case is called. There is the momentary bustle and confusion as preceding counsels hastily pack their papers to move out of the way, while Court attendants deliver to each justice the briefs and records of the case to be argued.

The Solicitor General has not designated one of his Washington assistants, as is usually the case, to argue the appeal, but rather the United States Attorney for the Southern District of New York, S. Hazard Gillespie. This indicates the importance which the government attaches to the case. Gillespie, who was a partner in the distinguished law firm founded by John W. Davis, before ascending to his high post, is a brilliant lawyer, and a former President of the New York State Bar Association.

It used to be mandatory for counsel to wear formal cutaway clothes when appearing before the Supreme Court. The rule has been relaxed so that it is optional, and one may wear a dark suit. But the Solicitor General's representatives still adhere to the formal attire.

Gillespie, straight, dignified, and eloquent, has barely stated the history of the case, explaining his jurisdictional right to be before this Court on direct appeal, when the barrage starts. The Chief Justice observes that the government's counsel claimed in the lower court that only 2 per cent interest had been paid on the loan. If that is so rather than the normal rate of interest "is that of no concern to us?" he asks.

Gillespie replies,

". . . I think, in fairness to the defendants, that we must consider the question as it was put to the Court in our jurisdictional statement, which was squarely . . . whether a loan comes within the foregoing prohibitions, and I think to expand the question as we outlined it to Your Honors when you noted probable jurisdiction would not be proper."

The Chief Justice frowns. Mr. Justice Clark wants to know whether the genuineness of the loan is not before the Court. Gillespie replies that it is not. The only question to be decided is "whether or not a loan, assuming it was a bona fide loan, came within the proscription of the statute." He attempts to go forward with his argument that a loan is a violation and that the indictment should not have been dismissed. But by now a gale is blowing at him and he cannot proceed. Mr. Justice Black wonders how the lower court could have pinned down the government to the admission that the transaction was a loan, by merely citing its trial brief. Gillespie again points out that these matters could have been reviewed by the Court of Appeals, but the government was so confident on the main legal issue that it chose to go directly to the Supreme Court and, therefore, had to forego these procedural contentions. He pleads that the Court maintain its jurisdiction by limiting itself to a review of the legal interpretation of the statute. He is confident the case would then be reversed and this would be of great value in enforcing the law.

Mr. Justice Black reads Guzzetta's statement to Judge Sugarman to the effect that while his brief calls the transaction a loan, it lacks some of the characteristics of a loan. How could the trial judge, without a finding by the jury, hold as a matter of law that it was a loan? Gillespie replies that the government has chosen to test the interpretation of the statute on the assumption that there was a valid loan, in order to obtain a speedy ruling upholding the statute. The real point from the government's view is that a loan should be held to be "a thing of value" and as much prohibited as a gift. This is what he has come prepared to argue. But it would be improper, he asserts, to raise factual issues which this Court could not decide and thus prejudice the needed decision on the law. Justices Brennan, Black, and Chief Justice Warren continue to pepper Gillespie with questions.

It would have been easy for him to bend to the storm and say that if the Court insisted, he could see nothing wrong with enlarging the issue as contained in the jurisdictional statement of the government's brief. But his integrity would not permit him to yield. I have rarely witnessed a more courageous stand by a lawyer. The attack never slackened, and he never wavered.

Suddenly, the red light flashes on his lectern, signaling that he must end whatever sentence he is uttering. Then the Court clerk announces a forty-five-minute recess for lunch.

There is a cafeteria in the basement of the courthouse, dedicated to courteous and efficient self-service. It seems as out of place in the surrounding marble splendor as a hamburger stand in the Taj Mahal. Long lines form in the corridor, moving slowly toward the clatter of trays.

Counsel who are in the midst of argument and those scheduled immediately thereafter, are considerately invited in advance by a Court attendant to order lunch, and at recess are led by him through a labyrinthine path to a private dining room where a large oval table seats about ten. The lawyers invariably hold their briefs or notes before them with one hand, while feeding themselves with the other. I doubt that any could tell what he has eaten, or rather what he has left untouched. I nominate this as the most nervous dining room in the world.

When we return, Gillespie continues his argument. As if a signal had been given during the recess, he is permitted to develop his contentions with little interruption. Only when he fervently insists that the amendment adding the word "lend" did not change the previous rule, is he subjected to a few searching questions. Finally, the red light blinks again and with finality.

It is my turn and my strategy has changed, due to the unanticipated events. Now the first effort must be to clear the atmosphere, which hangs heavy with judicial resistance. Otherwise, my argument, like Gillespie's, will be tolerated rather than accepted. So I endeavor to dissolve the Court's doubts by acknowledging them immediately and addressing myself to them.

It is conceded that the loan was repaid in full, and while we contend that full interest has been paid, this issue was not decided by a trial. How can it matter, when the government's notice of appeal presents the sole question to this Court as being whether a loan (and I read) "intending repayment of said money with interest," is a crime? No one doubts the intention to repay. The government concedes a bona fide loan on this appeal and under the authorities (U.S. *v.* Hvass, 355 U.S. 570 and U.S. *v.* Hood, 343 U.S. 148), the jurisdiction of the Court is limited to the question so presented. All that is before the Court is the construction of a statute. If the government wished to test the correctness of all the matters raised by the Court's questions to Mr. Gillespie, it could have done so in the Court of Appeals, and we would not be before the Supreme Court until the Court of Appeals had ruled on the very matters raised by the Chief Justice, and Mr. Justice Black. Mr. Gillespie spoke for the government. It was bound by his position. Was it fair to the defendants, who had no opportunity in their brief to answer matters not raised by the government, to be prejudiced before this Court?

I hastened to add that we appreciated the full moral impact of the Court's questions, and we were, therefore, eager to proceed to what we believed was the real moral issue involved in this appeal. Here was a statute that had an admirable purpose. It was to prevent trafficking between employer and labor representative to the disadvantage of workers. What it forbade was *malum prohibitum*—forbidden because of a statute, and not *malum in se*—inherently unlawful, like murder, stealing, or rape. In *malum in se* crimes, it is not necessary to give the citizen specific definition of what he may not do. He knows well enough that murder, theft, and the like are crimes, and have been so considered from the beginning of time. He needs no newer warnings than the Ten Commandments. But in *malum prohibitum* crimes, it is essential that the newly prohibited act be very clearly outlined so that no one may mistakenly transgress the law. For, in such situations, the very act forbidden was legal the day before the statute was passed. So, for example, a citizen would not automatically know that it was a crime, henceforth, to give a labor leader a gift. Such a *malum prohibitum* statute must, therefore, give the public fair warning in clear, everyday language of the precise acts thereby made criminal. How was a citizen to know, indeed, how was a lawyer to know (Judge Sugarman also had thought otherwise) that the statute which forbade the payment or delivery of money or other thing of value to a labor representative, applied to loans as well as gifts? Even Congress was not sure or it wouldn't have amended the statute to add the word "lend."

I quoted the language of the Court in the Cardiff case: "The vice of vagueness in criminal statutes is the treachery they conceal. . . . Words which are vague and fluid may be as much a trap for the innocent as the ancient laws of Caligula."

As the Supreme Court said in another case (U.S. *v.* Universal C.I.T. Credit Corp., 344 U.S. 218): "We should not derive outlawry from some ambiguous implication."

We drove the point home with analogies. A *malum prohibitum* statute forbade using the mails to transport obscene writings. A man was indicted for mailing an obscene *letter*. The Court dismissed the indictment. If the statute had intended to prohibit the sending of obscene letters, it should have said so and not rested on the general term "writings."

In another case, the statute made it a crime to ship a motor vehicle in interstate commerce, if the sender knew it was stolen. "Motor vehicle" was defined in the statute as any "self-propelled vehicle not designed for running on rails." A conviction for shipping a stolen airplane was reversed by the Supreme Court (McBoyle *v.* U.S. 283 U.S. 25). Mr. Justice Holmes wrote the opinion: "To make the warning fair . . . the line should be clear. When a rule of conduct is laid down in words that evoke in the common mind only the picture of vehicles moving on land, the statute should not be extended to aircraft simply because it may seem to us that a similar policy applies, or upon the speculation that if the legislature had thought of it, very likely broader words would have been used."

A statute which forbade carrying knives or blades of certain length was held not to apply to a razor. If the legislature meant to make that which was legal yesterday, a crime today, it had to give fair and precise warning, so that everyone would know exactly what he was no longer permitted to do. If it decided as a matter of public policy to prohibit razors, it should have said so explicitly.

These and many other illustrations were not technical. They rested on the broad principle that every individual was entitled to an unequivocal warning of the new sanctions imposed for acts which were formerly lawful, so that he did not wander into a criminal act unwittingly.

Not only was the argument sound, but we hoped it would appeal particularly to the very judges who were eager to burst the bonds of jurisdictional limitation in order to deal with the basic equities. Perhaps their deep concern for the protection of the individual from the tyranny of official power, as evidenced by their historic opinions safeguarding the precious rights of the individual, would offset their views as revealed in a flood of hostile questions.

The argument was ended, clients, associates, and friends met in the outside corridor in a customary huddle to exchange immediate reactions. The general feeling was one of uncertainty. Some thought the Court's silence after recess was a sign of receptivity. No one could be completely confident of the outcome. Yet our legal position seemed impeccable, and there was real hope that a closer study of the briefs would result in victory. After all, both government counsel and we agreed about the jurisdictional point, and the Court would have to overrule both of us to review matters we all thought were out of the case.

So Fruehauf and his wife returned to Detroit and we to New York, disappointed by the unexpected reaction of the Court, but by no means hopeless about the future. The next day, however, we received the most shattering surprise of all. It was a copy of a letter sent by the Solicitor General, J. Lee

Rankin, to the Court, in which he changed the position taken by his representative, Mr. Gillespie, and insisted that the Court ought to review not only the general question whether a bona fide loan was a violation of the statute, but whether this particular loan was.

We were stunned by this reversal of the government's position. So far as we were able to discover, this was the first time in the history of the Supreme Court that the Solicitor General had disavowed the argument of his government counsel made only the day before.

We wrote an indignant reply "challenging the propriety of a repudiation of a position so firmly asserted by the government's designated counsel upon the argument." We pointed out that Judge Sugarman had carefully preserved the government's right to appeal to the Court of Appeals and test his ruling that the loan was a genuine one, but the government had "deliberately elected to eliminate all questions other than the construction of the statute." We asserted that the government was bound by its Notice of Appeal and Brief, both of which were premised on the assumption of a bona fide loan.

The Solicitor General replied in another letter, contending that the Court had the right to construe the statute in the "context of the facts" before the lower court. So, long after the red light had blinked on the lectern, the argument raged on by letter.

Perspective is probably the most important word in the language. It often provides the explanation for conduct, which to some is justified and even noble, while to others is unwarranted and even unscrupulous. Also, perspective will give hopeful shades to the same fact which others consider a slide to defeat. So, we were divided into two camps. One thought the Court would resent the government's somersault, which revealed the bankruptcy of its position. The other thought that the government's adjustment to the view of some of the justices, no matter how belated and unorthodox, doomed our case.

One month later, the decision came down. By a vote of 8 to 1, the Supreme Court reversed the dismissal and sent the case back for a trial before judge and jury. The majority opinion was written by Mr. Justice Frankfurter. To our astonishment, he, the supreme legal technician, used all his vaunted skills to justify the abandonment of the age-old rule that the

Court was bound by the legal question posed by the government when it chose to so limit itself by direct appeal. Indeed, he did not really abandon this rule. He skirted it with ingenious reasoning so complex and inventive that we read it a dozen times and still were perplexed by its tortuous path. He even held that since the government went beyond the legal question it had posed, the Supreme Court had no jurisdiction, and having none, it nevertheless reversed! This conclusion he rationalized by resort to another statute which we all thought was inapplicable. Thus, he conceded that the district judge's ruling was "impermissible" as such, and "constitutes an insufficient basis to justify the exercise of this Court's jurisdiction on direct appeal." But he did not think this "requires us to penalize the government by dismissing this appeal *simpliciter*."

The opinion carefully outlined Gillespie's position that the loan, for purposes of this appeal, was bona fide and paid tribute to "his honorable impulse," but noted that not even the Solicitor General's representative could prevent the government from arguing all possible theories of the loan transaction. The opinion then cast the appeal in the role of seeking an advisory opinion, where the facts were unfocused and cloudy, and cited sound authority for the proposition that the Supreme Court will not give advisory judgments.

The most startling section of the opinion was the extensive argument that "the question put to the Court was unclear," and its suggestion that the government might at the trial adopt one or more of five different views why the loan factually was a violation of the statute. Although neither the prosecutor nor anyone else had even dreamed of many of these alternatives, Mr. Justice Frankfurter, in a typically brilliant demonstration of agility, suggested the following possibilities:

"1. That the loan was a sham, to cover up a gift or bribe.

"2. That the acceptance of only half the interest due (an assumption from the government's brief) constituted a gift of the other half to Dave Beck.

"3. That the rate of interest being lower than the going commercial rate (another unproven assumption) constituted a gift to Beck of the difference.

"4. That the giving of an unsecured loan which couldn't have been gotten through 'normal financing channels' constituted a thing of value, the benefit of the money in hand.

"5. That a loan, no matter what kind, is a violation of the statute."

Then turning on the Solicitor General, whom he had already said had destroyed the jurisdiction of the Court by his stand, he charged also that he "does not leave it unequivocally clear" which of these theories he claims he was precluded from by Judge Sugarman's decision.

Mr. Justice Frankfurter's virtuosity in attacking both sides brought an echo to me of an anecdote about a lawyer who was an inspired forensic genius, and who could argue both sides of any case with devastating skill. Having grown old and somewhat forgetful, he argued an appeal, presenting by error his opponent's case. He did so with overwhelming logic, until his associate tugged his coat and whispered that he was running for a touchdown in the wrong direction. Quickly, he recovered and said, "These are the arguments my learned adversary will make. Now let me demonstrate how completely fallacious they are."

The majority opinion was almost thirteen printed pages in length. Mr. Justice Stewart wrote a one-page dissenting opinion. It was as clear as it was concise. The government was limited to the legal question it posed on its direct appeal. He cited four Supreme Court cases to support this view. Also, as was decided in the Petrillo case, "The government's appeal does not open the whole case." He concluded:

"I think the issue whether a loan of money came within the proscriptions of the statute is before us now and should be decided.

"I further think this is the only issue properly before us."

But eight justices thought otherwise, and so we were headed back to a full-scale trial.

Once again long evenings devoted to preparation with clients and witnesses regarding the past history of facts, documents, statements to government representatives, and testimony before the Senate Committee. Once again scouring of records and immersion in legal research. Once again accelerated preparation which orbits from daylight through evening hours in one continuous sweep. Once again nervousness of clients increased by the psychological blow of a reversal by the Supreme Court. Is it only psychological? Now we face new theories of possible guilt listed by Mr. Justice Frankfurter, which a prosecutor will be pleased to embrace, and a presiding judge to honor, as the last word from on high.

Once again trial day is upon us. But the cast is not the same. The presiding judge is Wilfred Feinberg, newly appointed to the bench by President Kennedy. He is a balding, tall man in his forties, but looks younger. He has a soft voice and his manner is diffident as befits his scholarliness. He quickly impresses us with the cardinal virtues of a judge, patience to listen and fairness, resolute enough to withstand the argumentative storms which rage around him. As the long trial proceeds, and even though he rules against defense counsel on what we consider crucial matters, bringing forth eruptions of protest, he remains imperturbably courteous, sensitive to our concern, and so equitable in his dispositions, that our differences with him never become a grievance or diminish our admiration for his learning and sense of justice. Indeed, as we shall see, he is not above reversing himself on some rulings, when convinced by either side that new developments warrant it. Like all worthy men, his pride in being right is greater than his pride in being consistent.

There is also a new prosecutor. He is Thomas Day Edwards, a man of rare talent, but it is such men, rather than the mediocre ones, who work hardest. His mastery of the facts is complete. He knows dozens of documents and their dates by heart. He is a storehouse of legal knowledge. The mere mention of a precedent brings forth from him a recollection of the facts of that case and the resultant applicability or non-applicability to the immediate trial. As the case proceeds, we have the feeling that even in his three years at Harvard, he must have spent all his time preparing for this one trial. At the very end of the case, he presents a huge chart depicting the factual complications, the like of which none of us has ever seen. It consists of a number of celluloid overlays, each with differently colored data, so that as each page is turned, the new developments are superimposed upon the original facts which remain visible underneath. In this graphic way, the involved transactions grow before one's eyes like a slow movie. His legal ingenuity is no less, and, despite a quiet, dispassionate manner, he has the advocate's talent of holding his feet during a storm. A doughty and dangerous adversary—indeed, he is flanked by an assistant, John Mills, and others.

The defendants and their counsel enter the large wood-paneled courtroom through the front doors—but not Dave Beck, who is led in by a marshal from the rear, because he is still serving a jail sentence for a prior crime and is locked in a cell in the basement of the building. Even lunch is brought to him by his attorneys, Charles S. Burdell and James D. Walsh, so that he can have non-prison fare during their conferences in his cell. Beck appears wan and dispirited, but not crushed. He is the only one who loves to be in the courtroom. Sitting at defense table like all the others gives him the illusion of freedom. But who knows what the inner pain from incarceration is to a sixty-nine-year-old man who has tasted power and eminence? At one point in the trial, his lawyers report that he is suffering a kidney stone attack, and may have to be moved to the prison ward in Bellevue Hospital, thus postponing the trial. But he overcomes the pain and except for an added layer of pallor, looks the same and appears in court to the end.

He provides the chief prejudicial factor to a fair trial for the other defendants. The newspapers and their cameras focus on him. Also, the radio and television reports constantly use him as the frame of reference for the trial. He is the dramatic center of the controversy, and prospective jurors may well be contaminated by the hostile attitude toward him, thus condemning Fruehauf and Seymour, who are tied to and tried with him.

So, before we pick a jury, we move to sever the trial, to try Beck separately. But the judge points out that Beck would have to appear in Fruehauf's case anyhow. He denies our motion but promises to weed out from the jury anyone who knows Beck has been convicted and is serving a sentence.

There are other possible prejudices to be avoided. Government pensioners might tend to favor a case brought by "United States of America." One woman concedes she receives a pension "for my son. I am a Gold Star Mother." She is accepted, but some others on government payroll are challenged. Another prospective juror admits "I am a little prejudiced against unions." He is immediately excused from service, because "a little prejudice" will completely disrupt the sensitive scales of justice. However, an employee of Harper & Row, publishers of *The Enemy Within* by Robert Kennedy, aimed at corrupt union leaders, and which mentions Dave Beck and even the loan by Roy Fruehauf and Burge Seymour to him, is kept on the jury, over our protest, because he assures the judge that he has not read and will not be affected by the book. Although the defendants have ten challenges without cause, we have exhausted them and cannot remove him.

So it takes almost two full days before twelve jurors and four alternates are selected and solemnly sworn in to be the ultimate judges of whether our clients go to jail and their families are disgraced, or are vindicated. Their fate is now in the hands of these strangers.

The prosecutor then rises to make his opening statement to the jury outlining the government's case. Before he has finished his second sentence we are on our feet charging the injection of prejudice into the case.

> MR. EDWARDS: Now, ladies and gentlemen, this prosecution has been prepared by the United States Attorney's Office in cooperation with the Federal Bureau of Investigation, and the gentleman whom you have seen sitting next to me, and is sitting next to me now, is Mr. George Hand, who is a special agent—

> MR. NIZER: I object to this, Your Honor. I thought that the course to be taken was not to link the Federal Bureau of Investigation with this case, and if any witness were called we would have adequate opportunity to protect our client's rights.

> THE COURT: Mr. Edwards is identifying the person sitting there so they may not speculate whether he is a lawyer who should have been introduced.

> The jury is directed, of course, not to give any greater weight to the fact that a person may be a member of the Federal Bureau of Investigation or any other law-enforcement bureau.

But the next morning and before the jury take their seats, we press the matter vigorously, asking for a mistrial, so that in the early stage of the trial a new unprejudiced beginning might be effected.

> MR. NIZER: This was a calculated statement to give the jury the impression that the F.B.I. had organized the case . . . so you have not only the austere name of the government of the United States, but you have the F.B.I. thrown into this situation at the very opening to the jury. . . .

This morning the New York *Times* made full reference to the fact that Mr. Beck received a jail sentence.

In all this atmosphere counsel for the government doesn't practice restraint but tries to inject deliberately the prejudice of the F.B.I. preparing this case.

MR. EDWARDS: . . . I have the right to identify the people at the counsel table. . . . There will be one or more F.B.I. agents who will be witnesses in this case. . . . It is a completely frivolous motion.

The judge denies the motion for a mistrial but offers

to again admonish the jury that the fact that the F.B.I. worked with the government in this case should in their minds give no greater weight to the government's case . . . . and, if you want me to, I will again attempt to make that clear.

MR. NIZER: Yes, Your Honor, anything that would ameliorate the situation would please us.

THE COURT: Do all the defendants join in that request?

They all did, and the judge later made an emphatic statement to the jury to that effect.

As Edwards' opening statement continued we learned for the first time that the government had adopted one of Mr. Justice Frankfurter's suggestions, and was charging that while an ordinary loan might not be a violation of the statute, this was not such a loan. It was "an enormous one-sided favor," because Beck could not have obtained it through ordinary banking channels. There was no collateral, and no intention to collect interest, and that "although it was called a loan, the motive behind it . . . was a gift." Edwards promised to call bankers to the stand to prove that Beck could not on his own credit have obtained the two hundred thousand dollars. So one of Mr. Justice Frankfurter's invisible brainchildren was now running around in the courtroom. It was so elusive that we despaired of putting our hands on it. How was one to demonstrate that a loan was not a "one-sided favor," or that unless there was collateral it became tainted as if it were a gift?

Fortunately, Mr. Justice Frankfurter's opinion itself provided the means to contain the wraith we would now be chasing. He had conditioned all of his suggested theories of guilt upon the legal principle that they must not be at variance with the indictment. He reserved the right to the defendants to assert the classic contention that they must be tried for the crime charged, and that any substantial variance in the proof warranted a dismissal. So, not in the presence of the jury, we moved immediately to dismiss the case on the ground that the government's theory of "a unilateral tremendous favor" to Beck was a fatal variance from the indictment which accused us not of the making of a "one-sided" loan, but of paying and delivering two hundred thousand dollars to Beck. We cited cases which were thrown out for less variance than our case; for example, where an indictment charged interference with the shipment of sand, but the proof was that there was also interference with the shipment of steel. Had the grand jury known this was the accusation, it might have required evidence to support the charge, which might not have been available.

In another case, an employer was charged with giving money to a labor leader. At the trial, however, the government offered evidence that the employer had not given money to the labor representative but had paid life insurance premiums on his behalf and that of another person to an insurance company. This was held to be a fatal variance, requiring dismissal of the case. The defendant had no opportunity to prepare a defense to this accusation. Furthermore, a grand jury, which indicted because it was told cash was paid over, might not have indicted on these facts. So I argue that,

"no grand jury . . . would have indicted these men of impeccable reputation because the interest might be one thousand dollars [more than was paid] according to the government's theory, or because the collateral wasn't satisfactory to the government's high financial understanding of these transactions. . . .

"The way they got the indictment is by saying that these men paid and delivered two hundred thousand dollars to Beck. . . .

"In the sand and steel case, the Court said, 'If that is what you mean, say so. You can't make one charge and subject these people to another.' But never has there been a case as clear as this where two hundred thousand dollars is alleged to have been paid and now we come down to one-sided favors. . . ."

We ask the court to read the grand jury minutes, for we are

certain that the notion of a one-sided favor was not even mentioned there.

But to no avail. The judge denies our motion and holds that in his opinion this is not a "substantial variance" and he will let the jury decide the case.

The legal tide is clearly running against us. It is, however, in the course of my opening statement to the jury that we are struck by a tidal wave. We do not think we can survive. It towers over us almost without warning.

> MR. NIZER: In business relationships there are gifts given which are, we know as a matter of common sense, perfectly all right. I don't know of any dress manufacturer who doesn't give a gift to a buyer. There is nothing illegal about that. . . .
>
> But now we are brought here on the charge that under this indictment we had no right to give a labor leader a gift. Well it isn't a gift. But what was legal yesterday before this statute and becomes illegal tomorrow, even if it were a gift . . . requires at least that the government prove its case in a way so that every citizen knows what he is forbidden to do.
>
> The laws of this country are not traps. And I say to you that the evidence in this case will clearly indicate that neither Mr. Seymour nor Mr. Fruehauf . . . had any reason to think that this advance of two hundred thousand dollars as a loan to Mr. Beck under these circumstances was a wrongful, illegal act, and it would be outrageous to say that it was.

Then comes the blow.

> THE COURT: Mr. Nizer, I am going to have to interrupt.
>
> Ladies and gentlemen of the jury, as you will hear from me later on, the question of whether the defendants knew this was a wrongful act has nothing whatsoever to do with a violation of this statute. The elements of the crime I will charge you at the proper time, but one of the elements that is not in this crime is that the defendants knew consciously that they were doing something that violated the law. The government does not have to prove that.

Four defense lawyers are on their feet shouting their exceptions to the court's statement.

I turn to the stenographer's minutes of the prosecutor's opening statement the day before that "the motive behind the loan" was the motive behind a gift, and insist on my right to discuss our motives. The judge, calm despite the outbursts, assures me that I may discuss motives, but that

"conscious wrongdoing was not an element in this case. I do not intend to interfere with your opening in any other way."

We are in vital disagreement with the court, and our passions are running high, but I do not want the jury to obtain a false impression.

"Ladies and gentlemen, please don't understand my indignation, which comes from my heart, to be in any way disrespect either for Mr. Edwards, who is doing his duty, certainly not for the brilliant judge who presides here. If I speak with indignation, it is a lawyer's zeal for his client when he believes in his cause. I respect the judge's rulings and will comply with them at all times."

After I conclude, young Edwin Weisl, Jr., makes an opening statement on behalf of Burge Seymour. Weisl is replacing Cyrus Vance, who has accepted a government post as general counsel with the Defense Department. His intensity combined with a shy manner are suitable adornments for his keen legal mind. He is an appealing figure as he asks the jury to "dispel the cloud" which has hung for several years over his client, now almost seventy years old.

Then Charles Burdell, whose creased face and tough voice are incongruously topped by thick blondish hair, speaks to the jury not only as the lawyer but as a long-time friend of Dave Beck. He traces Beck's career from a laundry truck driver to the head of one of the most powerful unions in the world. He notes that he has engaged in real estate ventures in Seattle which have made him a millionaire and, therefore, had the ability to borrow moneys without collateral.

Professor Charles Seligson, seasoned, reasoned, and unemotional, opens for the Fruehauf Trailer Company. His bald head and eyeglasses academically poised on his nose contrast sharply with Weisl's dark hair flowing over his forehead toward his large black eyes. And even in sharper contrast is Mortimer Sullivan, lifelong friend of Seymour, but who on the record appears as attorney for his corporations, Associated Transport, Inc. and Brown Equipment Manufacturing Co. Sullivan, grayhaired, with bluff manner and blooming metallic voice, which doesn't diminish his charm, pours sarcasm or wit upon the occasion whenever he considers it right. Surely, we have a diversification of appeals to the jury.

When the openings are complete and the government begins to put witnesses on the stand, defense lawyers meet in the evening to take stock of our position. We agree that the court's rulings have put us in a distressful position. If the test is whether the loan constituted "a favor" to Beck, what is there for the jury to decide? Obviously, any loan is in a sense "a favor" to the borrower. He needs money, and even if he puts up collateral and pays interest, it is still a desirable transaction from his viewpoint. As I say later to the judge, making this the issue is like stuffing the ballot box against us. As to the distinction of a "one-sided favor," what does this mean? Since Beck turned to his friends instead of to his Seattle banks, and in the light of the surrounding feelings about him and the Teamsters, will not this question be decided against us?

Far worse, the judge's ruling, that consciousness of guilt is not a necessary element of this crime, removes the last barrier of defense, the innocent motive of the transaction. Certainly, if all the government has to prove is that we made a loan to Beck and that it constituted a favor to him, and the fact that we didn't know it might violate the statute is irrelevant, we are in the posture of conceding in advance all the facts necessary to conviction.

But a trial lawyer cannot afford the luxury of surrender. We determine to assail the judge with briefs which will cause him to change his mind about what "willfulness" means in the statute. My law partners Paul Martinson, Al Smith, and their associates Herbert Bobrow and George Berger, as well as Professor Seligson's associate Albert I. Schmalholtz and others, are set up as a team to do special research on this subject during the evenings, while we try to hold the line in the courtroom. Judge Feinberg has relied on the Ryan case to the effect that "conscious wrongdoing" is irrelevant. We study the briefs filed in that case, find other decisions not reported in the books, and philosophically develop the meaning of the statutory words "did knowingly and willfully" pay a thing of value to a labor representative.

Three days later we raise the subject again with the judge, who fortunately never closes the door to his mind. We argue that the language in the Ryan case referred to the defense by the employer that he didn't intend to profit from the cash gifts he gave to a labor leader. The court properly ruled that guilty frame of mind (*mens rea*) or conscious wrongdoing could not be avoided because one didn't expect to gain from his wrongful act. He knowingly violated the statute and if he didn't profit thereby that was no excuse. But it didn't mean that knowledge of wrongdoing was not a necessary element of the crime. We advise the court that we are preparing a brief on this esoteric subject.

THE COURT: I understand your argument very clearly, Mr. Nizer, and it is a very serious question in this case, and I intend, after listening to Mr. Edwards, to give this matter serious thought again. . . . When will I receive that material?

MR. NIZER: We will give it to you tomorrow, so that over the weekend Your Honor will have an opportunity as I know Your Honor loves to read these briefs over weekends.

THE COURT: I share the same joy in reading them over the weekend as you do in preparing them over the weekend.

Four days and three briefs later, we engage again in that subtlest of all warfare, the intellectual thrust for the judge's mind. By this time, six witnesses had testified for the government, and the testimony of one of them was used by us as if it were a phalanx to pry open the question anew.

Edwards had developed the fact that when Seymour's corporation advanced part of the loan to Beck, the voucher described the purpose as a loan to the "Beck-ACT Committee," which, of course, it was not. On cross-examination by Weisl and Sullivan, it was established that all of the original books of entry of the corporation correctly described the transaction as a loan to Dave Beck. The voucher entry was changed because it passed through many hands of the general office staff, and it was not thought advisable to expose such a transaction for general gossip. Nevertheless, it was an embarrassing entry, and Edwards quite understandably bore down heavily upon it as "concealment," "fraud," and "false bookkeeping." When the voucher, which was probably his most damaging item was offered in evidence, we had another opportunity to strike back on the main issue of willfulness. It is as exciting to attempt to turn disadvantage into triumph as to transform a noxious culture into a beneficent medicine.

MR. NIZER: . . . In view of the rule which was announced to the jury, that willfulness had nothing to do with this case . . . then the ACT Committee evidence should be stricken out. . . . They can't have it both ways. They can't put in evidence on the ground of willfulness and then claim willfulness is not an issue.

THE COURT: I will agree with that, the government can't have it both ways, Mr. Nizer.

MR. EDWARDS: Your Honor, I agree we can't have it both ways, but certainly evidence of concealment is relevant for several reasons whether or not we have to prove the defendants actually knew about this law. . . . It goes to show that this was understood by all as an irregular transaction, not a normal commercial bargain being struck in the ordinary way for the benefit of these corporations but a one-sided favor being passed to Beck. . . .

The court admitted the voucher. We had failed again. But no one is defeated until he stops trying. Two days and two briefs later, the government offered Seymour's testimony before a Seattle grand jury, when he appeared merely as a witness in an investigation of Beck's affairs. Once more, the purpose was to refer to his voucher entry that the loan was given to the ACT Committee.

MR. NIZER: This entire reference to ACT . . . ought to be eliminated, unless as we still fervently hope, and we are submitting some other briefs over the weekend, unless Your Honor . . . should give us a ruling with respect to willfulness in accordance with the cases we are relying on. Then the voucher becomes relevant material. In other words, did this show conscious wrongdoing in the light that the law forbade it?

It is at least an argument. But under the present ruling all references to the ACT Committee, I think should be out.

THE COURT: Mr. Edwards, would you address yourself to the proposition as to why reference to ACT is relevant if conscious wrongdoing is not an element?

As the prosecutor proceeded to expound his theories, we realized that we had subconsciously reached his mind rather than the court's. Or perhaps he chose to avoid legal error, and if a choice had to be made, he preferred to hold on to his "concealment evidence."

MR. EDWARDS: . . . If the government shows conscious wrongdoing . . . anything in the nature of concealment—consciousness of guilt is evidence of guilt. If you show that a man is conscious of the fact that he is doing something illegal that goes to show a consciousness that he is violating the law. . . .

THE COURT: Mr. Edwards, it seems to me that you are making a very good argument in support of Mr. Nizer's position.

MR. EDWARDS: Well, I don't intend to, Your Honor.

THE COURT: Mr. Nizer's opening statement which you objected to and which I admonished the jury about was that the government couldn't prove conscious wrongdoing here and I told the jury that conscious wrongdoing is not an element in this crime and is not an element in this case.

Was I wrong, according to you?

MR. EDWARDS: No, Your Honor. . . . Although the government does not need to show conscious wrongdoing, we are going to show knowledge of the forbidden relationship . . . by showing that the defendants knew they were engaging in an illegal transaction. . . .

THE COURT: . . . You can't say you have a right to prove they were doing something wrong and say the defendants can't prove the contrary, which will open the door to all kinds of evidence.

MR. EDWARDS: If a defendant testified "I had no idea I was breaking the law or doing anything wrong," that would be admissible. . . .

These words which would have sounded normal coming from our lips, were incredible from our adversary. Night after night we had toiled on briefs trying to make this point acceptable. Day after day we had attempted oral persuasion of the judge. Now suddenly we heard the prosecutor say he agreed with us in principle. Only decorum, demanded in a courtroom, prevented defense counsel from throwing their arms around each other exuberantly. Instead, we exchanged furtive glances of triumph, while our faces remained unsmiling. Now, at least, we had an issue to go to the jury. They could decide whether our clients knew or didn't know they were breaking the law when they made a loan. We knew that the truthful answer to this question would be favorable. The whole complexion of the case had changed.

The judge perceived the full meaning of the government's concession. With characteristic fairness he called Edwards' attention emphatically to the change wrought in the case, and even faced up to the necessity of correcting his own statement to the jury, which had startled us during my opening address.

> THE COURT: You understand that if you take this position that defendants are certainly entitled to introduce evidence to show that these gentlemen would not have violated the law if they had known what the law was, would not have violated the law if anyone had called it to their attention?
>
> MR. EDWARDS: Yes.
>
> THE COURT: You understand that?
>
> MR. EDWARDS: I do, Your Honor, and that does not surprise me, I may say . . . I have never supposed that the defendants would be prevented from testifying that they didn't know they were doing anything illegal. The conscious wrongdoing is relevant because it shows knowledge of all the required elements of the crime. . . .
>
> THE COURT: I think your position at this time is clear. You also realize that in view of the statement that I made to the jury that I am going to have to make another statement to the jury explaining that while conscious wrongdoing may not be the ultimate issue in the case . . . it is certainly an issue in the case if you introduce this evidence, so they don't get any wrong implication from what I said earlier.
>
> MR. EDWARDS: I think that is right, Your Honor, I don't know if it is necessary at this time, before you charge the jury, to indicate that to them.
>
> THE COURT: Well, I think it is necessary in view of what happened at the opening.

We did not know whether our clients fully understood how the intricate discussion of "willfulness" had affected their chance for liberty. Sitting in the courtroom day after day, while the testimony of witnesses swirled around them, and dozens of exhibits were tediously marked, they may well have become dulled to the refinements of various meanings of willfulness and conscious knowledge. Indeed such a discussion might have been better suited to a class in philosophy —did conscious wrongdoing mean merely that the defendant knew the man to whom he was handing the money was a labor representative, and that he represented employees of the defendant, or did it mean that in addition to all this he knew there was a law which forbade these acts? Now we had won the point that it meant both. We could show that Fruehauf and Seymour had no idea that it was, under the statute, a crime to make a loan to Beck. Such are the abstruse precepts on which the process of justice turns.

The topography of a trial often consists of twin rivers running side by side, one labeled The Facts and the other The Law. It is when they merge to form a steady stream in the same direction that their force becomes irresistible.

While we were thrashing about in legal water, trying to overcome its surge against our destination, the factual stream was running strongly in our direction. Witness after witness put on the stand by the government, yielded on cross-examination and established facts which we had hoped to prove in defense. This was not due to our skill but to the government's plight in being obliged to prove its case through many witnesses not hostilely disposed to us. They were scrupulous about their oaths, but had little hesitancy in reciting events of which they had knowledge, whenever the court removed the barrier of inadmissibility.

So, the prosecutor had subpoenaed Simon Wampold from Seattle to prove that he, as Beck's attorney, had visited Fruehauf and asked him "to assist in placing a loan" of two hundred thousand dollars. On cross-examination, the government's theory that Beck could not raise moneys through ordinary channels was dealt a severe blow when Wampold testified that Beck offered to "put up some government bonds as security."

Furthermore, in response to our prodding, Wampold established the prior one-and-a-half-million-dollar loan by the Teamsters Union to Fruehauf, and its full repayment with interest. Edwards, changing tack, objected strenuously that "the prior loan and the surrounding circumstances are not relevant to any issue in this case." But we urged its immediate materiality because it contradicted the government's theory that the loan of two hundred thousand dollars was given to Beck as a labor leader; rather it was given to him in gratitude for his prior assistance when Fruehauf needed money in his proxy contest. Before we were through we had firmly placed into the record every detail of the million-and-a-half-dollar transaction; the fact that the Teamsters Union had thirty million dollars from which it invested, or loaned to third persons; the fact that the million-and-a-half-dollar loan was processed by the legal and finance committee of the union, and was publicly announced. The district attorney deftly countered with the question whether the two-hundred-thousand-dollar loan was likewise publicized. Of course, it wasn't. Nevertheless, we did not have to await our defense to prove these facts.

A doubt was beginning to germinate in our minds as to whether we would have to put in any defense, if other government witnesses supplied the facts we planned to present. Thus, when the government produced Joseph Konowe, administrative assistant to the president of the Teamsters Union, to offer the constitution of the union into evidence, we were able to establish through him that the local unions were autonomous, made their own contracts, which ran into the thousands on behalf of 1,300,000 members, arbitrated their disputes locally, and even called strikes, without submission to Beck's authority as president. Consequently we could argue that Beck was not the bargaining labor representative with whom the Fruehauf Trailer Company dealt, in the sense that the statute forbade gifts to such representatives.

We scored even more heavily when the government put on the stand two bankers to establish that they had refused to lend Beck two hundred thousand dollars. The inference was that our client's loan to him was therefore an "extraordinary favor" not available in ordinary commercial channels.

The first was Barnum L. Colton, President of the National Bank of Washington, D.C., who testified that Alfons Landa had inquired of him whether a loan of two hundred thousand dollars would be made to Dave Beck. No such loan was made.

But, on cross-examination, he asserted that no financial statement of Beck or Fruehauf had been submitted and the matter was never even processed.

  MR. NIZER: . . . So far as this transaction is concerned neither you nor any committee of the bank passed upon the financial adequacy or inadequacy of Mr. Beck.

A. That is right.

Furthermore, he conceded that the reputation of the borrower is important and might result in an uncollateralized loan, and that at the time of the inquiry "Mr. Beck had an outstanding reputation as the president of a very large labor union."

Could we have done better if we had called Mr. Colton as a defense witness?

Then followed William T. Van Doren, President of Liberty National Bank of Washington. Landa had also asked him about a loan to Beck, but he refused because the loan limit was two hundred thousand dollars, or 10 per cent of the capital and surplus of the bank, and he didn't wish to make "a loan up to our legal limit to somebody who didn't even bank with us." Once more, it wasn't Beck's defective credit which defeated the loan.

A third banker was called. He was William Lonsdale, Vice President of Manufacturers Hanover Trust Company, which had ultimately made the loan of two hundred thousand dollars to Beck, thus replacing Fruehauf and Seymour's intermediary advance to him. The government's purpose was to show that the "low" 4 per cent interest charged by this bank was due to the high balance which Seymour's company had on deposit. The inference was that the rate of interest would otherwise have been higher and, therefore, that the 4 per cent interest rate on Fruehauf and Seymour's loan to Beck was "a special favor" to him.

We had intended to call an expert banker in our defense to prove the normalcy of the 4 per cent interest charge at that time. Here was another opportunity to support our defense through a government witness.

On cross-examination, I showed the witness the *Federal Reserve Bulletin* issued by the Board of Governors of the Federal Reserve System in Washington, which was "the bible" for bankers to determine interest rates throughout the country. Since interest is lower for large loans than for small ones, the *Bulletin* classified the average rates for different-sized loans.

What was the prime interest rate in 1954 for a two-hundred-thousand-dollar loan which was unsecured? Less than 4 per cent, he answered, indeed only 3.19 per cent.

Q. So a 4 per cent interest certainly wasn't a very

cheap or extraordinarily low rate in June 1954, was it?
A. No, sir.

Furthermore, the fact that Beck was an important labor leader of impeccable reputation, at that time, drawing a salary of fifty thousand dollars, in addition to expenses, would be factors in favor of a loan to him.

This evidence was so conclusive that toward the end of the case, when we were striking at the deficiencies of the government's contentions, Edwards said:

"I concede that the government has not proved that the 4 per cent rate was inadequate."

Many analogies have been drawn between trials and dramas, and one of the rules applicable to both is that it is advisable to have a strong ending. The government was, therefore, saving its most impressive witnesses for the last. They were an F.B.I. agent and two special agents of the Intelligence Division of the Internal Revenue Service. Their awesome titles, as well as their testimony of interviews with Fruehauf and Seymour, provided the greatest threat to the defendants. However, as is always the case—the greatest opportunity as well, for if we could draw significant admissions from such witnesses, or cast doubt on their stories, the impact on the jury would be correspondingly greater. It is one of the curious facts of a challenge, whether in personal relationship, business, sports, or professional contest, that the greatest triumphs hover near the edge of the precipice. It is when the "impossible" is overcome that victory is most rewarding. That is why most court victories result from the breaking of a powerful hostile witness, and not from the affirmative testimony of one's own witness. A fact dragged out of an adversary by a slashing attack is unadulterated by his self-interest. Its distilled purity is irresistibly persuasive. So although Edwards was moving from the uncomfortable terrain of unfriendly witnesses to his own supporting cast, our concern was mixed with hope. We were prepared for the attack. Even the jurors changed their posture from relaxed, swivel-chair motion to still, forward positions.

Eugene W. Harper, special agent for the Internal Revenue Service, Intelligence Division, took the stand. In 1955 he had interviewed Burge Seymour in the presence of a stenographer, and Seymour had signed and sworn to the question and answer transcript. Thus it was possible for the government to present Seymour's testimony even though he might never take the stand in this trial.

Seymour's statement was read to the jury, chiefly because it contained the admission that he knew the loan to Beck was inaccurately described on the check requisition as an ACT transaction. He explained that he did not wish "the personnel of his company to know the details of the loan." Weisl and Sullivan had previously established that all the original books of entry had correct descriptions of the loan as one to Dave Beck. So there wasn't much new prejudice in the revelation.

Now, however, there was a chance to tackle the government agent who had obtained the statement. Even though this evidence was offered only against Seymour and his companies and not again Fruehauf, I asked permission to cross-examine because there were references to Fruehauf in it.

Q. Mr. Seymour had no attorney present at the time you questioned him, did he, sir?

A. He did not.

Q. He just submitted himself to you and Mr. Watson, and when you told him about his constitutional rights not to speak, he said, "I will answer anything I can," didn't he?

A. He did.

There was a reference in the statement to "prior financial dealings between Dave Beck and Fruehauf." We tried to make him identify these as the million-and-a-half-dollar loan, but the best we could get was that he didn't remember one way or the other. No harm. We ventured on a new tack for a vital admission. He conceded that at the time he interviewed Seymour, he knew that the two hundred thousand dollars was a loan and not a gift. And he admitted that even then he knew the loan had been repaid in full. So now we had the concession that at the very first interview the government learned that the transaction was genuine. Indeed, repayment of the loan had already taken place.

There was one other goal. From the very beginning we had been plagued with the government contentions that Beck had not paid full interest on his loan. At the first trial, the prosecutor claimed that only half of the interest had been paid. This gave rise to one of Mr. Justice Frankfurter's theories that the forgiveness of the other half constituted a gift, and, therefore, violated the statute. We claimed that full interest of four thousand dollars had been paid. The reason for the confusion was that interest had also accumulated on the loan from Manufacturers Trust Company, which replaced the Fruehauf-Seymour loan. Subsequent interest payment had to be allocated across both periods, and the government's interpretation of unpaid interest thus became possible.

Now we had a special agent of the Intelligence Division of the Internal Revenue Service on the stand. Could we bend this expert to our interpretation, so that the ghost of unpaid interest would be banished from the trial? We would try.

After a considerable struggle, which must have bored the jury since it involved detailed references to notes, checks, dates, and pursuit down dry detours, we suddenly emerged upon a clearing and an exciting confrontation and surrender.

> Q. The note was for six months . . . and 4 per cent interest on that would be four thousand dollars exactly?
>
> A. Yes.
>
> Q. And you knew that the repayment of the two hundred thousand dollars included a sum of a four thousand dollar sum? In other words four thousand dollars interest was paid, . . . is that correct?
>
> A. Yes.

After Claude J. Watson, a special agent of the Internal Revenue Service, who had accompanied Harper, had testified with similar results, the government put an F.B.I. agent on the stand. He was lean and clean-looking, with authoritative and dignified bearing as befitted his service. He had been in the F.B.I. for twenty years and was also a lawyer. His name, Harvard Heystek, alliteratively suggested the combination of learning and action. His testimony was offered solely against Roy Fruehauf, because he had interviewed him in 1957 in the presence of Fruehauf's lawyers at that time, Clark Clifford and Carson Glass, both of Washington, D.C. He had filed a report of this interview, but now he testified orally as to what Fruehauf had admitted to him. Once more, the government was able to put a defendant's testimony into the record, even though he might not ultimately testify in defense.

Heystek quoted Fruehauf as telling him that the loan to Beck was a favor, not a usual business transaction, and that he didn't expect to receive interest. Nevertheless, he received four thousand dollars interest but he told Heystek this was three thousand dollars short of the amount due.

When I arose to cross-examine the witness, there were certain areas of attack which we had prepared. But no one could have guessed the developments which would ensue. This is the difference between direct examination and cross-examination. There is seldom a surprise in the first. It runs according to plan. There is almost always an unexpected development on the second. If it occurred would it be favorable or destructive?

We began with a few probing questions to indicate that the witness had little independent recollection of the interview about which he had testified. He conceded rereading his written reports "possibly more than a dozen times" before taking the stand.

Q. You studied them very closely, right?

A. Yes, sir.

Q. And you also conferred with government counsel with respect to these matters?

A. I discussed the facts of the interview with counsel, yes.

Q. Did he emphasize the importance of testimony with respect to interest, particularly?

A. I don't recall that he did. . . . There was a discussion and a detailed discussion of interest, yes.

His typewritten report contained many statements made by Fruehauf which were favorable to our case. These, of course, we had him elaborate. He had learned that only 285 Fruehauf employees out of about ten thousand belonged to Beck's Teamsters Union; and that there were over one hundred contracts with other unions.

We established the true motive of the loan to be gratitude, not an insidious bribe.

Q. Did Fruehauf tell you that that loan of a million and a half dollars had assured the continued corporate existence of the Fruehauf Company?

A. Yes, sir.

Q. And that Mr. Fruehauf for that reason was grateful to Mr. Beck as President of the International Union of having made possible this aid to Fruehauf Trailer Company?

A. In effect, yes.

Q. And that it was only that gratitude and no other relationship with the union of any kind that was responsible for this two-hundred-thousand-dollar transaction later? They told you that?

A. I think that was the position they took, yes.

He recalled that Fruehauf had been asked merely to help "place" the two-hundred-thousand-dollar loan with a bank, not to make it himself, and that Fruehauf and Seymour merely filled in until the loan was so placed with Manufacturers Trust Company.

Q. . . . Do you remember the word "interim" being used?

A. Yes, I do remember that.

Q. This interim transaction they told you they thought would be very brief . . . a few days or a week or two. . . .

A. That was my understanding.

There was always the possibility that he had made handwritten notes of his conference with Fruehauf, and that their production might add something valuable to the final typewritten report. It soon developed that he had made such written notes. When we asked for them, he said they had been destroyed. When? Probably a week or two after he made them. This was worth exploration, but we didn't expect that the digging process would produce the interesting artifacts it did.

At first he couldn't estimate the number of pages of his written notes. He explained that at the time of the conference he had before him "the printed record of the—." I did not permit him to finish the sentence, because he obviously was about to mention the volume of the Senate hearings at which Senator John F. Kennedy had questioned Fruehauf. The prosecutor and we had tentatively agreed to eliminate any reference to these hearings because of the prejudice they might create for both sides. On one hand, Senator Kennedy had commented that a loan did not violate the law. Yet, he and other senators had questioned the propriety of such transaction, and the possible amendment of the statute to rule them out in the future. Now my inquiry into the witness's handwritten notes had almost resulted in his blurting out innocently that he had made notes on "the printed record of the"—Senate hearings volume. A cross-examiner must have speedy reactions in an emergency not unlike a driver of a car. A typical illustration is presented by a witness in an ordinary accident suit, who under cross-examination innocently drags into his reply the fact that he spoke to an insurance company adjuster. The words "insurance company" are prejudicial to the defendant and a mistrial results, because a jury may be generous with its award if it knows it won't come out of the defendant's pocket. The cross-examiner must sense from the nature of the answer that fatal words are about to be uttered, and must stop the witness instantly. So the records shows how close we were to the cliff when I asked Heystek:

Q. How many pages were the personal notes that you made . . . in your own handwriting?

A. I couldn't estimate the pages because it was done in this way: I had had available to me at the time of the conference the printed record of the—

Q. No, for reasons which the court will uphold, I think, you should not go into collateral matters.

How many pages, that is my question?

A. I had made notes previously to which I appended notes on specific items as I went along.

He finally estimated there were ten or twelve pages and they were kept in a file drawer.

Q. So you went back approximately a week . . . later and took out these papers from the working file that you kept for working papers and destroyed them?

A. I destroyed them some time after that, I couldn't give you a date on it.

At about this time, the court adjourned for the day. As always, we obtained the stenographic minutes late that evening and studied them closely for the continued cross-examination the next morning. But we had not anticipated how useful they would be.

We started our attack on the theory that having made notes on a printed volume (the identity of which we would keep out of the record), he could only destroy the notes by destroying that volume as well. To our astonishment, the questions concerning this seeming improbability brought us a different prize.

Q. Did you not tell us yesterday that you actually had the volume in your hand and made some notes in that volume? Didn't you so testify yesterday?

A. No, sir. . . . I testified that I had the volume and
and made some notes from it, yes.

Q. From it. Did you append any notes to it?

A. No, sir.

Q. Let me read to you from page 1681 of your testimony yesterday:

> "I had made notes previously to which I appended
> notes on specific items as I went along."

Did you make that answer yesterday?

A. I made no reference to appending—

Q. Wait a minute. Did you make that answer? Please answer my question.

A. No, sir, not as to one word in there at least.

Q. . . . What word didn't you say yesterday as taken down by the stenographer?

A. "Appended."

Q. What was the word you claim you said yesterday?

A. I don't know exactly.

I moved to the stenographer and put my hand on his shoulder.

Q. And the stenographer, you claim, was wrong yesterday in taking it down that way?

A. I am making no claim whatever.

Q. Well, I call your attention to the fact that I am reading the official stenographer's minutes taken yesterday of your testimony. You still say that he was wrong in taking this word "appended"?

A. Yes, sir.

We could not have hoped for a more propitious moment to begin the query about the most damaging point of his testimony, namely, that Fruehauf had conceded that he had not been paid full 4 per cent interest.

Once more we entered a forest of details about the interim loan from Fruehauf and Seymour to Beck, and the loan from Manufacturers Trust Company which replaced it. At times we were lost in the thicket of unremembered facts. At other times we lost contact with each other over a disputed date and had to retrace our steps to the point we had previously reached. Several time I despaired of ever finding the proper road out of the darkness. But persistently we pushed forward and finally the witness had no other place to go but to our desired goal.

Q. You are not asserting that the check of four thousand dollars is three thousand dollars short?

A. No, sir.

Q. . . . You consider . . . that the four-thousand-dollar check from Mr. Beck . . . was the payment to be applied to the loan . . . for the interest; is that correct, as you understand it?

A. As far as I know, yes.

So again a government witness asserted that full interest had been paid by Beck.

On redirect examination, Edwards clarified the witness's previous answer about his handwritten notes by having him explain that he did not make notes on the printed volume, but rather wrote down some of its contents on separate pages to which he added further notes; also that his testimony was based on what Fruehauf had told him.

An opportunity was thus afforded for further cross-examination.

Q. And you had put these original notes in a regular file that you kept in your office in the regular course of your work, hadn't you?

A. No, sir.

Q. What file had you put them in?

A. I had put them in no file.

Q. Didn't you testify yesterday you put them in a file?

A. No, sir.

Q. And that you took them out from a file several weeks later to destroy?

A. No, sir.

Q. Well, let's see page 1684.

"Q. And you kept them in your desk?

"A. No, sir.

"Q. Where?

"A. In a file drawer maintained for the purpose in the office."

Did you make that answer yesterday?

A. A file drawer where I maintained a workbox.

Q. Where you what?

A. Maintained a workbox, I believe I said.

Q. When you said "file drawer," didn't you intend to mean there was a file that you maintained of these original notes in a drawer in your desk; didn't you intend that to mean a file?

A. No, sir, I meant a filing cabinet with a drawer containing a workbox where certain things are kept.

Q. So you were referring to a filing cabinet that you kept this in?

A. In brief, a metal cabinet with drawers, yes.

Q. And when you said a moment ago that you didn't testify yesterday that you kept them in a file, that was incorrect, wasn't it?

A. I distinguished the file from the filing drawer.

So it went. It was for the jury to evaluate the witness's testimony. But before we left him, we again emphasized his destruction of the original notes.

Q. Now you didn't destroy everything that was in that file drawer, did you?

A. No, sir.

Q. You kept some of your original reports, didn't you?

A. I doubt it very much.

Q. But you wouldn't say no to that, would you?

A. I couldn't say no.

Q. Was there any special reason why you selected this particular original document to destroy that you know of?

A. No, sir. It was a general practice of mine.

But a few minutes later:

Q. Was there a standard, uniform practice to destroy the original notes?

A. No, sir.

The government rested. There was an important piece of unfinished business to complete. As we have seen, Judge Feinberg had reversed himself on the issue whether defendants' knowledge of the law was admissible. His new ruling was that we would be permitted to show that our clients had no idea that a loan to Beck was a violation of law. He even volunteered to withdraw his contrary instruction to the jury at the early stage of the case, when I was making my opening statement.

Now Sullivan pressed this advantage in a practical way. We had not asked the government witnesses, many of whom were employees of Seymour's companies, whether they knew anything about Section 186 of the Labor Relations Act or that a loan to Beck might violate the statute. The court, consistent with its new ruling, stated that Mr. Edwards would have to recall his witnesses, so that defense counsel could inquire into their knowledge of the state of the law. Since some of these witnesses came from far distances, there was danger of delay. Besides, it would be equivalent psychologically to beginning the case all over again. This crisis blossomed into a stipulation in which both sides agreed that if the witnesses were recalled, they would testify (without the government conceding the truth thereof) that they had no idea that the loan transaction might violate the law! Thus, it was unnecessary to bring back the previous witnesses. This remarkable written stipulation was later read to the jury. Now, toward the very end of the trial, it seemed that the two streams, The Law and The Facts, were merging and flowing harmoniously in our direction.

Perhaps we could persuade the court that the government had failed to make out a sufficient case to submit to the jury, and that as a matter of law it ought to be dismissed, as Judge Sugarman had previously done.

Judge Feinberg, either because he recognized the weight of our contentions, or because he had a scholar's curiosity to exhaust all possibilities, set aside almost two full days for argument to dismiss the case. I attacked the government's basic theory that the loan violated the statute because it was a "one-sided favor."

"Please observe, Your Honor, these adjectives. Once it's a 'tremendous' favor; once it's 'enormous,' once it's 'extremely valuable.'

"The use of these adjectives in themselves constitute a constitutional objection to the entire theory. No jury can decide what is enormous or what is tremendous. . . . it is not a specific enough definition of the act which is alleged to be a crime to fit the constitutional objections to vagueness and uncertainty, particularly in a *malum prohibitum* statute where that which was legal yesterday becomes illegal today and a citizen should be put on fair notice as to precisely what he cannot do."

We poked at the vulnerability of the government's plastically changing positions. Now it contended that Fruehauf never intended to collect interest and it was *that* which constituted a violation of the statute.

"This is not even in Mr. Justice Frankfurter's five conjectures. . . . The government has added one.

"All right. Let's take it at that. I will follow Mr. Edwards down his path wherever it winds."

THE COURT: Maybe Mr. Edwards went to Harvard too.

MR. EDWARDS: I read all Mr. Justice Frankfurter's books, Your Honor.

MR. NIZER: I may say as a Columbia man that I have nothing but admiration and envy for the Harvard scholars and students.

Such occasional banter did not disguise the earnestness with which both sides urged their contentions on the court. Professor Seligson argued the venue point—namely, that the case was brought in the wrong district, and also that it was barred by the statute of limitations. Weisl and Sullivan also moved to dismiss, and Edwards had the burden of answering all of us.

When the thunder had died down, the court announced that it would reserve decision on our motions for judgment of acquittal. The fact that the judge did not deny our motions was significant. He would permit the case to go to the jury. If it decided for us, there was nothing left to rule upon. If it decided against us, the judge by his "reserved decision" had left open the possibility that he would overrule the jury and grant our motion for acquittal as a matter of law.

Still, we had to submit our fate to the jury, and the question arose whether we should put in defense testimony or boldly rest on the government's proof. The decision had to be made overnight and announced the next morning. Our clients had been fully prepared to testify, and all witness on our behalf also stood ready. But did we need a defense? Every fact which Fruehauf, Seymour, or Beck would wish to present had been established out of the mouths of government witnesses. Every document which we would desire to produce had already been marked in evidence. Our clients could only repeat the evidence already in the record, and then be subjected to cross-examination. Beck had special reason not to take the stand. If he did, the prosecutor could question him about his prior conviction, which had been so zealously kept from the jury. Once he chose to testify, his record would become admissible to attack his credibility. Fruehauf and Seymour had impeccable reputations and nothing to fear, but what purpose would be served in having Seymour cross-examined about the ACT Committee entry, or Fruehauf questioned about his testimony before the Senate committee, thus advising the jury that he had been called before it?

The lawyers held their own council of war and came to the unanimous conclusion that the government's case was defective, and that in any event we could not improve our position by repeating that which we had already drawn out of the government's witnesses. However, the responsibility for such a decision was so great that we could not make it without the clients' consent. If the jury decided in our favor, our judgment would be honored, but suppose it decided against us? Recrimination was almost inevitable. Would not our clients be justified in saying, "If only you hadn't been so audacious, and permitted us to testify, the result might well have been different." At least we had to offer our clients a choice, even though we knew it was limited by our firm advice.

However, duty which sheds itself of responsibility for decision, is unperformed. No matter how great the risk, the lawyer must rely on his judgment, a word we substitute for an imponderable bundle of past experience and psychological factors, all unconsciously sifted and evaluated to give insight into the future. If the ingredients of this process are adulterated, or their evaluation defective, we call the result bad judgment. If the cerebration points in the right direction, we call it wisdom. "Judgment," "wisdom"—these are semantic disguises for a mysterious process too involved to dissect scientifically. It is a realm to be explored, as unknown as outer space, but less enticing because it is not fraught with the perils which lure us as much as the search for knowledge. Perhaps we could stimulate the effort to invade man's inner continent by the realization that such an inquiry into what slows man's moral progress while he races ahead centuries in mechanical proficiency, may turn out to be as daring an enterprise as his flights into infinite space.

Fruehauf, Seymour, and their counsel met in my office for a long evening of discussion and decision. The advantages of announcing the next morning that we rested on the government's case were fully set forth. We offered the compromise proposal of putting in a brief defense limited solely to eminent character witnesses. In view of the standing of both defendants, we had an imposing list of distinguished men and women who would testify that each enjoyed a splendid reputation for veracity in his community.

We also pointed out that the defendants didn't have to testify that they were not aware of a statute which might forbid the loan to Beck. This fact was before the jury in another form. The stipulation agreed upon by Mr. Edwards and ourselves stated that certain witnesses who had previously testified, would, if recalled, for further cross-examination, testify that in June 1954

"they *had no idea,* nor to their knowledge did *any of the defendants have any idea,* that a loan of two hundred thousand dollars by the defendants . . . to Dave Beck would be a violation of law."

Among those listed in the stipulation who would so testify were two lawyers, Simon Wampold and Alfons Landa. If they didn't think such a loan transgressed Section 186, how could anyone assume that Fruehauf or Seymour would know otherwise? Furthermore, the stipulation included the fact that none of these witnesses thought that Fruehauf or Seymour had any idea that they might be violating the law. How much more could Fruehauf and Seymour add by a personal disclaimer from the stand?

Nevertheless, our clients disagreed. For years they had lived a disgraced life, the indictment having enveloped them in an odorous smog which accompanied them wherever they moved. They had looked forward to the day when they could take the stand to set forth their honorable motives. They wanted to contribute personally to their vindication. They didn't seek merely an acquittal. This would be escape. They wished to face the charge like men, and obtain moral restoration as well as legal victory.

Counsel were heartened by so principled an attitude, but our eye was on the verdict and our professional duty was to do that which promised the best result. We still saw nothing to be gained by repetition on the stand of what had gone before. The jury had observed the defendants for weeks, and we could in summation do justice to their personalities, without subjecting them to cross-examination and some possible burst of anger when harassed by insinuations which they so deeply resented.

We proposed a resolution of the problem. Suppose when

we announced that we rested we would make a clear record with proper emphasis of our clients' determination to testify. Would not this eliminate any inference that they shunned the witness stand because of a doubt about their innocence? Furthermore, we would call no other witnesses, not even character witnesses, in order to underline counsels' view that there was no case requiring any defense at all.

This plan was accepted. The next morning, I addressed the court:

"We have, Your Honor, searched the record from beginning to end very meticulously, and in the judgment of counsel there is no direct evidence on any of the requisite issues on which the government has the burden of proof; and to the extent that there may be found any, it is so trivial, inconsequential and remote from any issue, that that is an additional reason for our conviction that the government had failed to make out any case whatsoever.

"Our only obstacle to resting, and I hope Your Honor will permit me to say this in justice to our clients, were the protests of Mr. Fruehauf personally and Mr. Burge Seymour, personally. . . . By that, I mean that these gentlemen, in view of their impeccable reputations and high standing, have felt under such pressure of this indictment, the fact that it was announced, unfortunately, as if they had given some bribe . . . to a labor leader, which we actually know, even the government is fair enough to concede—was a loan made and repaid in full long before any investigating authority of any kind ever went in this matter."

After developing the innocence of the transaction, I turned to our clients' present position.

"Under these circumstances, Mr. Fruehauf and Mr. Seymour insisted on their right to take the stand and tell these facts out of their own mouths so that no one would think that if we rested it was because they didn't want to take the stand or feared to take the stand, an implication they were afraid might be drawn.

"We comforted them finally by telling them that not only was it our judgment that there was no charge here that required answer but that we would not put any other witnesses on the stand, so that . . . nobody could get the impression that they chose not to go on, but rather it was counsel's instruction that there was no case here to meet.

"It was with great reluctance on the absolute insistence of counsel, who are trying to do their duty, that these gentlemen finally agreed. This was not an easy struggle and I appreciate Your Honor's permission to put it on the record, otherwise I don't think we would be allowed to rest by our clients.

"So that into the late hours our struggle was not with the case or with the evidence which we deem totally insufficient, but with our clients."

We read the stipulation to the jury asserting that our clients "had no idea" that a loan to Beck might violate any law, watching the jurors' faces closely. Apparently, they were surprised at this development in view of the court's previous instruction to them. It was a grand flourish upon which the symphony of evidence ended. Then we laid down our baton and rested.

Now the time had come for summation. It is a wonderful moment for the lawyer. It gives him freedom to interpret and clarify; to criticize and expose; to balance and synthesize— freedom to pull together isolated bits of testimony and give them the entirety which bears the image of truth. During the trial, the lawyer hopes the jury fully sees the point of this or that involved piece of evidence or remembers a prior bit of testimony which gives meaning to a later exhibit or answer. Fearing that the jury doesn't, he is frustrated by the restrictions upon him. He presents, but he may not comment. He is silenced by the rules of procedure. But then the time to sum up comes. The heavy restraints are removed from him, and he feels as if he can breathe again. Then he can engage in the infinite art of persuasion. Like all arts, it is as variable as personality. Sullivan mixed hard-steeled sarcasm with sentiment. Weisl's presentation was devoid of artifice, stressing simplicity, the garb of truth. Seligson delivered a calm and pleasant lecture, instructing without arrogance. Burdell bounced back and forth between ridicule and informal invective.

The prosecutor, Edwards, adopted the attitude of objectivity, marshaling the facts with icy precision, while eschewing any conclusion in most instances, leaving the choice of alternatives to the jury. But all the while the facts were presented in such a way as to exclude all reasonable avenues except conviction. It is a favorite device of some prosecutors to adopt this subtle form of cajolery; to be above the passions of battle, as if the spokesman for the United States of America was too conscious of the dignity of his position to harangue the jury.

Edwards had the great advantage of speaking last. This was due to the fact that the government was the plaintiff and had the burden of proof. Such party opens and closes. As defendants, we would have no opportunity to reply. The danger was that his final argument might make inroads and linger in the jury's mind, even though adequate answers might be available. Every summation presents its challenges for solution. I concentrated on this problem. How could we create an unspoken reply?

I adopted what might be called a Pavlovian technique to train the jury to react almost automatically to certain words and arguments which we knew the prosecutor would use.

So, after spending almost a whole day demonstrating that the government had not only failed to prove its case, but that its witnesses had actually disproved its contentions, I turned to the special problem. I advised the jury that Mr. Edwards would sum up last, that we would have no opportunity to reply, and that we had to rely on the jury to recall the answers to his arguments. Then I attempted to anticipate each of Edwards' arguments, doing my utmost to phrase them in his language and style, and implored the jury to react immediately by recalling the answers which I repeated in skeleton form. So, for example, if Edwards told them that this loan was a "tremendous favor," not available as an ordinary banking transaction, I called for an immediate reflex recollection, first, that the bank officers who testified contradicted this theory; and second, that they might ask themselves why hadn't the government produced Beck's financial statement when its witness, Lake, of the Seattle bank, was on the stand? Was it because they knew it would show he had collateral and could have had a bank loan?

If Edwards argued that Beck didn't pay full interest— "please in your own minds speak back to him"; didn't his own witnesses admit that full interest of four thousand dollars had been paid?

If Edwards talked about concealment, I hoped "the moment you hear that word, you will have a reflex reaction" remembering first that all evidence in this case was voluntarily presented by the defendants to the government; second, that all original books of entry described the transaction as a Beck loan; third, that if there had been an intent to conceal, the loan could have been set up to one of Beck's subsidiary corporations, and this was not done. So if Edwards utters the word concealment or disguise, "let these three flagposts and the banners on them, remind you of the truth, that the two-hundred-thousand-dollar loan was at all times revealed."

If Edwards talked about improper motive, I prayed for a reflex reaction that honest gratitude for a prior favor and not labor advantage was the motive; that Fruehauf had only 289 employees out of ten thousand who belonged to the Teamsters Union; that there were no labor advantages to him before or after the loan.

In this way, we continued to present echoes of words not yet spoken by the prosecutor and to condition the jury to respond by awakening its memory to our answers. By repetition and emphasis, we tried to create associations in the jury's mind between the accusation and reply. Thus, our enforced silence would be replaced by an inner voice which we attempted to evoke.

Psychologically this device placed a burden on the prosecutor. His arguments would collide with their own anticipated echoes and trigger replies, which while unuttered, would be loud in the jury's mind.

The high-voltage emotions of a trial will either favor or destroy one of the litigants. They are a potent force not to be ignored on the theory that a calm dissertation of the facts will suffice. But they cannot be invoked by artifice. Oratory will not bring them into being or channel them. Only when the jury had been impressed by the hard facts can it be swept by sentiment and emotion to an accelerated resolution.

The lawyer who substitutes emotional appeal for persuasive fact will be astonished by the contemptuous resistance of the jury. On the other hand, the lawyer who fails to cap his factual strength with an emotional appeal for justice stunts his own achievement.

So we hoped that the jury had been intellectually weaned to our cause, but this momentum ought not to be handicapped by inhibition about emotionalism. We pointed to Ruth Fruehauf, who had shared her husband's good life, filled with achievement, and now must suffer the indignity of living through a trial, as if her husband and father of her children were a criminal. The jury's eyes turned to her but she succeeded in maintaining composure.

We quoted a famous case which stated that "a good reputation has always been regarded as a cherished possession among the peoples of civilized communities."

The Fruehaufs had lived under a cloud ever since he was charged with a crime. Such a cloud can be suffocating. In this sense, the jury had life-giving power, and no worthier recipient could be before them than Roy Fruehauf. We pleaded with the jury to restore Fruehauf's reputation which had been unjustly besmirched; to give him back his honor because that was the only real thing a man can hand down to his children; to send him back to his community in Detroit fully vindicated.

> *He who loses his wealth loses little.*
> *He who loses his health loses much.*
> *He who loses his reputation loses everything.*

We pleaded, we prayed, for a verdict of not guilty.

The next morning the judge instructed the jury about the applicable legal principles. His charge was lucid and learned and the jury followed it closely—on one occasion, asking him to repeat his words. He explained that "at the beginning of the case I interrupted Mr. Nizer" on the subject of willfulness, and he wanted to "correct that impression now." The government had made state of mind an issue and that is why the stipulation was admitted stating that the defendants "had no idea" that they were forbidden by statute to make a loan. Nevertheless:

"In order to find defendants guilty it is not necessary that you find that they made this loan with intent to influence or corrupt Dave Beck.

"It is not necessary for you to find that defendants made the loan with knowledge that they were violating the law."

We differed, of course, even with this revised concept of willfulness, and we feared its impact upon the jurors. Weren't they virtually being put in a position which excluded all except a verdict of guilty?

At 1:35 P.M. the jury was directed to retire and they left the jury box, as they had done dozens of times during the four weeks of the trial, but this time without an admonition not to discuss the case. They would return with words which would elate or doom us. United States Marshals suddenly arrived on the scene to take charge in case of a conviction.

All but Dave Beck, whose cell was his dining room, went to a nearby restaurant to begin the ordeal of waiting. Seymour and Fruehauf expressed everyone's anxiety when they said they wished it were several hours later. How significant the phrase "to kill time" is. To do so is not murder. It is suicide. It is metaphysical violence against one's own existence and, therefore, reveals the desperation of the supplicant.

We knew the jury would not even begin deliberations until about three o'clock, when it returned from lunch. So for several hours, the suspense was controlled, like a low, steady organ tone, underneath our chatter. Thereafter and until about five o'clock, the organ tone was more ominous but still not too irritating because it was natural that the jury should take considerable time to review and discuss the mass of testimony and mountain of exhibits. But every minute thereafter the organ tones rose in pitch and discordant volume, as we paced the long, bleak corridors of the Federal Court House. Our nerves were becoming frayed by the fierce music which we felt rather than heard. Fruehauf's courageous manner, expressed in flippancy now and then, began to give way as the noises stirred turbulence within him. His eyes narrowed, giving the impression that they were swollen. Ruth clutched his arm warmly as she tried to keep step with his uneven pace, now slowing, now walking speedily, as if driven by the rhythm of the inner screeching sounds. Seymour frequently sat on a wooden bench with Sullivan. His demeanor was philosophical almost to the point of resignation, but the sides of his face sagged as time ticked on. The lawyers gathered in various combinations and strode down the corridors, unhurriedly but with sufficient vigor to avoid a funereal step. At times we would join our clients and predict that a verdict would soon be coming, explaining that after all, the jury did have a large record to digest. But our efforts to be comforting grew feebler as the hours passed. Seven, eight, and nine o'clock went by. The hours had not been killed. They tarried the full length of their life span, and brought with them an ever-rising crescendo of tension noises.

One of the younger associates suggested that the lengthy deliberations might mean a disagreement. The clients shuddered at this thought. It meant temporary escape, but could they live through another such heart-pounding experience?

By ten o'clock, the suspense becomes a roaring cacophony. Alarm was rampant. Just when we wondered how much longer we could stand the ordeal, a court attendant appeared mysteriously from nowhere and announced: "Jury returning. Everyone in the courtroom please."

We hastened to our seats, where we sat stiffly, pulses throbbing, while the noises within were now uncontrollably shrill. The judge mounted the bench somewhat breathlessly in his haste, gesturing to all to sit down, as if the event was too meaningful for formal procedure. Then the jurors entered, this time last, as befitted their importance at that moment. They did not sit down but faced the judge, avoiding all eyes which they knew were on them.

THE CLERK: Members of the jury, will you answer to your names . . .

The roll call seemed interminable. What kind of torture was this?

THE CLERK: Mr. Foreman, have you arrived at a verdict?

THE FOREMAN: We have.

THE CLERK: How do you find?

THE FOREMAN: We find Roy Fruehauf, Fruehauf Trailer, Mr. Burge Seymour, Associated Trucking, Brown Equipment, and Dave Beck not guilty.

The last two words were a sharp thrust which released unbearable anxieties accumulated over a period of three years. There was an explosive sound of joy. The inner fierce music stopped abruptly. Ignoring the clerk who was completing the formalities by repeating the verdict, Ruth and Roy Fruehauf embraced. She pressed her head against his chest and closed her eyes. They just held each other tightly without saying a word. So they continued to stand as if they were a frozen tableau.

Dave Beck was being congratulated by his lawyers, but his pinched face had a sad look, like that of a father who hears everyone around him cheering the ending of a war, but knows that his son won't return. Beck knew that in a few moments he would be led back to prison.

The greatest emotion came from a quite unexpected quarter. Mortimer Sullivan, the devoted personal friend of Seymour, broke into sobs. The judge, as he told me later, was so moved by the scene that he left the bench abruptly, to hide his own feelings.

Edwards and his associate gathered their briefcases and strode quickly out of the courtroom. The defense lawyers made their own chain of congratulatory handshakes. Later, the clients conferred their tearful embraces on counsel. Everyone was too exhausted to continue the evening, but Fruehauf and Seymour announced that there would be a departure cocktail gathering at Roy's hotel suite the next evening. By that time the victory had sunk in and quickened the flow of sentiments. Fruehauf was his jovial, appealing self again. As if he were attending a sales convention, he moved skillfully around the room, chuckling and chatting amiably with everyone. One felt his strength, but what was winning about him was a boyish quality. His face, with slightly upturned nose, had the shiny look of a boy when he is scrubbed. His hair was plastered down as if it were brown silk and his corpulence (not too noticeable because of his broad, tenor-like frame) made his bubbling gaiety more appropriate. Ruth's even-featured beauty, which contrasted her dark hair with fair pink skin and gleaming white smile, complemented the celebration.

Seymour could no longer maintain his pretense of dourness. He was all smiles, and graciousness. Although no one needed the encouragement of the drinks, they did not hinder the uninhibited compliments and toasts which were sung from every quarter.

When the Fruehaufs returned to Detroit, they found that they had been restored to their prior enviable position in the community, but not in the Fruehauf Trailer Company. A new president had been installed during the long legal blackout. New management had achieved its own momentum. Roy could not accept a secondary place in the company founded by his father and built by him and his brothers.

Dauntlessly, he decided to go into another business of his own. He organized Roy Fruehauf, Inc. to haul earth, sand, and gravel to and from road building and other construction operations. To do so he ordered trailers of unprecedented size and joined them into a train, each of which could haul five times as much material as conventional dumps. Thus he was able to win bids over competitors, and obtained sixteen million dollars of contracts in five Midwestern states. Fruehauf's dream, like his father's before him, was transformed into a reality by his energy, bold concepts, and mechanical brilliance. In a short time his firm operated the largest earth-hauling fleet in the nation, and also became the largest supplier of sand and gravel in the metropolitan area of Detroit. He built ninety-two "trains," each costing fifty thousand dollars, and not the least of his satisfactions as a large stockholder of the Fruehauf Trailer Company must have been that he became one of its largest customers!

I do not believe in extrasensory perception, but I am sure that such a coincidence as I am about to relate is responsible for the skeptic's uncertainty, and the believer's clinging adherence.

On Sunday, November 7, 1965, I was at work on this chapter. I was propped up in bed, which is electrically controlled to assume all positions, and therefore particularly convenient for longhand writing. My electric pencil sharpener was beside me, also my electric heating control, light switches, television remote control, and telephones on each side of me (some day a lawyer-author will be found electrocuted in his bed), and I had reached the last ten pages of this chapter when I paused as I wrote the name Fruehauf. I wondered what the ordeal he had endured had taken out of him. I knew the collapse he had suffered when the first impact of indictment struck him; how he had come out of the darkness to find the brilliant light after a court dismissal, only to be plunged back into the domain of terror by a Supreme Court reversal and the anguish of a new trial; and now final vindication and a restored life accompanied by friendship, community recognition, a triumphant new business success; and above all the love and warmth of his family. Yet how does one measure what inner resources might have been depleted? What injury had been done to the psyche which affects the mysterious life forces? Perhaps, at the age of fifty-seven, he had grown stronger from his experience. The hardest wood is always found on the mountaintop where the trees are subjected to storms. Would it be discreet to even write about all this? In any event, it was interesting rumination and it propelled me to telephone him, obtain some facts about his new business, and advise him that this chapter, which he had suggested I write and was eager to see, would soon be in his hands. I reached for the telephone to make the call. It rang before I could lift the receiver. I answered. It was a long-disance call from Detroit. The voice said he was Don Graham and that Ruth Fruehauf had asked him to tell me that Roy Fruehauf had suffered a cerebral hemorrhage and had just died.

Chapter Four

JOHN HENRY FAULK

In 1955 an off-Broadway show took place on Broadway at the Hotel Astor in New York City, exceeding in emotional impact any performance given in the past decade. The lines were original and unrehearsed. The actors and actresses were stars exhorting their audiences to Americanism, either by condemning blacklisting in the theatrical profession, or by extolling the exposure of performers with communistic leanings. The scene was the meeting of the New York Local of American Federation of Television and Radio Artists, a union known as AFTRA.

The principles involved in the debate were crucial. They presented a microcosm of a challenging issue which has confronted our country since communism first threatened to infiltrate and corrode our society, namely: What abuses of our constitutional privileges are justified for the purpose of preserving those privileges? The issue is broader than whether the end justifies the means. For the ends are not as beneficial as those who are willing to close their eyes to amoral methods would have it. There are unintended ends: the destruction of the inviolate right to be presumed innocent until proven guilty; to be confronted by one's accuser and have the right to examine and answer; above all, to prevent the invasion of man's right to think and speak without fear. When these ends also result from improper means, how prohibitive the price! Then not only is the moral precept violated, but there is not even the inconsequential solace of a desirable pragmatic result.

However, life never presents itself in generic concepts. It consists of incidents which are not ordered neatly in categories of precious rights. Rather they are the day-by-day tragedies of jobs refused, rent unpaid, children taunted about their parent's patriotism, friendships abandoned to prevent the stigma of association, love strained by adversity, and worst of all, the inner struggle to avoid martyrdom, to surrender self-respect to conformity, to acquiesce in the great protective silence.

The actors and actresses who spoke with great emotion about their ordeal stirred the meeting to a pitch of uncontrollable excitement. For years the issue of blacklisting in the television and radio industry had been brewing. Now it burst into the open. One hundred sixty-seven members had signed a resolution to condemn Aware Inc., an outside organization, which had repeatedly accused certain actors and actresses of having "pink" or "Communist Front" records, resulting in their being blacklisted and rendered unemployable.

The director and "research consultant" of Aware Inc. was Vincent Hartnett, who previously had been the principal author of *Red Channels*, a book listing the "political activities" of performers. This book was reputed to have been the "bible" used by advertising agencies and networks to "check" the records of actors and actresses and in many instances barred the accused from work, without confrontation or the opportunity to deny or explain. Now the same Vincent Hartnett was doing similar research for pay, for sponsors or advertising agencies. The entire television and radio industry seemed to be in the grip of blacklisting practices. No one had yet proven or disproven these charges. Ultimately a trial before a judge and jury provided the opportunity, in true American fashion, to unravel the mystery. The burden of piercing the reluctance of witnesses to expose the truth was so heavy that six years of research and legal procedures were necessary to meet the requirements of positive proof in a courtroom.

The rumblings of the great storm began at the feverish meetings of AFTRA, where a resolution had been placed before the body to condemn Aware Inc. for interfering with the union's activities, and causing the blacklisting of members. A stenographic report of these meetings was kept by the union. These minutes later became a court exhibit. They tell a more vivid story than any playwright could fashion from his imagination.

An actor, Leslie Barrett, told of his experience in the following words:

"I have here a journal I have been writing.

" 'December 17, 1954, 3:15 in the morning. It is impossible for me to sleep as it has been for 3 or 4 nights now because of a letter from a certain Mr. Vincent Hartnett on December 11; I have been experiencing nothing but grief and anxiety. I can neither hold my food nor can I sleep.'

"It started December 9 after a union meeting. To my left was seated a person who greeted me and whom I answered 'hello.' In back of this person, a gentleman I never saw before seemed to be studying me, or was it my imagination? The meeting ended and I left dejected and miserable, the reason being that the tenor of these meetings is fraught with fear, distrust and acrimonious debate. There is disagreement, but few if any will speak out. Why? 'Because I have a little list,' so the saying goes, and if your name is listed you do not work.

"Needless to say, this situation is deplorable. One is afraid to look at anyone, to speak to anyone, to protest on the floor or to anyone. You come in silently, you leave silently, and I left followed by a feeling of revulsion that was almost nauseous.

"Strange as it may seem, I sensed I was being followed. After five or six blocks, I turned around and stared into the face of the man who was sitting behind the 'political' person in point. It is a terrible experience. Two days later I received this letter:

" 'Dear Mr. Barrett:

" 'In preparing a book on the Left Theater, I came across certain information regarding you. A photograph of the 1952 New York May Day Parade shows you marching.

" 'It is always possible that people have in good faith supported certain causes and come to realize that their support was misplaced. Therefore I am writing you to ascertain if there has been any change in your position.

" 'You are, of course, under no obligation to reply to this letter. As a matter of fact, I am under no obligation to write to you. However, my aim is to be scrupulously fair and to establish the facts. If I do not hear from you, I must conclude that your marching in the 1952 May Day Parade is still an accurate index of your position and sympathies.

" 'I am enclosing a 3 cent stamp for a reply.

" 'Very truly yours

Vincent Hartnett'

"I was stunned. I saw my livelihood taken from me and myself the center of doubt in hundreds of people's minds who never would have the opportunity to learn the facts. Unless I cooperated! For I later heard from reliable sources that this man represents a widespread, powerful group that insists on your 'cooperating' their way or you do not work.

"The next day I spoke to a union official of AFTRA and asked him who Vincent Hartnett was. His face froze. I showed him the letter.

" 'Is it true?' he asked.

" 'Of course not,' I replied. 'The man is mad!' I asked again who he was.

"This official said, he was formerly with *Red Channels,* but he left them. He is allied with a Syracuse chain grocer and certain posts of the American Legion.

"He went on to tell me that I should answer him and not let this pass, for this is a powerful man in our profession. This union official made it clear that in all his years of union activity nothing has made him so sick as this one man."

Barrett went on to relate that he visited the F.B.I., assured it he had never attended a May Day Parade, and asked for clearance.

He was told that this was not its function. It was an investigative agency and not a judicial body which made decisions. Its files could not even be seen without presidential directives.

"I was told further that if anyone had anything of interest, they were the proper authorities to come to and not private citizens or groups." (*Applause*)

Barrett had his lawyer write to Hartnett assuring him that he had never marched in a May Day Parade, nor ever had "sympathy or leanings" for communism. He received the following reply:

"Dear Mr. Barrett:

"To my surprise I received today a letter dated December 13 from Mr. Klein, a lawyer. I say I was surprised because I wrote to you, not to Mr. Klein or any member of your family.

"I was according you a privilege of commenting on certain information in my possession, and I hoped for the courtesy of a reply from you, not from Mr. Klein.

"As things stand at this point, I have not received from you any reply to my December 9th letter. I have no way of establishing that Mr. Klein is authorized to speak for you or that he has accurately transmitted to me your statement.

"Parenthetically, is this the same Harvey L. Klein who is listed as having signed Communist Party nominating petitions in 1939-40?

"Enclosed is a photograph of a group of marchers in the New York May Day Parade in 1952. The gentleman underneath the left arrow looks like you. Possibly I am mistaken. There may be some other actor in New York who closely resembles you. I have no desire to harass you.

"My only desire is to establish the facts. Frankly, I am disappointed up to this point. In my previous experience in similar cases, people who had nothing to hide did not pull a lawyer into the discussion. They simply and candidly denied or affirmed the evidence. I hope you will be equally candid and direct. You will find me most sympathetic and understanding.

"Sincerely yours,
Vincent Hartnett"

Barrett now found his lawyer under attack too:

"Not wishing to have my lawyer's practice possibly ruined by lies . . . I told him I would handle it from now on. My lawyer wished a denial placed on record concerning him, so I did answer by letter, and I received this reply:

" 'Dear Mr. Barrett:

" ' I am happy to receive your personal warranty of the statements made in the December 13 letter of Attorney Harvey L. Klein to me. I am also happy to hear that he is not the individual of the same name with the affiliations noted in the letter of December 14 to you.

" 'I appreciate your writing me, and I hope you incurred no

expense by the unnecessary move of calling in a lawyer. This only muddied the waters.

" 'Frankly, two people in radio and tv who know you thought the man pictured in the May Day Parade photo was you. Research to establish a positive identification of the man is continuing.

> " 'Sincerely yours,
> Vincent Hartnett' "

Vincent Hartnett was not even a member of AFTRA, and was not present at this meeting. But Godfrey Schmidt, a prominent lawyer and president of Aware Inc., was present. He was subjected to heckling from some of the members.

> MEMBER: I would like to know, is Mr. Schmidt an actor or isn't he? Isn't that the only way you become a member of AFTRA? . . .
>
> MR. MC KEE: Mr. Schmidt has a card as an associate member of AFTRA.
>
> MEMBER: Does he have a song-and-dance act?

Schmidt pointed out that he had "worked as the WNBC Story Teller for twenty-eight performances for pay," and was therefore properly a member of AFTRA. He took the floor to argue that:

"A man has a right as an American citizen to recognize the peril of this day, to recognize that Communist conspiracy has encircled its coils about all of the decency behind the Iron Curtain and is trying to subvert this country too, and when a group of candidates present themselves to you for your support, it is highly relevant, no matter who tells the story, that their record should be laid bare, that you should understand that people who were foolish enough to be beguiled by Communist propaganda are precisely not the people to be entrusted with office in this great organization." (*Applause*)

He argued that the word "blacklisting" was ambiguous and meant three different things. First it meant discrimination against employees because of union activities. Aware was against this kind of blacklisting. Second, it meant "smear tactics and lies to run down someone's reputation." That too, he condemned.

"In the third case, there is a clear intent expressed here that another type of activity should be denominated blacklisting. That is to say, to tell the truth, ladies and gentlemen!

Every single line of this is the unchallengeable truth, and the best proof of it that none of you will dare, if you feel aggrieved, bring it to court, as you could. (*Applause and boos*)

"Ladies and gentlemen, I can cope with applause because I know it won't last long, but catcalls and boos and the language of the menagerie is not my line. I can't refute it."

MEMBER: That is presumptuous and ill-mannered. . .

MR. SCHMIDT: . . . The time has come for Americans to stand up and be counted . . . that is why Aware was organized. It has a fine set of principles and a good program. . . . Thank you! (*Applause*)

Schmidt's challenge did not go unanswered.

MISS ELAINE ELDRIDGE: I am not qualified to compete with so eminent and articulate a lawyer as Mr. Schmidt. But, in my very humble way, I will try to say the few words that I must. . . .

She said she was one of thirteen members listed in Aware's newsletter for "such amazing subversive activities as belonging to the Actors Studio" or signing a petition to save the life of a Negro, Willie McGee.

"There must be hundreds and hundreds of actors . . . who were students at the Dramatic Workshop, which, by the way had a Board of Education Charter. . . . Are all of these people to be listed . . . for having a Dramatic Workshop record . . . or an Actors Studio record? . . .

"Or, are you married to one of those energetic citizens who concern themselves with problems of present-day society and espouse social causes of one kind or another, feeling that no one can question what cause it may be because that is what makes us a democratic America? If you are not now, you may in the future fall in love, as people will, and marry such a dangerous, un-American person, which is the reason one of our candidates was cited. . . . In that event, you, too, would be subject to victimization by this organization. . . .

"If you are invited to speak at the burial of a fellow actor, will you have to decline the honor for fear such deceased actor's political views are unpopular with or opposed to this organization's.

"Forgive me if I appear a little emotional about it, but I was one of the people named because I had accepted two years ago a telephone call from the National Committee of Arts, Sciences and Professions, asking me if I would be willing to teach on their staff. I said yes, and I went to one meeting at which the program was to be organized, and it fell through. I never heard anything further from it. . . . So I think it is a little presumptuous and perhaps a little premature on the part of Mr. Schmidt to consider all these people as dangers and menaces to our society. I assure you I don't think I am. I will let you judge. Thank you!" (*Applause*)

Another actress, Miss Kenney, took the floor to point out that dues paid to some of the organizations being discussed went ultimately "toward the Communist Party Fund":

"In other words, you would be contributing toward the destruction of your own country, your own Constitution. If you have not thought of it that way think about it. If you have not read the other side of the picture . . . read it and find out first what fools they are making of you." (*Applause*)

MISS STEPHANIE ELLIOTT: ". . . I am a young actress. I have only been in the business about seven or eight years, and I am a young member of AFTRA, about two years. I have never spoken to you before and I am scared to death of you, but my point is this. I was in a play at the Greenwich Mews Theater, I studied at the Dramatic Workshop.

"I do feel strongly if I am going to be stopped from studying where I want to or working with actors I have regard for, there is something wrong, something frightening, something that makes me cringe, makes me afraid, afraid of everybody who feels this way, who feels I should be stopped. . . .

"I am young. I haven't got a name yet like a lot of other people. . . . Maybe there was a political faction at the Workshop. I don't know. I was interested in becoming a better actress . . . perfecting my art. I am not interested in politics, Mr. Schmidt's or anybody else's politics.

"But when politics comes into it and makes me afraid to study with somebody, I think it is shameful. . . . I am interested in being a free American citizen, allowed to perfect my art, and I feel that Aware and whoever else is connected with it is not allowing me to do this.

"I don't want this in my country. . . ." (*Applause*)

So the debate raged until midnight. Then there was a cessation of hostilities. Dwight Weist moved to adjourn and suggested that the discussion and vote on the resolution to condemn Aware be continued at the next meeting. Both factions welcomed the opportunity to regroup their forces for the showdown one month later.

Seated silently in the rear of the room was a radio and television performer, subjected, like other listeners, to the waves of arguments which swept through the room. He felt intense resentment or passionate approval but had no premonition that it was he who would be engulfed in the contesting issues: that he was destined to be martyrized because of a personal challenge he was to throw into the faces of the most powerful forces; and that fate had marked him to be the instrumentality through which the historic debate on blacklisting would be determined in a judicial forum.

His name was John Henry Faulk.

The entire entertainment industry was seething with discussion of the issues which had been raised. It awaited May 24, 1955, the date on which 489 actors and actresses of AFTRA filed into City Center Theatre for final argument and decision.

President Travis Johnson presided with scrupulous impartiality, recognizing the speakers from the opposing camps alternately.

After the resolution had again been read referring to Aware Inc.'s "scandalous attack" on an entire slate of candidates for AFTRA office "by the now familar smear methods of inference and innuendo from alleged 'public records'" which "deprived actors of jobs" and concluding

"RESOLVED, that Aware Inc. be condemned for interfering in the internal affairs of our union."

the proponents sprang their first surprise. They announced that since the previous meeting, the Council of Actors' Equity Association (legitimate theater), with Mr. Ralph Bellamy presiding, had voted unanimously to condemn the action of Aware Inc.

The opponents countered with a surprise of their own. Miss Kim Hunter, a distinguished actress, who was generally considered to belong to the "liberal" group and opposed to Aware Inc., sent a telegram in its favor. It was not until years later that Miss Hunter testified tearfully from the witness stand that this telegram had been extracted from her against her will by Vincent Hartnett in order that she (an Academy Award winner the previous year) might work again!

Then the cannonading of the previous meeting continued.

Bill Keene told of his friend who owned a factory, discovered that his foreman was a Kleagle in the Ku Klux Klan, and promptly discharged him:

"Was my friend within his rights to fire the man? Of course he was!

"If a man were being considered for the presidency of a bank, and I knew that he was an embezzler or associated with embezzlers would it not be my duty to give the facts to the responsible people?

. . . And on the question of communism, if the people are given the facts, we believe the verdict will be, 'I don't want that guy in my living room!' "

VINTON HAYWORTH: "AFTRA is characterized as 'an outside organization,' but do those people who wrote this have the decency to tell you the truth that seven other members of AFTRA who signed that letter were according to sworn testimony, members of another outside organization? Yes . . . outside the bounds of honor, yes, outside the United States— the Communist Party. . . . You bet they didn't! And nowhere in the letter do you see a proposal to condemn these seven identified members nor the Communist Party. Isn't that strange?"

Rex Marshall asked why if the accusations were not true, suit wasn't brought? He likened the opposition to "a group of accused criminals saying to the Police Department, 'We can't refute the charges but we certainly deplore the investigation.' "

MISS NANCY POLLOCK: ". . . It is difficult for me to sit by and listen to these flagrant lies and remain calm and unemotional about it. . . .

"I am one of the members indicted . . . in Aware. Several times the question has been asked . . . why doesn't someone deny the charges? Well, I hereby deny those charges and I call those who made them, thieves and liars. Ladies and gentlemen, they are trying to steal my good name . . . they are doing it by devious, dishonest methods.

"They have me down as being a teacher for the arts and professions. I never taught there in my life, but that is not important. The fact is that by association—and this is what they try to push down our throats—they or people of their ilk, will destroy us, and what is more important to me than Equity or AFTRA, they will destroy our nation. . . .

"Must I stand here, as I have never done in all my life, and beat my breast and swear to you that I honestly and truly slept only with the man I have been married to? Must I beat my breast and tell you that I love my nation and would die for it and certainly as gladly as any of them? . . ."

Bud Collyer argued that it was the militant anti-Communist who often lost work.

So the meeting continued to be buffeted by emotional contentiousness. Even the president's ruling that, as in all previous matters, there would be no secret voting, was appealed from, and defeated 167 to 159. Ballots were secretly marked and cast, and after all the precautions had been taken of designating two tellers from each side, the votes were counted and the result announced. The resolution condemning Aware was carried 197 votes to 149.

Aware's adherents did not accept their defeat docilely. They demanded that a referendum be taken by mail of all members, so that the "minority" who had attended the meeting should not prevail. This was done. The members were bombarded by mail from both sides. The vote was 982 to 514 to condemn Aware.

By challenging the fairly close vote at the meeting, Aware had brought about its own condemnation by an almost 2 to 1 margin of the entire membership. Thus it gave momentum to a move to fulfill the mandate which that vote constituted. The incumbent officers and directors, who were mainly adherents of Aware, had to be ousted, so that the evils they had condoned or perpetrated would be eliminated.

A new slate was to be put up for election. But who should the "reform" candidates be? To keep the issue against blacklisting clear, it was essential that the new ticket should be vigorously anti-Communist. Otherwise, Aware would contend that Communist sympathizers were using the blacklisting issue as a blind to gain control of union affairs. If there were any pro-Communists in the union, they were an insignificant few. The overwhelming majority of the members, whether opposed to or in favor of Aware, detested communism. The new slate would have to reflect this fact, so that no one could becloud the true issue, which was Aware's activities and blacklisting. Whoever invented the phrase "red herring" didn't realize that the future would give it a literal political meaning.

Candidates were chosen who had always been anti-Communist but who were just as determinedly against Aware's and Hartnett's activities. They were Charles Collingwood, the distinguished CBS commentator, Garry Moore, an outstanding television and radio personality, Orson Bean, a rising young comedian, John Henry Faulk, a successful radio and television performer, and many others, like Martha Wright, Janice Rule, Dennis Patrick, Faye Emerson, Earl Rogers, Luis Van Rooten. They called themselves the "middle-of-the-road" candidates, opposing communism and blacklisting alike. They issued "A Declaration of Independents" in which they declared:

"As loyal Americans we are unalterably opposed to communism and all other totalitarian ideologies."

They pledged:

"To oppose denial of employment by discriminatory and intimidating practices, especially by outside organizations."

The furious election campaign which followed transcended mere union issues, and evoked intense public interest. The New York *Times*, for example (in a column by Jack Gould), commented on the new resistance to pressure groups, like Aware:

"A commercial cloud was cast over the anti-Communism of Aware by the confirmation by Vincent Hartnett, a director of the organization, that he was professionally engaged in reviewing the political background of artists at the rate of $5 a head."

Every persuasive device to win the election was used, from appeals clothed in dire threats, to predictions of disaster, clothed in sweet reason; from declarations of patriotism to justify rabid talk, to accusations of disloyalty in the name of loyalty. When the assaults on the voters' minds had ended, the sublime moment came when the voters revealed how they had resisted the overwhelming sorties and had managed to maintain balance in the emotional storm. The cold mathematics of tabulation constituted their final judgment. It was an overwhelming sweep in favor of the middle-of-the-road ticket. Out of thirty-five directors to be chosen, the Independents elected twenty-seven. Not only was Aware Inc. condemned, but its adherents were cast out of office. Complete control was won by the opposition. Charles Collingwood was designated the new president. John Henry Faulk and Orson Bean were elected vice presidents in the new administration.

The press hailed the victory of the middlers as a triumph for sanity and civil rights. Editorials in the New York *Times*, *Herald Tribune*, and other newspapers and trade papers complimented the entertainment industry on having cleansed itself of a vigilante group and of the excesses of super-patriotism.

The decision was not accepted with either resignation or good sportsmanship by Aware Inc., Vincent Hartnett, or their ally Laurence A. Johnson, "the grocer from Syracuse" (who provided the economic sanctions which helped make Hartnett's reports effective). Driven by fierce convictions of patriotism, love of power, and in the case of Hartnett, by the threat of economic extinction as well, they were determined to bring down those who had driven them out of office. They did not intend to wait for the next election in the hope of reversing the decision by democratic process. They were intent upon destroying their enemies immediately. They were ready to revenge themselves by using the very methods of accusation and blacklisting which had brought about their defeat.

Of all the candidates on the middle-of-the-road slate, the one who had received the highest number of votes was John Henry Faulk. At meetings, which only later were exposed, Aware Inc., Vincent Hartnett, and Laurence A. Johnson planned specifically to aim their guns at Faulk. They did so in a special *News Bulletin*.

They succeeded beyond their fondest dreams. They pulverized him out of the entertainment industry and left him unemployed and unemployable for 6½ years. They ruined his reputation and left him and his family in a state of starvation. They made a ghastly lesson of him, so that all others who dared to challenge them in the future would be terrorized by his example.

In the next annual election, they were returned to power. There were no "independents" to defy them. Their triumph was complete.

It was too complete. Others previously reduced to Faulk's state of desperation had committed suicide or slunk away. But they had chosen the wrong man to humiliate and destroy. In the great American tradition, which even they should have admired, Faulk rejected the role of a defeated martyr, refused to acknowledge his comatose enfeeblement, and actually attacked his tormentors. He demanded their condemnation. Scorning compromise, he insisted on complete judicial vindication. The result was a contest the like of which has not been seen in the annals of American trials.

First, how did Aware Inc. manage to ruin Faulk and throw him off the airwaves? It was done with a printed bulletin, a piece of paper which packed the firepower of a megaton bomb. It was cleverly worded and appeared to be so accurately documented that it was virtually impossible to resist the conclusion that Faulk had hypocritically posed as a loyal American, but now stood exposed as a Communist or a Communist sympathizer.

The crucial paragraph read:

"John Henry Faulk was quoted as saying that 'all middlers were chosen for their opposition to Communism as well as their opposition to Aware.' In most cases, this may well be true. But how about Faulk himself? What is his public record?"

There followed seven deadly specifications:

"1. According to the *Daily Worker* (the Communist newspaper) of April 22, 1946, 'Jack Faulk' was to appear at Club 65, 13 Astor Place, N.Y.C.—a favorite site of pro-Communist affairs.

"2. According to the *Daily Worker* of April 17, 1947 'Johnny Faulk' was to appear as an entertainer at the opening of 'Headline Cabaret' sponsored by Stage for Action (officially designated a Communist front). The late Philip Loeb was billed as emcee.

"3. According to the *Daily Worker* of April 5, 1948 'John Faulk' contributed cabaret material to 'Show-Time for Wallace' revues staged by the Progressive Citizens of America (officially designated as a Communist Front) in support of Henry A. Wallace's candidacy for the presidency of the U.S. Although Wallace was the officially endorsed candidate of the Communist Party, by no means all his supporters were Communists or pro-Communists. What is in question here is support of any candidate given through a Communist-Front set up.

"4. A program dated April 25, 1946 named 'John Faulk' as a scheduled entertainer (with identified Communist Earl Robinson and two non-Communists) under the auspices of the Independent Citizens Committee of the Arts, Sciences and Professions (officially designated a Communist Front, and predecessor of the Progressive Citizens of America).

"5. Vol. 3, Nos. 1 & 2, of the Bulletin of People's Songs (officially designated a Communist Front) named Faulk as one who had sent greetings to People's Songs on its second anniversary.

"6. 'Johnny Faulk' was listed in a circular as an entertainer or speaker (with Paul Robeson and two others) to appear at 'Spotlight on Wallace' to be held in Room 200 of the Jefferson School of Social Science on February 16, 1948. The Jefferson School has been found by the Federal Government to be what it is, the official training school of the Communist conspiracy in New York.

"7. 'John H. Faulk' was a U.S. sponsor of the American Continental Congress for Peace, staged in Mexico City, September 5–10, 1949, as shown by the official 'call.' The Congress was later described by the House Committee on Un-American Activities as 'another phase in the Communist world "peace" campaign, aimed at consolidating anti-American forces throughout the Western Hemisphere.' "

These "revelations" were followed by a rhetorical question: "Will John Henry Faulk, an AFTRA Vice President, discharge his responsibility to enforce the AFTRA constitutional amendment and National Rule against Communists and those who defy the Congress when asked if they are Communists?" Only those toughened in heart and mind by repeated disillusionment are devoid of all gullibility. Most people accept the printed word as substantial truth; not because they are naïve, but rather because they are sufficiently sophisticated to know that one cannot print a complete lie about another with impunity. They assume that the risk of libel would curb extreme irresponsibility. The very daring of the perpetrator establishes credence for him. So the paradox comes about that the more grievous the lie, the more believable it may become.

However, Hartnett, Johnson, and Aware Inc. did not rely merely on the shock of accusation to create acceptance. They set about actively to implement the campaign of the insidious word with more pragmatic assaults.

They circulated the *Bulletin* not only to their members but to 2285 others on a special mailing list calculated to do Faulk the greatest harm. They mailed it to all television and radio networks, their news departments, and to their top executives. Faulk's employer, Columbia Broadcasting System, and its president thus received this report with its finger pointing menacingly at their employee.

They sent it to leading newspapers and the editors of their radio and television departments.

They circulated it to leading advertising agencies and to

executives who placed hundreds of millions of dollars of advertising on the networks, and had to select and approve the actors who participate in them.

They sent the *Bulletin* directly to leading sponsors like Colgate-Palmolive, General Foods, and many others.

They forwarded it to the National Grocers' Association and various national advertising associations.

They circulated it to leading columnists like Walter Winchell, George Sokolsky, Fulton Lewis, Jr., and many, many others so that "items" might appear about the exposure of John Henry Faulk.

Then they invaded the Governmental departments with the *Bulletin*—the F.B.I., J. Edgar Hoover, the House Un-American Activities Committee, its chairman and counsel, Senator Eastland, the Department of Justice, various district attorneys' offices, and police departments.

They circulated it to the motion picture companies and their executives, book publishers, theater producers, and various theatrical unions.

When one realizes the public's abhorrence of communism and applies it to the broadcasting industry, whose every breath is dedicated to winning favor with the listeners, one understands the hypersensitivity of advertisers. They quake when the rating of viewing audience dips ever so slightly. These subtle quivers of public disfavor are sufficient to cause turmoil among the agencies responsible for the huge expenditures. One can therefore imagine the convulsions which result from a seismograph reading of the charge of communism. Waves of hysteria swept through the industry.

Faulk's sponsors began to cancel out their programs. Libby Frozen Foods, which constituted almost 15 per cent of his radio advertising (eight spots a week), terminated a long and successful relationship with him. So did the Nestlé Company, Libby's Canned Foods, Diamond Crystal Salt, Nucoa, Rheingold Beer, and others. As for new jobs, he never obtained a television engagement from the day the *Bulletin* was issued to the end of the trial, a period of 6½ years (except for one isolated guest appearance on a Jack Parr program).

Faulk had no warning of the issuance of the *Bulletin*. He returned one day from a stroll in the park to be told on the telephone by a New York *Times* reporter, Val Adams, that Aware had issued a document charging him with Communist affiliation. Like a soldier surprised by a bursting shell, he could not immediately measure its fragmentation power. Perhaps it was more noise than flying shrapnel. He learned its devastating effect soon enough. From desperation calls by his business superiors to new appraising looks even from his friends, he knew that his world was collapsing around him.

He decided to seek legal protection. So I met him for the first time in my office and had an opportunity to evaluate the man and the cause he bespoke.

Faulk made an excellent appearance. His features were clean-cut, but the over-all impression was of likableness rather than handsomeness. He was of medium height and looked much younger than his forty-two years. His tweed jacket, neatly knotted black tie, against a colored striped shirt, and pipe (with all the elaborate ritual of filling it aromatically from an oilskin bag, tapping it into the bowl, and lighting it with a tilted small flamethrower) gave a hint of his dual personality—a teacher at a university, which he had been, and an entertainer who also had to peddle his sponsor's wares.

The first surprise came when he spoke. There was a decided Texas accent, but the speech was more picturesque than the drawl. His gift of impersonating Southern characters (such as his "Uncle Lee") constantly intruded into his conversation, so that without warning in the midst of a serious discussion one was wafted into some homily or quaint expression accompanied by faithful accent and high-pitched veracity. This gave startling virtuosity to his speech, as if he were expressing himself on two levels at the same time. But unfailing charm and good will made the inconsistent mood of his talk quite palatable. One never felt that he had a comedian's vice of sacrificing thought for the satisfaction of a jest. Rather they complemented each other with such ease that one shared his concluding chuckle.

Whatever conflict there had once been between the college professor and the humorous commentator had resolved itself in a pattern which was now part of his personality. I learned to accept and enjoy his Southern ruralisms. I developed a glossary of his meanings. "The goose hangs high" meant that he and his family were well and in good spirits, though he used the phrase when I knew a goose on the table would be very welcome. "My dear," even when addressed to a man, merely was an expression of friendship, not a term of endearment. (Some men use "sweetheart" in the same impersonal sense as if they had said "buddy.") "Chopping in tall cotton" was his way of saying that the going was rough. "It's a hard fight with a short stick" meant the odds were against him. "Like a hound dog caught sucking eggs" described a man who had been caught red-handed. "Yelled like a scalded pup" expressed desperate shrillness. "He will lie on credit when he could tell the truth for cash" was his description of a compulsive liar who enjoys fibbing. Once, when he was being examined before trial, he was asked whether he attributed blame for his plight to the defendants Aware Inc. and Hartnett, or to the defendant Laurence A. Johnson. His answer was, "You don't debate over whether you get bit by a rattlesnake or a copperhead." So I continued to be educated in piquant phrases.

Faulk was unfailingly courteous and genial in manner. Politeness was not a burdensome amenity but a natural and joyous habit.

All this created a considerable trial problem. I do not believe a plaintiff should ever be frivolous while testifying. Psychologically it tends to diminish his grievance. If he can jest about the matter there is less reason for the jury to pour out its sympathy for his plight. It is the defendant who profits when the atmosphere in the courtroom is lightened by laughter. The minimizing impression then is that "we can all smile. The plaintiff's claim has been exaggerated. Let us not lose our sense of humor over him."

Also we tend to associate solemnity with profundity and humor with irresponsibility. Candidates for political office have learned this rule of public reaction and hide their wit for private occasions. We associate the jokemaker with the jester. His cap and bells represent buffoonery and finally elicit derision.

Consequently, I insisted that Faulk, when he testified, avoid all the colorful Southern-fried aphorisms, and recite the facts in a straight-forward, serious manner. I feared that otherwise he might be mistaken for a mere comedian, intent on performing, and diverting attention from the great cause he was fighting. I probably erred in this advice. It is not easy for a man to change his style. He felt constricted. He caught himself making some colorful allusion in broadened Southern accents and hesitated, looking guiltily at me. Paradoxically his affectations had become natural to him (is this not one of the secrets of charm?) and when he had to avoid them, he felt pinched. Late in the evening when we prepared for the next day's session, the poor man, in perfect good humor, would give vent to hilarious imitations, and make keen observations in Josh Billings or Will Rogers style, teasing us that on the morrow he would be prosaically correct. If there were any in the courtroom who had been delighted by him on the air, they must have shared his disappointment at being as solemn as the circumstances required.

But his airy and amiable manner did not mean that Faulk wasn't a man of deep conviction and feeling. He saw himself as a man chosen by accident to fight for a great principle, and he was determined to do battle to a finish, irrespective of the consequences.

Originally it was contemplated that others who had been maligned in the *Bulletin*, would join with him in bringing suit. But when they decided not to litigate, Faulk quietly accepted the burden alone. Nor was that decision made of necessity by his personal plight, for in the beginning Faulk still held on to his radio work, and was not yet aware of the devastation which was to overtake him. But like all courageous and undaunted men, if he had to fight alone, he would. Surrender was not in him. We shall see repeated evidence of this quiet American grit at times when alternatives were available which were almost irresistible in the relief they offered.

Faulk's prior history was a record of scholarship and patriotism. His family represented the kind of American spirit which was the essence of conservatism. From it stemmed the initiative which in later years was called liberalism. His father, a devout Methodist, got into trouble when he fought bigots who stoned Catholics. John was reared in the tradition of activated idealism (whose Texas hero was Professor J. Frank Dobie, after whom he named his son).

He was educated at the University of Texas, where he received his B.A. and M.A. degrees. He continued his studies for a Doctor of Philosophy degree. While working on his thesis, he received an appointment as instructor in English at the university.

He had always been fascinated by American folklore. Negro preachers used to deliver their sermons in an imaginative, dramatic, and musical manner. Faulk roamed far to study this extraordinary form of Americana, for these sermons or homilies, filled with flights of poetic imagery and feeling, were fast becoming obsolete. He not only recorded these unique preachments but learned to recite them in all their beauty and musical intonation. This perhaps was his first, rather accidental initiation as an entertainer. He was called upon to perform in singsong, accent, and native diction Delilah's shearing of Samson's locks, or David's triumph against Goliath, who roared his defiance in Negro dialect. Faulk's research earned for him a Julius Rosenwald Fellowship. His achievements also came to the attention of Dr. Thaddeus Stevens of the Rockefeller Foundation, which granted him a fellowship. His recordings and collection of Negro sermons are now housed in the archives of the Library of Congress.

When the Japanese attacked Pearl Harbor, Faulk attempted immediately to enlist in the United States Army. He had a cast in his right eye, which made it blind, and he was rejected. Determined to do his duty, he succeeded in joining the Merchant Marine. He spent several months on board a tanker ferrying high-test airplane gasoline from New York to England. Nazi submarines and bombers took note of these journeys and saw to it that they were not unhazardous. A number of ships in Faulk's convoy were sunk. His own ship was damaged and laid up in port. Restlessly, he joined the American Red Cros. and accepted a position as Assistant Field Director in Egypt.

By 1944, the Army's standards for physical fitness had been reduced and Faulk again volunteered. This time he was accepted for limited service as a G.I. He received his basic training and was assigned to Camp Swift in Texas, as a psychiatric social worker. While there, he was invited to address a gathering of F.B.I. agents in Austin, Texas, and did so. Later his lecture work included appearances before the Daughters of the American Revolution, Yale, Harvard, and Fordham universities, and churches of all denominations. His chief subject was "The American Heritage."

Faulk was a Democrat and had always voted for his party. He was an intimate friend of Sam Rayburn, who knew him from childhood; of President Lyndon Johnson, long before he became Vice President; and other distinguished Texans.

None of this found its way into Aware's *Bulletin* or Hartnett's or Laurence A. Johnson's condemnatory letters about

Faulk. One would think that even zealots, who considered it their sacred duty to report on a stranger's loyalty to his country, could not overlook such a record. Would they have ignored it if Faulk had sought to evade Army service or, because of his blind eye, had busied himself with personal enrichment or aggrandizement? Aside from the issue raised by the claim of any self-appointed and self-anointed private group to take over the governmental tasks of the F.B.I. and other agencies, what shall be said of so unfair and unbalanced an "investigation" which insinuates evil while ignoring the contradictory facts? This points up realistically the wisdom of affording the accused the oportunity to confront his accuser and answer him. Otherwise, selective presentation, even if true, can be a distortion of the whole truth.

All in all, my impression of Faulk was of the highest. Indeed, if we had to create a plaintiff to test the false charge of communism, we could not have imagined a better one than this Texan, who derived his Southern drawl honestly from a lifetime spent in Austin (where one would have to import a Communist to find one), and who garnished his lively personableness with scholarly attainments.

The next question involved the nature of his case. Would it be merely a libel suit because he had been maligned? This would be comparatively simple. Or would it be a challenge and exposure of the black-listing technique which was said to permeate the entertainment industry, terrorizing not only artists, but the world's largest advertising agencies, national broadcasting networks, and leading American corporations, who were sponsors? Faulk saw the expanded issue and his eyes were ablaze with determination to do battle on the larger scale. He was ready to fight for the principle of ridding the entertainment world from compulsory obeisance to private vigilanteism; of protecting all artists in the future from obliteration of their careers because they would not bend a knee to some unknown tyrant, or who did not even have the opportunity to know the charge which had blotted out a lifetime of study and artistic ambition. Faulk felt that he had become the instrumentality to strike a decisive blow for these American principles. He was ready to bear any burden to wage war against the dark boycott. This was not lip service on his part. No man could have suffered more than he was compelled to do, but he never faltered, regretted, or bemoaned his fate or sacrifices.

On the contrary, in extraordinary good humor, and with quiet resolve, he insisted upon pressing the attack, even when we were so moved by his suffering and that of his wife and children, that we debated the alternative of retreat and reasonable compromise which opened up to him at one time. I shall supply the details of this incident at a more appropriate time in this recital.

We, too, warmed to the challenge against blacklisting, but had to warn Faulk that denials, or tight-lipped silence by participants were as inevitable as in an investigation of a racket, where the victims as well as the wrongdoers fear to speak.

The problem of hard proof was not the only obstacle. There would be a patriotic smoke screen thrown across our path, which would dim the true issues.

Finally, even if it were true, how could a jury be persuaded that a few men, acting privately, could capture the entire entertainment industry and compel it to adopt their un-American standards of secret accusation, secretly enforced?

This was the task undertaken. To understand how so few could seduce a powerful industry, a few explanations are essential, even in anticipation of the revelations at the trial.

Laurence A. Johnson had become famous in the broadcasting industry as "that grocer from Syracuse," who it was ominously hinted could drive any entertainer off the air. He owned a chain of six supermarkets, but he was also an official in the National Association of Supermarkets and boasted an indirect control of thousands of product outlets throughout the nation. He was a white-haired, kindly looking man in the seventies, who was convinced that Communists were infiltrating radio and television. He was dedicated, no doubt by sincere conviction, to the task of waging war against the corruption of pure American airwaves. He also was motivated by the acquisition of power, which his activities gave him, over famous artists, great advertising agencies, and the national networks. We shall see how he gloried in the life-and-death sentences he could pronounce against outstanding entertainers; how one of them flew to his citadel in Syracuse to plead for mercy; and how Johnson brought his prize to his supermarkets to present him for autographs to his customers.

In an industry so hypersensitive to criticism that a few

postcards, judiciously sent, could shake a sponsor or a network to its foundations, Johnson learned the value of prolific mailings. He also recognized the value of special letterheads, whose title and patriotic slogans would strike terror in the hearts of those who wanted "no trouble."

So he made an alliance with the local Syracuse American Legion Post, Number 41 of the Onondaga County American Legion, and through his intimate friend John K. Dungey, the Chairman of the Anti-Subversive Committee of that American Legion Post, induced the sending of letters on that imposing letterhead to recalcitrants who at first resisted his meddling. He also organized a committee of his supermarket employees with the high-sounding title of Veterans Action Committee of Syracuse Supermarkets. At his beckoning, a sponsor or network would receive a fiery protest against some actor, on a red, white, and blue letterhead, signed by Francis W. Neuser, Commander. Of course, few knew that Neuser was Johnson's fruit and vegetable buyer.

Johnson used other ingenious devices to enlarge his influence. He printed "ballots" which would give the patrons in his stores the opportunity to vote, as to whether they would buy the toothpaste, for example, of a company which "supports Stalin's little creatures," or the competitive product of an anti-Communist company. In some instances, a sponsor who would not remove an artist from the air (even after condemnation by Aware Inc, and Hartnett and letters from the Syracuse American Legion Post, and the Veterans Action Committee) would be advised by Johnson that he intended to let the public decide by fair vote, whether they would buy the product of those who aided the Communist conspiracy or the competitor's product. A sample ballot was enclosed. It was about as fairly worded as a ballot in a Russian election.

As if this were not enough, Laurence A. Johnson was indefatigable in his personal visits to advertising agencies, sponsors, networks, and as we shall see, even to the General Manager of the Metropolitan Opera House. His imposing age and presence, gracious personality and patriotic talk, combined with the threats of "barring the offender's product from the shelves" of hundreds of stores, or promoting protest and boycott by the American Legion (not the national organization for which, of course, he did not speak) and other patriotic organizations, called for more gumption on the part of the sponsor, or its advertising agency, or the network, itself, than any of them could muster. In a highly competitive, ulcer-producing business, dependent on wheedling approval from the listener, the antagonistic buzz of a fly sounds like a clap of thunder. What then of the enormous din Johnson could create? Whatever resistance there was in the beginning was quickly broken down. The safe way was to comply with Aware's warnings, with Hartnett's reports, and with Johnson's demands that Hartnett's findings be enforced. Loud pronouncements of patriotic objectives soothed the conscience of all involved, even though it was not easy to make a virtue out of a nasty un-American procedure, which by its nature was secret and conspiratorial.

Everyone denied there was a blacklist, but when an artist had been so attacked, his name would never be cleared by other advertising agencies, and he found himself mysteriously uninvited for any role. Even talent agents were flabbergasted by the dawning recognition, over a period of months, that their erstwhile star, who had been in universal demand, had "suddenly developed leprosy." He could not be "sold" for a dime. As insiders, they knew what had happened, but they rarely could trace it, and besides, discretion required that they do not ask too many questions, or they might fall out of favor too. So it came about that surrender was the rule of the day.

Like Archimedes, who proclaimed that if he had a long enough lever he could lift the world, Johnson, Hartnett, and Aware Inc. discovered that in the hypersensitive entertainment industry any protest constituted leverage out of all proportion to its source or validity, and that they could lift the entire industry and shake loose any artist who displeased them.

They succeeded in subduing broadcasting, the fifth-largest industry in the United States, to illegal boycott, in conspiratorial silence. Who would speak? Could we obtain competent proof of all this?

Johnson depended on others to inform him that a performer's "record" disqualified his appearance in public. He conceived it his duty to apply economic sanctions. So Aware and Hartnett found their alliance with Johnson highly useful. They accused, and their accusation was equivalent to a verdict. He was powerful in enforcing the judgment, privately pronounced.

Johnson's chief informant originally had been Harvey

Matusow, a former Communist, who was used repeatedly as a paid government witness to identify "comrades." After many deadly finger-pointings, which resulted in convictions, Matusow astonished the Department of Justice, Senate committees, and the public at large by confessing that he had often invented his testimony. Matusow's admission of perjury should not have been as startling as it was, for I have always believed that a man's acceptance of communism (provided it is not an uninformed, short-lived, youthful indiscretion) renders him unworthy of trust, even when he later becomes a professional anti-Communist. Communism, despite its pretended garb of economic idealism, is another form of the oldest tyranny in history, which subjugates the individual, forfeits his freedom, and deprives him of self-expression. Any man who could adopt such a credo has a defect of character which is not likely to be cured by disillusionment.

The government indicted Harvey Matusow for perjury. The informer was tried for the self-confessed lies which permeated his previous sworn testimony. Roy Cohn appeared as a witness against him, vigorously denying knowledge or encouragement of Matusow's perjurious infamy. The jury convicted Matusow. The United States Attorney, who prosecuted the case brilliantly, was Thomas A. Bolan. Later, Cohn and Bolan became partners in private law practice. Still later, they became lawyers for Aware Inc., Vincent Hartnett, and Johnson, and tried the case against Faulk. So the streams of human events run into each other, creating curious crosscurrents.

When Matusow was discredited by conviction and imprisonment, Johnson turned to Vincent Hartnett in his stead. Their collaboration involved Johnson's strong fist in enforcing Aware's and Hartnett's condemnation of Faulk.

Their tactics were shrewd and brutally direct. For example, Mr. Harris Perlstein, the President of Pabst Brewing Company, one of Faulk's sponsors, received a letter from the Onondaga County American Legion, which set forth the following patriotic observations:

"Dear Mr. Perlstein:

"These are indeed trying times not only in the field of international politics but also in the TV and radio field.

"For International Communism to succeed in bringing the rest of the world under the yoke of their conspiracy they must gain complete control of the airwaves. The Communists are working around the clock to accomplish this.

"They must also raise money to finance their operations. As an example four Communist Fronts in the entertainment field raised over a million dollars for the Communist cause.

"The American Legion for years has realized the efforts that Communists are exerting in the field of entertainment and has gone on record not to support programs that feature Communists or individuals who have supported Communist causes.

"Therefore, we respectfully call to your attention one of your salesmen, John Henry Faulk, whose program comes through WCBS Radio, New York City—5:05 to 6 P.M. Monday through Friday.

"We are enclosing data from publication Aware on a John Henry Faulk and would like to know if this is the same John Henry Faulk who has this WCBS program.

"We of the American Legion sincerely hope that you will look into this situation and will be waiting a reply since we want to have our facts straight as to the person in question and his sponsor. . . ."

> "Very truly yours,
> John K. Dungey, Chairman
> Anti-Subversive Committee
> Onondaga County American Legion
> 1842 Bellevue Avenue
> Syracuse, New York"

The letter carried the notation that copies of it had been sent to Mr. L. A. Johnson, Mr. Francis W. Neuser, Commander of a Post of Veterans of Foreign Wars, and Mr. Wayne Murphy, National Americanism Commission, American Legion, Indianapolis, Indiana.

When one examines closely the series of syllogisms by which Faulk is impaled as a traitor, the phrase "poison pen letter" is too benign a description for this document. The letter ascends the steps of logic one by one with such artful speed, that the deception is blurred and the final leap seems inevitably right. First there is the assertion that to conquer the world, the Communists must "gain complete control of the airwaves," and that they are "working around the clock" to accomplish this. This is either an indictment of the national networks as having been infiltrated by the enemy, or of artists who are filling programs with Communist propaganda. There is not an iota of truth in either assumption.

The next step proceeds from the first. "Over a million dollars" has been raised to finance the Communists by "four Communist Fronts in the entertainment field." No specification is offered. The succeeding step is subtle, sleight of hand. "The American Legion . . . has gone on record not to support programs that feature Communists or individuals who have supported Communist causes." Thus, the local Syracuse Post throws around its shoulders the cloak of the National American Legion, giving the letter a national stamp of a foremost patriotic organization.

Then follows a breathlessly agile leap to the word "Therefore." Suddenly, "Therefore" becomes the terrible connecting link which carries Faulk into the center of a seething international conspiracy by communism to seize the world. "*Therefore,* we respectfully call to your attention one of your salesmen, John Henry Faulk . . ."

The letter is accompanied by Aware's *Bulletin,* which sets forth the accusations against Faulk.

The dagger having been struck deep, the letter turns cute: "We . . . would like to know if this is the same John Henry Faulk who has this WCBS program." A reply is requested only "since we want to have our facts straight as to the person in question and *his sponsor.*" Even while genuflecting, a gun is flashed at the head of the sponsor. If he continues to employ Faulk, the American Legion (the distinction between the local post and the national organization has already been blurred to extinction) will have "our facts straight" about Pabst Brewing Company. It, too, will then be involved in the conspiracy of communism "in bringing the rest of the world under the yoke of their conspiracy."

Even the list of those to whom copies have been sent constitutes an insidious magnification of the attack.

The identical letter was sent to other sponsors of Faulk, who in five years of broadcasting had preached his favorite theme, The American Heritage, salted and spiced with patriotic homilies and "the glories of the U.S.A." He had never engaged in any political comment.

It was only much later that we learned of the hysterical scurrying around by sponsors and their denunciations of their hapless advertising agencies, for having gotten them into such a scrape with leading patriotic organizations, all on account of an entertainer who, innocent or not, certainly was not irreplaceable.

We based our libel charges on this letter as well as on the Aware *Bulletin*.

Johnson did not rely on the Post Office alone. He "carried the mail" himself. Word spread that he was "up and down Madison Avenue" visiting agencies and sponsors and demanding Faulk's scalp. Despite these tugs on the lever, sufficient to have shaken the foremost stars off the broadcasting world, Faulk hung on. The reason was that there were others who were applying levers in the opposite direction and maintaining a precarious balance for a while.

Who were they? One was Charles Collingwood, the new President of AFTRA. He would not stand still while Faulk was destroyed, because his slate had ousted the Aware group from power. As he later testified at the trial, he visited the President of WCBS Radio, Mr. Arthur Hull Hays, and made it clear that if Faulk were let out, the union would demand a full investigation of the circumstances, including the conduct of advertising agencies and sponsors. Although Collingwood was himself a valued performer on CBS, he could not, he said, permit blacklisting to destroy one of the officers of the union, who had been elected to eliminate it. This statement in the presence of WCBS counsel, Jules Brauner, meant that Faulk could not be disposed of quietly. A Maxim silencer is essential to a blacklisting gun, or it may attract the attention of too many curious citizens. The customary reward for surrender to blacklisting was "avoidance of trouble," and the achievement of "peace of mind" (if conscience was not too obstreperous). But if firing Faulk meant a public exposure of the circumstances, involving important advertising agencies and their clients, the price was too high.

Edward R. Murrow, the famous commentator who had once dared to X-ray Senator Joseph McCarthy on a television screen, also intervened on behalf of Faulk. Although he was a director of Columbia Broadcasting System, Inc., he was more interested in the Bill of Rights than in a bill of particulars of an employer's rights.

Perhaps these influential overtures were unnecessary. Mr. Hays declared that he, too, was opposed to blacklisting and that he considered the meddling of vigilantes presumptuous and un-American. He gave assurance that Faulk would not be discharged because of the pressures which had been exerted against him.

They discussed the need for an antidote to the poisons which were being spread, and decided that Faulk should sign an affidavit of history and of his anti-communism. He had previously signed two such affidavits; one when he joined CBS, as all its artists had; and the second when he became an officer of the union, as the law required. Nevertheless, to paraphrase one of the speakers at the AFTRA union debate, he beat his breast again in public, swearing that he was a loyal American. Sponsors and agencies, who made anxious inquiries, were given copies of his affidavit. Salesmen who sold "spots" on Faulk's program carried his affidavit with them as defensive persuasion.

So it came about that when Faulk instituted suit in June 1956, he was still broadcasting on WCBS Radio, as he had for five years, although all other appearances on television and special assignments fell away, as if Aware, Hartnett, and Johnson had pressed an electric button which shattered his expanded activity and income.

The complaint in the action was not limited to libel. It charged a conspiracy. It accused the defendants, Aware Inc., Vincent Hartnett, and Laurence A. Johnson with having struck at Faulk because he had participated in an effort to dislodge them from their perch of power. It was a legal declaration of war on the nefarious practices which pervaded the entertainment industry, and which it bluntly called a racket.

The key language was that the defendants conspired maliciously to defame and injure Faulk, to destroy his livelihood, to remove him as an officer of AFTRA by certain "racketeering practices."

The gantlet had been thrown down for a battle to a finish. The issue involved nothing less than the extermination of the entire machinery for reviewing an artist's record of loyalty. Whether it was called blacklisting or patriotic precaution, the validity of the precedure would be legally tested.

Most debates or arguments end inconclusively, because the issue is not clearly defined. There is confusion of terms and consequent confusion of argument. Relevant and irrelevant contentions bypass each other without the collision necessary to evaluate their force. One side addresses itself to tangential matter, believing it is the core of the dispute. The other refuses to engage in side issues, and is charged with default. Unless the matter to be decided is sharply focused, the eye strays, the tongue is futile, and the mind struggles for comprehension.

The law recognizes this. Its technique, for defining the issue to be tried, is to compel the plaintiff to set forth his claim with certain minimum requirements of clarity, and to compel the defendant to file his answer, admitting or denying each allegation of the complaint, and also setting forth any special defenses he may have. The complaint and answer are called the pleadings in a case, and when the time for trial arrives, the presiding judge reads these pleadings and knows the issue between the parties. So do they. He is then able to determine what evidence is relevant and what is not. The jury is instructed what precise questions of fact are to be determined. It is as if a fence were built around the area of dispute. Neither side will be permitted to wander off in other pastures. Demagoguery, passion, sympathy are out of bounds. The controversy, as defined in the pleadings, must be decided on the merits.

In a simple case, this method of refining the dispute to its essence, works like a charm. If A sues B for an unpaid loan, the complaint sets forth the date and amount of the loan, the promise to repay by a certain time, and the failure to do so despite demand. The answer may either deny the making of the loan or, admitting it, allege repayment. The pleadings have narrowed the issue to be tried with specificity.

But in a complicated case, particularly where complete or partial defenses, as they are called, may be interposed, the effort to pinpoint the issues is extremely difficult.

The law, therefore, permits either side, long before trial, to question the validity of the pleadings, seeking to strike out a defense as non-existent in law, or as inadequately stated, or to dismiss the complaint because it does not set forth a legal grievance. These preliminary contests are called motions. Sometimes the litigants are not content with the judge's decision of these motions, and appeal to the Appellate Division (consisting of five judges in New York State, and varying numbers in other states). Sometimes even the appellate court's decision does not quench the loser's confidence in his position, and he appeals to the highest court in the State (the Court of Appeals, consisting of seven judges in New York, and in other states, different numbers of judges). All this, just on the pleadings, and before the case has even come to trial, or a word of testimony taken. Yet it is not technical hocus-pocus, as an uninformed layman may conclude. This is the law's way of clearing away the confusing underbrush which encumbers disputes. It is the struggle, essential to justice, to define the issues; to clarify the legal limits of the contest; to limit the admission of evidence to that which is relevant to the controversy; to exclude testimony which is inflammatory, and not material to the real question before the court. In short, it is fallible man's effort, based on centuries of experience, to provide as well as he can, pure justice unadulterated by confusion and prejudice.

The pleadings in a libel suit are unusually complicated. The plaintiff is permitted to spell out the libel by "innuendo." This means that even though the words used may not in themselves be libelous, the fair meaning which a reader would derive from them in their context is libelous. So, for example, the Aware *Bulletin* conceded that most of the middler candidates were anti-Communist. However, it went on to ask, "But how about Faulk himself? What is his public record?" These words are not in themselves defamatory, but we pleaded the innuendo, that they meant Faulk was a Communist or a pro-Communist and fellow traveler. The defendants had the right to deny the innuendo. They could plead that the meaning given to the words by the plaintiff was imaginary or strained. This would raise an issue for determination.

Even more complicated are the defenses available in a libel suit. Aware, Hartnett, and Johnson pleaded a complete assortment of them. We considered them invalid and confusing. The question arose whether we should move to strike them from the answer or sit by until the trial and argue their invalidity at that time. If we waited, the chances of a trial judge eliminating a defense were not bright. The judge might well ask why we had not tested the legal question at an earlier time, when an appeal could be taken by the losing party, and a final decision obtained which would become "the law of the case" binding on the trial judge. Also, if the issues were delimited in advance, then Faulk would not be harassed on his examination before trial with irrelevant questions. Otherwise, the tendency of the court on an examination before trial is to permit liberal questioning, so long as the pleadings stand in their broad state. These were the reasons in favor of addressing motions to the answer.

On the other hand, if we made such motions, there would be great delays. The legal reasons why we considered the defenses invalid would invite contrary contentions. There would be oral arguments, extensive briefs, time for the judge to write his opinion, and thereafter possible appeals. While we were thus considering the most advisable course, a totally unexpected event occurred which made up our minds for us. We were shocked by a decision in another case which came down from the New York Court of Appeals, and which seemed on the surface to destroy the basis for Faulk's suit. It was the case of Julian *v.* American Business Consultants, Inc. The blow fell on July 11, 1956, only five days after Hartnett and Aware had filed their answer in the Faulk case. Before we could even begin our struggle for vindication, there fell into the laps of the defendants a decision which they could effectively argue put Faulk out of court.

A radio actor, Joe Julian, had sued the publishers of *Red Channels* for libel because it listed him in its pages, thereby, he claimed, creating the false inference that he was either a Communist, fellow traveler, or a dupe of the "Reds," and preventing him from obtaining employment. Only two items were printed under Julian's name: that he had attended a meeting of the National Council of Arts, Sciences and Professions, and another meeting at the Hotel Commodore to abolish the House Un-American Activities Committee. Unlike Faulk, who denied being at the functions which he was charged with attending, Julian admitted that the listings of him were true, and even that the organizations involved turned out to be Communist Fronts, but asserted that he had always been anti-Communist. *Red Channels* contended that it had not accused him of being a Communist or dupe, but merely stated his record. It argued that the importance of the issue involving the Communists' attempt to infiltrate radio and television justified it in listing even those who were unwittingly aiding the enemy.

The case came to trial in the New York State Supreme Court, and at the end of the plaintiff's evidence, Judge Irving

H. Saypol would not permit the case to be submitted to a jury. He dismissed the complaint as a matter of law. The Appellate Division (five judges) unanimously affirmed. The case then went to the Court of Appeals, the highest court of New York State. That court by a 5 to 2 vote upheld the decision. The majority opinion pointed out that Julian, despite the listing, had continued to receive employment from the major networks. Even though his income declined, he had no right to silence criticism on a matter of keen public interest:

"Those who demand the right of free speech . . . should not seek to deny the same right to their critics . . . Public debate should be encouraged, not stifled."

A dissenting opinion was written by Judge Stanley H. Fuld and concurred in by the present Chief Judge Charles S. Desmond, which referred to the testimony of a producer for the Columbia Broadcasting System that there was a "widespread" custom in the radio and television industry not to hire anyone listed in *Red Channels:*

"We quarantine everybody in the book. We cannot take any chances."

The minority opinion pointed out that if *Red Channels* is considered as a whole, from the drawing on its cover, showing a lurid red hand smothering a microphone, to its preachments about the danger of Communist infiltration, the general impression would be given to any reader that everyone listed was a violator of American principles. The disclaimer in the opening section of the book, that many patriotic entertainers are misled, did not save it from the vice of evil implication: "A publisher may not brand his victim with suspicion and then avoid liability by attempting to foist upon the reader the burden and responsibility of ascertaining whether or not there is anything to the charge."

At least, concluded the minority, all this presented questions of fact which a jury should have decided. The case should not have been thrown out by the judge.

Although the dissenting judges of this great court (of which Mr. Justice Benjamin Cardozo had once been Chief Judge) argued their point of view cogently, the fact remained that eleven judges who had passed on the Julian case (one trial judge, five Appellate Division and five Court of Appeals judges) disagreed with the two dissenters.

Whenever a court of last resort, such as the United States Supreme Court, writes a lengthy, reasoned minority decision, the pain of the losing litigant is greatly assuaged. The fact that great minds can differ on philosophical approaches to law (Chief Justice Charles Evans Hughes once said he "never expected the Court to rise to the icy stratosphere of certainty") gives comfort to the defeated, because at least his position was found to be respectable. More than this, in view of the history of the Court of Appeals in which minority doctrines have on many occasions later become the majority view, the wound of defeat may be borne with a martyr's fortitude. Even bitter rejection can be sweetened by anticipation that in the future, the victim will be seen to have been right. It is human nature to persist in such a hope, because even if it is a delusion, its pursuit protects one's ego and pride. "Someday, you'll see . . ." is the prophecy of the loser which enables him to retreat from the scene of despair with flags flying triumphantly.

In any event, we were confronted by an enormous road-block at the very inception of our journey.

We seem to live in a sea in which the actions of others, unknown to us and no matter how remote, affect the waves which move us. If during Hitler's beer hall *putsch*, he had fallen to the sidewalk a little more slowly and the bullets which flew over him had struck him, how many millions of people now dead would still be alive? If a Secret Service agent had made a "routine" check of a storage building in the line of President Kennedy's ride in Dallas and found Oswald waiting in a room with a gun, how would the future of the United States and the world have been affected? It is impossible to fathom the endless alternatives of other historical events, but we know that our lives are a constant accommodation to forces which we did not set in motion. However, this does not mean that we are not masters of our own destiny.

Allowing for the turbulent or benign tides which are part of life, we master ourselves to the extent that we adjust to them. This appears to be the rule of nature, the challenge to overcome our environment and ourselves. In the process of our development, in the ascent from animalism to reason, we also get a glimpse of a higher purpose, which though mysterious, is the essence of religious conviction.

The law, which mirrors man's struggle to bring rational

order into life, illustrates in its way the effect of external events on our hopes for justice.

Recognizing that a rule established in one conflict may vitally affect other litigants, who had no opportunity to present their arguments, the law permits them to intervene. A lawyer may apply to a court to be permitted to appear *amicus curiae*, as "friend of the court," to argue in a case in which his client is not directly involved. Since, however, he has a keen interest in the principle about to be established, the courts will often hear him and permit him to file briefs. The phrase *amicus curiae* is not without humor. Theoretically, the lawyer wishes to aid the court, as its friend, to come to a correct decision. Actually, all parties are aware of his proper concern for his client's interest. Many an expression has been diverted from its true purpose by a touch of elegant phrasing. Whenever a lawyer rises to address the court, it is traditional for him to begin, "May it please the court." Actually, what he means is, "May it persuade the court."

Certain it was that we could not permit the Julian case to hover over our heads, casting a shadow of uncertainty. To await trial and then be confronted with the possibility that the decision in the Julian case precluded us from relief, involved a nerve-wracking ordeal. In addition, there were years of preparation and examinations before trial ahead of us. Were we to go through all the painful preliminaries without a clear end in view? We were confident that the Julian case was distinguishable from ours and, therefore, not applicable.

This is the interpretive aspect of law: the philosophical approach which gives values to differences of fact. If they are substantial enough the court will recognize the inapplicability of a rule made in a dissimilar situation. If, however, as lawyers say, there is only a distinction without a difference, the rule will be binding, for we know that rarely are two cases precisely parallel in fact.

We were determined to point out the difference with a distinction immediately. We would learn in advance what our fate was, and by testing the decision through appeal, if necessary, present the trial judge with a binding decision of the highest authority.

So we addressed a series of motions to the defendants' pleading, seeking to strike out various defenses they had set up. We knew the counterattack would be based on the

Julian case, to dismiss our complaint because we had not even stated a cause of action, or at least that the defenses were valid and precluded recovery.

This involved us in a struggle preliminary to the trial of two years—precious years they were. Some recital of these events is necessary in order that there be a fuller understanding of the trial itself. The young man who dreams of being a trial lawyer, declaiming heroically before a jury, usually ignores the equally exciting intellectual endeavors which precede the trial. It is through the tunnel of legalisms that one emerges into the fierce dramatic light in the courtroom.

Also, the layman will acquire a higher regard for the law when he understands that its so-called technical procedures are matters of substance, and philosophical substance at that. The process of justice is not a roll of thunder. It is the painful, meticulous placing of brick by brick, with the ideal of the final, shining structure always in mind.

So perhaps it will not be unrewarding to review the motions which contributed to that final edifice. First we moved to dismiss the defense of truth. When the defendants justify their publication on the ground that it is true, they must specify the facts which they will prove. They cannot rely on a generality that the claimed libel is the truth, because this would be merely a repetition of the libel. They must commit themselves with sufficient detail, so the plaintiff will not be surprised at the trial. The Aware *Bulletin* and the letter to sponsors were lengthy documents. What precisely did the defendants claim was true in these documents, and what facts did they assert to support that truth? None. Furthermore, a general plea of truth might mean merely that the *Daily Worker* contained the item saying Faulk entertained at a certain function, but the real question was not whether that newspaper so wrote, but whether he did so. Did the defendants dare to set forth the fact of his attendance? If he was not there, the *Bulletin* was still defamatory, even if the defendants repeated a falsehood from a newspaper. In short, the defense of truth must be coextensive with the libel, and set forth the truth with particulars.

Finally, the defendants had garnished this defense with assertions of patriotic motives. These were totally beside the point. There are other partial defenses which the law permits to plead lack of evil motive. In a plea of truth, the sole question is whether the publication was in fact true, not the innocence which motivated the error.

State Supreme Court Justice Saul S. Streit, before whom these motions were argued by Godfrey Schmidt and myself, struck out the defense of truth as inadequately pleaded. In his opinion, he wrote:

"The defense contents itself with the conclusory and omnibus assertion that all of the statements of fact contained in said article are true. No attempt is made to state affirmatively the particular facts claimed to be true."

We also moved to strike out the defense of "fair comment." What is such a defense? The law of libel impinges on the concept of free speech. As Justice Oliver Wendell Holmes once expressed it, "The right of free speech does not give one the right to yell 'fire' in a crowded theatre." So, too, free speech does not give one the right to call another man a thief or a Communist. Although we circumscribe the absolute right of free speech in various ways, we are zealous to prevent undue restrictions upon it. The defense of "fair comment" preserves the right to criticize reasonably. So the law balances our social objectives. On one hand it is concerned that reputation shall not be destroyed, for it is as precious in the human scale as life and limb. On the other hand, it does not wish the privilege of free speech to be unduly hampered. It is with such niceties that the rule of fair comment has been fashioned. A person accused of libel is immune if the defense of "fair comment" can be established by him. To do so, the law requires first that the comment asserted is based on facts truly stated; second, that corrupt or dishonorable motives are not ascribed to the person criticized, unless they are warranted by facts truly stated; and third, that the comment is the honest expression of the writer's real opinion. In short, the true facts must be stated and the comment, based upon them, must be fair.

Judge Streit held that the plea of fair comment failed to meet any of these requirements. He granted our motion to strike.

The defendants had also pleaded that the issue of communism was a proper matter for public concern, and that the right of free speech entitled them to criticize Faulk as an entertainer and union official. Therefore they concluded they were immune from suit. This defense they called "qualified privilege." They embellished it with incontestable allegations about the evils of communism and the need to protect our institutions. The defendants waved the flag, and while it is glorious, and we were as eager to salute it as anyone else, the question was whether all this was relevant to the real issue in the case.

We moved to strike this defense because "qualified privilege" did not apply to the facts of our case. That defense is available only in special circumstances where there is a certain kind of private relationship between the parties. For example, if a prior employer is asked by a prospective employer to give his opinion about a job applicant and he libels him, he may not be sued, provided he did not act maliciously. Qualified privilege also protects a credit agency which answers a proper inquiry. Even if its report is mistaken, if the error was not maliciously made, no liability will attach. It protects a bank which advises another bank (non-maliciously) that the depositor does not warrant a loan. The reason for these exceptions to the ordinary rule of libel is that the law considers it desirable that such services should be rendered provided they are private and not tainted with malice. The social good outweighs the risk to the individual. It is another illustration of the law's endeavor to balance the public interest against private right. But we argued that the extraordinary shield of "qualified privilege" could not be so extended to the Faulk situation. Here there was no private communication. The Aware *Bulletin* was widely distributed to public media. Also there was no special relationship between Aware or Hartnett with Faulk. Mere public interest does not wipe out the law of libel.

To say that patriotism and free speech permitted Aware or Hartnett to libel an entertainer (even if it was not malicious, which it was), would be an outrageous doctrine. It would mean, for example, that because narcotics traffic is a publicly recognized evil, one had the right under the doctrine of free speech to accuse an innocent man of being a drug peddler and then plead "qualified privilege."

Judge Streit struck out this defense as well. He pointed out that the defense of fair comment sufficiently protects a defendant who has written about a matter of public interest.

Now came the crucial test. The defendants, as anticipated,

asked the court to throw our case out of court. Their brief argued:

"The defendants rely on the Julian case . . . in challenging the insufficiency of the complaint here."

They pointed out that the Aware *Bulletin* explicitly stated: "*Middlers not Communist.*"

"Aware does not suggest that the 'middle-of-the-road' slate was a Communist slate. It was not."

They, therefore, insisted that the rest of the *Bulletin* could not be distorted by innuendo to be an accusation that Faulk was a Communist.

They hailed the Julian case as a legal landmark which proclaimed their full right to comment upon and criticize an entertainer's character. They denied that they had committed any libel, particularly in the light of the public interest involved in cleansing broadcasting from even innocent dupes of the Reds.

We pointed out the distinctions between the Julian case and the Faulk case. We had come to grips with the problem. We would know whether our suit had died aborning. The court's decision came in a lengthy, finely reasoned opinion.

It has been held by our highest courts that a false charge that a man is a Communist is libelous. "It is of little moment whether the statement describes plaintiff as a communist or as one having communistic sympathies and affiliations for [as Judge Learned Hand had said in a previous case] 'any difference is in degree only.'"

Judge Streit held that the enumeration of Faulk's alleged activities was designed to picture him as a Communist or one associated with Communists.

Then he addressed himself to the Julian case, where there was no accusation of either communism or pro-Communist sympathies. In the Faulk case, Aware's *Bulletin* "is directed against plaintiff, by name, as one whose record of participation in Communist Front functions and affairs is such as to discredit his statement that he is opposed to Communism.

"The court accordingly holds that a good cause of action in libel is stated."

The defendants appealed this decision to the Appellate Division. The complex issues were argued out in printed briefs which represented the most scholarly research of the law which the opposing sides could muster. In addition, Godfrey Schmidt and I addressed oral arguments to the court, which augmented the briefs and also permitted the five judges to fire questions at us. These exchanges were lively. In the friction of discussion, there are often sparks which illuminate the subject matter. After the oral argument, the court retired to reflect upon the printed arguments laden with cold precedents, and the oral arguments, lit by the passions of advocacy. Later it rendered its decision.

The court unanimously affirmed Judge Streit on all counts. It upheld our complaint as stating a cause of action, and it agreed that the various defenses had been properly stricken from the answer.

One would have thought that this long and arduous legal struggle had established our right to sue and to limit the controversy to the real issues. But we didn't count on the persistence of our adversaries.

As is customary when defenses are stricken out, the court granted the defendants twenty days to plead over again. For if a properly stated defense is available, justice requires that the defendants be not deprived of it, even though their earlier pleading was invalid. While the law demands that the issues be confined to relevance, it does not wish to forfeit any litigant's rights. The objective is not punishment but propriety.

So Aware and Hartnett filed amended answers. But lo and behold these were even more offensive than those stricken out. As if in defiance of the court's rulings, and to demonstrate that our curbing efforts could not succeed, they did not narrow the issues as directed. Rather they expanded on the terrors of communism, their own patriotic objectives, "historical" analysis of the Russian Revolution, and for good measure added several new defenses, called "Provocation" and "The Right to Reply." When we got through reading the new answers, we felt we were more deeply in the mire of confusion and demagoguery than we had been before our "victory."

Writings sometimes evoke a summary image. Despite the formalistic language in these legal documents, I could almost see a picture of the defendants laughing and thumbing their noses at us derisively.

Resignation, induced by exhaustion, is not an escape available to a litigant any more than to a combatant in any other war. We moved again to strike out the defenses and filed a brief of more than eighty pages. The matter came up before Supreme Court Judge Walter A. Lynch, and once again we had oral argument.

One paragraph in the answer boasted that the defendants' findings of subversive activities "coincided with those of Congress, the Supreme Court and the President" and even cited Executive Orders and the A.F.L.-C.I.O. constitution. It concluded that communism constituted a menace and that the defendants therefore "engaged in efforts at exposing the activities" of those who spread Communist ideology. But in another paragraph of Johnson's answer he alleged that he "at no time charged plaintiff with being a communist or communist sympathizer."

Then what was the relevance of the lecture on the evil of communism in a case where the defendants asserted that Faulk was not pro-Communist?

Judge Lynch rarely lost his good-natured smile, as if he were amused by the verbal dialectics of attorneys appearing before him. But his benign manner, which was made more fatherly by his kindly Irish face topped by gray hair, was somewhat deceptive. It sheathed a sharp, appraising mind, and even sharper questions despite the soft tone. He selected paragraphs from the answer which recited at length the advent of Lenin in March 1919 and the history of communism in the United States, and asked our adversary whether he considered evidence on this subject matter would be admissible at the trial. If so, for what purpose?

He indicated that the amended answers filed by the defendants were evasions of the ruling made by the Appellate Division. When the argument was concluded, we had good reason to believe that Judge Lynch would write an opinion striking the new defenses and insisting upon compliance with the previous decision.

A month went by. Then came the startling news that Judge Lynch had suddenly died from a heart attack. We had to make the motion all over again. This time it came up before Judge Jacob Markowitz.

After study of the voluminous briefs, he handed down a written opinion. The defense of truth, he pointed out, required only such allegations of fact as would permit a jury to find that Faulk was interested in furthering the cause of communism and associated with organizations espousing that cause:

"Instead of limiting itself to pleading such facts . . . the defense comprising 70 paragraphs covering 28 pages is devoted . . . to wholly immaterial and irrelevant matters . . ."

The judge reviewed the scope of these excursions, including the "Report on Blacklisting" by the Ford Fund for the Republic Inc., critical appraisals of that report in Congress and elsewhere and the history of communism in Russia and then in the United States.

All this, wrote the judge, can only serve to confuse the issue, and if permitted to remain in the answer "would allow the admission of evidence in their support which could inflame and prejudice as well as mislead the jury . . . ." He struck out the answer of truth or justification as improperly pleaded.

He also struck out the defense of fair comment on the same ground that Judge Streit had previously asserted and the five judges of the Appellate Division had affirmed.

The plea of "qualified privilege," despite the face-lifting which had been given it, was as defective as previously and was stricken from the answer.

The court then addressed itself to the newly pleaded defense that the defendants Aware Inc. and Hartnett had the "right of reply" to the attack by the middlers, including Faulk, upon their practices of blacklisting.

The law recognizes such a defense, but only if the reply is limited in scope to the plaintiff's attack. It may not go beyond that to libel the plaintiff with respect to other matters. So, for example, if a political candidate is attacked as being dishonest, he may reply that the accuser is a liar, but he may not, under the guise of reply, falsely accuse him of being an adulterer or an embezzler and be immune from a libel suit. The defamation in the reply must not be disproportionate to the original charge. The court held that the middlers' attack on blacklisting did not warrant the false accusation that Faulk was pro-Communist. If, indeed, he was, then the defense of truth would sufficiently protect the defendants, but the defense of reply was stricken.

Finally, Judge Markowitz dealt with the defense of provocation. This is a partial defense only. If a defendant has been attacked, and in the heat of passion defames his assailant, the jury may consider these circumstances in assessing damages. But the two requirements for this defense were absent in the Faulk case; there was no provocative attack by Faulk, and the retort was not in the heat of passion. It was deliberately planned more than a month after the election. There was no outburst before temper had a chance to cool. The court struck out this defense too.

The defendants had finally been subdued in the struggle on the pleadings.

Faulk's right to sue, despite the Julian case, had become "the law of the case." In addition, the defenses had been pared down, so that the defendants would be barred at the trial from shooting patriotic fireworks, the smoke of which might blind the jury to the real issues in the case. We had lost almost two years in this effort to clear away the obstructions to a fair trial. The sacrifice of time was not too great, so long as Faulk continued to be employed on CBS Radio and earned a living. But after the Appellate Division had struck down the false shields of the defendants, they finally succeeded in destroying Faulk's only remaining source of income. Faulk's two protectors had disappeared from the scene. Collingwood was no longer President of AFTRA, and Edward R. Murrow had terminated his official relationship with CBS.

Faulk was fired. This economic blow, like everything else in this case, came in an extraordinary manner. It made our legal progress seem quite hollow.

In June 1957, Faulk's superior at WCBS, Sam Slate, told him that the network might appropriate part of his time slot for the Ford Motor Company starring Arthur Godfrey. However, in view of Faulk's six-year successful relationship with the station, he was assured of either the remaining one-half hour, or a new one-hour slot of time which would be carved out for him. In the meantime, he deserved the vacation which he was about to take on the island of Jamaica. They bade him affectionate farewell as he left for his holiday.

While Faulk and his family were deriving pleasure from their idyllic repose in the sun, which contrasted with the turbulence of New York City and the tensions of broadcasting, CBS notified Faulk's agent, Gerald Dickler, that his client's employment was terminated. Dickler had the unpleasant task of requesting Faulk's immediate return, not as he might have thought, because of the pressure of work, but to face the bleak fact that holiday expenses and unemployment were incompatible.

What happened when Faulk faced the CBS executives will be revealed hereafter when they testified and were cross-examined. While stunned by the peculiar timing and suddenness of his discharge, Faulk was not bitter. Being naturally buoyant and optimistic, he was confident that all was for the best. He had received many attractive offers through the years, which out of loyalty to CBS he had declined. He was loath to believe that his established talents would not be snapped up.

I watched with growing dismay the effects upon him, as door after door closed to him. The tragic process was heightened by several enthusiastic offers he continued to receive, and the inevitable mysterious cooling off, accompanied by lame excuses. One could see his increased effort to keep his spirits as the pattern of total unemployability became clearer each day. He was finally reduced to asking for a ten-dollar-a-day stand-in job (to pose under the lights while the star rested), but even this was unavailable.

His struggle to earn a dollar became more gruesome each day, and his inability to do so created not only economic distress, but a burden on his spirit which was enough to break a man's mind as well as his heart.

We met regularly with Faulk and his theatrical agents, but the news was as black as blacklisting. Our fevers rose as fantastic evidence fell into our hands, such as a letter from a prospective employer to the New York outlet of its broadcasting network, which was mistakenly addressed to Faulk. But the realities of long unemployment pressed itself upon us. How would Faulk sustain his wife and four children? How long could he borrow from friends?

Now that the issues had been joined in the pleadings, examinations before trial of each side were arranged. We had the right to question under oath Vincent Hartnett, Aware Inc. through a director, Paul Milton, and Laurence A. Johnson. We did so. The defendants then had the right, which they exercised, of examining John Henry Faulk before trial. Such examinations are intended to afford both sides an opportunity to review the evidence so that they will not be surprised at the trial. They prevent judicial procedure from becoming a game of chance.

Examinations are considered part of the legal process and are held in the courthouse, However, no judge presides, because it is desirable to save his time for actual trial work. If a dispute arises about the propriety of a question, it may be referred to a judge for a ruling. Usually these questions are accumulated, so as to save the attorney a continuous journey to the judge's chambers.

In view of the absence of a judge, it has become customary for the lawyers to arrange examinations in the examining lawyer's offices, thus substituting convenient quarters for the somewhat drab examination rooms set aside in the courthouse.

So it was that I met Vincent Hartnett for the first time in my office when he arrived with his attorney for examination before trial. Faulk was present simply as an observer, and peculiarly enough this was the first time he and Hartnett had met.

The man who was principally responsible for Faulk's plight, and Faulk, who was now determined to destroy Hartnett's influence, had never seen each other. It was a curious inversion of a personal struggle with impersonal overtones. It emphasized that principles rather than personalities were the center of the dispute. All this changed, of course, during the clashes at the trial, when both were subjected to intense cross-examination.

The only reason that I was not completely surprised by Vincent Hartnett's appearance was that I had learned how rare it was for the image we form of a man from his reputation, to accord with reality. Also, mystery acts like a magnifying glass enlarging a man's stature. The unknown is not only fearsome, it tends to create glamor around what in fact may be commonplace. I suppose that is because imagination fulfills our inner wishes, and these are inclined toward romanticizing power.

So here was the arch villain of the piece (according to our view), and he couldn't have been cast worse. He was a frail, timid little man of about forty years of age, no more than 130 pounds in weight and less than average height. His dark eyes looked frightened, and his voice was thin and hesitant. He had an almost lipless mouth, which gave an outward curve to his cheeks. How fortunate he was to have kept out of sight and permitted his awesome work to strike terror into the hearts of those whose obedience he needed. I sometimes think that the most valuable by-product of a lawsuit against the tyrants of the day is that it flushes them out of their private haunts and subjects them to public scrutiny. The shrinking process is quite prophylactic.

After Hartnett was sworn in by the official stenographer, I began the examination which was to probe into the source or, as it turned out, lack of source for his accusations in the Aware *Bulletin*, and also how he generally operated his business of researching the political records of artists. The sessions were lengthy and were adjourned for brief periods to suit the convenience of the witness and the lawyers. In order to accelerate the procedure when I was otherwise engaged, my law partner Paul Martinson conducted many of the examinations of the witnesses.

One day when I was examining Hartnett, a startling development occurred. It virtually ended the lawsuit by confession, apology, and penitent reparation. In view of the bitterness which had previously marked these examinations, the incident was totally unexpected.

It was preceded by a series of questions concerning the charge that "According to the *Daily Worker* . . . 'Jack Faulk' was to appear at Club 65, . . . a favorite site of pro-Communist affairs." Hartnett had conceded that he never checked with any of the entertainers, who appeared at this function, whether John Henry Faulk had been present, even though their names were listed in the *Daily Worker* announcement; that he had never heard John Henry Faulk referred to as "Jack Faulk"; that he had not checked to determine whether there wasn't a Negro entertainer by the name of Jack Faulk who had attended this completely Negro show, and so forth through a deeply searching series of inquiries. Grudgingly he began to concede that he might have been in error. Also in the course of being hammered about the exclusion from the air of those who innocently might have lent their names to one or two fine-sounding organizations which were later condemned as Communist Fronts, he almost ruefully declared that he might have been too severe in his judgment in such cases, and that he now held a more tolerant view.

It was not merely the admissions wrung from him which

impressed me. These, of course, were valuable and would be stored away for cross-examination at the trial. What came through was a weakened resistance, and lesser determination to defy and to justify. Perhaps it was conscience shining through, or a pragmatic desire to escape from the lawsuit. But the answers created a new vibration in the air, different from those we had been accustomed to for many weeks.

The stenographic record of the hearing will best describe the psychological road which we traveled and the unpredictable destination to which it led:

> Q. You said a few moments ago, Mr. Hartnett, that at one time you were a crusader and you had an intolerant attitude on some of these subjects, but as time went on you grew to be more tolerant. You recall the substance of that testimony? That is correct?
>
> A. Yes.
>
> Q. You also said that because a man innocently had joined some Communist-Front movement . . . you wouldn't want to see him barred from . . . employment, because of that? You remember that?
>
> A. Yes.
>
> Q. . . . You know that for many, many years Faulk was on commercial paid television programs? You knew that?
>
> A. Yes, sir.
>
> Q. And you know that he has been off that since this litigation has been pending?
>
> A. Yes.
>
> Q. And you have heard, at least, I don't mean that you know of your own personal knowledge . . . that he has been out of employment ever since this controversy has begun, and at least in the last number of months—
>
> MR. SCHMIDT: I submit that is not a proper question. I don't care what he heard. That is not the same as proof.
>
> MR. NIZER: Don't you know that to be a fact in a general way? I don't mean of personal investigation, you know that.
>
> MR. HARTNETT: Yes, I do.
>
> Q. You have already told us that at the time that you published Aware *Bulletin* (Exhibit A) . . . that you had no information concerning Faulk being either a Com-

munist or a pro-Communist sympathizer at all, isn't that so?

A. Yes.

Q. You also told us this morning that in view of certain questions which have been put and certain exhibits referred to . . . we have gone over only one of the charges . . . namely appearing at Club 65—you now say you have serious doubts about that being so in view of the questioning?

A. I don't know. Yes, the questioning does arouse a doubt.

Q. Have you taken any steps to issue any public statement, or statement to the television networks that used to employ or to the agencies who could give him employment, to say that "There was one charge, . . . at least one, which I now have some doubts about. I would like to have that checked further before you feel that this is correct?" Have you done anything like that to make amends or correct anything?

A. No, sir.

The next question was blocked by counsel's objection.

MR. SCHMIDT: . . . do you want to reframe the question?

MR. NIZER: I will reframe it.

Q. As I understand your position, even those things which are asserted in the Aware *Bulletin* (Exhibit A) . . . you didn't charge they were intentional pro-Communist action?

A. No, sir.

Q. . . . You have testified that if a man joined the Communist-Front associations, but unwittingly . . . it is not fair under your more tolerant view that you have developed in more recent years . . . for him to lose his employment. . . . Is that the substance of your testimony?

A. Yes, sir.

Q. I ask you, in view of the fact . . . that you don't charge even now that it was an intentional . . . joining of these alleged associations, whether you don't think that [his] being unemployed would be an injustice if it was due to that?

A. Yes, I think it would be.

Q. Would you be willing then, to correct that injustice?

A. Yes, sir.

MR. SCHMIDT: Wait a moment.

THE WITNESS: I don't mind answering it.

MR. SCHMIDT: The question was if it was due to that, and this is the big question, so far as I am concerned. . . . I want to know whether it applies to the second question.

MR. NIZER: Yes, it does.

THE WITNESS: Certainly. I felt sorry for him.

Q. And you still do?

A. Yes.

Q. Would you be willing even now to issue a public statement . . . which would go to television companies and to agencies that could give him employment, that "If this is the basis for your not giving him employment, I want you to know that . . . we are sorry, and he is clear as far as we are concerned?"

A. I think if that is his position, it should be publicized.

Q. You would be willing to lend your name to it?

A. Yes, I would.

Q. I am assuming that your counsel's silence means consent, and I am going to ask you, therefore, whether you will be good enough to prepare the kind of statement that you think would be fair and submit it to your counsel, so that both of you can tell me at the next session that you are ready to publish that. Are you ready to do that?

A. Yes, I would like to sit down with Mr. Schmidt, if I could.

MR. SCHMIDT: There is one reservation that I have, and I don't want my silence to be considered on that. I myself, don't believe that he lost his job because of the publication. Maybe you could prove that to me, but as of now I don't believe it.

MR. NIZER: It is not a question of belief, it is a matter of fact.

MR. SCHMIDT: All right, that is right.

MR. NIZER: It is not a typographical error.

MR. SCHMIDT: Then it should be easily demonstrated, and I have not seen any of the facts that demonstrate it. Therefore it is *post hoc ergo propter hoc.*

THE WITNESS: I think it is all unfortunate. As I knew from certain information, the Communists were not on Faulk's slate. I have enough experience now to know that. I think it is unfortunate that they blasted us to hell with all the stuff in the press, and we retorted, I think not too angrily on it, but it was one of these unfortunate things. I think it has taught us all a lesson that we had best try to get together.

MR. NIZER: This suit has now been pending about two years. It has been through the courts on motions, up on appeal. Have you ever considered as a defendant who has made this kind of a statement, issuing some kind of public statement expressing the feelings that you now have, that a mistake was made unfortunately, due to the heat, apparently, if I understand you correctly—I am trying to restate it fairly in substance—and that therefore you want to make amends and correct the error? Have you ever considered making such a statement with anyone?

A. I haven't, sir.

Q. This is the first time you have thought of it?

A. Yes.

Q. It just grew out of these questions?

A. Yes.

Q. Based on your past training and understanding of ethics and morals, if a mistake is made that injures a man in his reputation, in his livelihood, isn't it only fair, without any further inducement or questioning, to try to correct the injustice? Wouldn't you say that is a fair principle?

A. I would, sir. If there hadn't been any lawsuit, I would certainly like to sit down with him.

Q. Isn't the lawsuit a further reason why you should sit down with him? You don't blame a man for asserting his rights in the American tradition by starting a lawsuit, instead of going up and punching you in the nose? Isn't that a more civilized procedure?

A. Yes.

Q. So far as you are concerned, then, if someone wanted to employ Mr. Faulk today in television, if it were up to you, you would give your blessing not to bar him from it, isn't that so?

A. Yes, sir, but I think there are two angles. From the point of view of principle, yes; but I think also it would be very important for him to make a good public position, as I have always advised people. The statement would help, yes, but I think his own activity is the finest proof of all. I don't mean to be a member of Aware, or anything like that.

My retort was "That is nice," and I immediately regretted my sarcasm, because I feared it would break the mood of Hartnett's self-revelation and repentance. However, even in the flood of contrition, he still talked of his advising people to make a public statement, which would meet his standards of patriotism. He was not conscious of the arrogance contained in this gesture. The implication was that because of the special circumstances (the pressure of a lawsuit) he would go easy on Faulk, and not insist he join.

I could not refrain from delving into his mind.

Q. . . . assume that a citizen is innocent . . . he has not been a member of the Communist Party or pro-Communist Fronts, aiding this nefarious enemy of our country, and civilization and religions; assuming that he is innocent of that, you don't require it as a condition before he gets employment that he issue public statements of how he feels about this? You assume that every loyal American feels the same way. They don't have to issue statements about it, do they?

A. There is a question of public relations problem.

Q. You know, for example, that Mr. Faulk signed an affidavit such as is required under law of anybody who becomes a union official, that he be non-Communist? . . . You know that?

A. Not of my own personal knowledge.

Q. You would assume that he lived up to the law of the land when he became a union official?

A. Yes.

Q. . . . Have you looked into the question whether Mr. Faulk signed such . . . a sworn statement very willingly?

MR. SCHMIDT: There is no statement ever made that Faulk was a Communist.

MR. NIZER: I know that.

MR. SCHMIDT: That Communist-disavowal statement under the NLRA is simply that, a disavowal of Communist affiliations. Why should he look it up? He never said he was a Communist. . . . There is nothing in there except that he is not . . . in favor of Communist activity.

MR. NIZER: That is right. What more do you need of a loyal American?

MR. SCHMIDT: There is nothing in the material complained of that says he was a Communist or a pro-Communist.

MR. NIZER: I understand.

This emphasis was so pleasing to our ears that we wished to hear its echo from Hartnett's mouth as well. We were rewarded with more than we hoped for. Within a minute the most damning admission which can ever be made in a libel suit tumbled out of him.

MR. NIZER: Mr. Hartnett . . . let me repeat what your counsel has said, and I will put it in the form of a question to you, so you can state it on the record. As I understand your position, you have never charged Mr. Faulk with being a Communist, is that right? That is what your counsel is saying?

A. Yes.

Q. You adopt that, don't you?

A. Yes.

Q. And you never charged him with being pro-Communist. . . . I mean a pro-Communist sympathizer?

A. I was once sold a barrel of false information.

"I was once sold a barrel of false information!" I hoped my face did not reveal the shock as well as delight which these words evoked. He was confessing error. He, the great investigator, the researcher non-pareil—blamed someone else for selling him false information. I was tempted to inquire whether he was a mere recipient of gossip, who it was who "sold it" to him, why he failed to verify it, and whether the apparatus of finger-pointing which could destroy an artist's career, was so recklessly conducted that he could casually admit that someone had given him a wrong steer. Were other people's lives subject to such accidental error? But I ruled out such an attack. He had made this startling statement so offhandedly that it would have been unwise to alert him to withdrawal or modification, by revealing surprise or springing to attack. Instead, we pursued the subject as if we had not heard the explosion of his confession.

Q. Aside from false information . . .

MR. SCHMIDT: He is talking about up to the time of the complaint.

Q. I will clarify that. Aside from the fact that you say you were sold false information about him, you don't charge him with being a Communist today?

A. No, sir.

Q. If there was ever such a charge, you know it is false?

A. I do.

Q. . . . Now, I will ask you, in coming back to my prior question, and in the spirit of good faith with which we have exchanged this colloquy, . . . if Faulk today had an offer to appear on television for a paid, commercial proposition, so far as you are concerned, if your voice could be heard, or your writing . . . you would give your blessing to it and would want him to be employed?

A. Yes, I would.

MR. SCHMIDT: That goes for me, too.

Q. . . . you would approve my showing your answers to any employer who might be interested in Mr. Faulk and who might on the other hand be dissuaded from employing him because of this litigation, . . . you would be willing for me to give your answers to such an employer, as your blessing?

A. Yes.

Q. Would you be willing to write a letter to such employer . . . suppose he said "I would like to know whether Aware or Mr. Hartnett, who investigates these matters, would tell me that it is okay," would you . . . tell him that it is?

A. Yes.

Q. And you would so advise CBS, if they were interested in retaining him?

A. Yes.

Q. . . . Would you advise Mr. Johnson . . . "I am writing such a letter and I advise you to do so?"

THE WITNESS: I shouldn't advise him, should I?

MR. SCHMIDT: He is not asking what I would do, or what Johnson would do.

A. Yes.

Q. You would be glad to write him, and you would say, "I think you ought to clear" . . . I don't use it in an invidious sense . . . "to give your blessing as far as loyalty, to endorse Mr. Faulk for any position that anyone wants to hire him for?" . . .

A. Yes.

Q. Would you advise the American Legion . . . if they were interested?

A. Yes.

Q. Would you so advise . . . Mr. Schmidt to do so, as President of Aware Inc.?

A. It seems logical, yes.

MR. NIZER: Would you do the same, Mr. Schmidt, or haven't I a right to ask you?

MR. SCHMIDT: Sure, you have a right and I told you I never wanted to help unfairly hurt anybody. I am still not persuaded that he was hurt by us, but that is another matter. Maybe you can persuade me.

MR. NIZER: . . . What I ask is . . . would you join Mr. Hartnett, as President of Aware Inc. in writing to any prospective employer of John Henry Faulk that so far as . . . your organization is concerned, you give your blessing to his being employed, or appearing on radio and television?

MR. SCHMIDT: Certainly. I can only conceive of one reason why—

MR. NIZER: You can give me the reason later . . .

MR. SCHMIDT: I want to explain it.

MR. NIZER: Let me first ask the direct question. . . . Would you also so advise Mr. Johnson?

MR. SCHMIDT: Certainly.

MR. NIZER: And any American Legion Post, or anyone else?

MR. SCHMIDT: It is the same logic. . . . If it applies to one, in honesty it has to apply to all. But I say to you the only reason I can conceive of people . . . saying to John Henry Faulk, "I am not going to hire you," is either that he is a poor entertainer, and I have never seen him . . . and I have no opinion on that, or that he is a Communist or pro-Communist. I don't think there is any other possible reason. . . . I never said that he is a Communist or a pro-Communist.

MR. NIZER: The court has held that the fair innuendo of what you said is just that.

MR. SCHMIDT: I don't agree.

MR. NIZER: The Appellate Court, and the lower court twice have ruled on that. . . . But you say you are not convinced?

MR. SCHMIDT: Right. That is a fact question of causal connection.

MR. NIZER: Let me put it this way without . . . now trying to give you the evidence. . . This man was employed with the highest rating, very successful, tremendous number of sponsors. You all know that, and now he cannot earn a nickel. His wife had to go out and get a job as a secretary to support her children and pay the rent. He had been made offers, and every time an offer is made somebody brings up this litigation. . . . Your charge is deemed a blacklist of him. . . .

There is a cloud over his head, whether he is a loyal American, and they won't employ him.

You say, "Give me proof, I don't believe it." It is not all a typographical error.

You are a successful lawyer, teacher and a distinguished member of the bar, and suddenly one day because of something being published about your patriotism you don't have a client for next year, and for you to say, "Prove it to me and not that Mr. Godfrey Schmidt is a bad lawyer," is preposterous.

Here is a man who didn't become a bad entertainer overnight.

I don't say anything about wiping out my lawsuit. . . .

This man is absolutely barred because of the cloud that you have created upon him in these publications, and . . . if you write that letter, at least you have a hope that he will be employed and incidentally, it will cut down damages if we are right in this lawsuit.

We adjourned the examination, and Mr. Schmidt and I went to lunch to discuss the turn of events. It was apparent that the defenses had for all practical purposes been abandoned. Hartnett's and Schmidt's readiness to restore Faulk's employability was an additional step toward settlement. Only two other items remained. Would the defendants issue a strong statement of retraction and apology and pay a sum which would indemnify Faulk for his losses? The first presented no difficulty. He told me that I could even draft the statement. But as to payment, he said Aware Inc. had no funds, Hartnett very limited funds, and Johnson would not contribute anything to the settlement.

My impression was that Johnson had relied on the accuracy of the Aware *Bulletin* and Hartnett's research, and that he held them responsible for his plight in having been involved in a lawsuit. This speculation seemed to be borne out by subsequent developments as well. At all times, Aware and Hartnett appeared reluctant to approach Johnson, as if it was their duty to relieve him of any concern in this matter. They, therefore, feared to irritate him by suggesting that he contribute to a settlement. Nevertheless, a small sum, perhaps ten thousand dollars could be raised, and, of course, Faulk's career would be opened again to him.

When I reported these developments, Faulk was elated by the admissions in the testimony, particularly Hartnett's, "I was once sold a barrel of false information"; I knew that he had set his heart on a conclusive verdict at a trial rather than a compromise out of court, and so I wanted to prevent his pride from interfering with a practical solution. He seemed to be concerned about our views, as attorneys, of him, and I assured him that it was no surrender of his ideals to end the case on such terms. "You have a wife and four children. They are suffering and who knows how long it will be before we reach trial. Many delaying tactics have already been employed and may continue. We must think of their welfare. No one on high has designated you to be a martyr. Here is a chance to resume your career with honor. You will earn large sums and repay your debts. You need not be concerned about any fees to us. We would be pleased to see you restored in your profession. The retraction will be as strong as you wish it to be. You will have triumphed in the public eye. We do not say this is as satisfactory a conclusion as a verdict and, therefore, we do not say you ought to accept this solution, but we do think you should consider this earnestly."

The relationship between client and attorney is a delicate one when it comes to settlement recommendations. The client's wishes should prevail, but to what extent must allowance be made for the fact that being emotionally involved, he should be protected against himself? How far should the lawyer go in giving strong guidance? When the client disagrees and future developments prove him wrong, may he not harbor the feeling that his lawyers, who were more objective, should have prevented him from having his way?

In any event, the proposal for settlement in the Faulk case was sufficiently sacrificial of the original objectives and so unattractive in money terms, that we did not consider it our duty to insist on its acceptance. Our presentation was designed to remove psychological factors militating against it, so that Faulk could make the decision on the basic merits. We, therefore, eagerly awaited his reaction.

It was firm and unqualified. He had not begun this lawsuit for the sole purpose of restoring his career and getting some money. He also wanted to destroy the practice of blacklisting, so that other artists would never be subjected to its fatal sting. If he accepted this settlement, Aware, Hartnett, and Johnson would remain in business at the usual stand. They would merely have extricated themselves from a tough spot, by admitting an error, and virtually without even the sacrifice of money gotten rid of a lawsuit, which after two years of hard contest had put them in an unfavorable position. They would escape exposure in a courtroom.

As to the continued suffering of himself and his family, he spoke with measured emphasis. "I think I am lucky. Few people have the opportunity that I have of representing American ideals in legal contest; of fighting a great cause, perhaps even a historic one. Whatever sacrifice my family and I will have to make is not great compared to the sacrifices many other Americans have made for principle. We won't starve. If I have to become a taxi driver, I'll do it. I mean this, quite literally. I'll earn a living as a cabdriver if I have to. But I want to see this through."

Then, with great sensitivity, he asked whether the burdens we would have to bear would be too much of a sacrifice for us? If so, he understood, and would reconsider.

There was no heroic posture in his statement. There was no consciousness of patriotic fervor. He spoke with utter sincerity. I doubt that I have ever heard more moving sentiments simply spoken. I had to restrain myself from revealing how deeply stirred I was. Of course I relieved him of any doubt about our determination to stay with the contest. In my effort to give him every reasonable propulsion to objective appraisal, I had not intended to imply that we would welcome release from battle.

He implored us to finish the task, and assured us that no matter what the outcome, he would never regret the sacrifice involved. We agreed that his decision was right.

We need not have. It turned out that no settlement was available on any terms. Less than two weeks after Hartnett's examination session, we received a letter from Roy M. Cohn advising us that he had been substituted as counsel for the defendants, and that he was leaving for the Far East that same afternoon and would return early in August.

Not only had Godfrey Schmidt disappeared from the scene as counsel, but quite cavalierly we were informed that new counsel was taking a trip and that we would be delayed several months before continuing the examinations. Several months—while Faulk continued to be unemployed.

Upon the resumption of his examination, Hartnett repudiated all the concessions he had made, and testified, "Mr. Nizer had me wondering myself. I was pretty well brainwashed. I began wondering what was what. I checked further, and I found out that the Faulk mentioned in Club 65 was John Faulk of CBS."

Although it was conclusively proven at the trial that Faulk was never there, this claim of brainwashing was used to withdraw Hartnett's previous admissions that an injustice had been done Faulk. Even the stipulations of previous counsel to produce certain documents were disavowed. Hartnett was repeatedly instructed by his new lawyers not to answer questions put to him on the examination. He would not return for examination unless compelled to do so by court order. He moved to terminate the examination on the ground that it was unnecessarily prolonged. Every inch of the way was obstructed and contested. A strategy of resistance was executed with remarkable ingenuity. We watched the months fritter away, with guerrilla warfare requiring numerous applications to the court. Each of these was heartbreaking, because we lost time even though relief was almost invariably obtained. A period of bitterness set in, which continued for years and then through the trial.

So, for example, it was necessary to ask the court to rule on Hartnett's refusals to answer and produce documents. After extensive briefs, Supreme Court Justice Sidney Fine ruled that Hartnett must produce Aware's membership list and its mailing list:

". . . Indeed, his former counsel agreed, during the examination to supply . . . a copy."

Hartnett's claim that he should not be required to get copies of the *Daily Worker* from a public library was rejected by the court, because of "Hartnett's admission at page 577 that he is in possession of the copies in question."

The court also directed Hartnett to answer questions about his finances and income "for the purpose of showing that the defendants extorted money . . . as alleged in the Amended Complaint."

Dozens of other documents were ordered produced, and hundreds of questions ordered to be answered.

Repeatedly, Hartnett failed to show up for examination. The remedy was to strike out his answer as punishment for his willful defaults. We so moved. Supreme Court Justice Aaron Steuer granted the relief unless Hartnett "appeared for resumption of the examination [the very next day] and the examination proceeded during court hours without interruption until concluded."

Hartnett then appeared for a few sessions but refused to answer so many questions that we were more frustrated than informed.

Hartnett's counsel moved to terminate the examination on grounds that it was oppressive. Supreme Court Justice George Tilzer directed the examination to proceed. Though he also stated there was "no doubt the examination is necessarily broad and comprehensive in scope," he critically suggested that it be limited "to such matters as are material and necessary."

Now we had to move to compel Hartnett to answer the questions, on which he had remained mute under his lawyer's instructions. Supreme Court Justice Samuel Hofstadter passed on hundreds of questions, sustaining objections to some and overruling objections to others.

Once more Hartnett balked in answering questions, and then refused to appear. Once more we moved to strike his answer unless he complied with the prior orders. Supreme Court Justice Edgar J. Nathan granted the motion unless Hartnett appeared immediately. He did, but again was told by his counsel to be silent as to certain questions.

Doggedly we again moved to compel him to answer. Supreme Court Justice Owen McGivern referred to Hartnett's attendance at twenty-two sessions, and the twenty-five hundred pages of his testimony, to the fact that two other judges had urged expedition of the conclusion of the examination, and Hartnett's claim that his health was being impaired by the extensiveness of the examination (though the judge observed "no medical proof of this contention appears . . ."). Judge McGivern directed Hartnett to appear and conclude his examination by answering certain specified questions, and producing documents which the court listed.

Similar difficulties were encountered when we examined Aware Inc. through its director, Paul R. Milton. Another motion to compel answers had to be made. Justice Samuel Gold required him to do so.

For months it was impossible to pin down a date for the examination of Laurence A. Johnson. Finally, the court ordered his appearance on a specific date. The same difficulties of obtaining answers or documents were encountered. Justice Matthew M. Levy appointed Special Referee Nathan B. Gurock to preside over the examination sessions so that immediate rulings could be obtained to protect both sides. Referee Gurock died, and application had to be made to proceed without a referee and submit objections to the court.

So it went, for weeks, months, yes, and years. Ten Supreme Court justices (Fine, Steuer, McGivern, Hofstadter, Tilzer, Nathan, Saypol, Gold, Levy, and Epstein) had made separate decisions during these examinations, and we hadn't even reached trial.

All legal rights, such as examinations before trial, carry within them the seeds of unforeseen new conflicts. On one hand, the examiner insists on the full exercise of his inquisitorial right. On the other hand, the person examined claims harassment and oppression. It is only fair that the court should be called upon to rule upon these contentions. But this requires an understanding of complicated issues raised by the pleadings, and involves rulings as to relevancy, often preceded by weeks of study by the court. So there are miniature trials within trials, and the contest burgeons like spreading fires.

It is easy to criticize the resulting delays, and belabor one side for "overzealousness," or the other for "obstruction." But what is the solution? Shall we abandon the remedy of examination because in a difficult, hotly contested case, it becomes burdensome?

Not dissimilar is our concern with the length of trials. Some of them last months, and recently several took more than a year. Shall we limit either party's right to present more than a certain number of witnesses (even though they are not merely corroborative, in which event the court has a right to exclude them)? Shall we curtail the right of cross-examination, or the number of documents which may be offered? Obviously, such remedies would violate the precepts of a fair trial. The seeker for truth is no respecter of time or effort. He glories in evidence, in reconstructed fact, in explorations in advance of trial to prevent injustice through surprise or lack of preparation. We may take comfort from the fact that, in the overwhelming number of cases, the issues are simple, and these problems do not arise; examinations before trial are brief and without proliferating contests.

In those few extraordinary causes, where the issues transcend mere individual grievance, and where the important principles involved evoke unique persistence, the procedure becomes cumbersome and time-consuming. Perhaps the exceptional nature of this type of case should make us more tolerant of the sacrifices entailed in prosecuting or defending it.

However one may view such a detached reasonable approach, it was no comfort to Faulk. We sent him lengthy reports of the legal skirmishes. We forwarded to him legal briefs eighty and a hundred pages in length, to busy him with the developments of the contest he was waging. We titillated him with the many judicial decisions. But the stark fact was that he was unemployed and would remain so, unless a trial was had, and a jury decided for him. How eager we were to have him and his witnesses tell their story to twelve men and women, then unknown, but who, one day, would be seated in a jury box. How much more eager we were to reach that wondrous day when we could face Hartnett, Milton, and Johnson on the stand and question them.

In the meantime Faulk was unable to earn a dollar in his profession. Loans became more and more difficult to manipulate. Debts mounted. Yet he bore up without a complaint.

He still announced with gallant gaiety that "the goose hangs high."

His friends could not be deceived. They knew that unless his troubles were bridged, Faulk, despite his courage, might never see the promised land of a trial and verdict.

Several union members and friends without Faulk's knowledge or permission, approached some prominent citizens concerning his plight and the great cause he represented. They arranged a meeting at the home of Mr. Herbert Steinmann, to which a special group was invited to raise funds for Faulk and his family.

Mrs. Eleanor Roosevelt, Myrna Loy, Dore Schary, Max Youngstein, Matty Fox, Eli Landau, and others attended. First on the agenda was a legal report. I recounted the lengthy struggle to reduce the pleadings to properly triable issues and then the skirmishes over the right of examination. Then going on, I recited Hartnett's hour of confession, followed by the change of lawyer and retraction of the previous recantation. Although the procedures described were ramified and the journey through the labyrinth of legal arguments not easy, the audience's intense interest in the cause lent excitement to the events.

Still we felt frustrated because such progress as we had made was merely to clear the path for the ultimate test which would occur at the trial. In the meantime we were all confronted by the human rather than legal obstacles which stood in the way of victory. The greater the oppression, the greater the need for relief, and yet the very effectiveness of the blacklist against Faulk might prevent him from lasting to the day of judgment.

Very tall persons like De Gaulle often use their height consciously, as if they were destined by nature to tower over ordinary mortals. Mrs. Roosevelt's straight tallness had a humble quality, as if it represented the grandeur of the common man and common woman. Her coiffure and dress were as old-fashioned as her words were new. Age had put lumps in her face, but magically they made contours of kindliness and beauty. Her smile connoted warmth with a touch of bravery, rather than joy, and her voice ballooned upward, as her enthusiasm caused her to drop the ballast of local discipline.

She literally spoke from and with her heart. The simplicity of her words did not hide her profound perception. She eschewed verbal effects as if the problems in life were too important to waste time on selective vocabulary. She saw the essence of things, and expressed it with such unadorned words that they seemed irresistibly right because of their lack of affectation. Just as she had seen and talked boldly about civil rights, when the timid thought she was "radical" and provocative (if only we had listened to her then, what grief our country could have avoided), so she saw in Faulk's case an extension of the hysteria created by Senator McCarthy, who exploited our common concern over communism and its treachery. She concluded her remarks (she never made an address) with example rather than exhortation. She announced that she was contributing $250.00, and sat down to search for her pen and checkbook in her large purse, oblivious to the applause.

Others made their pledges. Faulk accepted this support on the condition that it was a loan which he vowed to repay.

One knows from a quickening of the pulse that the day of trial has arrived. There is the physical bustle to drain off the nervous energy. Special briefcases, designed to hold large quantities, are packed with dozens of volumes of examination minutes, law briefs, and exhibits, and carted into a hired automobile which will daily transfer them to the courtroom and back again to the office for evening work. These are in the special care of our associate, George Berger, who becomes expert during the ensuing weeks in recapturing every stray piece of paper and restoring it to its proper resting place in voluminous files. When we retire at two or three in the morning, he stays behind in the office for an hour to change chaos into order and put the finishing touches on a legal brief due the next morning. "Housekeeping" during a complicated trial is a considerable task, and ultimately the lawyers and even the judge turn to the assistant on each side for the miraculous instantaneous production of a single sheet from thousands among which it is lodged, or pinpointing in the trial minutes an exhibit number which is buried in volumes of testimony.

The court attendants set up large tables for counsel, to

accommodate the bulky records. They provide water bottles and a stack of paper cups, which invariably tip over and flood the table, as if the documents needed cooling off (so we bring our own decanter and glasses).

Seating arrangements are made so that trial counsel may have two or three assistants next to him and the client at the end of the table. Storage space for permanent files is provided. It is as if we were moving into a house and settling down for a long stay.

We learn that Roy M. Cohn will not try the case for the defendants. His partner, Thomas A. Bolan, will be chief trial counsel, assisted by attorney John F. Lang (tall, dark, and friendly), a former F.B.I. agent, and by Vincent Hartnett himself, who is industrious in keeping the files, and making and handing notes to his attorneys. Next to him occasionally sits another lawyer, Mr. Alexander C. Dick, who has replaced Godfrey Schmidt as President of Aware, Inc.

Facing them across the same wide table, I sit at the end nearer the jury. Next to me, my law partner Paul Martinson (who has been fighting the cause from the beginning and is slightly stooped with scholarliness), then George Berger with the files above and below the table, as if he were playing an organ, and next to him, John Henry Faulk. He is directly opposite Hartnett, a fitting physical confrontation, which will be matched by their testimony.

Bolan has smooth bronze hair, a florid complexion, eyes for which a painter would use burnt ocher and which are suitable for the red hair he must have had in his youth before maturity and pomade darkened it. He is only about forty-odd years old, with handsome, clean-cut, uncurved features. He makes the mistake of looking beetle-browed and worried, instead of revealing a white line of teeth in a smile that lights up his face with charm and good nature.

A full day and a half is taken to select a jury of twelve and two alternates. The jurors are a vague blur the first day or two, as if a painter had daubed an abstraction of faces on a canvas. But as they respond with varying interest and emotion to the testimony, they seem to come forward into sharp focus. After a while their personalities become so sharply etched, that although counsel may do no more than greet them in the morning with a nod, we know and talk about the reactions of each one by name or number. ("Did you see Juror No. 8 nod his head when Faulk answered the judge's question?" or "Juror No. 3 almost jumped out of his seat when Hartnett said he couldn't rely on Government agencies to drive Communists off the air.")

When a lawyer selects jurors, he scans their faces, evaluates their voices, appraises their diction, observes their clothes, senses their empathy, weighs their mannerisms, all to determine whether they will be favorably inclined to his client and cause. He does not seek mere objectivity. Since each side selects those who have most favorable predilections to it, an average impartiality is thereby approximated. This is the law's device to avoid prejudice. "Each litigant," said an Italian legal philosopher, "shows his best profile. Justice sees truth full face."

One of the most helpful clues to a lawyer when he is analyzing a prospective juror, is the newspaper he has carried with him into court. A reader of the New York *Times* or *Herald Tribune* may well be a different kind of person than a reader of the *Daily News*. If a lawyer is lucky, the juror, waiting for hours in the back of the room before he is called, may be spotted reading a magazine. Is it *The New Yorker, Time, True, Modern Screen, U. S. News & World Report*, the *New Republic, Harper's*—and what conclusion shall we draw in relation to our case?

By itself the reading habits of a man may not be too significant, but when combined with other elements they can aid in analyzing him.

In some jurisdictions, jury lists are provided to counsel in advance, and the background is researched. For example, in Pennsylvania, we sit around a table and review the history of each prospective juror. Does he belong to a labor union? Has he his own shop? What kind of auto does he own? In what political party is he active? Is he married? What is his educational background? The reason most states do not follow this practice is that it makes possible advance knowledge and improper approach to a juror by some unscrupulous person. So once more, we see the difficulty of establishing policy. The advantages of one plan are offset by its dangers. That choice is made in each state which it believes best serves justice.

Supreme Court Justice Abraham N. Geller, formerly a judge of the highest criminal court, presided over the trial. He mounted the steps to the elevated judge's bench, his black robes registering his vigor by ballooning slightly be-hind him. He conducted a strict courtroom, demanding spectator decorum, and complete silence and unmovable-ness when the oath was administered to a witness. This dis-ciplinarian trait did not interfere with his innate kindliness and courtesy toward the jury, witnesses and counsel. He was only in his fifties—white hair, rimmed glasses, soft voice, and a face which had the cast and pallor of a scholar gave him distinction. As in most long trials, his patience was often taxed by counsel, but he was cautious enough to let off steam out-side of the hearing of the jury when we would be called into his robing room. The record will reveal some furious ex-changes in that room—then the return to the courtroom and a benign explanation to the jury that the delay was due to a necessary conference with counsel on some point of law.

So a judge must swallow his anger, despite provocation, for fear that otherwise he might prejudice the jury. Justice requires self-abnegation, among other godly attributes. Tem-per and judgment are mutual enemies. When they encounter each other, one or the other must be destroyed.

Justice Geller adopted a unique practice of instructing the jury on the law as the case unfolded, instead of waiting until the end of the case for the customary judge's charge to the jury. A better idea of his scholarliness and fairness can be gleaned from his guidance of the jury as new terrain was reached, such as the law of damages or the various defenses. At the very outset he explained to the jury what their func-tion was as contrasted to his own.

"When each of you was sworn in to be a juror, you were sworn in to be a judge, a judge of the facts in this case. It is as though each of you were wearing a robe as a judge, and I say that to you to impress upon you the im-portance of your responsibility as judges in this case, judges of the facts.

"I may not encroach upon your province as judges of the facts, and you may not encroach upon my province and responsibility as judge of the law in this case. Therefore, any notions that any of you may have as to what the law is or what it should be, or what someone told you it is, you must cast aside, and must unreservedly accept the law as laid down by the Court in this case."

This was a declaration of the separation of judge and

jury function, as essential to the Anglo-Saxon system of justice, as the separation of Church and State is essential to democracy.

The judge instructed the jury not to discuss the case as it progressed, with anyone else, or even among themselves. (One judge recently was carried away with his emphasis and instructed each juror not even to discuss the case with himself.) Justice Geller said:

"When jurors deliberate in a case, they are required to deliberate together, all of the twelve jurors . . . and exchanging points of view, not one or two or three, as you will be doing before the case is over. Moreover you will be doing it without the benefit of having heard all the evidence."

He warned them not to read the newspapers about the case, or listen to any radio or television reports of it.

"Jurors are supposed to get all of the evidence in a case in the courtroom, not outside the courtroom."

He explained the purpose of the opening statements about to be made by both counsel. They were not to be accepted as facts. Those could only come under oath from the witness stand.

"Opening statements might be said to be in the nature of contents in a book, so that you can follow the chapter and know what that chapter is about. It becomes more intelligible to you."

Then, as we neared that awesome moment when the testimony would be taken, he spelled out the noble enterprise in which we were all engaged.

"I should like you to keep in mind that all of us, you, the jury, I, the judge, and the lawyers are to try this case in the finest tradition of American justice, without fear or favor, without sympathy or prejudice, and with a sincere view to finding the truth in fairness in this case."

In the robing room, we moved to increase our claim for damages from five hundred thousand to one million dollars.

> MR. NIZER: At the time that the suit was instituted the plaintiff was still employed at CBS. Subsequently we learned, to our dismay, that not only was he to lose that employment, but he was to become unemployable. . . . Under those circumstances the damages which we had not anticipated would be as pervasive and extensive as they have turned out be, are now evi-

dent to us from actual experience over a period of about five years.

After briefs and arguments not in the presence of the jury, the motion to increase the claim for damages was granted.

The lawyers made opening statements to the jury. Finally I announced, "Mr. John Henry Faulk, will you please take the witness stand." He had waited six years for this moment. He walked past the counsel table, touching my shoulder in a disguised signal of good luck, and mounted the rostrum to the chair. The clerk held a Bible in front of him. Resting one hand on it, as if drawing strength from its touch, he took the oath. Then he sat down, flanked by the judge immediately on his right, the jurors on the left, and a packed courtroom in front, all eyeing him intently. Thus began the final stage of his fight for vindication and, indeed, survival.

I took him through the earlier stages of his life, his education, his teaching at the University of Texas, his Rosenwald fellowship, his Merchant Marine service (despite his blind eye since the age of seventeen), his Red Cross service in Egypt, and finally his G.I. service as psychiatric social worker at a hospital at Camp Swift.

He described his lectures to the F.B.I. as well as other organizations. About a half-hour later, the following inquiry came from our opponent.

MR. BOLAN: Excuse me for interrupting. Mr. Nizer, may we have the date of that talk before the F.B.I.?

MR. NIZER: Yes.

Q. Do you know just about when, the year and the month, of the F.B.I.?

A. I know it was 1945. It was during my period at the rehabilitation hospital.

This was the first signal that Bolan and particularly Lang, a former F.B.I. agent, didn't believe his testimony, and that there would be a careful checking. We were not wrong in this guess.

I drew from Faulk very early his views about communism.

Q. Did you at any time discuss foreign ideologies of any kind?

A. . . . No, except to hold them in considerable contempt. . . .

Q. Have your views at all times been the same about communism?

A. Yes, sir, they have . . . that it was a very antagonistic and very destructive philosophy, with which I held no brief whatever, never did and don't presently.

After Faulk was honorably discharged from the Army, he accepted an invitation of Davidson Taylor, vice president of CBS in charge of programming, to use his educational and humorous talents on radio (television was not yet in vogue). For one year he conducted a full network program called "Johnny's Front Porch." He traced his developing career through other programs; his CBS five-year stint; the R. J. Reynolds Tobacco Company program "Walk a Mile for a Camel" on which he was master of ceremonies; "Daniel Boone and His Adventures," an NBC network program; a program for the United States Signal Corps to promote enlistments, and many others.

"Overnight" stardom is usually the final recognition after years of training and development. Success is never sudden any more than disaster. The sudden heart attack is probably the culmination of twenty years or more of wrong diet which narrows and hardens the arteries with wastes. It is only the occlusion we take note of, instead of the years of wrong living which prepared it.

Faulk developed his skills on the lecture platform too. The Columbia Lecture Bureau booked him far and wide. Also, without fee he made addresses at Yale, Columbia, Fordham, and other universities; and for numerous good causes, Red Cross, Cerebral Palsy, Blood Donors, and churches of every faith and denomination. Circulars and newspaper reports of these events were offered in evidence— also numerous awards and plaques conferred on him. These and hundreds of clippings began to form a mound on the counsel table which blocked our view of Hartnett, as if Faulk's monument of distinction constituted a wall between us.

Since Faulk had not received a single television engagement after the issuance of the Aware *Bulletin*, it was necessary to show that he had established himself in this new medium before he was libeled. So he described his appearance on national CBS television for nine months on a program called "We Take Your Word," with John Daly as moderator, and Harriett Van Horne and Abe Burrows as the other panelists with him. They traced words back to their Greek, Latin, French, or Danish origins, deriving fun occasionally from the change of meaning in the course of time.

Faulk also appeared as a panelist on "Leave It to the Girls," an NBC television network show on Sunday nights. It was a Martha Rountree program with four female panelists, Maggie McNellis, Dorothy Kilgallen, Eloise MacElhone, and alternates like Elsa Maxwell. Faulk defended the male sex against their onslaughts.

    THE COURT: Did you ever win against all these women?
    THE WITNESS: No, sir, I don't recall a single victory. The idea was just to stay alive, Your Honor, not to win, just to survive on it.

Despite his disclaimer, this program was hailed as a superior comedy format in *Variety* magazine, "the bible of show business," and Faulk was singled out as a brilliant new star in the television firmament.

"Faulk was relaxed, natural, knew how to shade his satire, and emerged so warm a personality that he should cast his iconoscopes on wider wavelengths."

This review by Abel Green, the editor, was admitted in evidence and I read it to the jury.

Later Faulk became moderator of this program and invited some of his friends to participate as panelists. Governor Allan Shivers of Texas appeared with him. He described his other television programs, such as the CBS national network show "It's News to Me," with John Daly, Nina Foch, and Quentin Reynolds; "The Name's the Same" on the ABC national television network; he replaced Jack Paar on the CBS morning show for two hours every day on the CBS network; and many others. As for guest appearances, a sure sign of popularity, he appeared on the Virginia Graham, Wendy Barrie, Fannie Hurst, and other shows. He finally had his own television program called "The John Henry Faulk Show."

We turned back to radio. CBS ultimately fired Faulk. Would they claim it was due to his being a bad performer? It was important to demonstrate his previous success, so that the real reason for his discharge could be discerned by the jury. We were not yet certain how CBS executives would respond in this crisis. On the one hand they had admired Faulk. On the other, there were unceasing pressures on them from blacklisting sources. We shall see the cross-examination struggle which ensued. The defendants even put on the stand a publisher of radio and television ratings (those mathematical reports of a program's listening audience which control everyone's fate in broadcasting), and we had to engage him in cross-examination combat. In the meantime we sought to establish Faulk's great value to CBS in order to make its excuses for discharging him more implausible.

It so happened that Faulk was not content to sit on his broadcasting seat and promulgate his sales sermons. He visited many stores in person, and his fans flocked to see him and please him by buying his sponsors' products. In appreciation, the sponsors placed large advertisements in the newspapers of these events. We proved the circulation of these announcements to be in the hundreds of thousands. This chain of sales successes was completed by CBS, which printed and distributed beautiful folders of Faulk's achievements, in order to attract more sponsors.

We carefully developed these details and offered the documents to support them. One of the CBS promotion pieces had a teaser heading, "A pleasant disappointment to CBS Radio Merchandising director, Howard Lally." He had dispatched a photographer to a Flushing store to take a picture of a mass display of Hunt's Tomato Sauce, and in front of it Faulk signing autographs:

"Arriving at two p.m. the photographer found that 69 of the 75 cases in the featured display had been sold to eager customers. Only six cases were left for the remaining four hours of Saturday shopping. In other words, this was a merchandising effort so successful that it left no evidence for picture taking."

Photographs of Faulk at different stores, and eager crowds pressing around him, were received in evidence. So were trade magazines with photographs and articles about these merchandising triumphs. The proof showed that leading advertising agencies like Batten, Barton, Durstine & Osborn, Young & Rubicam, J. Walter Thompson, and many others received these trade publications regularly. The art of exploitation rarely includes understatement. So we did not suffer from CBS's description of its star:

"John Henry is about as persuasive a talker as they come. He's an authority on the language and lore of our American heritage.

"He developed his skill as a folk humorist while teaching at the University of Texas. He is one of the top rated personalities among New York major stations, is backed by extensive point of sales promotion in more than 900 metropolitan stores."

Like Pissarro's paintings which were composed of myriad dots, we continued for hours on end to place little evidence dots before the jury, in the hope that they would form a composition of great strength. The art of persuasion is rarely a flash of light which sweeps away the darkness of resistance. It is the cumulative effect of ceaseless tiny illuminations which attract the mind in a certain direction, until almost imperceptibly and slowly it has reached a conclusion.

So we continued with little dots; evidence that Faulk was master of ceremonies at the National Press Club on Congress night when all members of Congress and the United States Supreme Court attended. It was then Senator Lyndon B. Johnson, his old friend, who had invited Faulk to perform. We offered in evidence a national magazine called *T.V. Radio Mirror*, which printed a profile of Faulk, beginning: "You can take a man out of Texas but you can't take Texas out of a man. . . . We mean that in the nicest way," and other magazines which contained articles about him.

We proved that Faulk had addressed the Daughters of the American Revolution on Americanism Day and other occasions. They gave him a citation which was marked in evidence; also a citation from the March of Dimes, and acknowledgments from George Washington Centennial, Federation of Women's Clubs, various universities and churches; the Communion breakfasts of the St. George Association of the Fire Department of the City of New York, United Negro College Fund, the National Conference of Christians and Jews, the Y.W.C.A., Federation of Protestant Welfare Agencies, National Multiple Sclerosis Society, American Cancer Society, Children's Asthma Research Institute, N.A.A.C.P., and many, many others; all these documents were passed into the jury box.

It was interesting to observe the jurors as they scanned the documents. Sometimes one or two would pore over a particular exhibit, or point out a sentence to a fellow juror. Sometimes a juror would barely look at a document and pass it on to his neighbor, quite casually. We made mental notes of these reactions and they were the subject of much dinner conversation, as we attempted to read the slightest signs of what inroads we were making.

It takes years for a performer to acquire wide recognition and a following. He must make hundreds of appearances and see to it that they are of a character which build good will and a desire to see him again. Then, after setbacks and after meager rewards during the experimental period, the performer may emerge into star classification, with fame and huge salaries. There is rarely a gradual increase in his earnings. The financial progression is geometrical, but the preparation is slow mathematics. Faulk, despite his success, had not yet reached the extraordinary earnings of similar gifted performers. Our task was to prove that he was just about ready to emerge into the upper stratosphere when his career was cut off. We had to deal with his potential rather than with his proven record. For this reason it was essential to trace his arduous efforts and the record he had achieved. It took two court days for Faulk to depict this background. At the risk of boring the jury we continued to pile detail on detail, until the counsel table grew heavy with exhibits. Yet we had not even begun the story of the libel.

At this point we took him off the stand, and called the first witness who would break through the wall of silence about blacklisting. The judge gave us permission to call him out of order, because he was leaving for Europe the next day. Our adversaries and the entire courtroom must have sensed that startling testimony was in the offing.

David Susskind strode to the witness chair briskly, repeated the oath emphatically, and sat down straight on the edge of his chair, as if it would be necessary to spring forward.

He was about forty years old, but looked much younger. His hair (undecided between blond and gray), curling like the animated lines of his face, his light blue eyes slitting with emphasis, and his voice rising in querulousness, all registered intensity—and more intensity. His arms chopped the air as if he could not articulate fully (which he could), and therefore needed gesticulations to express what was inexpressible. Like a singer who is uncertain that he can reach a high C and stretches his arms upward to lift his voice, or an orator, like

Churchill, who stutters in advance of a most eloquent phrase, thus increasing its impact, Susskind flailed his arms helplessly, then made his point quite effortlessly nevertheless.

It was a delight to qualify him as an expert. Apparently, intensity (if it is combined with talent) pays off. Judged by his accomplishments he had already lived three lives.

After graduating from the University of Wisconsin and Harvard University *cum laude*, and serving the War Labor Board for a brief period as economic mediator, he joined the Navy as an ensign, and after engagements at Iwo Jima and Okinawa, emerged from the war a lieutenant (equivalent to captain in the Army).

Following a stint in the advertising departments of Warner Brothers and Universal Motion Picture Companies, he formed his own talent agency, representing actors, writers, directors, and other creative artists.

When in 1948, television nudged radio out of its monopolistic hold on the nation's ears, Susskind began a brilliant career of producing leading shows for the new medium. His "Philco Television Playhouse" ran fifty-two weeks a year for six years Sunday nights, on NBC. Among the stars who appeared on this series were Grace Kelly, Jason Robards, Jr., Kim Hunter, Kim Stanley, Julie Harris, Geraldine Page, Paul Newman, Tony Franciosa, Joanne Woodward, Franchot Tone, and Helen Hayes.

Susskind also produced "Armstrong Circle Theatre," which appeared for more then seven years on CBS. It won many awards. Over strenuous objection by counsel, we finally had some of them received in evidence, one reading:
"Awarded for services against aggressive communism from the Crusade for Freedom."

He produced the "DuPont Show of the Month," which ran on CBS for four years, and a series of "spectaculars," such as *The Moon and Sixpence* starring Sir Laurence Olivier, *Our Town* by Thornton Wilder, and hundreds of others.

Among his credits were thirty-nine two-hour programs, called "Play of the Week," which included *Medea* starring Judith Anderson and *The Cherry Orchard* starring Helen Hayes.

The quality of his productions can be gauged by the fact that they won more than one hundred awards, including two international awards presented by Princess Grace Rainier of Monaco.

But this was not all. He had produced several plays on Broadway such as *Rashomon* starring Claire Bloom, Rod Steiger, Oscar Homolka, and Akim Tamiroff. He had also produced motion pictures, starring Sidney Poitier in *Edge of the City* and *A Raisin in the Sun*, and Jackie Gleason, Anthony Quinn, Mickey Rooney, and Julie Harris in *Requiem for a Heavyweight*.

In addition to all this he had personally presided over a television discussion program called "Open End," lectured at the University of California, Harvard, Southeastern, and Louisiana State universities, and written articles. Only restrictions properly imposed by the court prevented us from offering more proof of his qualification as an expert. We were confident that his subsequent testimony would be considered authoritative.

Was blacklisting a mere theory or was it practiced in reality? We plunged into the mysterious waters surrounding the word.

Susskind had produced a show called "Appointment with Adventure." The sponsor was Camel Cigarettes (R. J. Reynolds Tobacco Company), and its agency was Young & Rubicam. He testified:

"When I sold the program to . . . Young & Rubicam, the condition of the sale was that all names of all personnel in all categories on every program were to be submitted for political clearance by Young & Rubicam, and nobody was to be hired until they approved and said, 'All right, hire such a person.' "

All names were submitted on the telephone, sometimes "ten or fifteen telephone calls a day." On the "Appointment with Adventure" program alone, he submitted about five thousand names for approval over a period of a year.

"I would guess approximately 33⅓ per cent, perhaps a little higher, came back politically rejected."

Bolan's objections kept coming with machine-gun regularity, but the witness was permitted to tell his conversation with the vice president of Young & Rubicam in charge of this program:

"I said, 'The production of the program is being seriously impaired. Human beings are suffering loss of employment without any substantiation, without any charges, without even their knowing that they can't be hired. . . .'

"And he said, 'I am helpless. . . . This is the practice. We have no choice, and we have to pay five dollars for every clearance and two dollars for every recheck. Do you think we like it? It's costing us a bloody fortune. . . . Cut down the number of directors and . . . writers because you are breaking us. It's five dollars a throw, and then two dollars a throw and you give eight actors for each role and four directors for each show . . . narrow it down.'

"I said, 'I can't narrow it down because I have learned that your percentage of rejections is so high I have to have alternative choices. . . . If this continues I will withdraw personally as the producer of the show.' "

Although this proof of blacklisting would have been admissible as general practice in the industry, we aimed for something much more specific. We wanted to tie this particular testimony about "Appointment with Adventure" to Hartnett, himself.

We read Hartnett's testimony at his examination before trial. He had an agreement with Young & Rubicam to check the names of artists submitted to him for this program:
". . . to see if there was any derogatory information. . . . For the first report it would be five dollars. For a longer report it may be twenty dollars or more. And then for a repeat on a name, ordinarily two dollars."

He received aproximately nine thousand dollars for his reports during the year when this program was being shown. When other admissions by Hartnett were read, even though they had been made several years before, they fitted into Susskind's testimony like a jigsaw puzzle. Truth has a reincarnation quality. It re-enacts itself again and again. So we read Hartnett's description of how names were submitted to him on the telephone daily by Young & Rubicam (he supplied the names of the callers—William D. Thompson, or his secretary, or Kenneth Bacon).

Although the caution of telephone use made a written blacklist scarce, Susskind startled the court by revealing a whitelist.

"When I sold the Borden Company, Young & Rubicam, a television program . . . called 'Justice,' a half-hour weekly series on NBC Thursday nights, based on cases from the Legal Aid Society, a condition of the sale was that a list of actors would be given me which numbered roughly 150, and that all roles on all programs in this series were to be filled from these politically cleared actors' names, and only such actors could be employed. . . .

"I said, 'It's impossible to cast a program from a list of 150-odd names. There are three thousand actors in the AFTRA Union in New York. There are ten thousand actors in the Screen Actors Guild. . . . Surely this 150 names will never permit me to do a program of any quality or workability. It's impossible.'

"He [vice president of Young & Rubicam] said, 'This whitelist is the only usable actors for this program. Take it or leave it. If you won't use this list, you don't have the sale. If you will use this list, you can have the sale.'

"I took the program. . . .'"

Later he received two more whitelists, enlarging the number of politically approved actors, writers, and directors to about 650. Unfortunately, not anticipating a trial years later, he had not kept the lists themselves, but he did have the covering letter. The court permitted it to go into evidence. It was on the letterhead of Young & Rubicam, Inc. I read it to the jury.

March 8, 1954

"Dear David:

"I have already sent you two lists with names of various performers, writers, etc. Attached is the third list.

"Regards.

"Sincerely,
David Levy"

Again we tied this testimony about the Borden Company to Hartnett, himself, by referring to his testimony on his examination before trial that he had received almost seven thousand dollars from the Borden Company one year and ten thousand dollars another.

We waited for the moment when Hartnett would take the stand in his own defense to develop the full story of how he obtained the Borden Company account.

In the meantime, we continued to push the door open on the blacklisting practices. What did Susskind say to the actors whom Hartnett had rejected?

". . . When I made the sale of 'Appointment with Adventure' and subsequently 'Justice,' and many other programs . . . it was stipulated that I was never to tell any rejectee why he was rejected."

The vice president in charge of the Borden account said to him:

". . . you are never to communicate to any principal . . . why. You are just to say you have changed your mind, or you are to say, 'I thought it over, and she is not tall enough,' or 'the leading man is too short.' Think of something artistic to tell them by way of an excuse. Never tell them that it has anything to do with political unreliability. . . ."

Q. And if they had applied for another part at a subsequent occasion, either on another show of yours, or any other show . . . would the same practice . . . be in existence at all times?

A. Yes, sir. . . . The practice was universal in television. Even if an actor had been cleared and therefore appeared time and again on a series, "he had to be re-cleared again on each occasion," and, of course, a fee paid.

No one was exempt. Even children had to be cleared politically.

MR. BOLAN: May I add that this witness be responsive? He was asked for an illustration.

THE WITNESS: I will give you an illustration. In the course of "Appointment with Adventure," . . . we required the services of a . . . seven- or eight-year-old . . . child actress. It was a backbreaking assignment to find a child who could act well enough to be in a professional program coast-to-coast.

We went to all the established sources, the talent agencies. . . .

MR. BOLAN: Your Honor, he was asked to give an illustration, and not a case history on a search for an actor or actress. Give us the illustration, not a whole story.

THE COURT: Overruled. I will allow it.

THE WITNESS: It was an extraordinarily difficult search involving going to the public school system, the United Nations schools. We finally found . . . an American child eight years old, female. That child's name came back unacceptable, politically unreliable.

There was a roar of exclamation and laughter in the court-room.

THE COURT: No, no. I will not tolerate any outburst of

that kind, or I will order the courtroom cleared. This is not a show. This is a courtroom.

THE WITNESS: I called up the executive in charge of the program at Young & Rubicam. I said, "You have ordered me not to protest, . . . but in the case of this eight-year-old child, it is just insane. She could not be part of any Communist conspiracy. She couldn't be politically unreliable. She couldn't even be political, and the search was so strenuous that I beg of you to tell me what it is you have on this child, because it must be wrong. It must be ludicrous." "I will call you back," he said.

He called me back and he said, "This is not to be taken as a precedent, but in this one case I will tell you that this child's father we regard as suspect, and therefore we will not permit the use of the child on the program," and we had to . . . find another child whose father was all right.

MR. BOLAN: I request that the jury be instructed that the testimony such as has just been given . . . that up to this moment there has been no evidence whatsoever that links such testimony with any of the defendants. . . .

MR. NIZER: All right. I will connect it. . . . Mr. Hartnett was examined on this subject, page 847 (examination before trial) . . .

"Q. Did you in the course of these duties for any clients also clear child actors?

"A. Yes. . . . Where a child apparently was the son or daughter of . . . people in the acting profession who had a record. . . . I know I did look for this particular stratagem. . . .

"Q. . . . when you discovered that the actor was a child, you didn't stop your research, but you did go ahead . . . to find out what there was against the child's parents, is that correct?

"A. . . . I would like to say that is part of the tragedy of the Communist movement, that even children are brought into the movement at an early age. . . .

"Q. Whom are they brought in by?

"A. I presume by their parents, sir, although some may start on their own. They are rather enterprising. Should I give an example?

"MR. BOLAN: No."

How much were sponsors to be blamed for yielding to these practices? Susskind explained:

"The broadcasting industry is incredibly and unusually sensitive and frightened. It is an industry dedicated to promoting good will. . . . The slightest whisper about an artist is damning and is murderous to the career of that artist."

> Q. And in your experience when, as you put it, a whisper about an artist goes through the advertising agencies that have to hire the artist, and through them to the sponsors, what is the result with respect to such controversy?
>
> A. That artist is rendered unemployable. . . . It was the effect of the guillotine. It chopped them off, economically. They were dead. They could not work.

We had reached the point of proving damages through expert opinion. Evidence of Faulk's past training and experience was already before the jury. The law permits the assessment of future probabilities. This depended on the opportunities in the industry and Faulk's potential. Some amount of crystal gazing into the future was involved, but the jury would determine to what extent the estimate was keen foresight, such as everyone must use even in a prosaic business venture, and how much was wild guess. The law knows no better way to allow damages for future loss. The jury's commen-sense evaluation of the expert's background and soundness is a leavening process in a field where no scientific computation is possible.

We stressed that Faulk was a television personality and that by 1956 there were about thirty million television sets in the United States. Said Susskind:

"Faulk could earn a living in radio, but the dynamic of his career, his progress in terms of money, fame, reputation depended . . . upon his relationship to the new television industry."

The quiz, fun show which was particularly effective in television required a particular kind of personality.

"He must have warmth, articulateness, a sense of humor, an identification with the audience—like Tennessee Ernie Ford, Garry Moore, Bud Collyer, Bill Cullen . . . Arthur Godfrey . . . Steve Allen, Johnny Carson."

Such performers as Jack Paar become more famous and

richer then straight dramatic actors, like Julie Harris or Frederick March, he testified.

Q. Based on your experience, how did John Henry Faulk fit into this category?

A. Having watched John Henry Faulk on radio and television, he was exceptionally gifted in this particular television arena, of the game, fun, quiz show. He was warm, witty, humorous, charming, bright, articulate. I think he was among the very best I had seen up to date in 1956 and 1955. . . .

Now we were ready for estimates of earnings.

Q. Are you familiar generally with the kind of income which the artists that you have mentioned earn in television, generally?

A. I am generally familiar with the income.

Q. What is the range of that kind of personality's income?

A. They range from a minimum of $150,000 to $200,000 a year, up to, in the case of Arthur Godfrey, and . . . a few others, a million dollars a year.

Success is a pyramidal structure. Such performers go on to multiply their income in motion pictures, Broadway plays, or writing a book. Nor is this all. Ultimately, they own their own television shows and profit from the residual income, that is, the repeated showings of their programs, as have Danny Thomas, Lucille Ball, Groucho Marx, and others.

The final question riveted down his opinion testimony that Faulk would have achieved a similar status of stardom.

Bolan asked that the jury be excused and then moved for a mistrial because Susskind's testimony, he claimed, was "inadmissible and completely inflammatory," in that he talked about blacklisting "with no relationship to any of the defendants."

We analyzed the long struggle before trial in which various judges had ruled against similar contentions by the defendants.

THE COURT: Irrespective of the fact that three other judges sustained the allegations and the right to examine on that, independently, I came to the same conclusion, and your motion for a mistrial is denied.

MR. BOLAN: May I have some additional time to prepare for the cross-examination?

THE COURT: Yes. We will take a short recess.

The first skirmish on cross-examination involved the question whether Susskind would consider it blacklisting to bar an identified Communist from television.

THE WITNESS: I don't know the theory of blacklisting except that it is private vigilanteism calculated to keep people off television.

However, he affirmed that a real Communist "would be dead as a duck [on television] and should be." Then the attack quickened.

Q. . . . did you ever employ a man who had been identified . . . by sworn testimony as a member of the Communist Party?

A. Identified by whom? If Harvey Matusow identified such a man; no . . . because he is a proven liar before a Congressional Committee. It depends . . . how was that man faced with his accuser. Was he allowed to bring counsel? Did they indict him . . .

He explained that the AFTRA Union provided that no Communist could belong to it, and that even one who had taken the Fifth Amendment was subject to disciplinary proceedings by the Union. Therefore he relied on AFTRA when he hired its members.

Q. You consider the Communist Party a political party?

A. I consider the Communist Party loathsome, abhorrent, dangerous, our deadliest enemy.

As to Susskind's high opinion of Faulk's earning ability:

Q. Turning to Mr. Faulk, of the thirty-five or fifty thousand artists that you employed, did you ever employ Mr. Faulk?

A. No, sir . . . because we—

Q. I did not ask why.

On redirect examination, we gave him an opportunity to explain. On dramatic shows he did not need such performers: "I have never engaged Garry Moore, Arthur Codfrey."

When Susskind left the stand, a different atmosphere existed in the courtroom. There was no longer any doubt that we could adduce evidence "from the inside" of blacklisting practices. His courage helped to open the door for other witnesses and greater revelations. It was against this background, that Faulk resumed the witness stand.

Slowly, like a barefooted man walking on a pebbled road, we trod over sharp objections to the description of the events which had engulfed him: the stormy meetings in AFTRA because Aware, Hartnett, and Johnson were "working together . . . attacking members for their patriotism"; Leslie Barrett's description of how Hartnett falsely hounded him for "marching in the 1952 May Day Parade" (at this point we filled in the mosaic by reading Hartnett's admission on his examination before trial):

". . . I wrote Leslie Barrett a letter."

Q. Did you write anything untrue?

A. Yes. . . . It was a kind of trick used by interrogators where one has reason to believe it is so, you put it as a fact and ask for an affirmation or denial. . . .

Q. You did testify [before a Congressional committee] that you should not have done it?

A. Yes.

We sketched AFTRA's condemnation of Aware; the successful campaign of the middle-of-the-road ticket; then the great retaliation—the publication of the *Bulletin* with its seven charges against Faulk.

The reverberations from the libel were immediate. Sam Slate, program director of CBS, and Carl Ward, its general manager, called an emergency meeting. Laurence Johnson of Syracuse was up and down Madison Avenue (the capital of the advertising agencies) pressuring Faulk's sponsors to drop him. Libby's Frozen Foods had canceled out that very day. Ward suggested:

"Perhaps we can stop the onslaught on you if you will . . . sign an affidavit . . . declaring your patriotism, and declaring this is all false, this *Bulletin*."

He did, even though only twenty-two days earlier he had signed an anti-Communist affidavit as required of all newly elected union officials. Then the offensive of the American Legion (Onondaga County) began. Faulk's sponsors received letters condemning him, and the agencies were at CBS's doors again, outraged because of their client's predicament. CBS sent Faulk to appease Young & Rubicam. An official told him that:

"Johnson and his racketeers . . . had a hold of me and . . . there was very little chance of me to be able to withstand them all. . . ."

We took Faulk off the stand for a few moments and put on Miss Alice Saunders, administrative assistant to the legal department of Young & Rubicam and in charge of its files. We obtained the letter from the Anti-Subversive Committee of the Onondaga County American Legion in Syracuse to Piel Brothers, CBS's letter to the agency citing Faulk's affidavit, and Young & Rubicam's letter to its client, Piel Brothers. The court accepted these documents in evidence, and they constituted a written chain of proof of the desperate efforts to prevent Faulk's sponsors from abandoning him.

Now we had reached the heartbeat of any libel suit, were the seven charges in Aware's *Bulletin* true or false?

Even the preliminary passages leading to the accusation were challenged by us.

The *Bulletin* said that the middlers attacked Aware but were "relatively silent on communism." I asked Faulk whether his slate was silent on communism.

> A. Absolutely not; exactly the reverse is true. . . . The leading plank in our platform . . . published in the New York *Herald* [*Tribune*] said we are unalterably opposed to communism.

That newspaper was put into evidence with a quote from Faulk that the middle-of-the-road slate was "chosen for their opposition to communism."

The *Bulletin* listed fourteen members who had refused to answer questions at a hearing of the House Un-American Activities Committee:

> Q. Did any of these members listed have anything to do with the middle-of-the-road slate?
>
> A. Not the slightest thing to do with it.
>
> Q. Have you ever in your life refused to answer any question concerning your patriotism or loyalty, or taken the Fifth Amendment in any way?
>
> A. I certainly have not, Mr. Nizer.

The *Bulletin* claimed that AFTRA's members were lured into condemning Aware "by misleading columns by John Crosby, New York *Herald Tribune*, and Jay Nelson Tuck, New York *Post*."

We offered these columns in evidence to permit the jury to determine whether they were misleading. Devastating, might have been a better description of them. Tuck's article was entitled "The Unholy Alliance in AFTRA and a Blacklist."

"It soon became clear that an actor need not be guilty of anything to be blacklisted. It was enough to be 'controversial.' . . . There were always at least a few people willing to let it be known that they were offended. As one director put it, three dirty postcards from a vacant lot were often enough. . . .

"On some programs, the blacklist soon gave way to a whitelist. . . ."

The *Bulletin* had imputed communism to the Faulk slate by asserting, "The middle-of-the-road ticket was first reported by the *Daily Worker* on November 15, 1955."

> Q. . . . is that correct?
> A. No. There again it's a distortion and an untruth.

We offered in evidence from Hartnett's file (the examination before trial was proving its worth every moment) two newspapers which had reported this story *before* the *Daily Worker* did.

The *Bulletin* asserted that most middler candidates might have been chosen for their anti-communism, "But how about Faulk himself? What is his public record?"

We could sense the jury leaning forward as we approached Faulk's answers to the seven charges in the *Bulletin*.

First, that "According to the *Daily Worker* . . . Jack Faulk was to appear at Club 65 . . . a favorite site of pro-Communist affairs."

> Q. Did you ever appear at Club 65 on that date or any other date?
> A. I did not.
> Q. Did you know at the time you received this *Bulletin* what Club 65 was?
> A. No, sir. I don't recall ever having heard of Club 65 until the defendants put out this *Bulletin*.
> Q. It says, "According to the *Daily Worker* . . ." Have you ever subscribed to the *Daily Worker*?
> A. I have not.
> Q. Have you ever read the *Daily Worker* prior to some articles I gave you with reference to this suit?
> A. I had not, sir.
> Q. Did you consider the *Daily Worker* a reliable newspaper?
> MR. BOLAN: I object.
> THE COURT: Overruled.
> A. I certainly do not, sir. . . . It's a propaganda sheet.

Q. This item says "Jack Faulk"—Have you ever been known as an entertainer or in private life as Jack Faulk?

A. No, sir . . . as John Henry Faulk or Johnny Faulk.

Q. Did Mr. Hartnett, or anybody on behalf of Aware, or . . . Mr. Johnson, get in touch with you to inquire whether you had been at Club 65. . . .

A. No, sir. They did not.

In similar categorical and all-inclusive denials, he replied to the second charge of the *Bulletin* that according to the *Daily Worker* he was to appear as an entertainer at the opening of Headline Cabaret, sponsored by Stage for Action, (officially designated a Communist Front).

Q. Did you appear as an entertainer for the Stage for Action?

A. No, sir. I did not.

Nor did he know whether it ever had been designated a Communist Front.

The date involved in this charge was April 20, 1947 and the place New York. We proved that Faulk was in Texas during that month of April. He attended a reception for the Texas State Legislature, and a photograph of Faulk together with Representative Jim Wright was taken with the marking on the back "Photo by Neil Douglas, Austin, Texas."

So again Faulk had been accused of being at a function which he proved he had not attended, or even known about.

The third charge stated that Faulk had "contributed cabaret material to 'Show-Time for Wallace' revues staged by the Progressive Citizens of America (officially designated as a Communist Front). . . ."

Faulk stated that he had contributed material for the revue and had been paid for it, as he had done for other organizations. But he was not a member of Progressive Citizens of America, and never paid dues to it.

He did not consider this organization a Communist Front: "I know amongst the founders was Mr. Harold Ickes, a member of Roosevelt's Cabinet. Mr. Henry Morgenthau, who was Secretary of the Treasury . . . amongst many other distinguished Americans and it had no relationship . . . with communism whatsoever."

Q. Was the material that you submitted for the cabaret show of any ideological or political character?

A. No, it was not. I guess you would call it just a funny

piece. I hope you would call it that, sir, but it had no slant to it. . . .

The fourth charge was the most insidious and revealed the malice of the defendants. It was like an innocently labeled bottle deliberately filled with deadly poison. It read:

"A program dated April 25, 1946 named 'John Faulk' as a scheduled entertainer (with identified Communist Earl Robinson and two non-Communists) under the auspices of the Independent Citizens Committee of the Arts, Sciences and Professions (officially designated a Communist Front . . .)."

The charge referred to "A program" which listed Faulk as an entertainer. It didn't reveal what function the program represented. We obtained the program from Hartnett's files.

Q. Will you tell us what the occasion was?

A. It was . . . the First Anniversary of the United Nations, sir, a dinner given in honor of that.

Q. Go ahead. Tell me more about it.

A. The honorees consisted of the entire Security Council . . .

THE COURT: The Security Council?

THE WITNESS: The Security Council of the United Nations. It was held at the Astor Hotel. It was sponsored by organizations such as the . . . American Association for University Women; The American Bar Association; The American Jewish Committee; National Y.M.C.A. and others.

It was presided over by the Honorable Trygve Lie . . . Secretary General of the United Nations at that time. It was attended by . . . Edward Stettinius, Secretary of State of the United States at the time.

Q. He addressed that function?

A. Yes, sir.

CBS had broadcast this program and had asked Faulk to entertain that evening.

. . . And I might say I was honored to do it. . . . Art Carney and Eddie Mayehoff and I did a bit together. . . .

Q. Were any of the facts you have told us about . . . set forth in the *Bulletin* issued by Aware and Hartnett?

A. No, sir. Out of all the names and sponsoring organizations, the only one Mr. Hartnett saw fit to mention was a man named Earl Robinson, who I never met before and who I did not invite.

Q. . . . Do you know . . . anything about him?

A. I know he was a song composer, and . . . he composed a song "Ballad for Americans" which was sung at the Republican National Convention. I know nothing about his Communist relationships, if indeed there are any.

"The program" was marked in evidence and passed among the jurors. Several of them looked across the counsel table at Hartnett. They would have a better opportunity to know his mind when we got to the cross-examination of him.

The fifth charge in the *Bulletin* was that Faulk had sent greetings to People's Songs (officially designated a Communist Front) on its second anniversary.

Q. . . . Did you in fact send greetings to People's Songs on its second anniversary?

A. No, sir, nor its first one either.

Q. Nor at any other one?

A. No, sir.

Nor did he know, if it was true at all, that People's Songs was a Communist Front. He described it as a group of folk singers who were "forerunners for the folk music craze that is now sweeping the country . . ."

The sixth charge accused Faulk of appearing with Paul Robeson on "Spotlight on Wallace," to be held in the Jefferson School of Social Science, which:

"has been found by the Federal Government to be what it is, the official training school of the Communist conspiracy in New York."

Q. . . . Is this a true statement?

A. No, sir. That is a completely false statement.

Q. Did you appear on the date they said, or any other date?

A. No, sir. I have never appeared there.

Q. Did you know where the Jefferson School of Social Science was located until this *Bulletin* was shown to you?

A. No, sir. I did not.

The date he was supposed to have appeared was February 16, 1948. The day before, Faulk was to appear at Yale University to address Jonathan Edwards College. But he caught the flu, and remained in bed over the weekend, including the day he was charged with being at the Jefferson School. Dr. Robert French, Master of Jonathan Edwards College, and Mr. Beek-

man, Canon of the Yale Graduate School, had written to Faulk
regretting that his illness had prevented his coming, and inviting him to come another time. What a fortunate flu that had
been. It created written disproof of the charge. A lie never
knows from what direction the truth will raise its head to
refute it.

The seventh charge was that Faulk "was a U.S. sponsor of
the American Continental Congress for Peace, staged in Mexico City . . . as shown by the official 'call,'" and that this Congress "was later described by the House Committee on Un-
American Activities as 'another phase in the Communist world
"peace" program . . .'"

> Q. Were you in fact a sponsor of that . . . Congress
> for Peace held in Mexico City?
> A. I was not.
> Q. Had you ever heard of it?
> A. I didn't even know they held one down there until
> that thing came out listing me.
> Q. Did you attend the . . . Congress?
> A. I did not.

Faulk's denials of the charges placed a heavy burden upon
the defendants to show either the truth of the charges, or
why those who professed to be researchers and investigators
had erred so grievously in so many instances. Was it all an inadvertent series of mistakes, or calculated concoction to destroy
Faulk? Even recklessness in publishing an untruth is equivalent in law to malice. How much more so deliberate falsity.
The day was approaching when the defendants would have
to take the stand and, under cross-examination, justify or confess.

In the course of the examination of Hartnett before trial, we
discovered that in the midst of the AFTRA election he had
written to the House Un-American Activities Committee making similar accusations against Faulk, as were later published
in the *Bulletin*. Obviously, this was an attempt to procure
Congressional inquiry into Faulk's conduct, at the very time
that he was appealing for votes on an anti-Communist platform. Neither Faulk nor we, as his counsel, had known of
this early effort to undermine him, until we discovered this
letter. I read it to the jury, and had him vigorously deny these
charges again.

Hartnett's letter had one new specification. He advised the

Congressional Committee that Faulk was listed in the cumulative index of that Committee. I asked him:

Q. Do you know who else is listed?

A. Yes. General Eisenhower, for one.

MR. BOLAN: I object, Your Honor.

THE COURT: Sustained.

MR. NIZER: May I read page 207 of Mr. Hartnett's testimony?

"Q. Do you know whether President Eisenhower's name was listed in the Un-American Activities index?

"A. Yes, sir.

"Q. He is?

"A. Yes, sir.

"Q. In connection with what?

"A. . . . I believe he sent his greetings to the National Council of American Soviet Friendship when he was still a general; possibly also for something like a Russian War Relief sponsorship."

Hartnett had also written letters to Kudner Advertising Agency and to others, condemning Faulk's record. These exhumed poisoned arrows were also shown to the jury. Then we showed Faulk his rotating schedules for broadcasting and he specified the names of various sponsors who had canceled his program or permitted it to lapse after expiration. Bolan strangely welcomed these rotating schedules, describing the Nucoa, Diamond Crystal Salt, and Rheingold Beer spots, and we suspected an attack based upon them. This turned out to be correct.

Faulk described the hundreds of times he had appeared on dozens of television programs before the *Bulletin* was published. Eight of these programs which ran as a series, featured him, or were in his name. Five of these eight were national network broadcasts. In the year before the *Bulletin* attacked him, he had been exposed on television screens about sixty-five hours in all, and before millions of viewers.

Q. After this *Bulletin* . . . was sent out, did you ever again appear on a commercial television show to this very day?

A. No, sir. I have not, with one possible exception, that was on the Jack Paar Show two or three years later. . . .

Television income, he testified, was about ten times more

lucrative to the performer than radio, and "I was placing the whole emphasis of my career on going into television."

He described how Charles Collingwood and Ed Murrow intervened to save his radio job, and how the multiplicity of small sponsors in radio, who took inexpensive spot commercials, made it easier to survive in radio than in television where one large sponsor with a huge budget was involved.

However, after being assured by his superior, Sam Slate, that "I would be the very last one that would ever leave CBS," he discovered he had been fired while on vacation with his family. His program was still commercially successful. His ratings were higher than when he began to broadcast.

Then we turned to the concluding phase of his direct testimony—the recital of the confident search for another job, the enthusiastic reception of offers to him, and the mysterious withdrawals at the last moment. It was a frustrating tale of doors opening to beautiful vistas, and closing shut suddenly as he was about to walk through them—indeed, at times, being shoved back after he had already been ushered through triumphantly.

The explanation for these recurrent rejections was always couched in some innocuous business terms. But we did not have to rely merely on the jury's insight that such curiously repeated last-moment changes of mind were too extraordinarily coincidental to meet the rule of probability, and that it was more likely that poisonous streams were flowing long distances to pollute the waters of Faulk's opportunities. We were able to offer proof rather than suspicion to the jury.

The most unexpected evidence fell into our hands, in a way which would have defied credibility—except that it really happened.

    Q. Did you in your effort to get regular employment contact all the networks?

    A. Yes, sir.

    Q. What were you told?

    A. No job.

His lecture bureau had been clamoring for his time, when he was on the air. Now he informed them that he had "worlds of available time," but suddenly, "with a cloud over my head," there was no demand.

However, a former program manager of CBS, Bill Schwartz,

had become manager of a Minneapolis station, WCCO. He had written Faulk, while he was on vacation, about an extraordinary opportunity at this large Midwestern radio station, at which Cedric Adams had been the leading personality. If Faulk was willing, as all young men should be, to go West, he would be made the star of the station. A one-hundred-thousand-dollar annual earning potential was offered. Faulk had been wooed before by other stations, but knew his future was in New York, the home of television. Now, without a job, he opened his mail to find this offer. He telephoned Schwartz, who immediately came to New York. Also, the general manager of WCCO flew in from Washington. Luck, they thought, had made Faulk available to them. They flew him and his wife to Minneapolis. Faulk appeared on every program of the station, to announce his new radio home. He and his wife also looked for a home to buy and settle down in Minneapolis. To whip up enthusiasm, a contest was held on the air, as to why one would like to travel to Faulk's home state of Texas, and the winner would be given a free trip. Faulk interviewed Minnesota's Governor Orville Freeman, later Secretary of Agriculture. Everything was set. Contracts were to be signed. Suddenly the enthusiasm which had enveloped the entire project vanished into thin air (non-broadcast), and it was suggested that Faulk and his wife should return to New York where he would be reached shortly.

Q. Did they call you to consummate the deal?

A. No, sir. I never heard from them again.

The pain of another collapsed opportunity was replaced by a new ray of hope. Station WOR, the leading radio station on the Mutual Broadcasting chain, had a large housewife audience in the early afternoon and needed a star like Faulk for that hour. Negotiations for his services proceeded with the urgency which marks an anxious buyer and a willing seller.

What intervened to stop the deal? We shifted suddenly to Hartnett's examination before trial. He had admitted speaking to Mr. Pat Winkler of the Mutual Broadcasting System.

"Q. What did Mr. Winkler say to you?

"A. He said that somebody at the network had proposed hiring Mr. Faulk. . . . He asked me if I had information about Mr. Faulk.

"Q. Did he make reference to the . . . lawsuit or the AFTRA dispute?

"A. I wanted him to understand there was a lawsuit going. . . . I didn't want to comment on Mr. Faulk other than to say we were being sued and I believed that the statements in the publication were true. . . ."

Of course, Faulk had not known until this examination that Hartnett had spoken to WOR's executive at the time when employment was about to become a reality.

I asked him:

Q. What happened to your negotiation with WOR . . . ?

A. It stopped just as suddenly as the WCCO one did.

With the consent of his manager, Gerald Dickler, Faulk engaged an additional agent, Jerome Hellman. They prepared a kinescope of his past shows on Goodson-Todman productions, to exhibit his prowess on film. It was submitted to NBC, but—no interest.

To earn some money, Faulk offered to do some commercials, leaving his name off. The assumption was that his name had become a curse. Perhaps a sponsor would buy his skill without identification. The advertising agencies laughed at the idea: "With your voice who do you think you'll fool?"

He went to see Oliver Presbry and Martha Rountree, who had produced "Meet the Press" and "Leave It to the Girls." They wanted to bring back the latter program on which Faulk had scored so heavily, but:

"After they had talked around the industry . . . they said my name was very controversial and it usually raised hackles on the neck of the people that they brought it up with in the advertising agencies and networks."

When he approached Miss Ruth Levine, an account executive of the advertising agency Benton & Bowles,

"She said that artists blacklisted off shows that Benton & Bowles did, had far less serious problems than I had . . . and so she felt it was almost pointless to pitch me to a sponsor. . . ."

Such oral revelations were frequent, but the written withdrawals of jobs always set forth some professed business reason for the change of heart. Blacklists operate either in silence or in innocent pretentions. Then—a break came.

Don Lee Broadcasting System, "The Nation's Greatest Regional Network," was situated in San Francisco, and was affiliated with the Mutual Broadcasting System. Its Vice President and General Manager, Wendell B. Campbell, knew of Faulk's talents and invited him to come to San Francisco to take over the afternoon shows. He wrote:

"If you are interested, then I'm going to ask you to call Bob Leder, Vice President and General Manager of WOR New York . . . to transcribe a half hour show, at least, which will be sent to me. . . . The ball is in your court now. . . . Please let me hear from you as soon as possible."

This letter was offered in evidence. I asked Faulk:

Q. Were you ready and eager to accept this post?

A. Yes, sir. I surely was. I had been unemployed for almost a year.

He made a transcription and sent it to the Coast. The fact that the post was three thousand miles away from New York heartened him. Perhaps the blacklist could not extend its tentacles that far. He was full of hope. Then arrived the usual letter:

"Johnny, at this point we will have to pass. I want you to understand that it wasn't because of our reaction to your work, it's just that some other things have come up which preclude our asking you to join us. . . .

"Sincerely,
Wendell B. Campbell."

But this time the story did not end there. Wendell Campbell had written a letter to Robert Leder, the Vice President of WOR in New York, stating his innermost mind. By mistake his secretary had addressed the envelope not to Leder, but to "John Henry Faulk, 118 West 79th Street, New York 24, New York." Freud's theory that errors are often the deliberate choice of the subconscious, might have applied here. Campbell was a good friend of Faulk's and wanted to employ him. Who knows—the girl who addressed the envelope might also have sympathized with Faulk's fight for principle.

In any event, Faulk opened the envelope addressed to him and found a letter to Leder which said that before employing Faulk he was "concerned with Johnny's legal problems with Aware Inc. but have been given to understand that these are all cleared up. If this is so, then we will be definitely interested in him."

Campbell's impression that the "legal problems were cleared up" might have stemmed from that portion of Hartnett's examination in which he confessed he had been "sold a barrel of false information" and that he would recommend Faulk's employment. Faulk had sent this passage to some of his friends. But as we have seen, after Roy M. Cohn and Thomas Bolan were substituted as counsel, Hartnett not only repudiated this position, but talked to an executive of WOR and told him that the charges against Faulk were true.

Faulk, on my instruction, kept the original envelope addressed to him, made a photostat copy of the enclosed letter, and forwarded the original letter to Robert Leder with a full explanation of the incident. Now, the envelope and photostated letter were marked in evidence. At last we had evidence in writing which showed why Faulk was receiving these heartbreaking setbacks.

When Faulk was a star, he, like other leading performers, had a "sit-in," one who gives the performer a rest by occupying his chair while the hot lights are adjusted, the camera focused, and the microphone "leveled." A sit-in gets ten dollars a day. Now, without any earnings for almost two years, his resources depleted, and a wife and children at home to feed, Faulk grew desperate. After another negative answer from Merton Copeland, producer of the "$64,000 Question" program, he humbled himself and asked for a sit-in job.

Q. And you were refused?

A. I don't like to say Mr. Copeland refused me. He said they had their regular ones, and if he could get a chance—he was embarrassed, sir, because he had known me before.

Even this blow did not break his spirit. He would not surrender the lawsuit which might be the price for his employability. But the realization that the most menial task in broadcasting was not available to him finally made him turn in other directions. He told his wife, "I believe they've got me surrounded."

He took a course in selling mutual funds for the Wellington Funds. It didn't work out. Through Senator William Benton, who owned the Encyclopedia Britannica, he tried to become an encyclopedia salesman. On the stand, despite our instructions, his wry humor was irrepressible.

Q. And did you take a course in some studies . . . ?

A. Oh, yes. . . . There are techniques to being an Encyclopedia Britannica salesman. They have a system. . . . It's a way of getting your foot in the door and holding it there so a lady can't close it when you sell her.

Q. Did you earn any money that way?

A. No, sir.

Like an animal that goes back to his lair, he decided to return with his family to his hometown, Austin, Texas. There, in the bosom of his family, he might be invulnerable from the doubts as to his loyalty, which the defendants had set in motion and which on mysterious wings pursued him everywhere. There was a tiny 250-watt radio station in Austin called KNOW, about as small as existed anywhere. It had only enough power to cover Austin "and not much more." He talked to Mr. Louis Cook, the manager of this station, and told him he was coming back and would be pleased to work for him. There could be no lower rung of the ladder in broadcasting. Of course KNOW was overwhelmed that its home boy who had become nationally famous would deign to appear for it. A written commitment was immediately forthcoming. It was marked in evidence. The arrangement was that he would obtain recordings from stars congratulating KNOW on acquiring John Henry Faulk. John Daly, Peter Lind Hayes, Mary Healy, Walter Cronkite, and others made such transcriptions. Faulk had his sister locate a home for him in South Austin where he had been reared. Then by air mail special delivery came a crushing letter:

"Dear John Henry:

"I regret to advise you that a matter, which I am not at liberty to disclose, involving some long range program planning for our station, has unexpectedly come up and makes it necessary for us to withdraw from any further negotiation or planning in connection with the proposed John Henry Faulk show on KNOW.

"I am sorry, too, for any inconvenience to you . . . that may have been caused by your efforts in making New York contacts and doing ground work in connection with the program. "We will just have to forget it. "Best regards,

"Sincerely,
Louis Cook"

"We will just have to forget it!" Even the city in which he was born and reared would not trust him. Slander, like leprosy, deprives the victim of any habitat. Culminating disasters came quickly one upon the other. His landlord served him with a dispossess notice for non-payment of rent. His electricity was about to be shut off. He took his family to Austin and over-crowded the house of one of his sisters, until he could lift his head above the inundating waters of despair.

With his wife he founded "an advertising agency." It oper-ated from his living room. One old friend was his account. With energy and gritted enthusiasm he succeeded in increas-ing his representation until he could move out of the house and even open an office, twelve by ten feet, for which he paid forty dollars a month rent.

For the year 1959, his wife and he, working at top pitch, grossed twenty-five hundred dollars. After expenses, this was, of course, inadequate to support his family even on an im-poverished standard. But he waited for the trial. We sent him lengthy reports of our crawling progress through a maze of legal proceedings. We bade him hold on until judgment day, and we did not mean that final day which comes to all, but that special day in the courts, which his courage and sacrifice had earned for him.

Finally we summoned him to New York, his wife and children staying behind. The trial day had come. Now he was completing his direct testimony. We put the concluding ques-tions to him:

Q. You told us that you had children. Will you give us their names and ages at that time?

A. There was Johanna. She's my oldest child. She was seven then. And Evelyn was six, and Frank Dobie, my son, was four.

Q. Did they attend school here?

A. Yes. P.S. 87 around the corner. . . .

Q. After you were let out by CBS, some time there-after, did your wife, Lynn, get a job?

A. Yes, sir.

THE COURT: Did your wife work before you were let out?

A. No sir. . . .

Q. Were there any immediate circumstances which induced her and you to have her go out and get a job? . . .

A. Sir, I had been unemployed since September 1957. We had a bank account at that time, a small one, that we coasted a spell on, and of course, I kept thinking each week I was going to get a job, and we went through Christmas, and the first of the year was dubious. We had a conference and agreed that she go out and try to get something, because it looked like I was completely off, and we ran out of funds completely. . . .

Q. What position did your wife take . . . ?

A. She was a kind of secretary-saleslady for a fixture company on 57th St.

Q. And who took care of the children while she was working?

A. Well, I did most of the time, when she was gone, and when she came home I would make my appointments, you know, to coincide with her coming back, so she could ride herd on the children. . . .

We translated his agony into loss of earnings, although we knew how inadequate a description this constituted. He had been averaging thirty-five thousand dollars a year income before he was let out by CBS. The year after he was fired, he earned $875 and this was solely from residuals on commercials made in previous years. He did not earn one cent from radio and television. Did he try to work?

You bet. I was straining myself night and day to get something, sir.

Q. In the year 1960, the next year, how much did you earn from radio and television . . . ?

A. Not a red cent.

Q. In the year 1961 how much did you earn from radio and television combined?

A. Not a penny.

The blacklist had been just as effective in 1962 right up to the day he was on the stand. He had earned nothing.

We were finished with his direct testimony. I announced, "Your witness." He has been on the witness stand six full days. But we knew that the gruesome years he had lived through had not ended his ordeal. He was about to face a long and exhaustive cross-examination, which our adversaries had prepared over the years. We were confident of the truth of our cause, but one never knows what surprises or contradictions may arise during cross-questioning. We therefore had prepared Faulk for any attack which we could anticipate. After each day's direct testimony, we would proceed to my office or home to review the thousands of facts, the hundreds of documents, which he ought to know, to avoid entrapment. We also drove him hard to speak to prospective witnesses, who still faltered and evaded commitment to tell what they knew.

Lawyers are accustomed to late hours during trial. They are conditioned, like trained athletes, to meet emotional drains as well as physical exhaustion. But clients are bewildered by the pace and become feeble and confused from sleeplessness combined with nervous strain. We could see Faulk turn pale in the late hours, and reach the point of non-absorption. Then I would send him home to get "a good night's rest." He would laugh at the advice, and bid us a cheerful "good morning" as he departed with eyes already half-closed. But he knew why we were driving him relentlessly, and he could see in the faces of my partner Martinson, and various associates who participated in preparation, that we did not spare ourselves either.

Now he was ready for cross-examination, but despite our preparation we had not foreseen the surprises which were coming.

The defendants believed in the ancient tactic that the best defense is an aggressive attack. The daring of their offensive, however, reached an intensity the like of which I had never before encountered.

Bolan immediately attempted to demean and ridicule Faulk. Hadn't he been merely a "disc jockey"? Faulk denied this.

> MR. BOLAN: I have noticed that Mr. Nizer and yourself have not used the term disc jockey at all up to this point. . . . Do you have any aversion to being described as a disc jockey?
>
> A. Not in the least, sir. I—
>
> Q. That is an answer. . . . Weren't you a member of the Fresh Air Disc Jockey Committee for the *Herald Tribune* Fresh Air Fund at one time?
>
> A. That is perfectly correct, sir.

Bolan proceeded to confront Faulk with reviews, articles, and contracts which referred to him as a disc jockey.

Faulk explained that a disc jockey is an authority on popular music, whereas he was not, that his was chiefly a talking program.

But the skirmishes concerning this description continued on and off during the lengthy cross-examination.

The plan to embarrass and shrink Faulk was waged in many ways. Articles which had made a derogatory comment about him were utilized as humiliating ammunition.

Q. Did you ever hear the term "professional Texan"?

A. Oh, indeed yes.

Q. Did you ever hear it in reference to you?

A. I think that I have, yes.

Q. What does the term mean?

A. I think in one instance someone writing a review of me, and I don't even recall who it was because it stung. It's very uncomplimentary as far as I am concerned.

It means one that is pompous and inflated and goes about boasting of Texas being the biggest and the best and the finest, and the sun rose and set there; that the first law of gravity was passed by the Texas State Legislature.

THE COURT: Aren't the Texans proud of being the biggest and the best?

THE WITNESS: I am infinitely proud. I am trying to characterize a pompous asinine fellow who has given Texas a rather wide-spread black eye, by the way, and is one of the points I made quite frequently on my program of these oil men, who say . . . they would buy Russia, lease it back to Khrushchev, and that sort of thing.

Bolan accused Faulk of exaggerating his Texas accent. Also,

Q. Wasn't it part of your act on CBS to act the part of an ignorant person rather than an intelligent one?

The court overruled my objection.

A. It certainly was not. . . . I referred frequently to my lectures at Yale University. I quoted Shakespeare . . . and John Milton quite frequently over the air. I do it on a folk level, that is quite true, but that's very different from conducting like a country bumpkin and that is what you are suggesting I did. I had a rather wide listening audience among university people, Princeton and Columbia University.

Bolan continued in this vein, asking him whether he hadn't gotten people to think of him as "an ignoramus."

Suddenly Faulk was asked whether Slate was a very good friend of his? Did he consider his superiors at CBS, Slate and

Ward, "truthful and honest persons?" This was an ominous indication to us that they would be witnesses for the defendants and bear out the defendants' theory that Faulk was fired because his popularity had waned, not because of the libel and blacklist. We had hoped that his former employers would support Faulk in his crisis, but we realized their dilemma if they "confessed" that they had finally yielded to Hartnett's and Johnson's pressures. Now we knew from the nature of the questions that the defendants considered Slate and Ward their bulwark. Faulk countered these questions cautiously at first:

> Mr. Slate is a truthful and honest man, but . . . I don't want to go the whole hog there, and I tell you why . . . . executives who are very honest men frequently were impelled to take actions and positions that could be described as less than candid let us say. . . .
>
> Q. They were compelled to not tell the truth?
> A. Let us say withhold the truth.

But when he was pressed hard he retorted:

"I considered Mr. Slate to be a man under very profound emotional stress, sir, that he had to take an action that he abominated."

It was not until Slate and Ward took the stand as defendants' witnesses and we encountered them in cross-examination, that the jury could determine the business law of physics: The relationship between the pressure of business necessity and the pressure of conscience and integrity.

The attack quickened. Had not Faulk lied under oath when he testified that he had never had any difficulties with CBS?

> Q. In 1955 [before the libel] were you notified by WCBS that your ratings had dropped so low that your services were to be terminated?
> A. I was not.
> Q. Did CBS offer you an opportunity to resign in 1955 rather than be fired?
> A. They did not. . . .
> Q. Did you submit a letter of resignation?
> A. I did.

It was offered in evidence. We had to await redirect examination to complete this incident, which actually was favorable to Faulk. In the meantime we shared his discomfort, at the cloud of suspicion which hovered over his head, due to a half-truth, which can be as insidious as a whole lie.

Faulk was pummeled about the *Pulse* ratings of the popularity of his show. The defendants contended that his ratings had declined perilously.

Faulk replied:

> A. Throughout my stay at CBS my ratings went up and down. They would shift. Everyone else's did so, too. I was always in the top ten listed in the *Pulse* ratings.

These questions, too, were like a mere overture to the opera—and a comic opera it turned out to be. For the defendant later put the *Pulse* publisher on the stand as an expert, and for the first time the validity of ratings was tested by severe cross-examination.

The strategy of attacking the plaintiff, as if he were the wrongdoer, included the accusation that he had brought this suit to get publicity which would improve his "sagging ratings." He was prodded about a "press release" which was issued when his complaint was filed. Had he hired a press agent by the name of Carl Ruff? He denied it, and explained that Charles Collingwood, the president of the union, had called in his own friend Ruff, to issue a statement merely restating the complaint in simple language, in the hope that public knowledge of the filing of the suit might deter the defendants from their continued drive on Faulk. CBS, at that time solicitous about Faulk's future, had advised this too. Then Bolan continued to harass him about the sincerity of the suit, charging that it was a mere publicity device. Faulk explained the fevered view people had of any charge involving communism in those days. He told the story of the agent who assured the employer that his actor was anti-Communist. "I don't care what kind of Communist he is. I won't employ him."

The defendants actually contended that Faulk was better off after the libel than before. CBS had renewed his contract for five years, ten months after he was attacked. The year after the libel bulletin was issued, Faulk's income increased.

> Q. In 1957, Mr. Faulk, did you earn more money from the radio profession than you had ever earned before in your life?
>
> A. Yes. . . .

This was a telling point and Bolan quite properly never let the jury forget it. Due to the intervention of Faulk's friends, Ed Murrow and Charles Collingwood, and also CBS's fortitude at the time, Faulk had been kept on his regular radio hour for over a year and a half after the libel. Then he was fired. But from a litigation standpoint we would have been better off had he lost his job immediately. For now we were caught in the vise of explaining how he could have prospered for a year after his reputation was destroyed. It was his future employability which was destroyed. He was like a man with a fatal disease, who nevertheless remains active for a year, and is told this proves he isn't sick at all. The time lapse, however, lent credence to the defendants' theory that Faulk suffered not from the libel but from his own incompetence. This was a cruel burden we had to bear, but was there ever a lawsuit that did not have nerve-wracking defects? Law doesn't run any more smoothly than love.

The defendants multiplied the devils of skepticism with every conceivable device. They quoted the complaint which asserted the loss of particular sponsors at a rate of eighteen spots a week. Bolan contended first that certain sponsors alleged to have canceled out did not do so, that others had not even been sponsors at the time of the libel, and that some who dropped out, later returned. This all-enveloping attack included a charge that he filled canceled spots so successfully that he was ahead of the game. It reminded me of the folk story of the woman who was charged with damaging a pot she had borrowed. Her defenses were first, that she never borrowed the pot; secondly, that she returned it in perfect condition; and third, that the pot was broken in the first place.

Hour after hour, for several days, Bolan hammered at Faulk's claim of loss of sponsors and replacements. The rotation schedules of CBS which showed his daily broadcasts, were presented to him and he was asked to pore over these documents and answer hundreds of questions put to him on the ebb and flow of sponsorship. At times Faulk reared, but he was held in tight rein.

> Q. . . . turning to the week of March 19 to 24, how many open spots were there in that week?
> A. None.
> Q. And for the week of April 2 to April 7?
> A. There were none.
> Q. And for the week of April 8 to 14?
> A. This is the week after Larry Johnson came down—
> MR. BOLAN: I object.

THE COURT: No, strike it out. Just answer the question.

A. There were ten.

We made careful notes for redirect examination of these matters, at which time Faulk could be given his head.

To show Faulk's relatively modest income from 1952 to 1957 (as compared with the testimony of his potential earnings), Bolan offered information from his income tax reports for those years. I did not object provided the income tax reports from 1958 through 1960, which revealed practically no income at all, were also received. The court permitted us to offer these latter reports, and the before-and-after picture revealed the devastation caused by the libel.

Finally, the defendants ventured on a series of questions which left us gasping with astonishment and then anger. It was the climax of their attack on Faulk, and its daring persuaded us that we were going to be faced with witnesses who would claim that Faulk was a member of the Communist Party!

A cross-examination attack is not unlike a storm. One can see the clouds gather. They become darker. Then there are frightening flashes followed by ear-shattering thunder. Bolan began rather quietly by probing into every detail of Faulk's movements while in the Merchant Marine; what port he landed in, and the exact dates of arrival and departure; when he was with the Red Cross, precisely what were his movements and on what dates. Later when he was a G.I. where did he stop, and for what precise periods of time. He answered quite readily, and I could see everybody at defendants' counsel table scribbling the data furiously as if they were under instruction not to miss a word. A campaign of contradiction was on the way.

The same curious inquisitiveness was applied to his talk to the F.B.I. Who invited him, on what date, at what hotel did it take place, how many were present, and other probing questions which revealed disbelief. Faulk remembered that Dallas Chief of Police Raymond D. Thorpe had invited him to make the talk to the F.B.I.

The next series of questions edged closer to the final attack. Did he know a man by the name of Eli Friedland? When did he first meet him?

Q. Did he ever spend any time in your home?

MR. NIZER: Objected to as totally irrelevant.

MR. BOLAN: . . . I am asking these as a foundation.

THE COURT: Yes, overruled.

A. Yes, he has.

Q. How often, when, where?

I objected.

THE COURT: I am accepting this in light of Mr. Bolan's statement, as preliminary to certain proof he wants to offer and inquire about.

These questions had the sound of shells whistling through space. Although ominous, perhaps they would pass over our heads. Then came the crashing detonation right in our midst.

Q. You have testified you have never been a member of the Communist Party, is that correct?

A. I have so testified. . . .

Q. Have you ever attended any meetings of the Communist Party?

A. I certainly have not.

Q. . . . I direct your attention to the month of February, the year 1944, Austin, Texas, and ask if you attended a Communist Party meeting at the home of one Ina May Bull?

A. I did not.

Q. Do you know Ina May Bull?

A. I do not.

Q. You have never heard that name?

A. I might have heard the name, but it doesn't ring a bell now.

Q. . . . Have you ever met Ina May Bull?

A. I think that I have, yes.

Q. Where and when?

A. I don't recall, somewhere, she was a citizen of Austin, as I recall, and a stenographer at the State Capitol. Beyond that I don't know anything about her.

Q. Have you ever been at her residence?

A. I don't recall ever having been at her residence.

Q. Was a party given in your honor at her home by the city branch of the Communist Party in February 1944?

A. Absolutely not.

Q. . . . Do you know a Ralph Weiner in Austin, Texas?

A. Ralph Weiner?

Q. Yes.

A. Never heard of him.

Q. Do you know a Max Strauss, in Austin, Texas?

A. I have heard that name, but I don't recall him now.

Q. Did you attend a Communist Party group of Austin, meeting at his home in April 1944?

A. I certainly did not. You know I didn't, too.

Faulk was furious at the imputations hurled at him. He had almost risen off his chair as he flung his angry retort at counsel. Faulk's easy, friendly manner had never altered up to this point. His flareup, based as it was upon an accusation of dishonor, gave a new insight into his character. Righteous indignation has a quality of fire in it, which can light a doubtful mind with persuasion. The jury saw a different Faulk during this critical exchange, and we believed they liked him. Bolan objected to the reference to himself, and the court struck it out. I had jumped up too, in protest against questions which, though denied, contained ugly insinuations. There was a general furor. The court pleaded that "you'd better not let your tempers get the best of you. I am saying that for my own benefit, too." We were summoned to the bench to cool off. But when Bolan resumed, he was unrelenting.

Q. Have you ever attended any meetings of the American Youth for Democracy?

A. Never.

Q. In March 1945, did you attend a Marxist study group sponsored by the Communist Party in Austin, Texas?

A. No, sir.

Q. . . . Was your friend, Eli Friedland, known to you to be a member of the Communist Party?

A. Absolutely not.

At the end of that court day, we were emotionally spent, from outraged anger and also alarm. None of us had any doubts about the truth of Faulk's denials. What we foresaw and feared was the production of witnesses who might falsely involve him. There might be other Matusows, who would finger a man unjustly and destroy him. What other conclusion could we form from this attack? Former counsel, Godfrey Schmidt, had said on the record that he never charged Faulk with being "a Communist or a pro-Communist." Hartnett had sworn in his examination before trial that he did not "charge Faulk with being a Communist or pro-Communist sympathizer." Yet now there was a complete reversal and direct accusations were made that he attended Communist meetings, and tendered "in his honor" too!

There is a rule of cross-examination, based not on law but psychology, that a lawyer should not put an incriminating question to a witness, unless he can overcome the denial with proof. For example, he should never ask a witness whether he has been convicted of a crime, unless he has in his possession a certified copy of the conviction.

I remember a lawyer for a bus company cross-examining a woman and asking her if she had been drunk at the time of the accident. She denied it vehemently, and no proof was ever offered to contradict her. The jury resented the attack upon her, and demonstrated it in their verdict. The doctrine of fair play is deeply ingrained in American tradition, and is a continuous force in every trial. A witness who makes a snide remark about another witness, or even at the cross-examiner, will injure his cause. A lawyer who attacks ruthlessly and without support for his accusation will be resented. A jury will understand the bold strokes of an advocate. It will admire his zeal and devotion to his client. But it will rarely forgive foul play, and it considers reckless accusations without even an attempt to prove them, hitting below the belt. Any lawyer who belabors a woman for her infidelity and fails to support the charge with substantial, cogent evidence, will feel the whiplash of a jury's denunciation. This principle applied equally to the damning accusation of communism. We had good reason to believe that counsel would not identify Ina May Bull, and others, and ask direct questions about Communist meetings, without putting them, and perhaps others, on the stand to denounce Faulk as a Red.

At about this time, too, John Lang, Bolan's assistant, disappeared from court for several days. Was he, a former F.B.I. agent, sleuthing in Austin? Telephone calls soon revealed that he was there. He had interviewed Police Chief Thorpe, who had completely confirmed Faulk's version of his address to the F.B.I. Thorpe advised us that he was willing, if necessary, to fly East and testify. At least we were prepared for our counterattack on this front. But where were the Ina May Bulls, the Max Strausses, the Ralph Weiners, who had been mentioned? So far as we could learn, not in Austin, and so we had no way of checking whether they had been approached by the defendants. This uncertainty rested heavily upon us, for nothing is more enervating than to anticipate a vicious attack from sources that can only be dimly perceived. There was only one comforting thought about the depressing events; if by any chance, the defendants had bluffed in asking these questions; if they had gambled on unnerving Faulk by facing him with rumors to test him out; if as Hartnett had already testified (in the Barrett incident) he practiced the trick of hurling a mere surmise at the accused as if it were a fact, to see whether it would draw a confession; then they had committed a grave error. Faulk had vehemently denied the accusations. What would the jury think if the defendants couldn't make good on their new libels? Might not the defendants, in their desperation, have insured us of a greater verdict than we had hoped for?

This seemed to be undue optimism. In the meantime, we expected a confrontation with hostile witnesses, who might destroy not only our lawsuit, but Faulk himself.

Redirect examination is designed to clear up any murkiness resulting from cross-examination. It is a form of rehabilitation of the witness. Faulk had been cross-questioned for five days. We felt that a very brief and sharp redirect examination would dramatically demonstrate his imperviousness. There were only a few matters which required an answer.

First, the defendants had proved that Faulk had resigned from CBS before the libel. Was this due to his failure as a performer, as they claimed? We demonstrated with a few questions that he had been offered a better post by Mrs. Lyndon Johnson's Texas stations, and had therefore quit CBS with regret. However, not only Slate and Ward, but Dr. Frank Stanton, President of CBS, had asked him to remain, and he yielded. They prepared a letter withdrawing his resignation and resuming his contract. He signed it. We read this exhibit to the jury. In one fell swoop, the impression that he had been forced to resign was reversed. CBS had pleaded with him to remain and he did.

Lengthy cross-examination had been aimed at Faulk's errors in claiming the loss of certain accounts. We proved that he had not cited all the sponsors he had lost and that the total dropouts exceeded his claim. As to the small number of spots available on his schedule after the libel, he said:

"I was living on borrowed time. Whether I lost three spots, sir, or thirty spots is very insignificant in terms of the fact that my entire career was shut out by the action of the defendants, completely and totally."

Concerning the claim that he started suit for the publicity purpose of lifting his sagging ratings, we asked him:

Q. What was your motive in bringing suit?

A. To vindicate my name and to remove the clouds that had been raised by these defendants over my integrity, the cloud that had been deadly to every artist that it had hit in this industry.

Faulk had been on the witness stand eleven days. He had constructed a foundation for his case, upon which we intended to build a triumphant structure. He had also suffered through a cross-questioning which ranged from ridicule to a challenge of his loyalty. We thought it appropriate that the final questions put to him should go to the essence of his conviction:

Q. Have you . . . ever been sympathetic to any Communist ideology, directly or indirectly?

A. No, sir, I have not.

Q. . . . Have you all your life believed in the principles of democracy of the Constitution of the United States . . . .

A. Yes, sir, I have.

Both sides were through with him. He stepped from the witness stand. He was pasty pale from his battle. As he walked behind me to his seat at the counsel table, once more he touched my shoulder lightly, and I thought with a tremulous hand. From that moment, he was a spectator, and he was to 'see a drama unfold which held his fate, but which he could no longer control.

Charles Collingwood was our next witness. He had been a Rhodes scholar, CBS correspondent in London and then to the United Nations. He was one of television's outstanding commentators and news analysts, and had presided over election night broadcasts. He had interviewed Winston Churchill, Charles de Gaulle, and other heads of state. Only a few months before, he had dealt with other kinds of royalty, that of achievement, John Glenn, and that of charm, Jacqueline Kennedy, when she toured the White House, sharing the history of her home with all Americans.

Collingwood was elegant in manner and diction, but without the accompanying affectations which draw attention thereto instead of to his words. He had an open, honest face and his reasoned tone was equal to his tonal resonance.

He explained why he had been caught up in AFTRA's fight against Aware Inc. and its blacklisting activities. Union members who were dominated by Aware, became "so preoccupied with looking under the bed . . . to find out whether some little dancer was a Communist," that they ignored the employment problems in a technologically changing industry. He ran on a middle-of-the-road ticket and became president of the union. When Faulk was attacked, Collingwood warned the president of WCBS that if Faulk, now second vice president of the union, was let out,

"we would take a very strong view of it, that I would have to hold hearings, because this would be a clear-cut case of blacklisting . . . . that the investigation . . . would also involve the agencies and clients. . . ."

Ed Murrow, he testified, added his powerful voice to the plea. With such mighty warriors on his side, Faulk kept his radio job for more than a year and a half. But the defendants never lifted the siege, and when he was finally compelled to venture out of CBS, he was cut down economically. Collingwood confirmed that Faulk's reputation for loyalty, patriotism, character, and integrity were "very high":

Q. What is the employment practice with respect to an artist who becomes involved in a controversy with respect to his loyalty?

A. Well, it really depends on how much guts the sponsor has, the network and the station . . . to stand up to the pressures which are brought against them. . . . The time of which we are speaking in most cases they didn't have very much guts.

It didn't matter whether the charge against the artist was true.

During the cross-examination, Collingwood maintained his best television imperturbable manner. Bolan asked him whether stars like Milton Berle, Sid Caesar, and Jackie Gleason didn't fade out of the picture. Collingwood countered that Jack Benny and Bob Hope had "carried over their radio popularity to television."

He admitted there were others like the American Legion who brought pressures, but insisted that Aware was the principal one from the union viewpoint. When Bolan sought his concession that the Aware *Bulletin* had not charged "you personally with any pro-Communist affiliations," he retorted sharply,

"I found the general imputation of what Aware had to say of me and the group to leave the impression that perhaps there was something wrong with my loyalties."

Thus, the cloak of suspicion which the defendants had cast over Faulk had also enveloped this impressive witness.

Collingwood was pummeled with questions as to how conclusive the proof of communism had to be before he would consider "blacklisting" improper.

He explained that he drew

"a strong line between someone who was proved to be a Communist, and those about whom charges were made that were not substantiated, which is a kind of vigilanteism and character destruction. . . ."

Tony Randall took the stand to the customary buzz of recognition. He stated his stage experience in *Inherit the Wind* and *Caesar and Cleopatra,* among other plays, and his motion picture experience, winding up with the then current *Pillow Talk* with Doris Day and Rock Hudson. He did not shed his stage personality simply because he was on the witness stand. Slender and mischievous of face, his dignity remained satirically hollow. His perplexity was exaggerated to the point of being feigned. His voice was pompously basso and rose to high-pitched querulousness. All combined to create charm and humor.

He testified that until the AFTRA resolution, actors were afraid to be seen voting against the Aware slate. After the condemnation of Aware by a 2 to 1 margin, we came "out from under the rocks so to speak. It seemed to show that if we organized we could beat them without being afraid."

On cross-examination, Bolan immediately picked up the phrase "from under the rocks" because of its evident uncomplimentary allusion to Randall—another typical illustration of why witnesses should not try to be comedians. Finally, Bolan faced him with a contradiction:

Q. Mr. Randall, you have testified that you came out from under the rocks after the referendum election in 1955. Now isn't it a fact, Mr. Randall, that you put your name on a sheet in support of the resolution before it was submitted to referendum vote, and I show you Exhibit FF?

Randall's light comedy touch extricated him as skillfully as it had involved him in the error. Blandly, he replied:

A. My word, I came out sooner than I thought.

On redirect examination, he expressed his revulsion to communism. There remained the impression that anti-Communist artists had, nevertheless, been intimidated by threat of reprisal from Aware, if they dared to defy it.

There was one defendant the jury had not even seen. Laurence Johnson had never appeared in the courtroom. At the beginning of the trial, he had sought an adjournment, claiming illness on the basis of a doctor's certificate. The court had denied the request on the ground that the certificate was inadequate. It was extraordinary for a defendant to absent himself completely. Our inquiries concerning his whereabouts or condition were parried without information. In the meantime, the clear strategy of the defendants was to insist that Johnson had not and could not be connected with plaintiff's accusations by any direct proof. If he were not in court, we could not put him on the stand as our witness in an effort to implicate him. Justice Geller had repeatedly warned us, that although Johnson's name had been brought into the evidence in various ways, there would have to be direct, sworn testimony connecting him with Faulk or the case against Johnson would be dismissed. Time and again, the judge cautioned the jury that the references to Johnson had been received subject to connection. Unless we could supply such testimony, the jury would be instructed to ignore all of the allusions to him.

Throughout the examination of Johnson before trial, he had denied any participation in the pressures upon Faulk. He had even denied control of the deeds of the Onondaga County American Legion Post, or of the Veterans Action Committee of Syracuse Supermarkets. The defendants seemed confident that we could not connect Johnson by proper legal evidence, and that he would be let out of the suit, leaving us (even if we won) with Aware and Hartnett, two financially worthless defendants.

Now the time had come to drag Johnson into the thick of the suit. The invaluable witnesses who could supply the missing link were Thomas D. Murray, account executive of the

Grey Advertising Agency and his superior, Samuel Dalsimer.

Murray had a disheveled, honest look in his face. He was one of those witnesses with an indefinable quality of absolute credibility. This gave added impact to his invaluable testimony.

When he was Vice President of the Coca-Cola Bottling Company of New York, in charge of its two-million-dollar annual advertising budget, he had sponsored Faulk on his WCBS radio program and found that he received "more laudatory mail from listeners than all the other fifteen performers" he used, combined.

Later Murray became a senior account executive of the Grey Advertising Agency, in charge of the account of the Hoffman Beverage Company, which was owned by the Pabst Brewing Company. He was pleased to learn that Faulk was sponsored by his client, because his performance "was as good for Hoffman as it had been for Coca-Cola."

One day Laurence Johnson of Syracuse telephoned him. He introduced himself as one who had influence over supermarkets which did a food business volume of eighteen to twenty million dollars annually:

"He then said . . . that he thought it was a disgrace that our company was using a Communist, John Henry Faulk, to advertise its products.

"I replied that I had no such knowledge about Mr. Faulk.

"And he said, 'Well, you had better get in line because a lot of people along Madison Avenue are getting in line. . . .'

"I said that I could not accept a telephone implication of this kind. I felt that there were legal ways of establishing whether or not Mr. Faulk, or for that matter, anyone else, was a Communist and that I had no intention of firing . . . a man who was a first-rate salesman for our product.

"Then he said, 'How would you like it if your client were to receive a letter from an American Legion Post up here?'

"And I said that I was a veteran myself and that I could not believe that the American Legion would lend itself to what I considered to be an obvious blackmail attempt and he said, 'Well, you will find out.'"

Johnson also talked advertising language to Murray. He threatened to remove Pabst beer from all display space. There are no clerks in supermarkets to make personal recommendations, and companies "spend a lot of money and effort" to obtain such "hard-won space" on the shelves. If a display is not there, explained Murray, "you are dead in that super-market. So this represented a tremendous threat to Pabst Brewing Company, but I mean tremendous. . . . That means you don't sell any merchandise." Johnson knew how to hit the vital nerve center of a sponsor.

Murray considered it his duty to report the incident of what he thought was a crank call, to his superior Dalsimer. Upon learning that the Johnson, who had telephoned, was "Larry Johnson of Syracuse," Dalsimer registered great alarm. "This could be dynamite," he said, "it could be very serious. You had better get on it fast and do something about it."

Murray realized that he had made a terrible error in defying Johnson. His was the plight of the private who talks back brashly to another soldier in the dark, only to be advised that he had offended a general.

He telephoned Johnson to make amends, but did not find him in his hotel room. With hat in hand, he dashed to the hotel in a taxi:

"Again no answer in Mr. Johnson's room. Then because frankly, I was very upset, I ran over to the desk clerk and I said, 'Can you help me find a Mr. Larry Johnson? I have to find him.'

"And the clerk said, 'He is standing right over there in the lobby with that other gentleman.'

"So I went over and I introduced myself to Mr. Johnson. I said, 'I am the Tom Murray who talked to you on the phone a while ago, Mr. Johnson, and I would like to discuss the matter with you further. . . .'

"And Mr. Johnson said, 'After the way you spoke to me, I want nothing further to do with you,' and with that he turned and with his companion left the hotel."

Murray and the Grey Advertising Agency had lost their chance. Johnson would not forgive their failure to knuckle down at once. They must be punished for talking back. Absolute obedience to Johnson's dictates was required and resistance, even by error, could not be countenanced. They would be taught a lesson. And indeed they were. The Pabst Brewing Company received a letter from the American Legion in Syracuse. It described how communism was gaining control of the American airwaves and then called attention to Pabst's "salesman, John Henry Faulk," enclosing Aware's *Bulletin* with the seven specifications of his "Communist record."

The President of the Pabst Brewing Company, Mr. Harris Perlstein, forwarded this incriminating letter to the Grey Advertising Agency, with what we can imagine was an appropriate comment on the embarrassment their conduct had caused their client. Murray was dispatched with these letters to Mr. Slate of CBS to complete the chain of "how come we are in this mess."

Since Johnson had threatened Murray with such a letter, it was received in evidence, together with the attached Aware *Bulletin*. Then, for the first time, we heard words from the judge which were music to our ears. He instructed the jury:

"You remember on a number of occasions, I said certain testimony was taken subject to connection. I explained there would have to be some independent proof connecting defendant Johnson with those letters of that [American Legion] Post to the sponsors.

"Now Mr. Murray's testimony is plaintiff's offer of such independent proof of his connection and you may now consider this evidence as to those letters as they affect defendant Johnson's responsibility."

When cross-examined, Murray no longer had reason to be obsequious about Johnson.

Q. When Mr. Johnson said to you that Mr. Faulk was a Communist, you didn't ask him what the basis of his statement was?

A. . . . Mr. Johnson had not qualified himself as an authority on such subjects. I thought he should be back wherever he comes from, selling baked beans. . . . By what right does a grocer call me up and tell me so and so is a Communist, "Get rid of him"?

I don't mind admitting I was kind of sore!

We felt as if a breath of fresh air had brushed across the courtroom. Bolan continued:

Q. Did you tell Johnson that there were courts of law to determine whether a person is a Communist?

A. I did.

Q. . . . You didn't ask him what the basis of his information was?

A. No, I did not. He volunteered the fact that Mr. Faulk had been written up in, I think, the *Daily Worker*, . . . but that cut no ice with me because Franklin D. Roosevelt was praised in the *Daily Worker*.

Murray was followed on the witness stand by his superior, Samuel Dalsimer. He immediately riveted down the testimony which the jury had just heard. "There are two sides to a coin," is the cry of those who claim antithesis. But here the two sides bore the same imprint and pressed the truth upon the viewer from each direction. Dalsimer was Executive Vice President of the Grey Advertising Agency, which did sixty million dollars' business annually for such clients as General Electric, Westinghouse, RCA, Greyhound, Procter & Gamble, and others. He was a tall, distinguished-looking man, as impressive in appearance as his achievements. The fact that such a man would be terrorized by a telephone call from a Syracuse grocer spoke volumes.

We had a surprise for the defendants. Dalsimer had encountered Johnson four years previously, and the story we drew from him was more shocking than the Faulk incident. It appeared that Dalsimer's agency represented the Block Drug Company, which manufactured Amm-i-dent Tooth Paste. Its competitor was Lever Brothers, whose product was Chlorodent Toothpaste. It was the first great chlorophyll battle. Dalsimer's client appealed to the public through a television program called "Danger," a melodramatic series which even dwarfed the risk from use of ordinary toothpastes. Laurence Johnson "monitored" this program. His eagle eye detected that one of the minor actors had been listed by *Counter Attack* as a Communist sympathizer. He sprung to the defense of the airwaves, which had just been polluted. He wrote a long letter to Mr. Block, which, of course, was turned over to Mr. Dalsimer. On Johnson's examination before trial, we had obtained his admission that he had sent this document. Now, over objection that it was an ancient incident, it went into evidence. It provided a remarkable window into Johnson's mind. Several months before he had complained to Dalsimer who "was very blunt with me . . . , practically told me to mind my own business, which, of course, he had a perfect right to do . . ." but—!

"I passed this information on to the Veterans Action Committee of Syracuse Supermarkets . . .

"I would like to make this offer to you."

He proposed to the Block Drug Company that the two competing toothpastes, Amm-i-dent and Chlorodent, be sold side by side for two weeks.

Then during the next two weeks a sign would be put on the Chlorodent stock saying that its competitor,
"Lever Bros. try not to use any of Stalin's little creatures in their advertising, but . . . endeavor to employ pro-American artists."

Block's company could put up its sign explaining why it uses "Communist Fronters" to advertise Amm-i-dent. To complete this fair poll, the Veterans Action Committee of Syracuse Supermarkets, "together with . . . Syracuse American Legion could post signs why they protest the use of Communist Fronters."

Johnson's conclusion would have made any dictator who ever rigged a ballot box swell with pride at his own restraint: "Wouldn't the buying public tell us by these tests whether they wanted to support Communist Fronts or not?

"Would not the results of such a test be of the utmost value to the thousands of supermarkets throughout America . . . ?"

The final touch of blackmail had the delicacy of a sledgehammer.
"This letter will be held awaiting your answer for a few days. Then copies will be sent to the following":

The succeeding list, which ranged from the Chamber of Commerce of the United States to the Sons of the American Revolution, and from the Catholic War Veterans to the Super Market Institute in Chicago, was calculated to impress upon the advertiser the inevitable question, "Isn't it easier to comply with Johnson's censure of some actor or actress than stand up to him and be involved in such a destructive campaign?" Martyrdom is a rare phenomenon at best, and one is not likely to find it among sponsors spending large sums to increase profits.

In the course of quoting Johnson, Dalsimer came within a prefix of that ominous word "blacklist." Johnson had said to him:
"There was going to be a good list and a bad one, and he . . . said I had missed the boat as far as getting on the good list was concerned."

On one occasion when Dalsimer met with Johnson he was accompanied by Harvey Matusow. When Johnson discovered that the television series called "Danger" was a CBS show, he opened fire on the entire network. He sent a letter to all retailers:

"Are the directors of the Columbia Broadcasting Company and President Frank Stanton trying to push Communist Fronters under the guise of advertising toothpaste? Why do they continually embarrass Block Drug Company by injecting Stalin's little creatures into CBS's owned show named Danger, sponsored by Ammident? . . .

"Is this the kind of testimonial for honesty and integrity we should expect of the Columbia Broadcasting Company?"

Johnson offered another objective poll to Stanton and CBS. He enclosed a questionnaire with a box for voting. It read: "Do you want any part of your purchase price of any products advertised on the Columbia Broadcasting System to be used to hire Communist Fronters?"

There were two squares for voting; one marked "Yes" and one marked "No." What could be fairer?

The letter concluded with a touching declaration of magnanimity if the vote should go against Johnson: "Can Mr. Frank Stanton deny responsibility for the appearance of Stalin's little creatures on Westinghouse, Block and Carter programs . . . ?

"If the American public decides in his favor we will surely acknowledge our error.

> "Very truly yours,
> Veterans Action
> Committee of
> Syracuse Supermarkets"

Johnson was proud of his handiwork. He mailed a copy to Hartnett with a handwritten note. It was unsigned, but he had to admit it was his writing at the examination before trial. It went into evidence, linking Johnson and Hartnett as if handcuffs were placed on their wrists.

Bolan had no difficulty eliciting the witness's bias against Johnson.

Q. And you had a dislike of Mr. Johnson . . . ?
A. Well, he made me pretty mad.

We called Kim Hunter, the noted actress, to the stand. As she stood taking her oath, only a few of us knew what courage it took for her to be there. She had been a victim of the blacklist herself. After starring in Tennessee Williams' *A Streetcar Named Desire* on the Broadway stage, she had enacted the same role of Stella in the motion picture. She won the Academy Award for the best supporting actress. Then, when she had reached the top rung of her profession, disaster struck her. She was blacklisted and became unemployable. With a rare exception, she couldn't get a job on stage, television, or motion pictures for three years. Her desperation was deeper because she didn't know the reason. No one accused her of any misconduct or disloyalty. A dark and mysterious door simply shut her out from her life's work. A blacklist is like a plague, whose origin and cause is unknown. One can only helplessly watch the devastation. Kim Hunter could only cry over a wasting career, not knowing why or what to do. It was only during the examination before trial of Hartnett that deadly letters about her were revealed, and we shall soon see that they were "lost" when we asked for them at the trial, and what a struggle it was to compel Hartnett to "find" them.

However, long before the Faulk trial, one of Kim Hunter's friends, William Dozier, a CBS executive producer, had surmised the source of her trouble. He referred her to Roy Brewer, of California, who made contact with Hartnett. The process of clearance began. But at what a price! She had to "confess," purge herself of wrongs she had not committed, and finally, in the AFTRA contest then pending with Aware, she had to send a telegram pleading that Aware be not condemned, when her whole being was filled with loathing for everything it stood for.

Having surrendered her principles she was taken off the blacklist and had no trouble working again. However, she was a sensitive and fine person, and the struggle within her did not abate.

When the Faulk case was instituted, we asked her whether she would testify. She explained that to do so would almost certainly put her back on the blacklist, and that she had not the stamina to go through that nightmarish experience again. She promised to think it over and consult with her husband. When the case came to trial years later, she volunteered to be a witness. It was not an easy decision. It meant revealing to all who knew her the expedient road she had taken to appease Hartnett, even though it involved a betrayal of her real convictions. Also, she was conscious of the risk that her career might be terminated in the resulting recriminations and retaliations. Nevertheless, she was determined to purge herself of inner doubts about her prior surrender to Hartnett.

This conflict was so intense that it virtually paralyzed her the moment she sat down in the witness chair. It was as if her emotions flooded her brain and numbed it. I was astonished to find that she could not focus on the simplest question. She stared at me helplessly and did not answer. The long silences were embarrassing. One could see her fighting hysteria, exhausting her energies so much that she could not speak. Only a slight quiver revealed the struggle. The judge also observed her torment.

    THE COURT: Miss Hunter, even though you are in a courtroom you can relax. Just assume that we are all in the living room. Just take it easy.

This eloquent actress, whose nostrils could convey emotions for which others used heaving chests, struggled haltingly to utter a few simple words. Still the story emerged.

When she learned that the three-year blight of her career might be ended by communication with Hartnett, she had her agent, Arthur P. Jacobs, write to him. Jacobs pointed out that "Miss Hunter is not sympathetic to the Left cause" and that she had appeared in Sidney Kingsley's play of Arthur Koestler's "violently anti-Communist . . . 'Darkness at Noon.'" He wanted to know whether there was "any information on her previous activities" and whether there "would be any costs involved in obtaining this information."

Hartnett replied that his files revealed that her name had been linked with Communist Front activities, and that he would furnish a complete report for two hundred dollars. She refused to pay.

"I said that . . . my life was an open book and I didn't feel I needed Mr. Hartnett's information or investigation and I certainly wasn't going to pay two hundred dollars for it."

We read into the record Hartnett's admission at his examination before trial, that he had attempted to extract this payment.

"Here's not Miss Hunter, but a public relations man . . . who makes five G's a year on this. On some accounts his probable retainer is fifty G's a year, and I said I would make a report for him, and I think I would be a complete ass if I did it for nothing."

Style can reveal the person as much as his deeds. Hartnett's "lingo" in this answer ("five G's," "complete ass") gave crude coloration to his conduct.

What was Miss Hunter's "dubious activity as recently as March 1953" which Hartnett referred to, as requiring "correction of her past mistakes?" It developed that she had contributed "five dollars or fifteen dollars" for the reprint of a series of articles in the New York *Post* by Oliver Pilat entitled "Blacklist—The Panic in TV-Radio." These articles had exposed Hartnett's *Red Channels* Activities," Laurence Johnson's "veto over employment of the two-billion-dollar radio and TV industry," and the participation of the Veterans Action Committee of Syracuse Supermarkets. She had forgotten about this trivial contribution, but this was her sin! If she only had known that she had been barred from tens of thousands of dollars of earnings and suffered oblivion in her profession because of that paltry sum. The defendants were remorseless. Like all tyrants, they were sensitive to exposure and unforgiving for any slight.

When she had come begging to Hartnett to restore her career, he demanded that she attend the AFTRA meeting and speak against the resolution condemning Aware, which was then pending.

"I said, 'Mr. Hartnett, it would be very difficult indeed for me to speak in support of Aware, because I am not in support of Aware Inc.' "

He generously reduced the price. She need only send a telegram. Thus, her stultification would not be in person. She yielded. The meeting was startled to receive a plea that

"you . . . think very carefully indeed before voting for this resolution. . . . AFTRA will have no recourse whatsoever if it places itself on record as . . . aiding the Communist conspiracy, even if this action is taken in the noble desire to aid and protect the innocent.

"Kim Hunter"

Only a few knew how this message had been obtained.

We later found in Hartnett's file his triumphant letter to Johnson:

"Dear Larry,

"Confidentially, I had a good telephone conversation this morning with Kim Hunter. . . .

". . . If she comes through tomorrow night at the AFTRA meeting as she promised she would do, you will hear the comrades shrieking all the way from New York to Syracuse. . . .

"Keep up the fight, Larry, you and your associates have done wonders.

"Sincerely,
"Vincent Hartnett"

We asked her whether after she sent the telegram she worked again. She replied, "I worked quite frequently after that, and to the present day."

We turned her over to cross-examination. It was obvious that she could be embarrassed by the fact that she had "lied" in her telegram, and in affidavits which she had been forced to submit. But we did not fear this encounter. A questionable witness may be destroyed by such admissions, but we relied upon the jury's distinguishing insight into Miss Hunter's character and the predicament she faced. If the cross-examiner emphasized the conflict between her beliefs and what she wrote, would he be discrediting her, or demonstrating the outrageous pressure to which she had been subjected? We did not have to wait long.

Q. Did Mr. Hartnett ask you to do anything you did not wish to do?

A. Yes.

Q. What was that?

A. I did not really wish to go on record in my union as opposing that resolution.

In the telegram she had argued that any member who had been libeled by AFTRA could sue.

Q. And did you state in that telegram something that you did not wish to state?

A. Well, yes . . . anybody who has been accused of pro-Communist tendencies by Aware Inc. has the right to go to court to prove his innocence, but there are few people who have the funds, and oh, the stamina to go through that. . . .

She was extremely agitated. Tears were flowing down her cheeks.

THE COURT: . . . Miss Hunter, we appreciate the stress under which you . . .

THE WITNESS: Yes, Your Honor.

THE COURT: Try to answer the questions calmly. If

you want to rest at any point you let me know. The
Court understands.

Nevertheless, her next answer was so unclear that the
judge asked her to "collect your thoughts and continue." She
replied, ". . . I don't follow my answer either."

Like a fighter whose brain sometimes clears from an additional blow, the cross-examination suddenly revived her.
Bolan tried to show that she had obtained work before she
sent the telegram to AFTRA.

> Q. And isn't it a fact that Mr. Hartnett marked you
> "pass" . . . a number of months prior to your sending
> the telegram?
>
> A. I don't know when he marked me "pass" as you
> say, or cleared. . . . All I know is that in that conversation
> on the phone I was left with the feeling that, kind of like
> a donkey with a carrot in front of his nose, that "You
> have had a taste of work, now do you want to continue
> working?"
>
> I wanted to continue working.

Besides the telegram, Hartnett had required an affidavit
from Kim Hunter in which she admitted the error of her ways.
It is difficult to understand why Communists or bitter anti-
Communists both believe that self-abasement is the minimum
requirement of the damned. Is it basically the cruelty of the
accuser which must be satisfied? Is he more interested in seeing his victim squirm than in conversion? The Russian trials,
at which intellectual founders of the Revolution were required to describe themselves as unprincipled wretches who
had betrayed their ideals, now see their counterpart when
anti-Communists prescribe self-flagellation as the only method
of purification. Sadism as the road to reform begets other evils,
such as the demand to confess lies rather than truth; to bypass the surrounding circumstances which change the entire
complexion of the act; to ignore the time element and judge
the deed by the absolute standards of hindsight; and
worst of all, to justify extremism and vigilanteism by forcing
the victim of the lynching to thank his oppressor by conceding his own evil.

Bolan read Kim Hunter's affidavit of self-degradation to
the jury. We wondered whether the jurors were sensitive
enough to appreciate that the compulsion which wrested

these words from her was the worst offense of the whole clearance system.

Although she repeatedly stated her opposition to Communist ideology, her affidavit contained such passages as: "Theater people . . . incline to be gullible, sentimental, and . . . politically naïve. . . . They are often fair game for . . . Communist-inspired operations. I was no exception. . . . Here is a list of these incidents, how I was drawn in and to what extent."

Was there need for such confession? What were the incidents for which such prostration was required?

Seven years earlier all actors had been circulated to attend a meeting to discuss the rights of ten Hollywood writers who had refused to answer questions put by the House Committee on Un-American Activities. Out of curiosity, she went and listened. It was an isolated instance. Yet now, almost a decade later, she made a humiliating sworn statement of regret.

Her second "confession" involved the use of her name in connection with "the problem of world peace" under the auspices of the National Council of Arts, Sciences and Professions. She never even attended a session.

The third misdeed was that she signed a petition in aid of Willie McGee, a Negro, "who was alleged to be suffering injustice at the hands of the Mississippi courts." She never attended the meeting. On redirect examination, she asserted that she had no regrets for this act, but in her affidavit she had to describe it as "misguided association with . . . the McGee case" which was making it difficult "for me to obtain employment in radio and television."

The final item on her *mea culpa* list was her sponsorship to the extent of approximately five dollars of the reprint of the New York *Post's* articles on blacklisting.

"I have since learned that this reprint was promoted by a faction in the union so radical . . . as to be considered pro-Communist. . . ." Thus, she was forced to crawl to her redemption.

She concluded her redirect testimony with an unequivocal statement that at no time in her life had she ever had any sympathy for Communist ideology.

She stepped down from the witness stand, her head proudly high, as if she had gained strength from the experience. We knew that she had aided our case, and we felt her ordeal was not unrewarded. She had regained her self-respect.

Joseph Cotten starred on a radio series called "The Private Files of Matthew Bell." It had no political content. One day the sponsor, Seabrook Farms, received a letter from the Syracuse American Legion Post, signed by Laurence Johnson, criticizing it for having "Stalin's little creatures" crawling over its products. It threatened a boycott of Seabrook not only in Johnson's supermarkets, but in other supermarket chains.

There is a famous case taught in all law schools in which a lit firecracker is tossed into a crowd. Each person who catches it throws it hysterically to someone else. Finally, it explodes and someone is injured. Who is responsible among the many who tossed it forward?

Johnson's or Hartnett's letter was like that firecracker. The sponsor, Seabrook Farms, immediately hurled it at its advertising agency, the firm of Hilton and Riggio. Now, Peter Hilton, the president, was on the witness stand. He had thrown the Johnson firecracker to the producer of the program, Music Corporation of America (MCA). It flung it at the star, Joseph Cotten. It passed to Leo Dorsey, counsel for Seabrook Farms.

Hilton wanted MCA to cancel the show. It refused. Instead, a meeting was arranged with Laurence Johnson.

In Seabrook Farms' private plane, its president, C. F. Seabrook, Joseph Cotten, Peter Hilton, and Leo Dorsey flew to Syracuse. They proceeded to Johnson's office in the rear of one of his supermarkets. There he held court, as prosecutor and judge. He informed all that the Veterans Action Committee of Syracuse Supermarkets had to protect the American way of life.

Mr. Seabrook cited his company's record during the war and assured Johnson that he would not knowingly support any Communist cause. Johnson rejected this generalization. He had to go by the "record" that there were Communist fellow travelers on the show.

No "record" was produced or cited. In the blacklisting court, such details are not needed. Weren't the pleaders before him fortunate to face their prosecutor? Others would not have known who he was.

Joseph Cotten "protested very vehemently." He cited his work during the war, showing letters which attested to his patriotic efforts in entertaining troops and selling war bonds. Johnson was unimpressed. He had his mysterious "record."

Finally, Hilton brought forth a compromise proposal. The

sponsor would give up one of its three commercials and substitute therefor a patriotic message about the need for protecting America's free institutions. Johnson accepted this offer grudgingly, not perceiving its irony. For would not such a plea best be enforced if the Johnsons and Hartnetts were prevented from violating the right of every American to be tried by his peers in accordance with due process of law? It probably would have stunned Johnson to realize that his private brand of super-patriotism more closely resembled communism's exaltation of the State's interests over the welfare of any citizen. The government's interest according to communism is interpreted and enforced by arbitrary edict of an unelected official who has seized power. Who had designated Johnson or Hartnett to condemn Joseph Cotten and his companions, who flew to Carnossa to appease the tyrant?

On the way back to the airport, Johnson's patriotism yielded to his business instinct. He stopped at one of his supermarkets and brought Joseph Cotten to his customers, offering them autographs. Cotten felt "very uncomfortable." His persecutor was exhibiting him as if he were a prize animal captured in a hunt. Indignity was thus added to insult.

The results were foreseeable. At the end of the thirteen weeks, Mr. Seabrook canceled the program. Hilton testified: "He made it clear that he held us responsible for the incident and our relations deteriorated immediately from that point on."

Hilton lost this account, which represented about a half million dollars a year billings and a profit of seventy-five thousand dollars a year.

Johnson followed up his contract. He asked Hilton to engage Harvey Matusow as a writer. Hilton was no longer in the mood to bend a knee. He refused.

The producer and director of Joseph Cotten's show was Hiram Brown. He testified that he had been summoned to Laurence Johnson's hotel suite by Matusow and told by Johnson that he, too, would lose his job if he didn't use "the right actors." Brown testified on the basis of thirty years' experience that a blacklist operated in radio and television. The actor was not told that he was rejected because of political affiliation. "The language was always devious."

On cross-examination, he was asked:

Q. Do you have a personal hatred of Mr. Hartnett?

A. I have.

It was, therefore, necessary on redirect examination to demonstrate the basis of the bias. Hartnett had listed him in *Red Channels*. Of the three items under his name two were of organizations, "I never in my life heard anything about." The third referred to his sponsorship of a dinner for Governor Herbert H. Lehman and Senator Meade, the regular Democratic candidates in the 1946 campaign. After asserting that his feelings about Hartnett had no effect on the truthfulness of his testimony, and his abhorrence of communism, he was excused from the stand.

Laurence Johnson and the Syracuse American Legion Post also tackled the Metropolitan Opera. But an opera is not a product which needs to be displayed in supermarkets, and they received a sharp rebuff.

We presented as a witness Reginald Allen, then director of operations for Lincoln Center for the Performing Arts, which includes the Philharmonic Hall, the new Metropolitan Opera House, the New York State Theater for the Dance, a Repertory Drama Theater, a Library Museum, and the Juilliard School of Music.

Allen had been a lieutenant commander on the carrier *Enterprise* during the war. He had been manager of the Philadelphia Orchestra under Leopold Stokowski and later business manager of the Metropolitan Opera House. He was an impressive, cultured American, with a traditional sense of patriotism. The collision between him and Laurence Johnson presented a fascinating contrast.

At the time that Allen was associated with the Metropolitan Opera, Laurence Johnson visited him and demanded that an artist by the name of Jack Gilford be removed from the touring company of *Die Fledermaus*, which was to play in Syracuse. Johnson had sent his customary shock troops in advance, in the form of a letter from the American Legion Post in Syracuse. Allen had replied in a letter which was admitted in evidence:

"We can, of course, assure you that the Metropolitan would not knowingly employ one, who, after a fair hearing in the manner of American justice before an impartial tribunal, was found to be engaged in activities hostile to our country. . . .

But the Metropolitan cannot sit as such a tribunal nor could it make such a decision on the basis of publications which are mere compilations from frequently dubious sources, compilations which in no wise represent the judgment of such a tribunal as we have mentioned, made under the conditions required by American justice."

Although Allen was not a lawyer, he and Rudolf Bing, the general manager of the Metropolitan Opera House, had stated brilliantly what the United States Supreme Court later held with respect to such compilations as that of the House Un-American Activities Committee, or indeed the so-called subversive list of organizations issued by the Attorney General without the opportunity for a trial of those organizations. Certainly, it applied to Hartnett's *Red Channels*.

Allen pointed out that the Legion admitted that Gilford had done "nothing illegal and . . . you do not claim he is a Communist." Then he struck hard and courageously at the arrogance and un-American technique which had been employed: "You are proposing that Gilford's loyalty to the United States and his right to hold a job anywhere be tried and determined by the Syracuse Post #41 of the American Legion. That, of course, is a matter of indirect concern to the Metropolitan which believes as strongly as you do in American concepts and a fair trial."

Now Johnson had come to reprimand Allen for his attitude and demand a change of position or there would be a boycott of the Metropolitan *Fledermaus* company when it came to Syracuse. Allen's description of Johnson as "extremely self-anointed and sanctimonious" was stricken out by the court as characterizations, but he made it clear that he finally escorted Johnson "out onto Broadway . . ."

Before he departed, Johnson left with Allen a photostatic copy of a letter from CBS concerning his protest against Gilford's appearance on an Arthur Godfrey program sponsored by Liggett & Myers Tobacco Company. It was a crawling apology from the President of CBS Television, J. L. Van Volkenburg, written to Johnson. It even thanked Johnson "for being instrumental in having this matter brought to our attention." Johnson treated this letter as if it were a trophy he had won, but Allen was unimpressed. Yet, later Allen had to travel to Syracuse to deal with the near riots which resulted from the publicized positions taken by Johnson and Post #41 against the *Fledermaus* company.

Every new domain attracts men to conquer it. The American and African continents have now been replaced by the limitless continent of space as an allure to adventurous man. In a smaller way the invention of television created a new domain of sight and sound, and the challenge to fill it. With increasing leisure, millions of Americans, who did not care to spend it in the company of their own minds, turned to the magic box. The demand for entertainment was there. Who would supply it? The acknowledged conquerors in the resulting struggle was the producing firm of Goodson-Todman Productions. It created such programs as "What's My Line?," "I've Got a Secret," "The Price Is Right," "Password," "To Tell the Truth," "The Name's the Same," "It's News to Me," and many, many others dating back to "Stop the Music."

At the time of the trial, Goodson-Todman had the astonishing number of thirty-two half-hour shows a week on major television networks. It had won thirty-five Emmy, Sylvania and Look awards. It was the acknowledged leader among television production firms.

Surely, if anyone could testify with authority about blacklisting, it was Mark Goodson, the head of this company. So it must have been another shock to the defendants when we announced that he would be our next witness.

Lawyers often ask whether a valuable witness is also impressive looking. Some outstanding experts are nervous, weasly looking men. Others are imposing. The effort to translate a witness's lifetime of experience into a few hours of testimony is aided by the visual impression he makes on the jury. Goodson was as effective in voice and appearance as in his expert knowledge. He was in his fifties, gray-templed, fine-featured, athletically sunburned, and articulately refined. He had a natural air of elegance, carefully cultivated by his clothes. He wore a dark suit, a striped or colored shirt, with white collar and precisely correct protruding cuffs, a paisley or checked silk handkerchief in his coat to match or deliberately contrast with his tie, a faint toilet water scent which could be detected by those close and which a distant observer would have imagined was there, and a white carnation in his lapel, which unembarrassedly announced his intention to be carefully groomed.

He had earned his Phi Beta Kappa key at the University of California, had been President of the New York Chapter of the Academy of Television Arts and Sciences, and had been a member of its National Board of Trustees.

He had, of course, hired thousands of performers, and the practice was to have them "cleared" in advance. When they were rejected, they were not told that unspecified "political affiliations" were responsible. They were blacklisted and never sought again. An artist might be able to refute an accusation, but how could he quarrel with silence? "Non-clearability," Goodson said, "meant unemployability."

It was when he became specific that his testimony took on special bite. Laurence Johnson had written to C. A. Swanson & Sons (frozen foods), a sponsor of "The Name's the Same." Leaning as usual on the Onondaga County American Legion, Johnson had indicted the actress Judy Holliday, who appeared on the panel of Goodson's television show. Finally, she was "cleared" by George Sokolsky.

Later, Hartnett attacked Abe Burrows (co-author of *How To Succeed in Business Without Really Trying*, and author of many other works in the theater), who had also appeared on Goodson's show. His attack was supported by "organized mail" which he could discern by the fact that the postcards which arrived had "similiar phrasing." Mr. Gilbert Swanson visited Goodson, and after careful review found that Burrows was anti-Communist and unjustly accused. They stood by him. But the attacks continued, and Burrows was appealed to by his own sponsor to withdraw, even though he was innocent.

Goodson explained,

"A sponsor is in business to sell his goods. He has no interest in being involved in causes. . . . The favorite slogan along Madison Avenue is 'Why buy yourself a headache. . . . There are a lot of other performers. Why bother with this one?' "

So many distinguished artists were rejected at one time or another that it would have been an honor to be included among them, were it not for the tragedy that such patriotic Americans should be pilloried. Lena Horne was barred at one time. Goodson testified that on other occasions, Oscar

Hammerstein, Richard Rodgers, Moss Hart, Jerome Robbins, Burt Lancaster, Leopold Stokowski, Leonard Bernstein, and General Dwight D. Eisenhower appeared on rejection lists. Someone once engaged in the exercise of listing the famous plays, books, music, and arts generally, of which we would have been deprived, if their creators had been stilled early enough by the Hartnetts and Johnsons. The resulting impoverishment of our society ought to be measured against the danger of polluting our entertainment media. Even if on occasion, a real Communist is speared by illegal blacklist, what an imbalance, we risk in the true values to society. Outrageous as the harrassment of famous artists was there was an unknown girl whose case was even more shocking.

She was a young English girl called Anna Lee. She had appeared on "It's News to Me," with John Henry Faulk as a regular panelist. One day the advertising agency informed Goodson that he must remove her from the show because "one of the clearance forms" showed she had some kind of "a record."

Though the practice was never to question or investigate such a report, Goodson determined in this instance to do so.

"I invited Anna Lee to lunch . . . and I said, 'Anna, what are your politics?'

"And she said, 'You mean in England? Well, I was a Churchill Conservative.'

"I said, 'What about your husband? Perhaps, they are tying you in with your husband.'

"She said, 'Well, he is a Texas Republican. . . . Why do you ask?'

"I said, 'There seems to be some misinformation.' "

Goodson insisted on breaking the wall of silence. He reported the facts to the agency and demanded a reconsideration. An exception was made and he was later advised that an error of identification had been made. It was another actress with a similar name who was intended to be blacklisted.

Then came the shock:

"But anyway, we want you to drop her, because we are concerned about the amount of mail that may come in, about the controversy involved, and so we would just as soon not have her anyway.

"And I said, 'But how can you take this girl and so completely step over her rights in this way?' And I got a little angry and red-faced and I said, 'As far as I am concerned, I am not going to drop her.'"

He left in defiance. When he got back to his office, he received a friendly warning to keep his temper in check, and go along in this matter, or he himself might come under suspicion!

When a blacklister alerts his victim that he may lose his job and that he would like to help him, one has a right to wonder what is going on behind the scene. Kenneth Roberts, a prominent radio and television announcer, received just such a letter from Hartnett winding up with, ". . . You will find it of the greatest importance to your career to get in touch with me without delay."

Now Roberts was on the witness stand revealing these mysterious events. Shortly after Hartnett's *Red Channels* had been published, a prominent civil liberties lawyer, Arthur Garfield Hays, had invited those listed in its pages to attend a meeting in his office. More than forty, including Roberts, came and were advised that they had legal rights against *Red Channels*. Hartnett was looking for someone to become an informant and report to him on the gathering threat to his publication. That is why he suddenly developed a sympathetic concern about Roberts. Perhaps, in return for "clearance," which would enable him to hold his job with a Philip Morris Cigarette-sponsored radio program, Roberts would act as a counterspy. It is inevitable that evil-doers should spawn other evils to maintain themselves. Once, Hartnett, using a hidden tape recorder, had snooped on a meeting of a union faction. Now he was hoping to place a human recorder in his enemy's midst. But Roberts would have none of it. Indeed, he wondered why Hartnett had not worried about the injustice to him *before* he listed his name in *Red Channels*, citing as a sin his presence at a political rally under the auspices of the Committee of Arts and Sciences, for so dangerous an enterprise as the re-election of Governor Herbert H. Lehman.

For five years after the Hays meeting there was silence. Then Hartnett suddenly revived his interest in Roberts. Could his purpose have been to frighten him off as a witness in our case? In any event, he wrote that an "informant" (never identified) had told him that six years earlier Roberts had attended a Communist Party Theater Group Meeting at the Royalton Hotel. Was this true? he asked innocently, while hurling the poisonous dart. Roberts assured him it was an absolute, unqualified lie, but when Hartnett continued the correspondence, persisting that his anonymous informant was reliable and was "angry" at the denial, Roberts exploded. He wrote:

"Your letters to me present a clear implication of threat and intimidation unless I admit to something of which I am not guilty, and throw myself at your mercy.

"I cannot help regarding your letters as an unwarranted invasion of my privacy, and an unprincipled attack upon my peace of mind. It is unthinkable for a private citizen to bandy unfounded charges of this nature against another under no more authority than that allowed by continuing to quote from an 'informant.'"

Roberts also went to the F.B.I. to complain, but the judge limited the testimony at this point on the ground that we were trying the Faulk case only, and that the evidence had been admitted to show Hartnett's practice but not to pursue Roberts' grievance. Still, the jury had gotten another glimpse into the darkness, which some misguided spirits called patriotism.

Putting a witness on the stand is like launching a boat—one cannot be sure that future storms will not take him off course. When Gerald Dickler, business manager for Faulk, sat down in the witness chair, we did not anticipate that cross-examination storms would toss him on unexpected routes. Fortunately, some ended in favorable harbors, which otherwise we could never have reached.

Dickler was no ordinary manager. What witnesses we had! He was a distinguished lawyer, partner of Leonard Hall, at one time national chairman of the Republican Party. He was author of a fine book on trials of historic characters, such as Joan of Arc and Galileo. He had guided the business carrers of H. V. Kaltenborn, Lowell Thomas, Norman Vincent Peale, Ron Cochran, Pauline Fredericks, and others. As a member of the Academy of Television Arts and Sciences, he was competent to give expert opinion on Faulk's talents and earning potentials. He established the fact that over a five-year period, CBS collected more than one million dollars in fees from Faulk's sponsors. Then he gave his opinion that had Faulk continued his career, he would have earned in a range of between $250,000 to $500,000 a year from radio and television alone, aside from auxiliary income derived from summer stock shows, books, articles, and personal appearances.

He, too, described the "clearance" system which prevailed in radio and television. Though it was "hush-hush," it "couldn't be concealed forever" from those active in the industry. He concluded the revelations of blacklisting with a telling sentence:

"Each agency executive who was involved with hiring, was reputed to have a little black book in a lower drawer which was frequently as not *Red Channels* or subsequent bulletins that were issued by clearance groups or individuals who were active in the business of 'investigating.' "

Whether the "record" was true or false didn't matter. If an artist was controversial, and, of course, being listed was enough to make him so, he was quarantined as if the bubonic plague had returned from the Middle Ages to claim him.

When Dickler was asked whether he still was Faulk's manager, he replied, "There isn't any business to manage."

One of the cardinal rules of cross-examination is not to challenge a truthful witness on facts he can elaborate. Obviously, Dickler was such a witness. But Bolan's first question was: "Who are the television stars who make five hundred thousand dollars per year?" He got the answer. Dickler reeled off the names of Garry Moore, Bud Collyer, Jackie Gleason, Jack Paar, Arthur Godfrey, and Dave Garroway. When the cross-examiner wanted to know the source of his knowledge about Garroway, Dickler told him that he represented him and had made his contract.

Far more daring was Bolan's demand that Dickler cite a single illustration of an artist who had been barred from the air because he was controversial.

THE WITNESS: You just want the names?

MR. BOLAN: Yes, and the illustration.

Now there was no stopping. We were headed for testimony we never dreamed we could get into the record. Dickler cited Jean Muir, who, with the exception of one "obscure" show, hadn't worked for seven years. Then he told the story of Philip Loeb, who had for years played Papa Goldberg on the television series "The Rise of the Goldbergs," and was dropped because he had become "controversial." He couldn't get any work in radio and television, and committed suicide!

He went on to tell about the magnificent actress Mady Christian, who had appeared in "I Remember Mama." She too was canceled out when she appeared on a "list," and "her life also ended in a tragic suicide." Dickler continued:

"Jack Gilford, Canada Lee, Sam Wanamaker, who had to go to England to find employment, Morris Carnovsky, who was off the air for a long, long time, Howard DeSilva, who still cannot, as far as I know, find employment in television . . . Pert Kelton. There were others and I could bring them to mind . . . Irene Wicker, the Singing Lady. . . ."

Thus, Dickler had been invited to give testimony which showed that some artists, uninformed of why they were exiled from their professions, desperately inflicted the penalty of death upon themselves. How many others were there who survived, but whose lives were curtailed or embittered by assailants unknown to them?

Garry Moore was our next witness. The world of entertainment is full of contrasts. The handsome type is offset by the homely one; the highly talented performer by the charming one who preens himself on not being able to sing, dance, or tell jokes; the announcer with golden resonance in his voice, by the star with a flat, soft tone. In the early days of radio, S. L. Rothafel introduced his acts in hushed, unvibrant sounds. Quite by accident, it was discovered that he stood out above all other announcers whose chief assets were lustrously booming voices. He became famous as Roxy. A theater as well as a vogue was founded in his name. He was so convinced that his voice "coming from the heart" had healing qualities, that he broadcast to hospitals, and many a patient wrote about the beneficent effect. A defect in his vocal equipment became a unique asset.

True, it is that sincerity is best conveyed by simplicity. To sing, "I love you" cannot equal Ronald Colman's or Charles Boyer's whisper of the same words, while the camera focused on their moist eyes.

Garry Moore was untheatrical, from crew cut hair to long nose and embarrassed grin. Indeed, he was so prosaically natural that it took art to maintain it in front of millions of viewers. Above all, his voice was shadowy, nonresonant, and easily recognized against the perfectly formed tones of announcers who spoke their lines as if they were singing. When he submitted himself to the X-ray of the television camera, his goodness photographed as clearly as his average features. Moore was a man of principle and character. Long before the storm for civil rights showered everyone with sensitivity, he had refused to stop at motels which barred any Negro in his company. Although never active or interested in union affairs, he was deeply concerned with the activities of Aware and Hartnett. He thought a union should busy itself obtaining employment for lesser performers, and increasing their minimum rates, rather than concentrating on a hunt for a few Communists, even if they existed. He was particularly offended by the un-American practice of accusing a man surreptitiously and not giving him a chance to defend himself. He was a Republican politically but a democrat in principle. So he had volunteered to run on the middle-of-the-road ticket with Charles Collingwood and John Henry Faulk, and now at considerable sacrifice to his manifold duties and some risk of his public standing, he threw himself into the cauldron of contest without a reservation.

He evaluated the skill of such performers as Faulk who have warm personalities, charm, and executive ability. Such performers last longer than the entertainers they introduce. There were only a handful, such as Arthur Godfrey, Art Linkletter, Dave Garroway, Bill Cullen, Hugh Downs.

THE COURT: How about Garry Moore?

THE WITNESS: No opinion, sir. (*Laughter*)

Moore stated with "reasonable certainty" (that is the principal requirement for an expert opinion; the law does not expect him to be absolutely certain) that Faulk would have earned "between two hundred thousand dollars upward to conceivably a million dollars" a year, had he remained on television.

The moment we turned Moore over to cross-examination, he had to call on his renowned felicity to meet an unexpected attack.

Q. Isn't it a fact that you are not able to state with reasonable certainty what your own income might be next year?

A. No, my contract is all signed for next year. I know exactly what it is going to be.

He was faced with an interview he gave in which he said he might be out of a job next year.

A. Yes. This was an effort to be modest. (*Laughter*)

Bolan got Moore to estimate that he had appeared in more than five thousand television shows.

Q. And has Mr. Faulk appeared in any of these with you?

A. No, he has not. John Henry Faulk is not the type of talent that I would hire on a show that I am on because he does the same thing I do and there isn't room for two of us on one show.

When the cross-examiner broadened his challenge, the fur really flew. Moore leaned forward, his casual voice suddenly eloquently hoarse with feeling:

"I was terribly frightened by what was happening to people, being blacklisted, suddenly becoming unemployable, for what reason they knew not, not even being confronted or told why they were made unemployable. It was a little like fighting with six men in a closet with the light out, and you can't tell who is hitting you."

Bolan threw his most difficult questions at him. Would he employ entertainers who were Communists, or had taken the Fifth Amendment? Didn't an employer have a right to know the record of any performer who wished to work for him?

A. . . . we never felt the employers did not have a right to know about anyone who worked for them. We only felt that if a man was accused of some one thing, he should be told that he was accused of it. He should be confronted and given a chance to prove or disprove, that he suddenly is not dropped for no reason that he knows about, nor is even told.

He illustrated his point with a poignant illustration of an aerialist who was barred, until Moore's persistence revealed that his name had been confused with someone else's. If Moore had taken the easy road and hired another aerialist— there were dozens available—the poor man might have been unemployed forever due to an error in identification.

When Moore stepped off the stand, I thought I detected a look of admiration on the faces of many jurors. It was silent applause more meaningful than any that he had obtained in a long career. For the rest of the trial, the image he had conjured up of six men beating an entertainer in a dark closet remained the best description of blacklisting.

The defendant, Laurence Johnson, had still not set foot in the courtroom. If he had any hope that we would fail to offer sufficient direct evidence connecting him with blacklisting, and thus relieve him of the necessity to testify, the next two witnesses crushed that strategy.

Francis C. Barton, Jr., formerly with CBS, and Benton & Bowles, was an executive of the Lennen & Newell Advertising Agency. It represented Schlitz Brewing Company of Milwaukee, which sponsored "The Schlitz Playhouse of Stars" on national television. Each week a dramatic show was presented. There was no recurring star or thread among the shows.

One day Schlitz received a telegram from Johnson charging that one of the minor characters in its TV show was a Communist. Schlitz referred the matter to its advertising agency, and Newell and Barton arranged a dinner meeting with Johnson at the Hampshire House, and found Matusow there too. Johnson demanded that the Schlitz shows, which had been filmed, not be shown. When Barton expressed his detestation of communism, but denied knowledge that any of the performers on the show were Communists, Johnson indignantly rejected his effort to save his films, while "our boys were dying in Korea."

Barton persisted that he would not simply scrap the films. "I wanted to know how he set himself up as an authority . . . . he got thoroughly angry with me and started to pound the table and raise his voice sufficiently to attract attention around the dining room, and then he calmed down."

How was the matter resolved? Barton agreed to remove from the credits on the shows already filmed any names Johnson specified and also agreed to engage Harvey Matusow to assist him in the future, to avoid hiring performers "with records."

He produced a check for $150.00 paid by Lennen & Newell to Matusow, who set up a card index of performers.

While Barton testified that he used the index technique thereafter, the watchful eye of Johnson continued to be on him. On cross-examination, he revealed that Johnson continued to call him and complain about the use of some actor.

So another great advertising agency of impeccable reputation and patriotism was forced to join the blacklist brigade. Step by step Johnson and Hartnett were seizing control of the airwaves and foisting upon the executives in the industry their secret apparatus for the elimination of artists, who they determined did not meet the required standards of patriotism. Only through such painstaking testimony (it was not easy to involve Barton in the trial—he had to be subpoenaed, but his high character and integrity assured us of the truth) was it possible to understand how a few men were able to tyrannize a great industry.

We felt guilty presenting the next witness. He had just been through a severe illness. He was feeble. The strain of testifying was an ordeal we offered to spare him, but with unheralded courage he stated he would come. Brevity did not diminish the impact of his story. He was Harry J. Blackburne, who, before he retired, had been for twenty-four years chain store and supermarket manager of Liebmann Breweries, which manufactured Rheingold beer and ale. He had previously been the manager for fourteen years of the real estate advertising section of the *Journal-American*, a New York newspaper.

Faulk was sponsored by Rheingold. In this instance, Laurence Johnson, picking his spots with devilish acumen, did not call the advertising agency, Foote, Cone & Belding, but Blackburne, who he knew would be deeply concerned with space display in supermarkets. He told him bluntly that "John Henry Faulk, whom Rheingold is sponsoring, is a Communist." Blackburne protested that this was not so.

On cross-examination, Blackburne asserted that every manufacturer cherished floor display space in supermarkets and that Johnson's threat had struck a vulnerable point.

After the usual throwing of the hot potato to the advertising agency and to CBS, the burned fingers were cooled when Faulk was canceled.

At this point, the fierce, steady screeches of sirens obliterated the voices in the courtroom. The judge screamed above the noise:

THE COURT: I take it the jurors know the good news that Carpenter is in orbit. . . . We can't compete with these sirens.

We sat down and waited for the invasion of noise to withdraw. I ruminated that man was piercing outer space, but here we were in a long struggle to explore the inner continents of man, and nobody was blowing any sirens to commemorate the event.

The truth is a passkey which can open the most intricate locks. The next witness appeared to be trapped in a contradiction, but the truth, even though somewhat embarrassing, opened the door and he walked out, his veracity unblemished. He was Lester Wolff, who conducted an advertising agency. Faulk had testified that after he was fired, he went searching for a job. Like so many others who sit on top of the world, he had learned that it turns over every twenty-four hours. He was willing to replace Wendy Barrie and work for scale, that is, a minimum price of eighty dollars a program. He had approached Wolff, who had told him that he canvassed his clients, but none of them would touch him because he was controversial.

Bolan and his law partner, Roy Cohn, had apparently checked every person mentioned by Faulk. When Cohn spoke to Wolff, he was told that he had not submitted Faulk's name to sponsors. So the defense thought it might call Wolff as a witness to contradict Faulk's testimony.

Yes before it could do so, we had put Wolff on the stand as our witness. Bolan asked for a brief recess to prepare cross-examination. Then he demanded to know of the witness whether Roy Cohn had not called Wolff and been told a different story than Faulk had related. The witness explained that although he had not submitted Faulk's name to sponsors, he had told Faulk that he had. The reason was that Wolff and his associates had met and decided that Faulk was unemployable; that it would be futile to submit his name to any sponsor. But to tell him that would be cruel.

"To ease his pain, shall we say, . . . we wanted to let him down easy. We did not want to tell him that we got together in the office and felt this was too great a risk for us to take."

So Wolff had told a white lie to Faulk, and Faulk had repeated it on the stand. But he had told the truth.

Unlike a play which is designed to build to a single climax, a trial is often an undisciplined profusion of climaxes. We concluded the plaintiff's case, by putting Everett Sloane on the stand. His testimony added a new sensation to the many which had buffeted the jury for many weeks. His revelations were given added impact by his dramatic voice and appearance. He had starred on "Philco Playhouse" as Van Gogh, and had given fierce character portrayals on "Kraft Theater," "United States Steel Hour," "Studio 1," "Playhouse 90," and also in motion pictures produced by the leading film companies.

Nature had equipped him for his profession. He was red-headed, but one did not notice his hair first. The carrot tints of his gaunt face established his coloration. One of his eyes focused slightly outward, and this strabismic effect gave him a glowering look of great intensity. Above all, a distinctive, gruff, but melodious voice used deliberately in a clipped, off-hand manner, lent dramatic effect to his most casual comment. The jury was quickly engrossed in his recital.

In 1952, he found that his income was sinking rapidly. He earned half of what he had made the year before, and the next year one-third. Such agencies as Batton, Barton, Durstine and Osborne, Young & Rubicam, and J. Walter Thompson, which had always sought his services eagerly, ceased to call him. Previously his motion picture work, and other engagements, had forced him to turn down offers continuously awaiting him, but now he found much time on his hands and a strange silence among prospective employers. He and his agents were slow to come to the conclusion that he was being blacklisted, but the suspicion of his plight became a reality by an accidental meeting with an author:

"He said, 'I recommended you yesterday for a part in the "Ford Theater" that I just wrote, . . . and they turned you down.'

"I said, 'Why?'

"He said, 'Because you are in *Red Channels*.'

"I said, 'I am not in *Red Channels*.'

"He said, 'I wasn't aware of that. They told me you were.'

"I said, 'You'd better go back and tell them I am not,' and so I called him the following day . . . and he said, 'You were right,' which of course I knew I was. 'You are not in *Red Channels*, but they say they must have confused you with Allen Sloane.'"

Q. What is your first name?

A. Everett.

Thus far it was just another case of mistaken identity, one of the gruesome by-products of stealth. But the novel aspect of his case was still to come:

"I found out . . . that if you worked for the UN Radio more than twice, that the third time . . . you were required to obtain the same status as a permanent employee, and that included submitting to an F.B.I. check."

Q. What did you do then?

A. And so, having already worked for the UN Radio twice, I sought a third employment from them, which I received.

In this way he obtained an F.B.I. check of his record. An impressive document was issued by the Secretary of State of the United States to the Secretary General of the United Nations, stating that after "a full field investigation . . . it has been determined there is no reasonable doubt as to the loyalty of this person to the Government of the United States." Armed with this extraordinary badge of patriotism, he ventured forth to take his name off the blacklist. He was advised to see Paul Milton, a director of Aware, who might tell him how to get cleared. What he did not know was that a year earlier Hartnett had written to Laurence Johnson condemning "Everett Sloane," so that more than mistaken identity was responsible for his plight.

Sloane's recital of his conversation with Paul Milton was an admixture of high drama, irony, and maddening humor which exceeded any script he had ever enacted.

"I said to Milton, 'As you know, I have been barred from employment with certain agencies . . . and in order to get over that situation I have had a full field check by the F.B.I. made and I have received a letter from the Civil Service Commission declaring me a loyal citizen; and since I have heard that you have been instrumental in clearing certain people, in what way I do not know, I would like very much for you to see this letter and tell me what is the best procedure to go through with it.'"

Paul Milton read the commendation from the Secretary of State carefully. Then said:

"'Well, I take this with a grain of salt.'

"Then I said, 'What do you mean by that?'

"He said, 'Well, we don't put much stock in it.'

"And I said, 'Who is "we"?'

"And he said, 'Aware Inc. . . .'

"I said . . . 'what is your objection to this document . . . ?'

"He said, 'Well, we at Aware have different standards of clearance than the United States Government's agencies. We are a little more stringent. We feel they are a little too lenient.'

"And I said, 'You mean to say that you set yourselves up as opposed to the United States Government in the matter of loyalty, which is, indeed, I would say, their province?'

"He said, 'Yes, we do.'

"I said, 'Well what would Aware Inc. suggest I do then, in view of the fact that this document doesn't seem to mean much to them, in order to be cleared so that I will work for all advertising agencies in the field?'

"And he said, 'Well, I suggest that you let me arrange a meeting for you with Mr. Hartnett, at which meeting perhaps you and he can evolve some statement that you can make that will be satisfactory to Mr. Hartnett and will also prove satisfactory to, perhaps, the people who are not presently hiring you.'"

I shuddered at the next question which asked what his reply was to this suggestion because when I had asked him the same question in the privacy of my home, he seared the walls with four-letter words which might have caused the United States Supreme Court to reverse its vaunted position on censorship and free speech. I warned him to practice self-discipline on the witness stand. But now when the question was put to him, I saw the rush of blood to his face making it the same color as his hair, and the same sputtering which made him stutter:

"I said go f-f-fly a kite."

I breathed with relief as I glanced at the women jurors.

"I told Mr. Milton that as far as I was concerned I was much more interested in the opinion of the United States Government than of Mr. Milton or Aware or Mr. Vincent Hartnett and that both their purpose and methods were immoral and illegal and that I would have nothing to do with them whatsoever, . . . and I walked out of the restaurant."

A question presented itself as Sloane finished his testimony: Was Aware unwittingly emulating the Communists, in their desire to set up a super government which would replace the F.B.I. and State Department in the performance of their duties?

Humor bubbles up through the dramatic tides of contest in the most unexpected ways. A blue-coated court attendant reported to Justice Geller that one of the jurors was taking notes. This resulted in a conference with counsel and then the judge's learned lecture to the jurors on the inadvisability of this practice. Although it was not forbidden, it sometimes gave the juror the notion, when he got into the jury room, that his arguments were entitled to more weight because he had memoranda to back up his recollection. This would upset the desired objective of free and equally balanced discussion. If a juror needed to have his memory refreshed, he could call for the particular testimony or exhibit and the stenographer would read it to all the jurors. Furthermore, while making notes the juror's attention might be diverted from other testimony, equally important. When the judge was through with his reasoned strictures, one of the women jurors surrendered the notes which she had made to the attendant to give them to the judge. He read them aloud:

"Oranges, grapefruit, vegetables, dry milk, meat, desserts, air mail stamps."

I am sure that no shopping list ever earned such a howl of laughter.

After another witness, Fred Mitchell, in charge of forty million dollars' broadcast advertising including the Colgate account, had confirmed Faulk's unemployability, we conferred at length with the court. Laurence Johnson had still not set foot into the courtroom. It was arranged that Bolan would advise the judge and us whether he would appear as a defense witness, and if not what remedies were available to us.

Now we had concluded the presentation of Faulk's case. Six weeks had passed, during which witness after witness had been paraded on the stand, and hundreds of documents marked in evidence. Six weeks, during which neither Faulk nor our battery of lawyers had spent a single evening, Saturday and Sunday included, away from the office, laboring there on the next morning's adventure in the courtroom. Six weeks during which witnesses whom we had implored to reveal their experiences had disappointed us, while others came forward courageously. Six weeks during which our emotions and hopes had been buffeted by good and ill fortune, in which our triumphs had been smothered by anxieties about the future, and the future dimmed by the uncertainties of the present. Six weeks in which the unmatched natural drama of antagonists, bitterly sincere in their opposing views, pleaded, declaimed, and shouted, while the court struggled to maintain the dispassionate atmosphere of justice. Six weeks in which not only the jurors' faces, but their moods and reactions became identifiable, and we strained to read the weather forecast of their judgment.

And now, after 3889 pages of testimony, dozens of legal briefs, prolixity in argument, and endless clatter of swords as we dueled with our opponents over the veracity of witnesses— all was brought to a halt with just two words—"Plaintiff rests." It was like a thrilling movement in a symphony, when violence is followed by violence, and then endlessly churned into long slow lyrical passages, suddenly brought to an abrupt end by two plucked string notes. The ear, accustomed to continuity of sound, can be shocked by silence.

The defense asked for a brief recess before it took over the burden of going forward. Now our feelings were really mixed. We were worried by the uncertainty of unexpected witnesses and possible startling counterattacks. But we were elated, to the point of tingling excitement, at the certainty that Hartnett (and we hoped Johnson) would take the stand, and at long last we could in open battle encounter those who loomed so large because of mystery, so powerful because of anonymity, and so invulnerable because of unaccountability. For Faulk, his real day in court was approaching. It was when his unknown enemies would, after seven years, finally have to face us and be subjected to the deep probing which only cross-examination can afford.

The defendants opended their defense with an impressive visual effect. Attendants brought in huge books which had been subpoenaed from CBS. They contained the logs of all broadcasts, which must be kept for the Federal Communications Commission. Thus they laid the foundation for the proof that despite cancellations, Faulk earned more money *after* the libel than he had ever before. The log books were about three feet wide and four feet long, and their gray canvas backs gave them the appearance of immense stone slabs. They were so heavy that the judge had two attendants haul them onto the counsel table.

Visual evidence sticks in the mind better than oral statement. We comprehend through the eye more easily than through the ear. That is why lawyers frequently use toy models of automobiles to explain an automobile collision, or skeletons to explain injuries. Even in complicated anti-trust litigations, colored charts are worth thousands of explanatory words. The old saying, seeing is believing, is true in court, although in church, the reverse is probably true. There, one must believe in order to see.

The defendants chose to put in a defense for Aware Inc. first. Paul Milton, a founder and director of Aware Inc. therefore took the stand. He was a pale man in his middle or late fifties, of medium height and blondish complexion with a mustache tending toward gray, and a frightened demeanor. He had been a writer for magazines and for such radio programs as "March of Time," "Mr. & Mrs. North," and "Treasury Agent." He had also written a number of novels, over a period of thirteen years. Then he had gone into real estate, where apparently he had prospered. But the transition had left him, like musicians who become businessmen or actresses who retire to be housewives, with an invisible trail of sadness. One's heart can be left empty while the pocket is filled. I knew an extremely wealthy businessman, whose eyes became young, and whose voice filled with excitement, when he related (as he frequently did) his early experiences as a cub reporter on the New York *World*. The hardest thing to retire from is glamor.

Milton's testimony put a wall of innocence and high motive around Aware Inc. It was a non-profit organization. It never had more than 350 members who maintained it by paying ten-dollar dues, and even then it had to resort to cocktail parties to finance itself. The Certificate of Incorporation stated that its purpose was to combat the Communist conspiracy.

Aware Inc. never received any money for clearing or screening artists, nor, he said, did it ever furnish a list of artists and their records to any employer.

Milton testified that he had collaborated with Hartnett in writing the Aware *Bulletin* which contained the seven charges against Faulk, but that he had done so in reliance on the data which Hartnett had supplied. The *Bulletin* had been submitted to the Board of Directors of Aware Inc. and also to its counsel, and all had approved it, having faith in Hartnett's research. He testified that Laurence Johnson had nothing to do with the preparation of the libel document.

Having put a virtuous face on Aware Inc., he turned to the only testimony in the direct case which had mentioned his name, that of Everett Sloane. He gave his version of the conversation when Sloane showed him the letter in which the

F.B.I. attested to his loyalty and asked how he could get off the blacklist.

"In general I suggested that he could circulate the letter, as I knew some other people in the business had been doing, to his employers, and he could take any other steps in his own behalf by puting himself on record wherever he wanted to."

We were so eager to cross-examine that I drew him out even while his own counsel was still questioning him. Each time I interrupted he came nearer to Sloane's version.

MR. BOLAN: Was Aware mentioned at that meeting? . . .

MR. NIZER: Have you finished the conversation? First may I ask if he finished his answer.

Q. All right; is there anything else you recall of that conversation? . . .

A. In general. I am trying to recall. It is a long time ago. I perhaps suggested if he had anything serious to say he would go to the F.B.I. . . .

Q. Did he discuss—

MR. NIZER: I still don't think he has finished. May I ask whether he has finished the entire conversation? . . .

THE WITNESS: I perhaps suggested that he meet with Vincent Hartnett, who was the best-informed documentarian in my acquaintance. . . .

So a little prodding, even before cross-examination, caused him to confirm the main point of Sloane's testimony, that the Government report of his loyalty was not enough, and that he ought to visit Hartnett. He denied that Sloane had told him "to go fly a kite," which, of course, I believed, knowing that Sloane was not given to such inexpressive language under the circumstances.

Did the defense think we would limit ourselves to the formal picture which it drew of Aware's position? The cross-examination which ensued covered three times as many pages in the record as the direct examination. Hartnett had a foretaste of what was in store for him.

Milton conceded that the *Bulletin* was sent to two thousand people, who were strategically placed with respect to the employment of any artist on radio, television, motion picture, or newspaper. Wasn't it Aware's purpose then to affect Faulk's employment? He denied this—but finally

A. It might, by no means certain.

I would not accept this partial concession, and faced him with his prior contradictory testimony on an examination before trial. Then I asked

Q. And you intended the influence upon their [employers'] conduct to be adverse to Mr. Faulk, isn't that a fact?

A. In this context it would have been, yes.

Defendants' favorite passage in the *Bulletin* was the statement that the middle-of-the-road slate was not Communistic. They used it as a shield against our charges. But there was a large crack in the shield. The very next sentence in the *Bulletin* was,

"But how about Faulk himself? What is his public record?"

There followed the seven specifications against him. Weren't these rhetorical questions written by Milton and Hartnett intended by them to be charges of pro-communism? He persisted for a while in his claim that the *Bulletin* was merely informative, not accusatory. Finally,

Q. . . . You were coming out against him, weren't you?

A. Yes, that is right.

On direct examination he had relieved Hartnett of responsibility for a certain sentence in the *Bulletin,* claiming that he himself had written it. He had forgotten, however, that in his examination before trial he had been unable to identify specifically what he wrote or what Hartnett wrote. We faced him with this contradiction.

Q. . . . In 1960 you weren't able to select any portion which you had written or contributed to the *Bulletin* [Exhibit 41], is that correct, now?

A. As you read it, yes, sir.

Q. And yet yesterday, which is two years later, you selected a specific sentence which counsel read to you . . . and said you had written that . . . ?

A. Yes, sir.

Q. Did you have any memoranda of any kind which refreshed your memory since 1960?

A. No, sir.

Q. Was your memory better yesterday than two years ago on this subject?

A. At this point, yes, it apparently was.

Q. You relied solely on memory, you had nothing to

refresh it except your memory, but it got better in two years, is that it?

A. On this point, yes.

We left it to the jury to assess his veracity, but we continued to chip away at it. One never knows when the blows on cross-examination, no matter how ineffectual some may be, cumulatively will cause a large crack in the defense façade. So for example, he denied that the *Bulletin* was a serious attack upon Faulk's loyalty and patriotism. When we confronted him with a contradictory statement in his examination before trial, he attempted to extricate himself in the following startling manner:

"There is no question of his patriotism or loyalty. They are separate things. There is nothing in there to indicate he could not have associated himself with twenty Communist Fronts and still . . . be a loyal and patriotic American."

When I could catch my breath at this delectable distinction I asked:

Q. Well, then, sir, knowing what you do about the entire background, up to this moment you consider Mr. Faulk a loyal and patriotic American, don't you?

MR. BOLAN: I object, Your Honor.

THE COURT: Overruled.

A. In so far as my knowledge of his career goes, yes.

Now, every vicious insinuation in the *Bulletin* became more offensive in view of the admission he had just made. So we turned to the language of the *Bulletin* which he had helped to draft, and the repeated use of the phrase "According to the *Daily Worker*," an obvious attempt to make it appear that only the Communist newspaper reported the contest in the union and therefore supported Faulk. The New York *Times*, the *Herald Tribune*, and other newspapers had reported the activities of the middle-of-the-road ticket, but Milton had deliberately omitted this fact. He was forced to concede this selectivity. Then was not Aware's purpose malicious? Was it not attempting to distort the truth? His effort to escape this conclusion resulted in an incredibly clumsy rationalization.

A. . . . The *Times* and *Tribune* had enormous circulation. They were carefully read by the trade, by the entire industry, and I assumed everybody knew. . . .

Q. . . . So you felt that the people who read it would remember having read the New York *Times* and *Tribune*, so it wasn't necessary to put it in [the *Bulletin*], is that it? . . . You left it to the reader to fill in the rest; is that correct?

A. Generally speaking yes. . . .

Q. You mean that the reason you left out the New York *Times*, Mr. Milton—let me understand you—and the *Tribune* and the *Daily Variety* and other newspapers I have shown you is because you assumed that everybody knew that and there was no need to refer to it in the *Bulletin*. . . .

A. Yes.

He had used the word "we" in one of his answers. He soon admitted that the Board of Aware Inc. had approved the *Bulletin's* text.

Since he had isolated the *Daily Worker* for citation, did he consider it a reliable newspaper?

It dawned upon him that to condemn it would remove another prop from the *Bulletin's* authenticity. This resulted in another intellectual contortion. He considered it "notorious" but not "unreliable."

Milton had scored heavily for the defense by eliminating Laurence Johnson from the preparation of the *Bulletin*. Now our task was to undo this damage. Milton conceded that Johnson was his "personal friend," visited at his home in New York, and knew that Milton was a leading figure in Aware.

We attempted to forge the link more firmly. He admitted that Johnson attended some meetings of Aware Inc., and that he had been present at an early meeting before Aware was even incorporated.

When we tried to connect Johnson and Hartnett as working associates, Milton shied away. But his own words in his examination before trial pushed him back into line, for he said that they "consulted very frequently."

When a witness finds that resistance is futile, he comes along with the cross-examiner docilely even where no contradictory proof is available. The truth has its own pressure and seeks release, when opportunity is afforded it to flow freely. So now Milton conceded that when Johnson was publicly attacked for blacklisting activities, Aware Inc. at its regular meeting offered to help him. He even acknowledged the tie-in between Aware and the American Legion Post of Syracuse and the Veterans Action Committee of Syracuse Supermarkets, and that Dungey and Neuser of those organizations were members of Aware Inc.

Finally he replied "That's right," to the question whether "Laurence Johnson and his Syracuse friends were active in screening or blacklisting performers, before Aware Inc. was organized?" He specifically included Dungey and Neuser "among others" as the Syracuse friends who effectuated the blacklist. We were really making progress.

Before Aware was organized, Milton had belonged to a similar group in a radio writers' union which sent out the "record" of writers to employers. He had been sued by one of the victims, but Justice Geller excluded this evidence as being too remote. However, Milton was faced with his prior testimony:

> Q. Isn't it fair then to say that people who are in disagreement with your faction you have been labeling as pro-Communists?
>
> A. We have, yes.

So despite Milton's benign appearance, he was revealed as the predecessor of Aware's tactics. Even before Aware was organized, Milton had worked with Laurence Johnson and inquired of his then assistant, Harvey Matusow, about data concerning certain individuals. He denied this, but was surprised by an envelope we produced, sent by him to Matusow, and the typewritten sheets which had filled it:

> Q. Does that refresh your recollection, sir, that you did communicate with Mr. Matusow to give you aid on alleged pro-Communistic activities of various others?
>
> A. Yes, on that occasion.

Capitalizing on the momentum of revelation, we drew out of him an incident which for the first time raised a serious question about his personal motives. We asked him whether some of the writers whose "records" he set forth lost their jobs.

> A. I don't know.
>
> Q. You don't know. Was there a man by the name of Sheldon Stark who, prior to your criticism and testimony about him, was employed in "Treasury Men in Action?"
>
> A. . . . I am not certain now.
>
> Q. Wasn't Mr. Hartnett the gentleman who acted as a consultant, as you would call it, to that program, "Treasury Men in Action?"
>
> A. I am not sure.

Q. Didn't you obtain a job on "Treasury Men in Action" after Mr. Stark lost his job?

MR. BOLAN: I object, Your Honor.

THE COURT: Overruled.

Q. My question is, did you?

A. Yes.

Although on redirect examination Bolan established that Milton did not acquire Stark's job until two months after he lost it, and therefore there was no immediate sequence between the accusation and the replacement by the accuser, it was for the jury to weigh the matter.

How different a few questions and answers can make a witness look. Cross-examination when it succeeds can pierce the most impressive exterior and reveal the character and motivation of the witness just as a fluoroscope machine unsentimentally depicts a raw pulsating heart. Milton had a sympathetic personality and it was risky to attack him frontally. But by now it was not too hazardous to inquire about the basis for his charges against Faulk. He admitted he had no information that Faulk had attended some of the functions the *Bulletin* said he had.

He had been told by Hartnett that the Progressive Citizens Committee was not a Communist Front but merely a "liberal front organization":

Q. Nevertheless you still wrote in the *Bulletin* [Exhibit 41] "Progressive Citizens of America, officially designated as a Communist Front," didn't you?

A. Yes.

The repeated use in the *Bulletin* of the phrase "officially designated as a Communist Front" turned out to be a fraudulent as well as irresponsible device. Milton admitted that it meant that some government agency or department had made such a finding, and if so that proper practice would have been to name the source of the designation in the *Bulletin*. I pressed him.

Q. In this case you didn't do it?

A. We didn't . . . it would have been clearer had we given the citations . . . the sources, I mean.

Q. It might have been so clear that the inaccuracy would have been shown; isn't that so? . . .

A. No, that was not the reason. It was space . . .

Q. You were trying to save space?

A. Some.

Q. I show you the original copy of the *Bulletin* and I call your attention to the fact that the last page still has at least a half-page empty, hasn't it?

A. That's right.

Q. So that you weren't lacking in space to put down the source of what you claimed was the official designation, were you?

A. Not lacking. We were trying to conserve.

Milton was like a man cornered, who tries to escape by running the wrong way and bashes his head in the bargain. We were encouraged to step up the pace of our questions. The *Bulletin* referred to a program of an event which named Faulk as an entertainer "with identified Communist Earl Robinson . . .":

Q. You knew before you wrote the *Bulletin,* that this event was a first-year salute to the United Nations?

A. Yes, sir.

Q. And you deliberately and purposefully omitted this fact when you wrote this item?

A. Yes.

Q. You also knew at that time that on this occasion the Secretary of State of the United States at that time, Edward Stettinius, was a speaker?

A. Yes.

Q. And you deliberately and purposefully omitted that from this time, didn't you?

A. That's right.

After referring by name to Trygve Lie and various ambassadors who attended this function, we obtained the same admission of his "deliberate and purposeful" omission of these facts from the *Bulletin.* The repetition irritated him:

A. We omitted it, period.

Q. Deliberately, period?

A. Well, not inadvertently.

Q. Not inadvertently?

A. That's right.

Later he balked at admitting that his purpose in writing this item was to accuse Faulk of a pro-Communist activity. But when faced with his own prior testimony on an examination before trial to precisely this effect, he reversed himself.

Q. Tell us, standing by itself, would it have any significance?

A. . . . it has some significance necessarily. It's a human act.

Q. Yes, it has significance in that it is a human act, even if you breathe, but I am saying, has it a pro-Communist significance just that a man is supposed to have either sent a greeting or attended that Continental Congress for Peace . . . ?

A. I don't think so by itself, depending on the man.

So it went. Reluctance, resistance, and occasional defiance, but almost always the grudging admission: The accusation that Faulk had opposed the anti-Communist faction in AFTRA was untrue; it was true that Faulk's broadcasts had no political content and, therefore, were not "subverting the airwaves," as charged in the American Legion letter.

There are some admissions which do not merely yield ground but virtually surrender the entire defense position. Such a concession came when he was asked whether Faulk would have been attacked by Aware if he had not run on a ticket which opposed Aware's slate in the AFTRA Union. Would Faulk's acts and record have been considered significant if he had not been a candidate?

A. They acquired significance because he was a candidate. . . . There were other people in AFTRA with much more substantial records that didn't draw this kind of attention to themselves and we didn't publicize that fact.

Not until summation were we able to analyze the full meaning of this answer. It reflected upon the sincerity of Aware's patriotic motives, because if Faulk was a menace to the airwaves, he should have been exposed according to Hartnett's and Johnson's theory, whether he ran for office in AFTRA or not. If the reason he was attacked was that he endangered Aware's control of AFTRA and Hartnett's collection of fees, then blacklisting was not even an unjustified means to a good end. The end too was inglorious.

We heard the words, "I call Mr. Vincent Hartnett as our next witness." Automatically, everyone at our side of the counsel table reached for folders and exhibits which would be necessary for cross-examination. The rustling noises interfered with administering the oath, during which the judge insisted on immovable silence. Our nervous energy came to rest, like a rapid motion picture which is stopped, leaving a frozen picture on the screen. Then when Hartnett sat down in the chair which seemed too large for him, we moved again. I observed once more his open but scared eyes, thin lips, and unimposing presence.

Lawyers plan the sequence of their witnesses, so that each one gets the benefit of the persuasive draft preceding him, like automobile racers who like to ride second and be pulled forward by the vacuum created by the leading car. Milton was undoubtedly put on the stand first to give Hartnett such an advantage. But as things turned out, we had gone far beyond Milton's description of Aware's "innocence" and drawn from him so many admissions, that Hartnett was now put to the task of carrying an additional burden of a colleague's concessions. In addition to his own problem, he would now find it necessary to differ with Milton if he was to avoid some crucial admissions. If he felt this pressure, it was not evident. He proceeded to give his impressive background.

He had received his B.A. and M.A. degrees from Notre Dame *maxima cum laude*. He became a writer for magazines, and in 1942 joined the United States Naval Reserve as an ensign. Four years later he was honorably discharged, having risen to the rank of lieutenant commander. He joined Philips H. Lord's organization, a packager of radio and TV programs such as "Gangbusters." It was then that he conceived the idea of accumulating files on political records of entertainers. The next step was for him to go into the business of supplying such data to the three major networks, sponsors, and advertising agencies who made it a practice "to check into any possible Communist Party or Communist Front affiliations of prospective employees." His first client was Borden's, which paid him twenty dollars for each name checked; then for a larger volume of business five dollars a name and two dollars if a name was repeated "a second or third time." Soon his customers included Lever Brothers, ABC, Young & Rubicam, Twentieth Century-Fox, and the Kudner Agency, among others. Nevertheless, his total income before expenses averaged only sixteen thousand dollars a year for five years.

Q. Did you ever receive any money from any performer for clearance or so-called clearance?

A. No, no.

He offered his explanation of the Kim Hunter incident, insisting that his report to her sponsor had given her a job, even before she sent the telegram to AFTRA.

He also produced a letter from the president of Philip Morris, Inc. thanking him for clearing Kenneth Roberts. He testified that he recommended that such performers as Lee J. Cobb and Frank Maxwell "be given a break."

While setting his best foot forward in an effort to show that he had aided artists to obtain employment, he was demonstrating his control of their destiny. It was this power which was unauthorized and evil, not merely its unreasonable use. He could have learned this from the anti-trust laws. We denounce the monopolist even if he doesn't raise prices. It is his power to do so at his own whim which the law condemns. In the same way, we abhor dictatorship even if the dictator is benevolent. He has usurped the will of the people and he cannot legitimize himself by exercising his stolen powers charitably. Hartnett seemed oblivious to all this as he preened himself on his good works. We would try later in cross-examination to pierce his notions, and even if he might be impervious to the educational process, we hoped to reach the jury's understanding of the real issues.

After a luncheon recess the following occurred:

MR. BOLAN: Your Honor, there are a few preliminary questions I did forget to ask Mr. Hartnett.

Q. Mr. Hartnett, are you married?

A. Yes.

Q. Do you have any children?

A. Six.

Q. With respect to Kim Hunter . . .

MR. NIZER: I move to strike out the answer, and it was answered so quickly that I wouldn't have even had a chance to blink.

THE COURT: Whether he had six children or no children or sixteen children has nothing to do with the issues in the case. I will let it stand with that instruction I just made.

MR. BOLAN: I would like to make the same request with respect to Mr. Faulk's children.

MR. NIZER: Your Honor, I think that is a highly improper statement. . . . In view of the fact that the issue with respect to the plaintiff is the suffering and injury to him, the reference to his family is pertinent in a libel action. It is not of the defendant.

THE COURT: That is as I understand the law.

Later, at summation time, Hartnett's children sat side by side in regular, increased sizes in a front row in the courtroom, until we asked the judge to direct them to seats less in the line of vision of the jury.

Before Bolan turned over his client for cross-examination, he dug the richest vein available to a defendant in a libel suit—reliance testimony. Even if the publication is false the defendant may mitigate damages by showing that he relied on what he read or heard. Ordinarily, such evidence is hearsay and inadmissible, for one cannot cross-examine a newspaper clipping or some gossip passed on by one who doesn't take the stand. But an exception is made in a libel case because one's honest reliance, even on a defective source, indicates lack of malice. It tends to prove the innocence of the mistake. Such evidence is worthless to establish truth, but it has some value in showing how the defamer was misled and that he was not motivated by sheer malice.

The plaintiff suffers during this phase of the case. Testimony before some State or Congressional committee may be read quoting some crackpot; a telephone conversation difficult to trace may be the source of his "knowledge"; a newspaper column may have caused him to believe. All these are read to the jury, and the plaintiff must pray that it will understand the judge's instruction that such "reliance" testimony never achieves the dignity of truth. So we went through agonizing hours while the record was flooded with an assortment of *Daily Worker* clippings, memos, House Un-American Activities Committee quotations, and oral communications and the like, which Hartnett claimed he relied on when he set forth the seven false specifications against Faulk. For example, he claimed that Mrs. J. B. Matthews told him that Faulk was listed in a *Bulletin of People's Songs* and that Wren, the "security expert" of the advertising agency of Batten, Barton, Durstine & Osborn, told him about Faulk appearing at the "notorious" Jefferson School. We later sprung a surprise, by producing Wren as our rebuttal witness to give the lie to this claim. Wren was so bitter that his gall spilled over the court-room, but that we shall come to later.

Finally, when the counsel table was loaded high with impressive "documentation" of Hartnett's reliance, his lawyer announced, "Your witness." We earnestly hoped to make him so.

As I faced him, he balanced himself in his chair as if to withstand the blows which might be coming. There was a faint smile on his lips which could either have represented confidence or defiance. We could only be sure that we had scored when he himself called out the point by concession.

He had written in the *Bulletin* that the middle-of-the-road ticket was first reported by the Communist *Daily Worker*. We showed him earlier articles in non-Communist newspapers.

Q. And so this statement in the *Bulletin* is inaccurate, isn't it . . . ?

A. In that sense, it is, yes.

Nor was this due to oversight or ignorance. The non-Communist article had been discussed by the Aware Board, and the minutes of the meeting compelled him to admit that he knew the true fact "months before" he wrote the untruth.

Realizing that he was prepared for cross-examination, we did not follow a consecutive line but darted at him from different directions, so as to upset his sense of anticipation, which might constrict the truth.

Q. Now, sir, we have had all of these booklets and citations offered on the subject of reliance all day today. You realize that citations of the House Un-American Activities Committee are not official designations, isn't that so?

A. No, I don't so realize.

Q. Haven't you so testified?

A. If you will refresh my recollection.

Q. Page 2330 (Examination before Trial) you were asked the following question:

"Q. And, of course, you realize that House Committee citations are not official designations?

"A. In that legal sense, that is correct."

He had insisted in direct examination that he only reported on artists when a client requested him to do so. He never volunteered information against anyone. Thus, he had sought to establish lack of personal venom. After a long struggle, he abandoned this pose of objectivity.

> Q. Did Young & Rubicam ask you about Mr. Faulk at all in the list of names that they gave you to check?
>
> A. Not to my recollection, no.
>
> Q. Nevertheless, when you wrote a report . . . you added that "John Henry Faulk has a significant Communist Front record," didn't you?
>
> A. Yes.

We clashed swords again as I demanded to know whether his purpose in volunteering this false statement was to influence that agency not to hire him. Grudgingly, he gave ground. He intended that "they should think twice."

> Q. And not only think twice, but think in connection with employing such a man; isn't that what it means?
>
> A. Yes, sir.

Hartnett had a file card for Faulk upon which he rubber stamped a series of mysterious initials. We decoded them. PETS meant Communist Party nominating petition; S-2 meant index to a publication entitled "Communist Activities Among Aliens and National Groups, Part II," issued by a Senate subcommittee; HMS stood for Harvey Matusow's testimony; C153 meant the 1953 index to published hearings of the Senate Subcommittee on Government Operations. HCUA meant House Committee on Un-American Activities. There were thirteen such sources which he had checked. Faulk's name did not appear in eleven of them. The other two were innocent references; one to a *Newsweek* article about Faulk, and the second to a theater clipping in the Public Library file. How Hartnett had struggled to find something incriminating about Faulk! Yet, when his thorough search revealed nothing, he listed false accusations nevertheless to destroy the man. How could he maintain the posture that even if he erred he was free from malice?

Indeed, his careful investigation had revealed that Faulk had enlisted in the Army despite his physical handicaps. I asked him:

> Q. That, of course, is an important factor in evaluating whether a man is patriotic or is associated with unloyal organizations, isn't it, that despite one blind eye he gets into the Armed Forces?
>
> A. Now, you have two elements in your question.

Q. Will you please answer them? Please don't quibble with me.

A. It would be evidence, I would say, generally speaking, of patriotism, yes.

But he never reported any of these facts to Aware, or in the *Bulletin*. So his malice was a two-sided coin—affirmative misrepresentations, and deliberate omissions of favorable data.

Hartnett was the author of *Red Channels*, which listed the "pro-Communist affiliations" of television and radio entertainers. All seven accusations against Faulk involved incidents which occurred before *Red Channels* was printed. If Hartnett really believed the charges against Faulk, would he not have included them in *Red Channels*?

Q. And, nevertheless, you never mentioned John Henry Faulk in *Red Channels*, did you?

A. I did not.

Hartnett followed *Red Channels* with a more comprehensive directory of political sin, called *File 13*. (He selected titles in cloak-and-dagger style, as if he were writing television melodramas.) He never mentioned Faulk in this volume, nor in a succeeding one; nor in still another reference work of his, called *Confidential Notebook*. Yet when Faulk ran on a union ticket which condemned blacklisting, Hartnett suddenly discovered ancient misdeeds which he had previously, by his publishing silence, deemed nonexistent or unworthy of credence. In a long series of cross-examination exchanges, we raised the specter of his own inconsistent conduct and forced him to contest with it. Is there a less enviable position for a witness than when he must combat himself while the cross-examiner awaits either loser with equal satisfaction?

Having obtained Hartnett's admissions that the accusations against Faulk had not previously been worthy of his attention, it was not too difficult to make him concede that even if Faulk had attended the occasions listed in the *Bulletin*, his doing so might be quite innocent. The surrender of the former position made untenable any contrary claim, particularly when we had a deadly quotation from his examination before trial.

Q. So that the conclusion . . . is that at the time the *Bulletin* was published, and for that matter to this day . . . you don't say that Faulk is a pro-Communist; is that what it amounts to in simple language?

A. We can break it down. At the time the *Bulletin* was prepared, I had no knowledge, I had no evidence to back up a charge that he was pro-Communist. He might have attended these things in good faith.

But how about Hartnett's good faith? The *Bulletin* cited a quotation by Faulk which it said had appeared in the *Daily Worker*. Actually, it was word-for-word from the Republican newspaper, the New York *Herald Tribune*. This was no innocent error.

Q. And you had the New York *Herald Tribune* in front of you when you wrote those words in quote, didn't you?

A. I most likely did, yes.

The *Bulletin* charged that the middle-of-the-road candidates were silent on communism. He knew otherwise.

Q. . . . it is a fact, is it not, that the middle-of-the-roaders ran on an anti-Communist ticket and so announced?

A. Yes.

Q. So that there is no doubt that they were not keeping silent about their position on communism . . . you agree to that?

A. Yes.

Similarly, how sincere was he in getting at the truth, when he continued to use Matusow as a source for accusation even after Matusow had recanted previous testimony and "been convicted and imprisoned for perjury?" Inevitably, there was comic relief in the midst of the drama.

Q. And when you looked at the Matusow testimony, you never found Mr. Faulk's name, did you?

A. I did not.

Q. But you found your own name, didn't you?

A. Yes, in testimony given by Matusow before the Senate committee.

We pursued his sense of humor. Had he not once been a member of an organization which subsequently appeared in the House Un-American Activities index as a Communist Front organization? No, it was only the California Un-American Activities Committee, called the Tenney Committee, which had declared the organization subversive. But, of course, he hastened to add that the Tenney Committee was not very reliable. He had previously cited it as a source on which he had relied! When a witness darts about avoiding cross-examination arrows, he is bound sooner or later to run into one which was not even shot at him.

Now it was possible to embarrass him with a question irrespective of his answer:

> Q. If you were preparing such a list, you would list yourself if you were consistent?

> A. No, because I never listed anyone solely for that one thing. I differ with the Tenney Committee.

So these reports with high-sounding names were not sacrosanct. He did not hesitate to differ with a finding by one of the most frequently cited committees. But had he extended this privilege to those he listed in *Red Channels* or *File 13*? He conceded that he had not.

Awe for committee names was the very foundation of blacklisting. What sponsor would look behind the title of Senate Internal Security Committee, or House Un-American Activities Committee index? Yet, now that it suited his purpose, it was Hartnett himself who debunked these titles. He admitted that being listed in the index of the House Un-American Activities Committee could be "of no significance."

> Q. As a matter of fact, you testified that President Eisenhower's name is listed, haven't you?

> A. Yes. . . . I believe the reference to former President Eisenhower was made on a letterhead introduced in the testimony of Bishop G. Bromley Oxman.

Yet, if President Eisenhower were to become a performer on radio and television (as indeed he did in the last Republican convention), you would list these citations . . . wouldn't you?

> A. Yes.

It would have been interesting to learn Hartnett's views, if he had attempted to write for or appear on radio or television, and found himself mysteriously unemployable, because some other "security officer," applying the usual technique, had reported that Hartnett was a member of an organization cited in the California Un-American Activities Committee (Tenney) report.

Hartnett had been under cross-examination for two days. The toll of battle is always greater when it involves retreat. He seemed tired, and the judge had to urge him to answer more loudly in the noisy courtroom, for the voice has a tendency to hide when its master is embarrassed. But all this was just the beginning. There were three more days of cross-examination awaiting him and a far more massive attack.

Conspiratorial structures often have windows which look out upon ugly courtyards. We succeeded in prying open one of these barred windows and the sight was shocking. Irresponsible magazines or trade papers have been known to print up in galley proof a vicious attack upon some executive, show it to him in advance, and extract a price for nonpublication or revision. We faced Hartnett with a charge which resembled this technique. He struggled to preserve his patriotic motivation. This is how he fared in the cross-examination battle.

He had written an article in an American Legion magazine attacking the Borden Company for using actors on its television program who had "Communist Front" affiliations.

Q. And that article, before it was published, was brought to the attention of the Borden Company, wasn't it?

A. No, I don't think it was.

Q. You had a conference with the Borden Company before that article was published, didn't you?

A. I did.

Q. As a result of that conference you were hired by the Borden Company that you had just written this article about?

MR. BOLAN: I object.

THE COURT: Overruled.

Q. Weren't you?

A. That I had just written the article about?

Q. Well, a short time before. I don't want to fence with you, Mr. Hartnett.

A. No, but I like to be exact on this.

Q. All right, sir, thank you. Let's be exact. Were you hired by the Borden Company?

A. I was.

Q. And were you hired . . . before that article in which you criticized the Borden Company was published?

A. I was.

Q. Then the article came out thereafter and praised the Borden Company, didn't it?

A. Both criticized and praised, I would say.

Q. By criticized, you mean that they had once had not so good a record, but now they were very patriotic?

A. It told the facts about the past infiltration and praised the Borden Company for taking measures and praised Pall Mall.

Q. The measures which you praised . . . was that they had hired you, correct?

A. No, that they had instituted their own policies. Part of this was retaining me.

Q. Yes. How much did they agree to pay you annually for your service?

A. The only thing that I can testify to certainly as to retainer basis was six thousand dollars a year at the moment.

Q. . . . In 1955 didn't you get ten thousand dollars from the Borden Company?

A. I did.

He had tried to keep the window partly closed by denying his approach to the Borden Company with the galley proof of his condemnatory article. I pushed hard at the window so that the jury could see the whole scene behind it.

Q. I asked you before whether, when you wrote this article which was critical of the Borden Company, you had brought it to their attention before you published it, and I think you told me that you had not.

A. I don't recall, sir, that I did bring it to their notice before the publication.

Q. I read to you from your examination before trial, page 2357:

Q. Did the Borden Company know about this article at the time you had it in galley proof?

A. I believe that I told Stewart Peabody, who was in effect Advertising Director of the Borden Company, that I had written such an article when he asked if I would serve them as a consultant. I felt that since he wished to retain me as a consultant, he should know that this article was in the works. It was scheduled for publication. I told him about it, as I recall, and it put me in a peculiar position as a journalist. Ethically, I certainly could not seek to withdraw the article I had written, so I felt that the solution to my problem was to go right along and have the article published even though it criticized

past performances of my client or its television show, and at the same time in fairness both to the Borden Company and the Pall Mall cigarettes which I didn't represent, I felt I should update the article, so that I did send that addition which you have read to the article which the editor incorporated in the article prior to publication, but after the thing, as I recall, had been in galley proof form."
Did you make that answer?

A. Yes, I did.

After the Borden Company retained him, he added the following to the article in italics:

"It is emphasized that Pall Mall and the Borden Company when alerted by Legionnaires and others to the situation . . . obviously finally took all appropriate measures to correct the situation."

The appropriate measures involved hiring Hartnett for pay!

The galley proof was further changed to sing a poem of glory to his new paying client:

"Judging from the fine talent now being used on 'Big Story' and 'T-Men' it seems evident that the sponsors, Borden in particular, have an effective policy not only of providing splendid entertainment but also of making positive contribution to Americanism. For this they deserve the support of all patriotic Americans."

The poor Borden Company certainly had a squeeze put on it. Laurence Johnson too visited it and suggested that Hartnett be hired. Hartnett conceded this but claimed that he had not known it at the time.

Q. You say that you found out only three weeks ago that Mr. Johnson had helped get you that job at Borden's?

A. Three or four weeks ago, yes, sir.

The trial was revealing an interesting economic assistance program among the patriots. Johnson had put pressure on Hilton and Barton to hire Matusow. Hartnett was the "adviser" to the sponsor which fired its writer Stark, whose job was then taken by Paul Milton. And now Hartnett was aided by Johnson in obtaining a "retainer arrangement" with Borden's. When Hartnett denied this mutual washing of hands, he was faced with a reply he had given on his examination before trial, when he was not fully alerted to the significance of the question:

A. Yes, at one period (knowing Laurence Johnson) did enhance my value to the client.

I shifted to an item of malice. The law permits a searching of the mind to discover ill will. For this reason even a letter or note written by the defendant may be examined to discover whether the hatred in his heart had flowed onto paper. Hartnett had written two drafts of the *Bulletin*. Where was the first one? Even though it was not used, it could reveal a fingerprint of his malice. He could only produce a part of a sheet numbered 2. The rest was missing. After a considerable struggle, he conceded that the first draft "was at least 50 per cent longer" than the *Bulletin*. He didn't have it and didn't remember whether it existed at the time the suit was begun.

But after a pummeling, aided by contradiction in his examination before trial, he conceded that he had destroyed it after Faulk sued. He did not even have a carbon copy of it, even though there was one of the second draft which became the *Bulletin*.

Hartnett seemed to be in bad luck with documents. In addition to those he had destroyed, he had lost some. When Kim Hunter was on the stand, we called for several letters Hartnett had written. We knew they existed because we had seen them at the examination before trial, but Bolan at that time had not permitted us to read them. So we simply marked them for identification and awaited the trial.

When Kim Hunter was testifying, we asked for these documents, but Hartnett could not find them. Now we cross-examined him about their loss.

Q. You remember one day you actually went home during a court day because they might be at your home?

A. I did.

Q. . . . Do you recall that a week went by while I was calling for these letters, and you and Mr. Bolan . . . were looking for them . . . ?

A. It probably was about a week, yes.

Q. And then I called for them one morning in the presence of the jury, and you said you couldn't find them?

A. . . . yes.

Q. . . . Then I put you on the stand. Do you recall that during my case?

A. Indeed I do.

At that time, Bolan had asked me whether I intended to

examine Hartnett, as our witness, about these letters, and when I told him that was my purpose, he asked the court to grant him another twenty-four hours to see if he could find them. We consented. Hartnett was taken off the stand without testifying. The next day, the letters were produced. Now we asked him where they had been.

A. They were in a special Kim Hunter file which I discovered. . . .

Q. On the very Kim Hunter matter, you produced many other letters that had been marked at the examination before trial, hadn't you?

A. Yes, I had.

Q. . . . And you isolated these three letters and put them in another file?

A. I did.

These letters revealed the names of more than seventy artists who were being checked by Hartnett on one occasion, and more than forty on another occasion. Little did this host of performers know that they were being tried, and many of them condemned, in absentia. "In my opinion," wrote Hartnett in his report to the American Broadcasting Company, "you would run a serious risk of adverse public opinion by featuring on your network James Thurber, Kim Hunter . . ." So James Thurber's fables could not be televised. Not only was the public deprived of his genius, but the insulting presumption was indulged in, that if it had been exposed to his work, it would be outraged and the network would suffer the consequences of "adverse public opinion." And James Thurber was supposed to be blind!

Of course this reference to Kim Hunter, who was referred to in all three letters, might be considered by the jury to be the real reason why Hartnett could not find them, until we put him on the stand as our witness to question him about their disappearance.

Laurence Johnson was still an absentee defendant. But in a certain sense Hartnett was his embodiment, as if the two figures were pasted together, only the outer surface being seen. We explored their relationship. Had he not turned to Johnson to help him keep certain artists off the air?

A. None come to mind, sir.

Q. Let me see if I can refresh your recollection. Did

you ever ask Mr. Larry Johnson to take action against Franchot Tone?

A. I don't know whether I asked him to take action. I remember writing him about Franchot Tone.

Q. Mr. Johnson wasn't in the theatrical profession, was he?

A. No.

Q. He was in the grocery business, right?

A. Yes.

Q. What were you writing to Mr. Laurence Johnson with respect to Franchot Tone?

A. . . . he had asked me for a report on Franchot Tone, which I furnished him. . . . I expressed an opinion that Franchot Tone should do more . . .

Q. Before he can appear on television?

A. Could be. I'm not sure of that.

Q. Could be. Did you ever write to Johnson, "If he refuses to take a public stand, then we can take necessary measures?"

A. Yes, that sounds right.

It was not easy to draw out of him a description of the "necessary measures." But we hoped that the tedious effort to do so would fill the jury with disgust rather than boredom. Ultimately, he conceded that it meant pressures by Johnson's organizations, draped in the colors, the denial of space on supermarket shelves, and terrorizing techniques such as providing ballots to customers who were offered the fair choice of voting for Americanism or communism.

Hartnett more readily conceded that he never protested against Johnson's boycotts as improper. On the contrary, he wrote him "congratulations on your wonderful work."

This "wonderful work," which kept artists off the air, was it authorized by the F.B.I., or any other governmental authority? No, no. Indeed, he didn't think much of their processes anyhow.

Q. You think that instead of leaving it to the government and the F.B.I. and the government authorities, that to do that would be very unrealistic, correct?

A. Absolutely.

There wasn't even consistency in his inconsistency. He did not hesitate to set up a secret alliance with the New York Police Department, seeking information about Faulk.

Q. You told Lieutenant Crain of the Police Department of the City of New York that the middle-of-the-road slate was helping communism, didn't you?

A. I don't recall saying that they were helping communism. Did I so testify?

Q. Page 1323 of Examination before Trial.

"Q. Did you say anything to the effect that the middle-of-the-road slate was helping communism?

"A. Yes, I think I did."

He admitted knowing that the opposite was the truth. Hartnett conceded having seventy talks with Lieutenant Crain about artists. He claimed that Paul Milton had made this secret arrangement with the police through Inspector Robb, but we read to him Milton's denial, and self-protective assertion that it would have been improper to do so. Of course, the police had no information about Faulk. Why should they? But the investigative attempt to get something criminal on Aware's enemies, was iniquitous in purpose, though empty in result.

There is something about the mentality of a blacklister which seeks gumshoe outlet. When some opponents of the AFTRA slate met at the Blue Ribbon Restaurant, Hartnett went there.

Q. And while you were attending it, you had on a shoulder holster microphone secretly to record what was being said?

A. Yes.

Q. . . . In other words, you considered your function there to spy on this group and get the recording of what was said?

A. Yes.

He had no license as a private detective. All of his activities stemmed from self-delegated authority.

The road of cross-examination became littered with contradictions. The refuse made the scene uglier.

Q. Mr. Johnson worked with Harvey Matusow in these activities . . . did he not?

A. Yes, I object to "work with." He obtained information from Matusow.

Q. I read to you from page 191 of your examination:

"Q. Did Laurence Johnson work with Matusow?

"A. Yes."

Q. Did you make that answer?

A. Yes, I accepted your nomenclature there, yes.

Although he had made 270 corrections before signing the examination before trial, he admitted he had never corrected or qualified this answer.

Hartnett considered the Syracuse American Legion Post and the Veterans Action Committee, "Johnson's boys." He so referred to them when he wrote to Johnson. "How would your boys feel about Ben Grauer in a show?"

He wrote to Johnson condemning the use of Susan Strasberg, then fifteen years old, because he had listed her father in his disreputable *File 13*. We hoped that the jury shared our conviction that there was no basis for believing that Franchot Tone, Ben Grauer and Lee Strasberg were disloyal.

Judge Cardozo once pointed out that character is seldom lost from wrong choices made in matters of consequence. The honorable man can resist temptation which challenges his integrity. It is the small, insignificant concessions which are unlikely to be known by others, which must be guarded against. These begin the breach in the wall of character, which is then subtly widened until all is lost. We found in Hartnett's career such a small incident which cast a demeaning light upon him and embarrassed him severely. He had written an article for a magazine not under his real name, but the name of Forman. Under this fictitious name, he referred to *Red Channels* and quoted from the attacks which had been made upon it in 166 American newspapers as "a vicious publication that destroys character by innuendo and veiled accusation," "a smear pamphlet," "a character assassination for profit." After setting forth these characterizations of his own publication, he then referred to Vincent Hartnett as if he were a third person, and praised him for the fine work he was doing.

It could all be chalked up to vanity and self-glorification, and may not in itself have been a major matter. But his indulgence in deception which permitted him under an assumed name to issue a defense of himself as if he were commenting objectively on a third person, might well be considered by the jury as depicting a man given to small unscrupulous acts and, therefore, more vulnerable to the accusation of the larger unscrupulousness—blacklisting.

After we had tied Hartnett to Johnson, Neuser, Dungey, and their organizations with detailed cords of activity, we exposed the recklessness of his seven accusations against Faulk, adding his own irresponsibility to the mound of falsity already built out of Paul Milton's admissions. We concluded (or so we thought) our attack with a climactic reading to him of his confession in the examination before trial that he had been "sold a barrel of false information" about Faulk.

Then we released him to the tender mercies of his own counsel for redirect examination. We would have the privilege of recross-examination if anything new was developed. This is ordinarily the petering-out period—a sort of last gasp, for by this time the witness has either been discredited beyond repair, or he has successfully withstood the attack and strengthened his hold on the case. Yet, such are the vagaries of trial dramas, that it was during redirect and recross-examination of Hartnett, that the greatest explosion of the trial occurred. It could not have been foreseen or planned.

During the second day of cross-examination I noticed that Hartnett would occasionally take a pink card out of his pocket, write something on it, put it back in his breast pocket, and proceed to answer my questions. At first I thought he was making notes for his counsel for redirect examination. Even this would be strange behavior by a witness. It is the lawyer who usually carries this burden, while the witness is preoccupied enough responding to hostile questions. But soon I observed that before Hartnett made these notes on his colored card, he had looked at the doors of the courtroom which were almost directly opposite him. On one occasion as I followed his eyes to the door, then to the clock on the wall, and then saw him unclip his fountain pen and write a note on a card, I interrupted cross-examination of a subject I was pursuing:

Q. Incidentally, you have made notes of people coming into the courtroom even while you have been on the stand, haven't you, and the time they have come into the courtroom, on those pink slips?

A. Yes.

Q. Did you write down the time they entered the courtroom?

A. I did.

Since comment on this incident had to await summation, I indulged in the only communication possible at the time—a long, meaningful look at the jury.

Now, several days later, Bolan was conducting redirect examination of Hartnett. He decided to exploit this incident to his own purpose.

Q. On cross-examination Mr. Nizer asked you if you were recording the names of the people who came into the courtroom during your testimony. Do you recall that?

A. I do.

Q. Who were the names of the people you wrote?

A. Elliot Sullivan, who was sitting next to Mrs. Faulk; John Randolph, Alan Manson, Jack Gilford, were some of them.

This struck me as extraordinary. Was attendance at a public trial to be included in some future report by Hartnett, as evidence of pro-communism? Hartnett had considered an artist's attendance at a funeral of an alleged pro-Communist activity which required listing in his reports. Now, apparently being present at a trial of Aware and Hartnett was proof of disloyalty to our country and warranted a notation with the precise time of entry. Aside from the neurotic illogic of the whole thing, for the crowded courtroom often held many members of Aware, I was particularly struck by Hartnett's reference to the fact that one of these visitors sat down next to Mrs. Faulk. What an exquisite extension of the doctrine of guilt by association. Now it was guilt by proximity. I marked his answer on my pad with several penciled stars, to remind me that this was worthy of recross-examination in depth. I needed no reminder. I had already decided to take a gamble which the prudent rules of cross-examination would have ruled out. But there are times when caution is the great risk, and besides, my anger was getting the better of me. Now the time for recross had come. Once more, I faced Hartnett, although we had thought we were through with him.

Q. You have said that when you were on the witness stand, when somebody came into the room you wrote down the name, and in answer to your counsel's question you gave the name of one person, Mr. Sullivan, and you added he sat right down next to Mrs. Faulk. Did you say that?

A. I did.

Q. Do you see Mrs. Faulk in the court now?

A. I believe she is the lady over there, I am not sure.

THE COURT: Which lady?

MR. NIZER: Will you stand up?

(A woman rose in the courtroom.)

MR. NIZER: What is your name, please?

THE WOMAN: Sofer. S-o-f-e-r.

There was a roar of laughter in the courtroom which rose and rolled on as the full realization of his blunder took over. I imagined the hilarity was also tinged with ridicule. The jury too revealed the shock underneath its own burst of mirth. Against this emotional background of derision, I shouted.

Q. Is that the way you identify people when you also choose—

Objection was sustained.

Q. Would you like to have a second chance at . . . identifying her? . . . Can you identify Mrs. Faulk in this courtroom now?

A. A certain lady was pointed out to me, described by Mr. Sibley as being Mrs. Faulk.

Q. Which one is that?

MR. BOLAN: He said Mr. Sibley of the New York *Times* pointed out—

MR. NIZER: Mr. Bolan, I am not asking you to testify.

THE COURT: Now wait a minute, Mr. Bolan. We want the answer from the witness.

A. It looked like her, Your Honor. I mistook her then.

Hartnett's reflex was typical. When he was caught in an egregious, embarrassing error, he immediately shifted the blame to someone else—Sibley, a New York *Times* reporter had misled him! Of course, this wasn't true. Sibley took the stand later, to deny vehemently that he had ever pointed out Mrs. Faulk to Hartnett or anyone else. He did not relish Hartnett's clutching at him to lift himself out of a hole. Hartnett, instead of taking his loss in a manly manner, revealed a persecution complex—a reporter had done him in by false identification.

What better way could we conclude with Hartnett than this incident? Its dramatic effect could not be adequately measured. It not only belied Sullivan's sitting down next to Mrs. Faulk (an unlikely event, if for no other reason than that the courtroom was usually crowded, and it would have been a coincidence if a seat next to her happened to be unoccupied); but it also was a shocking demonstration of the inaccuracy with which Hartnett fingered artists and marked them for destruction. An experiment had been improvised right in the courtroom, and Hartnett had revealed himself to be inaccurate, reckless, and irresponsible—and he had not even had the grace to admit his error. He immediately indicted someone else for his blunder.

There was a human as well as humorous undercurrent to the incident which only a few of us knew. It involved Mrs. Sofer, the lady who was mistakenly pointed out by Hartnett as Mrs. Faulk.

The ballet has its devoted followers who attend every performance, usually sitting in the same seat. They get to know the personal history of every performer and ultimately the performers themselves, for balletomanes even travel throughout the country, loyally attending every performance of the tour.

Exciting trials attract similar adherents—shall we call them trialomanes? In significant trials, counsel often become aware of one or more regular attendees. Even when we arrive early to deck the counsel table with documents, as if a feast were being prepared, these visitors are already there—usually in the same front-row seats. At first our suspicious natures cause us to wonder whether they are hostile witnesses. We even send out feelers, to avoid surprise. Soon we learn that they are simply following the trial, and their innocence encourages our friendliness. There is the daily greeting, sometimes the passing of a few light words in a corridor during ten-minute recesses, and ultimately, after weeks of eye acquaintance, brief discussions of their reactions to the day's developments.

Mrs. Sofer was a trialomane—at least during the Faulk case. She was a handsome-looking, auburn-haired, well-dressed, middle-aged woman who impressed her presence upon us by loyal attendance throughout the eleven weeks of the trial. As our acquaintance grew from formal nods to friendly greetings, she seemed to become a good will mascot, emotionally involved in the struggle. She came to court in a chauffeur-driven car. Sometimes witnesses needed a lift uptown, after the day ended, and she offered the courtesy of her car. When Faulk did not meet us in the morning to continue preparation on the way to court, her car would pick him up, and deliver him to the courtroom.

At lunchtime, we ate at a nearby restaurant called Gassner's, where we had a corner table which afforded us privacy, and also provided a large leather windowsill on which we parked documents to be discussed between gulps of food.

Our table was reserved for our legal staff, Faulk, and any witness who might need oral sustenance as well. Here we distinguished quickly between those, who being emotionally tense, ordered wiener schnitzel, beef à la mode, and other heavy dishes to dampen the fires, and those, like myself, who ordered cottage cheese, yogurt, and honey (sometimes a plate of soup for the warmth it gave to a worn throat) in order not to war with the inner fires. Mrs. Sofer never broke into this circle, but she had a table in another corner of the same restaurant, where Faulk's well-wishers could join her. We all became fond of her, as she suffered over our setbacks, and prospered when we scored. She was a refined woman, con stantly on the fringe of our struggle.

Of course, neither she, nor any of us dreamed that she would become part of the trial itself. So when Hartnett rose from the witness stand, scanned the room carefully, and, of all the people, pointed a finger at her, as Mrs. Faulk, she arose with dignity and upon my demand, called out her name, with ill-disguised emotion and glee. She hastened to spell it out at once, as if to pin down Hartnett's error with finality. She had been catapulted into the center of the drama, and in a triumphant role, too. What balletomane had ever been called upon to ascend the stage and dance *Giselle*? But Mrs. Sofer's name will go down imperishably in the law books as one who gave the lie, by the mere recital of her name, to the entire defense. The gale of laughter, which followed the one word she spoke, must have sounded like the world's applause in her ears. We were pleased with this unique triumph of a trialomane.

The reason Hartnett and his counsel appeared undismayed despite the fact that the trial evidently was going badly for them, was that they had three witnesses who they expected could destroy us. Two of them were top executives of CBS, who would testify that Faulk was fired because his popularity declined, not because of Aware's *Bulletin* or Hartnett's actions. The third was the publisher of *Pulse*, a rating service widely used in radio and television, which would scientifically bear out this theory that Faulk failed as a performer, and now was trying to blame Aware, Johnson, and Hartnett for his own inadequacy. These three witnesses were reputable executives of high standing. If they were believed, there could be no damage. At best, Faulk might succeed in obtaining a six cents nominal verdict on the theory that even if he was libeled, the loss of his job was due to other reasons.

In every lawsuit, counsel expects the disappointment of recalcitrant witnesses who refuse to cooperate. But we had not expected that CBS would have any such reluctance. After all, it had been the beneficiary of a long and successful relationship with Faulk, during which it had grossed more than one million dollars from his program.

We had broken through the resistance of large advertising agencies, who disliked becoming involved in a suit which exposed blacklisting and which called upon them to confess that they had participated in such practices under economic duress. Producers and packagers of shows, like Mark Goodson and David Susskind, had come forward heroically to reveal the industry's practices. Stars like Garry Moore, and Kim Hunter had volunteered their experiences. Strangers to Faulk, moved by his great cause, risked embarrassment, as well as economic injury, and came to testify. Of all those to be marshaled as witnesses, we were most confident that Faulk's superiors at CBS, Sam Slate and Carl Ward, would be available to us. Slate was not only Faulk's boss, but had become his close friend. They shared much in common, from Southern accent to views about broadcasting. Slate knew intimately the ordeal Faulk and his family had undergone through the unjust attacks upon him. He had responded with deeds as well as with sympathy. He was delighted that Ed Murrow and Charles Collingwood had supported Faulk, so that he could survive the assaults by Johnson and "his boys" for more than a year.

When Murrow and Collingwood were out of power, Faulk still leaned on Slate, who assured him he would always shield him. Later, when Faulk had to be let out because the unremitting pressures became too great, Slate was genuinely distressed. During preparation of the case, when we did not know whether we could lure any witnesses at all to the stand, our list always started with CBS—at least Slate and Ward would corroborate Faulk's story. As we approached trial, we learned to our consternation that Slate and Ward would not come forward for us, because we surmised to do so might expose the "security measures" which CBS, too, had taken against artists and to which it had yielded when applied from the outside. Faulk's entreaties failed, and this left a gaping hole in our case. We had intended to demonstrate what we knew was the truth, that Faulk had finally lost his post at CBS because the libels had made him controversial. This could best be done through CBS executives. Now not only would they be absent from our ranks, but they were going to appear as defense witnesses against us. We still could not be certain whether they were so unhappy with their role that they would soften their blows, or, whether, to protect the corporate image, they would go all out to blame Faulk's defective showmanship for his unemployment. The strategy of cross-examination could only be determined when we knew the witnesses' attitude. Indeed, Faulk was sure that Slate and Ward would never testify against him.

Now we saw Ward and Slate in the back of the courtroom, flanked solicitously by CBS lawyers. Obviously, it was the company's policy to reject any inference that it had participated in any blacklisting. As we discovered later, a theory had been carefully worked out to demonstrate that extensive program changes and Faulk's decline in ratings were responsible for his being let out. Whatever hopes we had that Slate and Ward would balk at playing this role for CBS, were shattered by the very announcement, "Mr. Ward, will you please take the stand." Bolan's voice had a ring of triumph in it. His manner and the straightened posture of his associates at the counsel table revealed the inner satisfaction and excitement which accompanied the announcement.

Soon we knew the worst. Ward was the tall, executive type, impressive in manner and unhesitating in the answers which he snapped. He gave an impression of direct objectivity, and Bolan quickly heightened that impression by revealing that he had been subpoenaed to testify. What a witness to tangle with. Yet we could not afford at this late hour to go down without applying every resource of cross-examination.

Ward had been General Manager at WCBS Radio in New York City during six years of Faulk's program, but he was promoted to another position long before Faulk was fired. So Sam Slate, who had announced Faulk's discharge, would testify to that critical period.

But Ward was dissatisfied with Faulk's performance long before the Aware *Bulletin* came out. Bolan was so tickled with his testimony that he used the obvious device of having it repeated. Said Ward:

> I told Mr. Faulk that the rating on the program did not represent what we would like to obtain from the time period, that as a result we probably were going to terminate his employment.

MR. BOLAN: Would you read that back, please.

THE COURT: Read it back.

(The last answer was read.)

Q. Would you continue, Mr. Ward.

A. I believe I told Mr. Faulk . . . of some frustration, aside from the ratings, . . . the manner in which the program was being handled.

MR. BOLAN: May I ask if the jury is able to hear?

THE WITNESS: I told Mr. Faulk that unless there were some unusual changes in the performance of the program, that we would probably terminate his employment.

Q. Was there any discussion as to giving Mr. Faulk an opportunity to resign?

A. There was.

To save his face so that "it would appear that he had resigned," they arranged to amend Faulk's contract so that either party could terminate on three weeks' notice. Then Faulk sent a letter of resignation saying he had found other employment. The letter was introduced into evidence.

The ratings which Ward had found unsatisfactory were those reported by *Pulse*, a publication used in the industry to sample every performer's audience, and to which CBS subscribed.

Having received all the answers he sought, Bolan announced, "I have no further questions." But we had a good many. The discussion with Faulk which Ward had testified about really arose from the fact that Faulk had changed the successful format of his one-man show, by turning to guests. He had hoped to develop more excitement by utilizing this well-known showmanship device. Ward had disagreed. I tried to develop this background by a friendly and even flattering approach.

Q. Was it unusual to criticize an artist for his format . . . which you felt could be improved upon to the benefit of his program?

A. Mr. Nizer, I don't know that we criticized them,

but we would make suggestions . . . and tell them how a program . . . could be improved.

Q. If I called it constructive criticism, would you then accept the word criticism?

A. Yes, sir.

Ward had insisted that Faulk give up his guests and go back to a one-man show. His reason for this could only do us good. So we asked him to justify his judgment.

I believe I told Mr. Faulk that I felt the attraction of his program was his own personality rather than the injecting of guests into the program itself.

Now he was only a step or two away from most favorable testimony. His answers were inevitable.

Q. Did you consider Faulk's personality unique?

A. Yes, sir, I did.

Q. And very effective as a professional performer?

A. I do.

Q. You did at that time too, did you not, Mr. Ward?

A. I felt that Mr. Faulk by virtue of being an unusual personality represented an opportunity for the station to develop some unusual audience attraction and radio following.

We showed him the many advertising folders issued by CBS hailing Faulk's audience pull and effectiveness. Next we attempted to tackle his argument on declining ratings.

Q. As it turned out, your constructive advice was right, according to the ratings, they went up after he went back to his old format; is that correct?

A. The ratings went up, Mr. Nizer.

But Ward also explained that from January 1957 through June there was a decline again.

Faulk's resignation was not a pretense to hide his discharge, was it? We showed him a trade paper which announced prominently on the front page that Faulk had been engaged by the Texas broadcasting chain as vice president and broadcaster with stock options as a special inducement. Of course, this was long before Aware's *Bulletin*. So Faulk had not been pushed out by CBS while he pretended to leave voluntarily. He had really been offered an important post as executive and artist at an important Texas broadcasting chain.

There was only one more admission necessary to complete Ward's transformation to a witness for the plaintiff. Fortunately, we had found a letter in the CBS files, which compelled him to come along with us. CBS had used Nielsen as a second rating service. *Pulse* and Nielsen varied in their reports, a precursor of the attacks available upon their sampling techniques. Of seventeen radio stations, Nielsen reported Faulk second.

Q. And he was ahead of the entire NBC lineup, was he not, sir?

A. Yes.

Dr. Frank Stanton, President of CBS, had called for an opinion about Faulk. Ward wrote him a memorandum which I showed him, and it unlocked his memory.

". . . because of the reputation of the Nielsen Service we had to give consideration to the showing that Mr. Faulk made."

Q. Did you recommend, therefore, that you wanted to continue to have Mr. Faulk after 1955 on your station?

A. . . . I told Dr. Stanton in the memorandum that we decided to continue the services of Mr. Faulk. . . .

Q. Right, sir. . . . Had you talked to John Henry Faulk about withdrawing his resignation and continuing on the station . . . ?

A. I did.

Q. And did he agree to do so ultimately?

A. He did.

We felt we had passed the first crisis.

Now, Sam Slate was called to the stand to finish the task Ward had failed to do. If ever a man was torn between loyalty to his employer and to his dear friend, it was Slate. His distress revealed itself in severe physical symptoms. His eyes blinked as if flashlights were being popped in front of them. His face twitched. His head jerked, as if his collar was choking him. His whole body seemed to squirm in restless movements. But above all, his voice rebelled. Mr. Slate, who at that very time was broadcasting the WCBS editorials, would become inaudible in the middle of a sentence as if the breath necessary to sustain it had been removed by his emotion. This caused a continuous crisis of admonition to him.

THE COURT: Mr. Slate, would you please keep your voice up? I want the jurors to hear you, and this is a noisy room. You have to speak up.

THE WITNESS: Sorry, Judge.

Later:

> THE COURT: Keep your voice up, please. . . .
>
> THE WITNESS: I'm sorry. . . . Judge, can you hear me?
>
> THE COURT: . . . I'm straining myself.

Still later:

> THE COURT: I am standing almost close to you and I barely hear you, and the jurors are motioning to me that they don't know what you are saying. Speak up, will you please, Mr. Slate? Shout.
>
> THE WITNESS: Yes, sir, I will shout.

Yet, a moment later:

> THE COURT: I barely hear you, and I am sitting very close to you.
>
> MR. BOLAN: Maybe we can turn off the fan.
>
> THE COURT: No, the fan is not noisy at all.

When we reached the cross-examination, his vocal cords approached paralysis.

> THE COURT: . . . I have to stand up and get close to you to catch every word, and I don't want to do that.
>
> THE WITNESS: Yes, sir. Maybe I better stand up.
>
> THE COURT: If you feel you can speak louder, I will let you stand up. Maybe you prefer the . . . English system of standing.
>
> THE WITNESS: . . . I will stand back so perhaps I can project it to you, too.
>
> THE COURT: All right.

It was pitiful to see him stand and hunch his shoulders in a great effort to make himself heard a few feet away. But, of course, Slate, who could thunder at a sales meeting, was not suffering from throat trouble.

Nevertheless, in spurts and wheezes, he testified in answer to Bolan's question that he told Faulk:

"because of the decline of ratings in the afternoon that we would unfortunately have to eliminate his show. We would not pick up his contract."

> Q. That decline in rating, what was that based on?
>
> A. It was based on *Pulse.*

He described the shifting of programs which cut across Faulk's hour and absorbed it. He stressed the decline in Faulk's popularity. He told Faulk all the reasons for his discharge, but, he said, he never mentioned the Aware *Bul-*

letin or Johnson's activities against him as being a factor in the slightest way.

Late in the afternoon he was turned over to us for cross-examination. The judge commented on the fact that it was "a brutally hot day" and that in twenty minutes we would recess until the next morning. The remaining time did not become cooler for Slate as we began to probe his story.

We turned to the events almost two years before Faulk was fired, to focus attention on the *Bulletin*, which Slate's testimony had ignored.

He could not deny the impact of the Aware-Hartnett-Johnson offensive and the deep concern it gave to CBS. He remembered the conferences with Ward, Faulk's denials of the charges in the *Bulletin*, and the resort to an affidavit by Faulk to appease alarmed clients. He conceded there were cancellations and that

"Mr. Ward felt that if we lost a great number of sponsors, we'd have to take a good hard look again to determine whether we could continue the show or not."

A little more prodding brought the name of Laurence Johnson from his lips and that "he was instrumental in having letters written to agencies." Again his voice failed him, and for a second time he asked for permission to stand.

We drew from him a recollection, whispery though it was, that CBS salesmen reported

"that Mr. Johnson was calling the agencies all up and down Madison Avenue."

Was it likely that this crisis left no mark at all on CBS, and that its subsequent shedding of Faulk had no relationship to it, as he now claimed?

The next step was to make him admit that the *Bulletin* had left a fatal mark on Faulk's brow, which any employer would recognize.

> Q. . . . These charges in this *Bulletin* . . . made Mr. Faulk controversial so far as any new employer was concerned; is that correct?
> A. I was aware of that, Mr. Nizer.
> THE COURT: I didn't hear that.
> MR. NIZER: "I was aware of that, Mr. Nizer." Thank you, sir.
> Q. . . . What is the effect of such controversiality on his getting new employment?

A. It certainly wouldn't help him any.

Q. I can't hear you.

THE COURT: I don't hear you.

MR. BOLAN: He said it certainly wouldn't help him any.

Q. No, I am sure of that, but would he become generally, in the practice of the industry, virtually unemployable for New York?

A. I would say it would be very, very difficult for him to get new jobs, Mr. Nizer.

This was true, he conceded, even if the controversial artist turned out ultimately to be innocent.

We tried to show that as a friend of Faulk he had advised him to accept any job he could far from New York. At first, he said:

A. I have no recollection of giving Johnny that advice.

But repetition stirred his recollection:

A. The only advice that I can remember giving Johnny, that it would be a good idea to get out of New York City. I don't remember where or what part of the country.

Next we challenged his theory that Faulk's decline in ratings was responsible for his joblessness. Martha Wright, the singer, had been moved up into part of Faulk's time when he was let out. But her *Pulse* ratings had declined during the very period when Faulk's had gone up. He struggled with the *Pulse* reports.

Ratings are given not only for individual artists, but also for a whole station during a segment of time, for example, from noon to 6:00 P.M. Such a rating measures the share of audience which a radio station attracts as against competing stations.

Q. Isn't it a fact that John Henry Faulk's position on share of audience was far better than the entire WCBS time segment from twelve to six?

A. I would doubt that, Mr. Nizer. I would have to see the figures.

THE COURT: I don't hear you.

After he repeated his doubt, we faced him with the *Pulse* ratings. Finally:

Q. No, no, please answer my question. Assuming the accuracy of these figures on *Pulse* ratings . . . Mr. Faulk's went up a point, didn't he, during the same period that WCBS went down?

A. That's correct.

My notes for cross-examination had a huge penciled star which I had made next to an answer Slate had given to Bolan. That night that star guided me to a review of the stenographic minutes (delivered at midnight) of his testimony. It involved a date. Ordinarily, errors in dates are of no consequence. We are all fallible on fixing time. But sometimes a date is crucial. It can reveal the falsity of entire testimony. For example, if the person claimed to have been involved in a conversation was out of the country at the time, the fiction of the testimony can be conclusively demonstrated instead of merely denied. What made the particular date critical in Slate's testimony was that he contended he had told Faulk in July 1957, that due to declining ratings and program changes his contract would not be renewed. Faulk and Dickler had testified that the very opposite was the fact, that Slate had never warned Faulk of any plan to discharge him, but on the contrary had assured him of his "spot" despite any program changes. Furthermore, Faulk and Dickler testified that while Faulk and his family were on vacation in Jamaica, Dickler was suddenly notified that Faulk was fired. Astonished by the news, Dickler had summoned Faulk back to the city. So here was a complete contradiction of fact. Had Slate told Faulk in advance he was through, or had Slate's hand been forced while Faulk basked in sunlight on a faraway beach believing that he was secure? The date that Slate gave for his version was pinned down time and again in his testimony as July 1957. But Faulk was out of the city by that time! When he withdrew the date, the approach became clear.

Q. Did you find out since yesterday that Mr. Faulk wasn't in the city of New York during the month of July . . . ?

A. Mr. Nizer—

THE COURT: The question is a simple one. Read the question to the witness. You can answer that yes or no.

A. Yes.

Q. By whom was it called to your attention, sir?

A. By one of my associates at CBS.

Q. Did you not yesterday time and again testify that

this conversation with Mr. Faulk took place in July 1957 . . . ?

A. I don't remember, Mr. Nizer.

Q. You don't remember since yesterday whether you so testified?

A. . . . I believe that is correct.

Q. So you had no conversation with Mr. Faulk concerning the subject matter you testified to yesterday in July 1957, did you?

A. I did not have any conversations with him until he returned from Jamaica, Mr. Nizer.

But by then he had already been fired, so how could you have warned him in advance of the "reasons" for CBS's alleged unhappiness?

We felt the timing was now right to suggest why CBS had adopted so hostile an attitude toward its own star, who it knew was victimized by a blacklist.

Q. The CBS organization during the years from . . . 1951 to 1956 had an executive whose duty it was also to act as what has been called screening or security officer; is that right?

A. I believe that's correct.

Q. And his name was Dan O'Shea?

A. I think so, Mr. Nizer.

Q. Under this system of screening, the network, before it would permit a performer to appear on it, would have to get a report either from some outside agency or internal checking with respect to the alleged political associations of that performer, is that right, sir? This was the practice? . . .

A. In a general way, I would say that was the practice.

On redirect examination, Bolan tried to pull Slate back into line. Faulk's *Pulse* rating had gone down from January to June 1957, immediately before his discharge, and this he said was one of the reasons for his being let out.

He also stressed the contemplated program changes, involving Arthur Godfrey, whose musical program required "a flow" of continued music from Martha Wright. As to controversiality, a lawsuit "would tend to make a performer controversial." So it was claimed it was not the wrong, but the remedy which had done Faulk in.

The price for redirect testimony is the opportunity for re-cross. Before the Godfrey show, Faulk had also been preceded by music—Lanny Ross's singing program. So he conceded that there was no difference in so far as "musical flow" was concerned.

We concluded cross-examination on his unlikely explanation for the firing of Faulk:

> Q. You mean to say that of all the factors you considered, Mr. Slate, . . . the one factor you didn't consider was the controversiality of this pending lawsuit and the subject matter of it? Is that your testimony?
>
> A. That is my testimony.
>
> MR. NIZER: That is all, sir.

Dr. Sydney Roslow had earned his doctorate degree in psychology. He was tall, gray-haired, and his professional demeanor lent dignity to his calling.

Dr. Roslow explained that *Pulse* was a research company in advertising and marketing which specialized in radio and television measurement. He described the techniques of this science. Interviewers presented questionnaires to men and women in their homes after certain programs had finished. These questionnaires were then processed to obtain percentage ratings. There were two categories, he explained. One was the straight rating of those who listened to certain programs. The other was "share of audience" rating which recorded only those homes which had had their radios turned on. In other words, of those who were actually listening to radio at the time, how many had preferred a particular program. There were also categories of in-home and out-of-home radios, like those in automobiles, which had restored radio's popularity, because the driver's eyes could still be kept on the road while his ears were filled. There were about twenty-five radio stations in the vicinity of New York City which were covered by *Pulse*. When the complicated statistics had been gathered and interpreted, they were published and sold to four networks and others.

Then he turned to Faulk. He had prepared a chart of straight ratings, share-of-audience ratings, and the rank among those with whom he competed during the same time segment. For the six-month period prior to Faulk's being fired by CBS, his ratings had been going down. From January to June, they had declined gradually from a rating of 4 to 3.1. This difference of .9 he projected to thirty-six thousand fewer homes listening to Faulk in July than in January. Faulk ranked fourth among his competitors, and his share of audience rating had also receded.

Dr. Roslow was turned over to us for cross-examination. We felt that not only was Faulk's fate involved, but that for the first time there would be a real look into the mystique of ratings. It was obvious to us that if all viewers could be questioned, the result would be significant. Even if 50 per cent or a much lesser number could be interviewed, the answers would be indicative of a trend. But, of course, the smaller the sampling, the greater the possibility of error. Our first attack was therefore directed not at the abstract theories of ratings, but at the application of these theories by *Pulse* to determine whether they were in sufficient depth to acquire validity.

Roslow soon admitted that his monthly reports were based on samplings of only one week. Three weeks were ignored.

During that one week, *Pulse* interviewers questioned four hundred people out of four million set owners concerning Faulk, a sampling of one one-thousandth of 1 per cent.

He conceded that the other major rating services, Hooper and Nielsen, occasionally differed substantially with each other and *Pulse*. Furthermore, he allowed up to a half-point error in his own report.

Since the entire drop in Faulk's rating from January to June was only about .9, would not the margin of error in itself eliminate the decline? He struggled with the figures, but like a wrestler who stops bridging himself and sinks on his shoulders, he made the final concession.

To expose the flimsy basis for the ratings, we translated these figures into persons. The entire drop in Faulk's rating would be "wiped out if fifteen more people out of four million were interviewed."

We gave him pad and pencil and asked him to compare Faulk's ratings for three months in 1955 with the same three months in 1957. The difference was only one-tenth of 1 per cent. The following testimony came close to condemning his own reports as unreliable.

> Q. Then wouldn't you consider one-tenth of 1 per cent very insignificant . . . ?

A. I consider it unreliable, not insignificant.

Q. Your own report unreliable?

A. I would consider the difference as being unreliable, not insignificant.

Q. You mean that your report would show a conclusion which you find is unreliable, is that it?

A. I didn't draw any conclusion.

We turned to the share-of-audience rating and found that Dr. Roslow's hand on *Pulse* was even more uncertain. The difference of one point would be changed if instead of twelve people being interviewed, a thirteenth had stated that he heard Faulk.

Ratings give the impression of refined precision as they report variations in decimal points. Yet the margin of error conceded by Dr. Roslow destroyed the scientific aura created by these minute calibrations.

Q. The margin of error in this share of audience is larger than the difference that you find between 1955 and 1957 on share-of-audience for Mr. Faulk, right?

A. Yes.

Since the sampling was so infinitesimal that one additional listener could add a whole point to a rating, did not sheer accident make ratings totally unreliable?

Q. When your name goes around to these homes, if someone is out, of course, there can be no interview. . . .

A. Yes, that's correct.

Q. If you go there at seven to eight, if somebody is out to dinner, that blocks off that interview, right?

A. Yes.

If that person happened to be a Faulk listener, and the next one was not, then, of course, the survey would be radically altered. Roslow would not concede. "I don't know what the effect would be," he replied.

We retraced all his findings on rank, and made him lift Faulk to first place by merely using his margin of error as an eraser to rub out the precise calibrations of one-tenth or two-tenths of a per cent. Often the addition of one Faulk listener would turn all his figures topsy-turvy.

There was still one more strategy available, to turn Dr. Roslow into a favorable witness for Faulk. He had been called as an expert to demonstrate that Faulk had failed CBS. Suppose we could show that CBS had failed Faulk?

Q. Now will you take a look at your CBS report . . . share-of-audience . . . for the entire WCBS time segment from 12 noon to 6:00 P.M.? There is a reduction of about nineteen to twenty per cent?

A. About twenty per cent.

Q. Look at the same period, taking exactly the same figures for share-of-audience for Mr. Faulk. That is a drop of about nine per cent, correct?

A. Yes.

Q. . . . In order to figure how WCBS did on all of its programs during that time segment, you would really have to take out the rating of Faulk in order to compare it with Faulk, is that right?

A. Yes.

Q. And if you took out John Henry Faulk's rating, then, of course, the drop of CBS would be larger than the twenty per cent, wouldn't it?

A. Yes.

The pull of the line was too strong for him. He conceded that between 1955 and June 1957, WCBS's decline in share-of-audience was more than twice as steep as John Henry Faulk's. Faulk had done much better than the station.

Suddenly the trial became a medical one. Doctors took the stand to testify concerning a rare disease. Anyone who entered the courtroom expecting to listen to a libel suit involving blacklisting, would have been sure that he wandered into a wrong room where a malpractice case, involving the esophagus was in process. How did this come about?

The drama of the courtroom knows no logical development. Like all human affairs, it is unpredictable, and undisciplined. It shoots out in all directions, creating suspense and excitement through the propulsion of life's forces, rather than by the planned design of an author. That is why the truth of a court trial is often stranger than the fiction of a most imaginative mind.

Laurence Johnson was responsible for the medical development. He had not yet shown his face in the courtroom. Our persistent demands had finally brought about the announcement of his attorney that he would not come to the trial at all. There is a rule of law that if a defendant in a civil case does not testify, the jury is permitted to draw the strongest inference against him which the opposing evidence allows. The jury may infer that had he testified he would not have contradicted the testimony of the plaintiff and his witnesses. This is the penalty imposed by law upon a defendant who does not take the stand and submit himself to cross-examination. There is only one escape from this rule. If the defendant can offer a legal excuse why he did not appear, and the jury believes him, then the inference that he could not contradict the charges against him, will not be drawn. The jury may excuse his absence and decide the case on the testimony before it.

Johnson offered as his excuse of not coming to testify, his illness, which, under doctor's orders, prevented him from submitting himself to the ordeal of the witness stand. Since we were skeptical that illness precluded his ability to testify, the court, with the consent of both counsel, directed that Johnson be examined medically, by each side, and that the doctors testify to his condition. The jury could weigh the medical contentions, and decide whether Johnson's excuse was valid, or whether the presumption should be indulged in, that he did not testify because he could not deny the testimony against him. Thus, we were catapulted into a medical contest.

Dr. Wardner D. Ayer, of Syracuse, New York, took the stand to testify for Johnson. He was a distinguished physician of more than forty-five years' experience, and was senior attending physician at University Hospital, senior attending physician in medicine at the Memorial Hospital in Syracuse, and consulting neurologist at the Psychopathic Hospital in Syracuse. He was Emeritus Professor of internal medicine and neurology at Syracuse University. He had written important papers on poliomyelitis, and hemorrhages of the brain, in which he had done pioneer work.

He had thoroughly examined Johnson and studied X-rays of his esophagus. He explained that the esophagus, or as it is sometimes called, the gut tube, starts at the back of the mouth and runs about eighteen inches to the stomach. When we swallow food, we can control it one-third of the way down and then it goes automatically into the stomach. Johnson had a constriction in the lower end of the esophagus, causing "an enormous dilation" immediately above it. The X-ray showed it clearly as if it were a balloon. It also showed that food was retained there. This accounted for his difficulty in swallowing, his burping of gas, and his regurgitation. He gave some of his other findings:

"rapid heart action, evident fatigue and nervousness, a top normal blood pressure, severe varicose veins, enlargement of the prostate with frequency of urination."

Then followed his conclusion:

Q. Are you able to state with a reasonable degree of certainty your medical opinion as to whether or not Mr. Johnson's health would be endangered if he testified at this trial?

A. In my opinion, yes, on the basis of nervous strain, and aggravation of the cardiospasm with the fact that he would be having pain, would be possibly regurgitating and vomiting under the stress of harsh—I don't say you are harsh—but of severe cross-examination.

He was finished. We then subjected him to cross-examination, the law's X-ray technique to reveal the truth.

Q. Doctor, how many times did you examine Mr. Laurence Johnson?

A. Once.

Q. That is the only time you have seen him in your life?

A. That is true. IIe was there two or three hours.

Q. . . . You knew that he was coming to you not to get medical aid . . . but so that you could testify in this case . . . ?

A. I suppose that is true.

Q. This esophagus condition is called what in medical language?

A. Cardiospasm. It is a spasm at the end of the esophagus. It is the cardiac end of the stomach.

Q. That is the area of gastroenterology, is it not?

A. Partly so.

Q. You haven't specialized in that field, have you, sir?

A. As an internist, we see enterological conditions just as frequently as we do many other parts of the body.

Q. Is the name for the condition that you have described esophageal achalasia . . . ?

A. I don't know that term. . . .

Q. You don't? Isn't that a well-known term?

A. No, that is not.

Q. Aside from being an internist . . . have you ever specialized in gastroenterology?

A. Not as a sharply defined specialty, of course not.

It turned out that in ten years, he had treated only seven cases involving this condition. Having demonstrated the difference between his high stature as a physician and his relative inexperience in the special field of gastroenterology, the cross-examination ground was better prepared for the next sequence of questions.

Q. When Mr. Johnson came in to your office, he came on his own steam, did he not?

A. Yes, he came walking in, that's true.

Q. And he undressed by himself without the aid of a nurse or anybody?

A. I think so.

Q. And thereafter he dressed himself?

A. He did.

Q. He was well-groomed . . . was he not?

A. I think so.

Q. And he was completely oriented in every way? He spoke intelligently to you, answered your questions sensibly, did he not?

A. I thought so.

Q. And he told you he had been in Africa in 1960?

A. Yes.

Q. . . . He also told you that last year he had written a book?

A. He did.

Q. Did he tell you that within the last two weeks he had traveled by himself to Rhode Island from Syracuse . . . ?

A. I think he told me he was going to see his daughter, who was ill, that he hadn't been there, to my knowledge.

Q. Did you ask him whether he was able to travel around freely? Didn't you put that as one of your questions?

A. I think so, probably yes.

Q. . . . Do you know that he has . . . traveled to New York to be examined yesterday?

A. I think I was told so this morning, yes.

Q. Did you ask him whether he drives a car?

A. Yes.

Q. And he does, does he not?

A. Yes.

Q. And carries on all the normal functions of the average man, with whatever ailments you have described?

A. No, he did not. He told me he couldn't.

Q. Well, driving a car is a normal function?

A. That is true.

Q. It requires alertness and coordination, does it not, sir?

A. Yes.

He claimed that Johnson "was a little uncertain and hesitant in his gait" even for a man seventy-three years old.

Q. You found no edema?

A. I did not.

Q. What does edema mean?

A. Swelling of the tissues, most often in the ankles, where we look for them.

Q. And that would indicate this lack of fluid or swelling that his heart action was good, would it not?

A. . . . There was not decompensation, that is right.

Q. . . . he told you that he occasionally vomits?

A. That is true.

Q. Is one of the ways of testing whether it is serious, whether there is loss of weight?

A. That is true.

Q. He had not lost weight.

A. That is my understanding.

Q. . . . And you told us before that he was two hours in your office. He didn't vomit during that period?

A. He was in pain.

Q. . . . Pain is subjective. He didn't vomit?

A. No he did not.

Q. And, of course, when a man undergoes a two-hour examination, he is somewhat nervous, is he not . . . ?

A. It depends on the doctor, sir. No, I don't think he was under great nervous strain.

Q. I think your eminence would make anybody nervous under examination, Doctor. Now you told us that his neck was flabby?

A. That is right.

Q. That isn't an extraordinary condition in any person above the age of fifty or sixty, is it?

A. Well, I think so.

Q. You understand that Mr. Johnson was to testify here, not appear for a beauty contest, Doctor?

A. Well, that—well. I won't qualify unless you ask me to.

Q. . . . You said that there was no indication of cranial nerves?

A. That is true.

Q. So that would mean that the reflexes of his eyes, his muscles of his face, complete control of his tongue and speech, right, sir?

A. That is right.

Q. And he had normal sensation on his skin and of his extremities . . . ?

A. Yes . . . that is true.

Q. And that is a sign of pretty good health for a man of seventy-three, isn't it?

A. Yes.

This answer in itself was almost enough for our purposes, because our position was not that he was a perfect specimen, but rather that despite his disease, he could testify, as indeed hundreds of witnesses do, who have heart conditions and other infirmities. But we continued to build the affirmative factors of his health. After a brief skirmish, he conceded that Johnson had "no weakness of the legs" or "difficulty with joints," or "shortness of breath." Nor had he suffered a heart attack. His heart was not enlarged. His liver and spleen were normal in size.

He was not familiar with the medical term "concentric constriction."

Q. Don't you know, Doctor, that concentric in plain layman's language . . . means smooth. It is a smooth outline?

A. I know that perfectly, but I never used—

Q. Please, please answer my question, sir.

A. I am trying to save you time.

He laughed.

THE COURT: Don't save time, please. This is not a laughing matter, Doctor.

THE WITNESS: I am sorry.

Q. . . . My last question was that concentric means smooth outline of whatever narrowing there is?

A. Yes, sir.

Q. When it is concentric or smooth, is that not an indication of lack of tumor or cancer in the condition as it then exists, sir . . . ?

A. Not necessarily.

Laurence Johnson had told him that he had his esophagus condition ten years, and he had conducted his supermarket business nevertheless.

Johnson had some indication of sugar, but he controlled his diabetic condition by diet and without resort to insulin.

Dr. Ayer had fought back so alertly during cross-examination, that I concluded with the question:

Q. Doctor, would you mind if I asked you how old you are?

A. I don't like to tell you. I am seventy-three, and I have not got a sagging neck.

THE COURT: All he asked you about was your age.

THE WITNESS: I know.

MR. NIZER: That is all, sir.

Then we presented our expert. Knowing that Johnson's illness was in the field of enterology, we had chosen one of the foremost specialists in the United States on this subject. He was Professor Jerome A. Marks, for ten years associate professor of clinical medicine at New York University, where he taught gastroenterology, or diseases of the digestive system. This included studies of the esophagus. He had contributed to medical books on this subject, and his eminence in this field had been recognized by electing him to the board of trustees of the American College of Gastroenterology, and president of two gastroenterology societies. When he had concluded the recital of his qualifications, Professor Marks' authoritativeness in this very field was evident.

Professor Marks described his examination of Johnson only twenty-four hours before. He had undressed, climbed on the table, descended, and dressed, all without aid. Johnson "spoke calmly and quietly. He seemed to recall quite well the details of his illness, going back fifteen years, and he was on the whole an exemplary patient."

Then came the key question:

Q. Can you state with reasonable certainty whether a

person of the age of Mr. Johnson, with a dilated or enlarged esophagus . . . is able to carry on work in a regular manner, . . . ?

A. In my experience patients with this condition are able to carry on their usual duties and occupations.

Q. If it is a woman who has this condition can she do her housework?

A. She does her housework.

Q. And if it is a man, can he go to work or drive a car or play golf?

A. He does, sir.

He pointed out that Johnson had not lost weight and this meant that despite occasional vomiting, he retained enough food "to nourish him adequately."

There are several new categories of drugs in the tranquilizer family, which have specific action against vomiting. He mentioned Compazine, Sparine, and Tigan. The significance of this testimony was, that even if Johnson were more prone to vomit than he was, there was a control which would be effective for many hours. Even without anti-emetics, could Professor Marks state with reasonable certainty whether Johnson would be able to testify in a lawsuit?

A. I should say with reasonable certainty that this man would be able to come into court and testify for any reasonable length of time.

The medical battle had ended. It seemed to us that the evidence pointed to the conclusion that Johnson could testify. This would mean that the jury could presume that his failure to do so was deliberate and due to his inability to contradict our testimony. But our satisfaction was premature. The jury never made this presumption. An incredible event occurred which shocked the judge, the lawyers, and the jury. After all of our hard work, it was Johnson who left our case in tatters. We shall soon come to this unforeseen incident.

The tensions of trial take their toll. Lawyers and litigants look haggard. I invariably lose weight—as much as ten pounds from a total of 144 pounds. Late hours of work added to a suspenseful court day, the anxieties of which often intrude into the few sleeping hours available, have a cumulative, exhausting effect. Saturdays and Sundays are welcomed not as days of rest, but as an opportunity for non-interrupted consecutive hours for preparations of briefs, interviews with witnesses, and planning of strategy. Trial work requires such complete dedication that it is not overdramatic to say that all trial lawyers leave a part of their lives behind them in each contest. When Supreme Court Chief Justice Harlan F. Stone was still Dean of Columbia University Law School, he gave a lecture to Columbia College graduates, like myself, who were about to enter the Law School. I set myself for a brilliant dissertation on the philosophy of law and its ideals. Instead, he stressed over and over again that the legal profession was so arduous, that the first requirement for being a successful lawyer was good health! I was disappointed at the time at what I thought was a misplaced emphasis. But I have learned since how wise was his judgment.

Justice Geller, at one of the conferences at the bench, told us that his reading of our briefs and his independent research, late every evening, followed by the inevitable exciting trial day requiring instantaneous rulings, had worn him down. One had only to look at the red rims of the lawyers' eyes and the pallor of fatigue in their faces to know how they felt. Even some of the jurors broke under the strain. Our forewoman was advised by her doctor that the mere burden of listening and evaluating, with all of the storms that raged around the witness stand in front of her, was too much for her health. The court excused her and substituted one of the alternates in her place. Now we only had one alternate left. It was risky to use him up, because if a third juror were to become ill, and there was no alternate, a mistrial would have to be declared, and the entire case tried all over again. The law guarantees every litigant twelve jurors in certain courts.

So we were deeply concerned when the judge advised us that he had received a desperate letter from one of the jurors. It read:

"Your Honor, I have gone to church and prayed for wisdom to come to the right decision. What we discussed this morning has put the last strain of worry on my mind. I would like to be excused from the jury panel. Have been ill the past two days with a sick stomach, but have put off going to the doctor because of the trial. I will go tonight. My closest friend committed suicide a few months before this trial began, and I have not gotten over that shock. Since I have been on this trial my work has suffered. That has been a big upset for me. I have a spinal condition that makes it most painful to sit for such long stretches of time in the cramped, uncomfortable chairs that we have been sitting in, and has caused much loss of sleep for me and pain at night.

"I am a good juror and have a most open mind. I have concentrated and with my total attention on this trial. I have learned, though, that it is contrary to my nature to sit in judgment, and whatever verdict I will come to will make me unhappy for a long time to come.

"Most Sincerely,"

The judge induced counsel to stipulate that the juror should be excused from further service, but that if another juror should drop out later, neither attorney would insist on a mistrial, and the remaining eleven jurors would decide the case. Instead of ten out of twelve jurors, ten out of eleven would be permitted to reach a verdict. Even though we had used up our reserves of two alternates, that contingency never arose.

The defendants had ended their defense, and they had not called Ina May Bull, or Eli Friedland, or Ralph Weiner, or Max Strauss to the stand to support their accusation that Faulk had attended Communist meetings in Texas. So they had taken a stab in the dark and having struck nothing, sought forgetfulness in silence. But we would not forget—when summation time came.

We had the right to present rebuttal witnesses, who had to be limited to new defense testimony. However, brevity was psychologically indicated. The strain of the trial had affected everyone. Jurors had been away from work for eleven weeks. The time had come for sharp, unprolonged thrusts. If the defendants cross-examined at length, they would have to bear the brunt of the jury's impatience.

So we put on the stand Ted Poston, a reporter for the New York *Post,* who had been a founder of the Amsterdam News Chapter of the Newspaper Guild, whose function had been held at Club 65. He testified that Faulk had not entertained there, as the Aware *Bulletin* claimed; also that it was an anti-Communist occasion, and that Club 65 was not "a site for Communist functions."

Poston was subjected to lengthy cross-examination to test his memory, but he recited the names of the entertainers and was certain that Faulk was not among them. There is an ancient legal joke about the prosecutor who announced that he has three witnesses who saw the defendant steal the horse.

The defendant retorts that he has twenty who did not see him take it. Proof of the negative is always difficult. Yet, although we could have rested on Aware's failure to demonstrate that Faulk had entertained at Club 65, we went further and proved by an official of that event, that Faulk was not there.

Then we put Jack A. Wren on the witness stand for only four questions. He was an account executive of Batten, Barton, Durstine & Osborn, Inc. and he denied telling Hartnett that Faulk was to appear at the Jefferson School. Thus, Hartnett's reliance testimony was severely weakened.

The defense was so taken aback by this surprise witness that they asked for "a moment" to plan cross-examination. The judge and jury fretted during the delay. Time shrinks patience.

THE COURT: Will you need much more time, Mr. Bolan?

MR. BOLAN: No, just a moment.

THE COURT: We have been waiting ten or twelve minutes.

Finally, cross-examination began. Wren's hostility was like a taut spring. The very first merely introductory question released a bitter tirade.

Q. Mr. Wren, what were your duties at BBD&O in late 1955?

A. Well, my duties, among other things, was to protect our clients against false charges made that we loaded our shows with Communists, by Vincent Hartnett, who made these charges against us, who wrote poison pen letters behind our backs to our clients, wrote to our officers accusing us of loading our shows with Communists.

A moment later Bolan asked what appeared to be an innocuous question. Wren's bald head thrust forward from his short body, caught the light from above, and seemed to aim a searchlight at his target, before he let loose another salvo which set the air aflame.

Q. Did you ever send any communications to Mr. Hartnett at any time?

A. It is entirely possible I sent communications to Mr. Hartnett in the early fifties, especially when Mr. Hartnett was engineering picket lines around our clients' shows, and I had to treat with him as a merchant treats with a racketeer who sells protection.

Q. Mr. Wren, it is obvious you don't like Mr. Hartnett,

but you need not say that in every answer. Did you have some personal disagreement with Mr. Hartnett at some time?

A. Yes, sir . . . not a personal disagreement, sir, a disagreement.

Q. . . . Isn't it a fact that you told Mr. Hartnett that if he testified that you gave him this [memorandum], that you would deny it under oath?

A. It is not a fact, sir. It is Mr. Hartnett's invention.

Bolan questioned him closely about an earlier friendly relationship with Hartnett and their communications with each other. There were letters addressed to Wren as "Jack" and signed by Hartnett as "Vince." Bolan asked him whether he wasn't a "security officer" for his agency.

A. It is not true. This is a term invented—I never had this title, and I think it was used by John Cogley of the Fund for the Republic. It is a title Mr. Hartnett adores. I have not this title.

When pressed about his correspondence with Hartnett, he burst forth again:

A. It is entirely possible because I had to deal with Mr. Hartnett since he generated pressure against our clients by claiming that we used Communists on our shows.

So it went. Was it not extraordinary that an official of one of the most distinguished advertising agencies in the world, should bear such venom toward Hartnett and his methods? It indicated that the large advertising agencies were not co-conspirators, but victims themselves of blacklisting.

Our final rebuttal witness was our own rating expert. We were determined to destroy the defendant's theory that CBS had discharged Faulk because his ratings slipped. Despite any success we might have had with Dr. Roslow, CBS executives had testified that they relied on *Pulse* figures, and we feared that if only a few jurors accepted this version, we were lost.

But we stormed our objective from an entirely different direction. We no longer attacked *Pulse*. We assumed for this purpose only, that *Pulse* was reliable, as CBS had done. Nevertheless, we contended that if properly interpreted, Faulk's ratings warranted his continuance.

We had chosen an outstanding authority in this field. He was Marvin Antonowsky, who, at the early age of thirty-one, had become vice president of Kenyon & Eckhardt, a leading advertising agency, in charge of media research and sales analysis, and responsible for the expenditure of one hundred million dollars of advertising. Later he joined Norman, Craig & Kummel as vice president in charge of advertising expenditures for such accounts as Colgate-Palmolive, Cheesebrough-Pond's, Chanel, Revlon, Hertz Rent-A-Car, and others.

Statistical data is a language all its own, and it is not easy to parse. Like a foreign language learned by the mind but not the ear, which requires the slowing process of translation for comprehension, figures and percentages are difficult to absorb. I find that if they are translated into visual images, they can be read and understood easily, because they are no longer unfamiliar symbols. So Antonowsky, who in his career had prepared presentation charts relating to more than six hundred million dollars of expenditures, worked with us in the late evenings, to prepare a series of huge charts, which would demonstrate our theories. Sometimes clarity is obtained by comparing different sizes of vertical bars, called chimneys. Drawn in scale with percentage figures above them and with different colors to represent Faulk and his competitors, one could see at a mere glance how one chimney towered over the one next to it, or later shrunk in size. Sometimes the device of a round ball, with different-colored slices, or sometimes a line on a graph ascending sharply gave the picture quickly. During preparation, we struggled to determine what comparisons to make and how to present them graphically, so that complex statistical theories could be comprehended at a mere glance.

We made huge cardboard charts, which would be visible to the juror sitting farthest from the witness chair. We set them up one after another on a large easel. Antonowsky, who was about six feet four inches, tall and thin, and looked like a huge chimney himself, was permitted to stand in front of the chart, while I, with a long pointer, directed his attention to the brilliant colored lines and circles. The moribund subject of statistics came alive, and the judge, as well as several of the jurors, stood up, better to observe the dramatic developments.

The first chart compared Faulk's ratings for six months before December 1956, when CBS renewed his contract, with those in 1957 when it fired him. They were exactly the same. This was true of both the straight rating and the share-of-audience rating. The chimneys looked like twins in size, and their equality refuted the theory that it was Faulk who had changed. They demonstrated that WCBS had acted inconsistently and, therefore, that some other factor had intervened. Obviously, it was the fact that Faulk had contracted the television disease called controversiality.

The next chart had horizontal lines, blue and red. The blue lines represented Faulk's share of audience for the same period in 1956 and 1957. They were the same length. The red lines represented a similar comparison of WCBS's share of audience. The second red line for 1957 was considerably shorter. It had shrunk 12 percent. Faulk had held on to his audience as against all competitors, better than WCBS had for all its programs during the same time segment.

Faulk's regular program had been followed a half-hour later by the singer, Martha Wright. When he was discharged, CBS moved her up into his time slot. So we presented two charts involving Miss Wright. The first was a comparison between Faulk's ratings and hers when she followed him by half an hour. His had gone up 9 per cent in straight rating and 20 per cent in share-of-audience rating between a six-month period in 1956 and the same six-month period in 1957, when he was fired. Her straight rating for the same periods had gone down 8 per cent and her share-of-audience rating had remained the same. The blue and orange lines seemed to ask the question, "Why would CBS remove him in her favor?" I echoed the question in legal form.

Q. Can you state with reasonable certainty which one would be recommended to a client on the basis of these figures.

ANTONOWSKY: I would say the Faulk show.

After Martha Wright had taken Faulk's place, she, of course, was reported on by *Pulse*. So our next chart compared her ratings for six months with those of Faulk for the same period, the year before, when he occupied the identical time.

Q. What does that comparison show?

A. It shows that Martha Wright had an 8 per cent lower share and a 14 per cent lower rating.

Antonowsky educated the jurors to a factor in sponsorship which had not yet been mentioned. It was chiefly this factor which had prompted his recommendation to Lincoln Mercury, which spent thirty million dollars a year for advertising, to continue "The Ed Sullivan Show" for seven years, or to induce

Lever Brothers to sponsor the television program "The Defenders." That factor was "cost per thousand." It represented the cost to the sponsor of reaching a thousand homes. "The lower the cost per thousand, the better the buy." This figure was obtained by dividing the cost of the program by the audience reached. But how did one know the cost? This information was furnished by a monthly publication called *Standard Rate and Data Service*. It set forth station rates for the purchase of time. The information is broken down into local and national stations, and varying time segments, each of which commands a different price. After Antonowsky testified that this publication "is the bible of anybody buying time," we offered it in evidence.

Then he let us in on another mystery in television. Irrespective of rating, a sponsor pays a premium for personality, because "he gets more personal sell."

THE COURT: Personal sell?

A. Yes. . . . As an example, we would pay probably twice as much for Tennessee Ernie Ford than we would pay, let's say, for Dick Clark, because we know that he sells goods. He builds an image for the product, and when you are selling packaged goods, you can see from month to month what happened.

Taking Ford as an example, currently in television has a very, very low rating, but he is sold out because he is a personality salesman, and he has proven that he can sell products.

He called Faulk a personality salesman, and, therefore, extremely valuable to a sponsor irrespective of what the ratings showed anyhow. He had prepared a tabulation of personality shows, and the cost per thousand of each:

Dorothy and Dick	$ .93
John Henry Faulk	.99
Jack Sterling	1.19
Bill Cullen	1.27
McCanns at Home	1.30
Martha Deane	1.39
Tex and Jinx	1.51

Only if the cost per thousand is more than $1.50 does the program become uneconomic. Not only was Faulk second-best on the list, but before his program could be deemed a failure, his rating would have to drop from 3.5 to 2 and his share-of-audience from 11 to 7. Of course, no such decline ever took place. The trivial variations of one-tenth and two-tenths of a 1 per cent, in Faulk's ratings, were swept away as meaningless by this Antonowsky analysis.

We turned over our expert and his multicolored charts for cross-examination.

Why had he not included Martha Wright's morning show in his analysis?

> A. There is a very good reason for that, because . . . in the morning you have women alone, and you cannot make a judgment . . . because two people select the dial in the evening.

Bolan had observed that we offered no chart of comparison between Arthur Godfrey, who took over a half-hour of Faulk's time, and Faulk. We had such a chart ready, but because the court was pressing us to conclude the case, we omitted it. When Bolan demanded to know how Godfrey had fared, the witness replied:

> A. We do have a chart which we can use . . . which shows that there is no significant pickup when Godfrey and Martha Wright replace him.

When the testimony was concluded, both sides made motions not in the presence of the jury.

We moved to dismiss the defense of truth, because the defendants had failed to submit sufficient evidence to warrant submission to the jury. Bolan contended that there was some testimony to support the seven charges in the *Bulletin*. We replied:

"Justification as a complete defense must be broad as the charge. . . . If you make a charge that a man robbed the Chase National Bank, then you put in justification that the man was in the Chase National Bank, even though he didn't rob it, it is no defense. You have to be co-extensive with the entire charge. . . ."

The court ruled that there was no evidence from which the jury could conclude that truth had been proved. He dismissed this defense, and also the defense of partial truth, and fair comment, which must also be based on facts truly stated. The defense of provocation met a similar fate. The element of retort in the heat of passion was missing. The defendants had calculatingly prepared the *Bulletin*. It was not an uncontrollable outburst in reply to attack.

The court cited the pretrial motions to strike the various defenses, which had been granted, and affirmed by the Appellate Division. As repleaded, the defendants had the burden of proving that Faulk actually attended the functions he was accused of in the *Bulletin*, that they were Communist Fronts, and that he knew or should have known that they were. The defendants failed in this proof. All their complete defenses were stricken out. They stood denuded. Only the partial defense of reliance survived. The jury could evaluate that defense in mitigation of punitive damages.

The judge called a conference of the lawyers to make arrangements for summation. Like duelists, the rules of combat were laid down. Bolan was granted a whole court day for his final address to the jury. Then I would have the next day. On the third day, the judge would charge the jurors, who would then retire to reach a verdict.

There is an anecdote of two duelists who agree to meet in another city to vindicate their honor with pistols. One buys a round-trip ticket, the other only a one-way ticket. He is twitted for lack of confidence, but he explains, "I always travel back on my opponent's ticket." This is the advantage of summing up last. It enables one to travel home on his adversary's ticket. The law always permits the plaintiff, who has the burden of proof, to have the final word. This balances his burden to open the case and submit his evidence, for the scrutiny of the defendant, who may then fashion his defense. By reversing this sequence in summation, the plaintiff is enabled to listen to his opponent, evaluate his strength, and adjust his final argument accordingly.

For more than nine of the eleven weeks the trial had been conducted in the Supreme Court Building in New York County, which had been constructed before air conditioning preserved spring indoors, while summer raged outside. So, we had sweltered in the courtroom during May and June, but Justice Geller had finally arranged to transfer the trial to the new Criminal Courts Building only a block away. It was as cool inside as the marble façade gave promise it would be. So, during the last two weeks of the contest, we were in a courtroom ordinarily assigned to criminal cases, a fact which we thought not entirely inappropriate in a symbolic sense.

Word had spread that the final arguments to the jury were to be made, and so the courtroom, which was several times larger than that in Supreme Court, was crowded to capacity, and visitors formed lines outside seeking admission.

In this public setting, John Faulk sat alongside of us at counsel table, ready to listen a whole day to our opponent's view of the case. Either because we had not anticipated the attack which would be launched against him, or because we had been too preoccupied, we failed to warn him that he might face the worst ordeal of the trial. The law grants immunity against slander to a lawyer just as it does to a legislator, while he is performing his duty. The reason is the same. We do not wish to inhibit the process of justice, or representation in Congress, by limiting free speech. If a Senator or President could be held liable for castigating those whom he believes are injuring the public interest, then he could not serve the nation to the fullest extent of his capacity. Neither could a lawyer serve his client adequately if he could not express himself freely in the courtroom. As between the public interest to be served by fearless talk from our elected officials, or lawyers or judges engaged in the process of justice, and the rights of a private citizen, we favor the former.

The only restriction upon excessive tirade is the reaction of the audience. If the electorate or jury believes the charges are reckless and mere vituperation, they mete out the worst punishment which the offender can receive. For what is worse for a public official than to be rejected at the polls, or for a litigant and his lawyer than to suffer defeat? So restraint is imposed by the retaliatory consequences. Experience has shown that a lawyer who seeks to persuade will not take the risk of angering the jury by vitriolic, unfair argument. However, the defendants continued even in summation to gamble on an all-out offensive instead of an ameliorating defense. Of course, if the jury could be incensed against Faulk, he would recover six cents, if he got anything at all. This was the defendants' strategy.

Faulk had looked upon summation as the culminating steps in his vindication. Many of his friends and family were present. Among them were the very people whom he wished to hold a high opinion of him. One can, therefore, imagine his shock when he heard himself denounced more bitterly than the *Bulletin* had ever dared to do. We, his protectors, did not stir a muscle as insults poured upon him hour after hour. He turned pale with inner fury. Was this what he had waited for, for six years? Was this the bright day of restored honor?

Bolan's summation began and ended with the charge that Faulk had lied at every turn of the case:

". . . I am going to start first with what I think is a very important issue and fact in this case; namely, that is, that the plaintiff, Mr. Faulk, has deliberately lied to you on numerous occasions in this case on matters of great importance. There are so many lies that it's hard to list them all. I will give you about nine or ten for a start and mention many more throughout my summation."

He set the pattern by quoting Ward's testimony that he had warned Faulk of his falling ratings. Then he contended that Faulk's earlier resignation from WCBS was not due to his new opportunity with the Texas Broadcasting Company. Faulk nudged me with the obvious answer, but I told him that the rules permitted no interrupting correction. "Tomorrow will be our day," I whispered. But thundering over this assurance were Bolan's words:

"Mr. Ward was telling the truth. Mr. Faulk was lying. I submit that just on this series of lies, they were so deliberate, so flagrant that you could question anything Mr. Faulk told you at this trial, but I am going to give you quite a few others. . . ."

In Texas, these would be fighting words, even if Bolan had smiled when he uttered them, which he did not do. The defense charged that discrepancies in the number of radio "spots" which Faulk claimed he lost and other "misstatements" were deliberate falsehoods:

"Mr. Faulk's lies spread over a tremendous area. Every area in which he testified, he lied or exaggerated. . . . Mr. Faulk made a number of other deliberate lies about the sponsors which he said went off his program as a result of the *Bulletin*."

The word "liar" and "lie" bounced off the marble walls in quickening succession and ricocheted around the room, striking Faulk's admirers and invariably Faulk himself, who seemed to be bleeding inside from the cutting blows.

Hour after hour, the tirade continued:

"Mr. Faulk in this area again lied under oath."

At the very end of his summation, Bolan returned to this

theme, but now it was orchestrated loudly as if to alter its familiarity, by sheer emphasis:

"Just a few remaining words. I think the basic question here is Mr. Faulk's credibility. Can you believe a man who has lied as deliberately as Mr. Faulk has done in this case under oath?"

With equal vehemence, Bolan contrasted Hartnett with Faulk. He argued that Hartnett was the soul of veracity. Despite our cross-examination, he literally gambled his case on this contention. He achieved magnificent emphasis by such extremism. But suppose the jury disagreed?

He threw the dice for all or nothing:

"I would like you to contrast Mr. Faulk's many lies with Mr. Hartnett's testimony under five days, approximately, of cross-examination. . . .

"I submit, ladies and gentlemen, that I doubt if you will ever come across a man as truthful and honest as Mr. Hartnett is; and I state this to you. I would gamble this entire case on your appraisal of Mr. Hartnett's frankness on the witness stand; without hesitation. I would gamble it."

So he did. More than ever we urgently needed the jury's rebuke of the defendants through a substantial verdict. Not only the old abuses for which we were suing, but the new denigration of Faulk's character required that Faulk be vindicated. We, too, had put his future in the scales, by submitting him to trial. Either he would emerge as the heroic instrument of justice for all artists, or be besmirched all over again, adding humiliation to his despair.

Combined with the strategy of defiance, the defendants engaged in long stretches of more responsible argument, which they made with great skill. In the world of persuasion, logic alone may not always be the victor. In a race between a contention, which travels with great speed if it is streamlined with simplicity, and an answer to it, encumbered with the weight of complexity, the former may reach the mind first and hold it. The Faulk case presented several such problems. There were vulnerabilities in our cause, which lent themselves to lightning breakthroughs. The defendants took full advantage of them. Our task was not only to answer the apparent discrepancies, but to so simplify the explanations that they acquired the seven-league boots of truth in outspeeding the challenger. For truth can put wings on the most sluggish feet.

For example, Bolan demonstrated with exhibits that

". . . The year after the publication of the *Bulletin,* was the best year of Faulk's career. . . . He got more sponsors then than he had ever had before in his life. He was almost 90 per cent full during that year. . . ."

This was true in radio, where the momentum of his prior years carried him forward for a while. He had the benefit of "across-the-board" seasonal advertising, such as that placed by automobile sponsors. Also CBS, due to Charles Collingwood and Ed Murrow's intervention, sought to hold the fort for Faulk. But in television, where he had no continuous program, he was immediately cut off, from the day the *Bulletin* appeared.

Even in radio, when the shield of Collingwood and Murrow was removed, he succumbed. But all this was an involved argument. Could it reach the jurors' minds with sufficient impact to overcome the simple cry of the defense, "Faulk suffered no damage. He prospered after the libel. How could it have hurt him?"

Said Bolan:

"You have heard of the great pressure, how influential these people were. . . . How do you explain all these sponsors flocking to Mr. Faulk as they had never flocked before? . . .

"From an exhibit in evidence as to Mr. Faulk's income, . . . his gross business income (after the *Bulletin* was published) was $36,238.85, the biggest gross that Mr. Faulk ever had."

Quite naturally, the defense preened itself on producing the CBS executives, Slate and Ward, as its witnesses. Bolan quoted Slate's testimony that he had fired Faulk because his ratings declined. The cross-examination of Slate was conveniently forgotten, a matter which would not be subject to similar amnesia the next day. In the meantime, Bolan urged that there was "no reason why Ward or Slate should lie. It is Mr. Faulk who is not telling the truth." Here again was the simple, easily comprehensible charge. We had to accept the burden of making the involved answer just as streamlined to achieve lucidity.

The defense cut through the complexity of *Pulse* ratings, Dr. Roslow's testimony, and Antonowsky's "fancy charts" with similar disdain. What difference did it make how accurate *Pulse* was—CBS relied on it and that was enough; that is why Faulk was let out, not for any other reason.

The most deceptive argument was the right of an employer

to "blacklist" an employee for certain reasons. Confusion on this issue has pervaded the nation to this day, and the defense exploited it with what appeared to be irresistible logic. The syllogism ran this way. True, a man has a right to plead the Fifth Amendment, that is, to refuse to answer on the ground that to do so might incriminate him. No court may punish him for exercising his constitutional right. But once this man is outside of the court of law, is the average citizen compelled to ignore the fact that he resorted to the Fifth Amendment? "What," asked Bolan, "would be the practical consequences?" He gave an illustration:

"If a man is asked, 'Did you steal ten thousand dollars from your former employer?' and he says, 'I refuse to answer on the ground that an answer may tend to incriminate me' . . . wouldn't a prospective employer be foolhardy if he didn't doubt the man's honesty?

"The same thing holds true with respect to asking a man if he is a member of the Communist Party. If he says, 'I refuse to answer because if I do so, my answer may tend to incriminate me,' I submit . . . it is a fact which the television and radio networks have the right to take into consideration. I submit it is not blacklisting as the plaintiffs seek to describe blacklisting. . . ."

Aside from the fact that Faulk had never pleaded the Fifth Amendment, nor had the slightest reluctance to answer any question about his political affiliations, so that the illustration was inapplicable to him, it was a fatally defective syllogism. We feared the temporary allure it might have for the jurors, and I ached to reply and tear down the false structure of reasoning—but our turn would not come until the morrow, and patience is just another discipline which advocacy imposes.

The defendants had two over-all objectives. One was to be vindicated in their "patriotic" endeavors to cleanse the airwaves. The other was to get Johnson out of the case, so that even if they lost, there would be no financially responsible person from whom to collect. Bolan now turned to this effort to eliminate Johnson from liability. He argued that there was no evidence at all that Laurence Johnson had anything to do with the preparation of the *Bulletin*. He contended that the testimony which attempted to connect Johnson with the claimed conspiracy was tenuous and remote.

Then to rebut the contention that Johnson's failure to testify warranted an inference against him, he bore down heavily on the medical testimony. It was true that Johnson drove a car, but,

"Driving a car might be relaxing. . . . It is the emotional strain which severely endangers the health."

That is why he said Johnson could not testify. The emotional strain would be too much for him. Even David Susskind, who had been accustomed to television programs, was nervous on the witness stand. Kim Hunter, he recalled, could hardly speak, she was so overcome.

"Remember Mr. Milton, how his hands shook? Remember Sam Slate of CBS . . . his hand shook. Even my hand is shaking a little bit now."

It was true that Johnson had testified at an examination before trial without ill effect, but, argued Bolan, this was a fairly relaxed type of hearing not in the presence of judge and jury.

So the hours of argument stretched out until the end of the day came. In final peroration, he stressed the three main points on which he had constructed his defense; Faulk was not to be believed; the *Bulletin* did not injure him because he earned more money during the next two years than ever before; and Johnson was not involved in the case.

At 5:30 P.M., he thanked the jury for its kind attention. His summation was ended. The court declared a recess until the next morning at 10:00 A.M.

Faulk had not been able to eat during the lunch hour. He was pale and beaten down by the attacks upon him. Now at the end of the day, he was even more depressed. Throughout the years of the contest, he had borne his suffering with remarkable courage and good humor. He had been sustained, even exhilarated, by the approach of judgment day. But now everything seemed to have collapsed around him. At the very end of the trial, he had been besmirched, taunted, vilified, and ridiculed for more than six hours of continuous attack. His frustration was so painful that he was almost in tears. His friends, and among them were, of course, his counsel, down to the clerks who carried the heavy bags out of the courtroom, suffered with him. We tried to assuage his deep pain, to explain the function of summation, the right of each lawyer to characterize and interpret the evidence for the jury. "This may cost the defense dearly," I comforted him. "They have gambled by attacking you and the jury may react with a large verdict. Wait until tomorrow. You will hear our answer, and you will feel better."

Our summation had to be adjusted to the tactics we had encountered. The defendants had not acted as perpetrators of a wrong who were defending themselves, but as aggressors who wielded a merciless sword against us. We would have to turn the sword back upon them and avenge the new as well as old injuries.

We arrived in court early next morning, but found the court-room already filled. We proceeded to set the stage physically for our effort. An attendant set a table in front of the jury box, on which we placed the twenty-odd volumes of typed testimony in various piles, each with a big red number upon the cover to correspond with my notes, so that I could quote specific testimony by selecting the volume readily. On each side of the table we lined up a large stack of exhibits, not in sequence of their numbers, but in the order in which my notes indicated I would use them. A decanter of water was left on the counsel table behind, to be used only when periodic ten-minute recesses were declared about every hour, or whenever the subject matter indicated a good stopping point. A speaker should avoid drinking water during his address because it breaks the audience's concentration on his words, and dissipates the spell of whatever emotion he may have created. Even hoarseness is preferable to such an intrusion. Surely, he would not nibble a sandwich to gain strength during his oration. And if the orator were a woman, would she stop to powder? Aesthetics aside, any diversionary act breaks the invisible strands betwen the listener and the speaker. "It is my duty to speak," said a preacher once, "and yours to listen. But if you finish before I do, please let me know." The orator should never by some artificial act help the audience finish before he does. Particularly ludicrous is the speaker who before he has even begun, ceremoniously lifts a glass of water, and drinks slowly. The only excuse I can find for such a public display of thirst-quenching is when the glass is filled with gin, and the speaker desperately needs to stoke his fortitude. Whenever a lawyer in the course of the trial oversteps the bounds of fairness, his adversary comforts himself that "he will pay the price" when the throttle is let out in summation. Where, as in the Faulk case, a conspiracy was charged, the final argument, like a chemical solution, had to make visible the connecting web of isolated facts. So for eleven weeks both sides nursed their frustrations with the knowledge that the summation would give the opportunity to clarify, characterize, and persuade.

Also, the longer the trial, the more need there is to refresh the jurors' memory. Both sides had presented thirty-five witnesses, whose testimony covered more than eight thousand pages of the record. Many of these witnesses may have been forgotten by the jury. I sometimes think it would be advisable to have photographs of witnesses to aid recall. Instead, it is again the function of a summation not only to review the evidence, but to picture the witnesses with vivid verbal strokes, relying upon some particular incident or answer which would revive the jury's recollection.

So the summation poses an enormous problem for every lawyer. He must organize, sift, dissect, evaluate, dramatize, and persuade, but, above all, he must not tire the jurors. Ordinarily, when a speaker doesn't strike oil in fifteen minutes, he should stop boring. Yet, the task of summation often requires an address lasting all day.

The lawyer must resort to every dignified device to make his flood of words an exciting experience. Colloquial usage to contrast with ringing phrases, appropriate jests or sarcasm when they give momentum to the point and not otherwise, an occasional descriptive vignette, may be employed. But they will not avail unless the summation is characterized by such sincerity and deep feeling that it sets the atmosphere aflame, and the fires leap into the jury box to set fire to the convictions of the jurors. Even all this gives only a glimpse, a mere glimpse, of the art of persuasion, which is composed of infinite psychological insights and myriad personality factors, which make us all feel inadequate to practice so mysterious and miraculous an art.

"May it please Your Honor, Mr. Foreman, ladies and gentlemen of the jury.

"First . . . let me thank you on behalf of John Henry Faulk, my client, myself, and my associates as counsel, for the extraordinary dedication to duty and patience that you have shown in serving on this case.

"This is not the ordinary service that you have rendered. It is far beyond the call of duty. You have been deprived of . . . attendance to your business at great sacrifice. We have been . . . sensitive to it. . . . We are very grateful. . . .

"There is one compensation that you may derive . . . which is also of an extraordinary nature, and that is . . . that you are participating in a case which has historic implications. . . . There are in the history of litigation just a few of these, . . . and, I stand here with a very deep sense of responsibility because I have the burden of presenting this case to you. . . . If during these long ten weeks, I have at any time taxed your patience because of the zeal of advocate . . . or had some contentions with counsel, I apologize for that. You must understand that we too have been under strain. For six years, we have waited for this day, six years. We have worked during those six years day and night . . . and so we too have been under strain, including the fact that last night there was no sleep at all. . . .

". . . We would have thought that, after everything that happened in this courtroom, there could have been a different position taken by the defendants. I would expect them to defend themselves, but they didn't have to spill their malice and hate in this courtroom. . . .

"Here we were, the learned court, whose research and learning on the complicated questions of libel law awed us all, instructing you that the defense of truth was stricken out. . . . Think of it. So strong is this case that after ten weeks . . . you haven't anything on which to decide that the defendants told the truth in these seven charges. They defaulted on it. . . .

"So they stood bare in this courtroom as libelers who had destroyed this man and his family. Don't you think it would have been the decent thing under these circumstances for the defendant to take the usual, proper position for a defendant, 'I was wrong, I am sorry'; a little repentance, 'but I didn't mean it, please don't soak me too heavily.' This is a proper stance for a defendant. I recognize the duty of Mr. Bolan.

"But no, even under those circumstances, they called my client a liar. . . . Any man would have had to hold on to himself. I admire Mr. Faulk for just keeping silent under that attack, because I had to grip my seat. At the last moment we are libeled again.

"And who is it that is held forth as a truthful man? Mr. Bolan says, 'I gamble my case on the integrity, on the truth of

Mr. Hartnett.' I accept that unhesitatingly. Why . . . the *Bulletin* that he wrote has already been held to be a complete lie. . . . So how can he be a truthful man? . . .

"MR. BOLAN: Your Honor, may I object to Mr. Nizer's characterization of His Honor's ruling. The exhibit was not held to be a complete lie. In fact, no part of it was held to be a lie. All that was said—

"THE COURT: It was held to be a libel by the court. Well, I covered that.

"MR. BOLAN: It was not held to be a lie in any part, Your Honor.

"THE COURT: No, overruled, overruled.

"MR. NIZER: I repeat that when a defense of truth is stricken out of a case and a defense of partial truth is stricken out of a case, that the document is not only libelous but a complete lie. I stand by that, and I wouldn't have been as strong about it, if they hadn't called Mr. Faulk a liar. And I repeat it."

In this way, we opened our final plea, striking at the audacity of the defendants who resorted to invective rather than apology. Our cry of outrage was not mere retort. It spelled out the defendants' malice, and if the jury was aroused by their tactics, they could translate their indignation into punitive damages.

For this reason, too, we turned at the outset to the accusation against Faulk made in the midst of trial.

"There is no issue of communism in this case. John Henry Faulk, from the first moment that he could understand and breathe, has been anti-Communist. . . .

"One of the bad days we had, and I will never forgive the defendants for this, was when they cross-examined him for hours, 'Did you know Ina May Bull in Austin, Texas?' 'Did you know there was a Communist meeting?' 'Were you there?'

"And he said, 'no, no, no.' Wouldn't you think they would bring in Ina May Bull, or was it just bull? . . . It is like having a woman on the stand and saying, 'Weren't you unfaithful in Austin, Texas?' and then forgetting about it.

"You don't ask that kind of question unless you have some evidence. You don't say to a man, 'Did you ever rob a bank in Baltimore?' and then you forget about it. . . .

"So communism is not the issue. We detest communism. It is

clear that communism is the great enemy, not only of our country and of all the free world, but of all decency.

"The shortest distance between the cradle and grave is communism, and I don't know how any man can believe in communism when communism doesn't believe in any man.

"There is no issue here of communism. The question is whether we will permit our government to protect us under proper judicial and other procedures, or whether we are going to permit private vigilantes like this gentleman seated here with the thin mouth and blue suit, who sneaks into the Blue Ribbon Restaurant, when there is a meeting of some union people, with a hidden microphone in his lapel. That is the question, are you going to permit private vigilanteism for profit?

"If he was a real patriot and he dug up any evidence, he would have sent it to the F.B.I. like all of us should, against a Communist. . . .

"The Communists don't have to be a majority to be dangerous. A minority is dangerous enough. And if any citizen has evidence of any kind, he should send it to the governmental authorities. Not this gentleman; he charged twenty dollars a throw."

(*Laughter*)

THE COURT: No, if there is laughter, I will empty the courtroom.

We turned to the argument that an employer should have the right not to hire a man who took the Fifth Amendment. Faulk was not in this category, but we wanted to come to grips with this question because his case involved important principles, and we were determined to meet the defendants on any extended ground they chose.

Of course, an employer has a right to refuse to hire a man even if he doesn't like the color of his tie, the way he slouches in a chair, his diction, his shifty eyes, or his having taken the Fifth Amendment. This is not blacklisting. It is an individual exercise of judgment, and even if based on mere caprice, is legal. But if he sends out a blacklist to all prospective employers, and threatens them with dire consequences, if they hire that man, then he is acting illegally. The benign right of individual choice turns cancerous if exercised conspiratorially with others. For example, a company acting alone may fix its prices even at exorbitant rates. But if it gets together with its competitors and fixes prices, it is guilty not only of a civil offense but of a criminal violation.

The philosophy behind this rule is that an eccentric employer rejecting an applicant for even a bizarre reason, does not deprive him of the opportunity of employment by others; and a company which is too greedy may simply price itself out of the market. It is when the competitive forces in the open market are dammed up, whether by blacklist, conspiracy, or other techniques, that the wrong occurs.

"This isn't even a case of mistaken fanaticism. . . . Someone once said that a fanatic is a man who, having lost sight of his objective, redoubles his efforts.

"Now they didn't lose sight of their objective. This was very calculated. They wanted to destroy Faulk, because in destroying Faulk blacklisting could continue and they could collect. . . .

"Hartnett charged three hundred dollars for a report on Arthur Miller. . . . Here is a great artist. If Arthur Miller did anything wrong the government should go after him . . . but . . . collecting three hundred dollars to pass Arthur Miller? . . .

"James Thurber, one of the great figures that we ought to be proud of in America. . . . Mr. Hartnett says he is a dangerous figure and collects twenty dollars. . . .

"And Emily Kimbrough, 'A Helen Hayes type of liberal, pass her, twenty dollars.' He is allowing her to work.

"And then, believe it or not, on that list, 'Santa Claus, five dollars.' Despite his red suit, he got passed by Mr. Hartnett.

"This is the man who can ruin your life by pointing a finger at you. . . .

"When a man points a finger at you, he ought to remember he's got four fingers pointing at himself. . . .

"Robert Frost once wrote a wonderful line. . . . 'The people I am most scared of are the people who are scared.'

"And these people who claim to be scared of communism are the people most to be scared of."

Conspiracies are not easy to prove. The law recognizes this. It does not expect evidence of a group of malefactors meeting surreptitiously in a cellar lit by candlelight. Circumstantial evidence of parallel action under conditions which would ordinarily not result in uniformity may be sufficient. (The fact that everyone carries an umbrella on a rainy day is not suspicious parallelism, but the fact that a number of competitors charge precisely the same price in a varying market may be.)

In the Faulk case there was direct evidence of conspiracy, and we made the most of it. The minutes of the Board Meeting of Aware Inc. contained the entry that the *Bulletin* was to be issued against Faulk. We held up the minutes, hammering its Exhibit No. 119 into the minds of the jurors, and read from it, "Mr. Milton is to contact Messrs. Neuser, Johnson and Dungey re: coming down from Syracuse to speak at the next membership meeting. . . ."

For hour after hour, we endeavor to breathe life into testimony embalmed in stenographer's minutes; we see Joseph Cotten flying to Syracuse to woo Laurence Johnson, who takes him to his supermarkets for autographs.

"His esophagus isn't bothering him then . . . but when he has to come into court and meet this charge, he suddenly gets esophagus trouble."

We read the names of some of the two thousand recipients of the *Bulletin* to show that newspapers, advertising agencies, motion picture companies, television and radio executives, police authorities, unions, etc.—twelve categories all received the description of Faulk as a Communist traitor.

"Is it any wonder that Mr. Faulk is as dead as a doornail? They covered every possible spot to injure him. . . . It's like knocking a man down and pumping twelve more bullets into him. These twelve categories are twelve more bullets just to make sure he is stone dead. . . ."

We hear again the striking phrase by a witness that from the moment Faulk was accused of being disloyal, he was a "walking corpse."

Summations must be constructed of simple declarative statements, the best conveyor belt for tightly reasoned argument. But there is also the exclamation point of exhortation:

"You have a chance in this case to give a clarion call to the world . . . to make an award of punitive damages in several million dollars, of compensatory damage over a million dollars.

"It doesn't matter whether it can be collected or not. Let the word go out that this sort of thing must stop. Give by your verdict a clear answer to the kind of un-Americanism which this case represents. Aren't we free people?"

We reviewed the Everett Sloane incident; his securing a

letter from a governmental agency attesting to his loyalty and Aware's Mr. Milton finding this inadequate. We read the letter and suggested, "If you want this in the jury room, it's Exhibit 103"—where there are hundreds of exhibits it is useful to have the jury concentrate on a few by number. Psychologically, memory is aided by unusual numbers. Perhaps that is why advertisers frequently refer to some ingredient in the product as K34, or G97. The mind is surprised by a number which has no logical pertinence, and therefore pauses over it, resulting in concentration which aids recall.

The court declared a ten-minute recess. There was the recognizable incoherent noise of sudden comments and shuffling of feet as hundreds of people rose from their seats to stretch and walk out, usually to smoke. Not being enslaved by cigarettes, I never leave the courtroom to be subjected to the good wishes and other observations by well-intentioned spectators or friends. Rather, I sit at counsel table, usually alone, to sip some water, and calmly review the notes for the next hour or two of argument. Little did any of us anticipate that the next recess would be accompanied by a crisis greater than any we had faced in the entire trial.

The jury returned. We stood again as the judge mounted the bench. Then we continued the process of recapturing the scenes of the trial.

We reached Hartnett's wrong identification of Mrs. Sofer as Mrs. Faulk.

"You remember there was a burst of laughter despite the court's admonition that this court must be conducted with the dignity it deserves. You couldn't help it. I think the jury laughed too. Laughter with embarrassment. Here is this great identifier who didn't even know who Mrs. Faulk was, who has been sitting here for all this time.

"He was like a man who had cancer. He was doomed to die in a year . . . and Mr. Bolan says, 'But wasn't he living during that year?'"

We review the seven charges in the *Bulletin* to arouse the jury to their horrendous falsity, and we hover for an extra moment over the accusation that Faulk appeared at a function with a "Communist," but not revealing it was a United Nations Anniversary Dinner. We cite as an analogy an accusation against a man for appearing at a function with an editor of

Pravda, the official Communist newspaper, without revealing that the occasion was a presidential press conference.

We read Hartnett's letter to Johnson gloating that an actor, Win Stracke, had been removed from Borden's television program, but admonishing Johnson,

"You can't print this; you will understand why, but I think you fellows should know."

"You can't print it. See, they have slaughtered somebody . . . so please don't print it, we may be sued and the fellow doesn't know who did it to him. . . . Lord knows where he is, in what Austin, Texas he is living today."

We refer to this letter as "an ugly exhibit, No. 135."

"When you are in the jury room ask for 135."

We remind the jury that Faulk presented nine witnesses who testified to Johnson's blacklisting activities, but that the defense had none. Even Johnson didn't deny the charges.

"Whether he is sick or not, let's make this clear, ladies and gentlemen, . . . a man cannot answer charges by not appearing. . . . The only question is whether there is an inference to be drawn from his not appearing."

I relate G. K. Chesterton's observation that when a man has something unimportant to do like building a bridge, he calls in a trained individual, but when he has a really important function to perform like doing justice between disputants, he relies on twelve people, with common sense.

"After all, isn't that what the founder of Christianity did? He gathered twelve around him."

The clock showed 3:30 P.M. It was time for a recess so that the jurors could rest their ears, and thus sharpen their attentiveness. So we drove toward a climactic conclusion of the Johnson issue.

"There is one point . . . which entitles you to draw an inference against Mr. Johnson's failure to appear. No court is heartless, least of all this court.

"You go into any court and say, . . . 'I have a witness here, and he has a heart condition. . . . May I ask that whenever he wishes a recess, he have it and that he doesn't testify for more than an hour or half-hour?'

"The court grants that. There is no reason why not. And if I knew that he had an esophagus [condition], all I might want to do is show him some letters and ask him if he signed them. He might have had the easiest time in the world.

"But he didn't want to be here to identify those letters. This was a plain pretense. This man who drives a car and can do everything else could have testified here, but like all bullies, they are also cowards.

"He had this esophagus condition ten years ago, and five and six years ago when he was crushing Mr. Faulk.

"The only trouble with him inside, is guts, not the esophagus, and he should have appeared here and defended himself and he didn't have the guts to do it. There is nothing the matter with his esophagus.

"May I have a recess at this time?"

THE COURT: Yes, I think so. We will reconvene soon.

At this precise moment, as I turned to sit down at counsel table, a young lady rushed into the inner enclosure, with haste which was heedless of collision, and with trembling hand thrust a note at Bolan. She blocked my path, so I stood still for a moment, though not without observing the anguish on her face which seemed to flow down her body and stiffen it with alarm.

Bolan opened the piece of paper and in an instant his face caught the color of its whiteness. He saw me standing there and without a word he handed me the note.

It read: "Laurence Johnson has just been found dead in a Bronx motel."

Had death intervened to destroy our case after all? Aside from our sympathy for Johnson's family, a host of question marks filled our heads. Would our claim against Johnson expire with him, and leave us with uncollectible judgments against the other defendants? Even worse, since we charged a conspiracy, and now one of the actors in it was dead, would there be a mistrial of the entire case? Could we afford to retry this case, either monetarily or emotionally? Could Faulk last through it again? Even if we could proceed with the trial against Hartnett and Aware Inc., what would be the reaction of the jury when it learned that Johnson, whom we belabored as a malingerer, had died while the accusation was still on our lips? Might sympathy for Johnson and resentment against us result in a defendants' verdict—or in a nominal one for the plaintiff?

Even the uncertainties of the bizarre situation in which we found ourselves could not agitate our spirits. We were stunned.

We asked for a conference with the judge in the robing room and passed the shocking report on to him. After expressing respectful regret which we all felt, for death is always too final an arbiter, he addressed himself to the immediate problem. First, could the information be kept from the jury, until we had determined the legal consequences? Reporters were summoned, but they had already telephoned their city desks. News, like a radio wave which travels around the world seven times in one second, cannot be recaptured. The judge dismissed the reporters with full understanding that they could not push the genie back into the bottle.

He took steps to verify the facts. Perhaps it was another Johnson who had died. After all, what would the Johnson of Syracuse be doing in a Bronx motel? Captain Fox, the chief of the court attendants, was summoned, and the judge also called Captain Gross of the Appellate Division to trace the facts through the Police Department. The report came back from Lieutenant Reagan that Laurence Johnson of 1202 Broad Street, Syracuse, New York (the correct address of the defendant), "male, white, about seventy-three years of age," had been found dead at 9:00 A.M. of that morning at Town & Country Motor Lodge, 2244 Tillotson Avenue, Bronx, and been removed to Jacobi Morgue at 2:55 P.M.

The judge suggested that counsel should alert their research staffs by telephone to immediate study of what the proper legal course should be where one of the defendants dies during summation. Then he requested me to continue my summation, without, of course, revealing Johnson's death. Before the next recess, he and his law secretary Abe Spindel would study the Civil Practice Act, and other authorities.

So counsel filed back into court again. The jury returned, apparently refreshed from its stretch, and oblivious to the tremors in the air which Johnson's death had caused.

Again there were three knocks on the door, democracy's substitute for bugles, to announce that the judge was entering. He climbed the few steps to his pulpit, more slowly as if he were weighed down by inner thought. Then he nodded, and like the wave of a conductor's wand, all who had risen on his entry, sat down. The tension in the huge, overpopulated courtroom was like a silent buzz of the terrible news which had flashed through the corridors and enveloped the spectators.

Despite this tragedy, the summation still had to be finished.

All trial lawyers must have a little of Pagliacci's blood in them. For they are called upon to present an exterior so different from the turbulence within them. How pleasant it would be if performance of duty was its own reward, not complicated by inner conflicts. Often, however, we are compelled to function on two levels, suppressing the distress within us, as if it were a corner of darkness which couldn't be lit.

No man or woman can escape such a predicament at some time in life. The death of a loved one, or some other disaster, lies like an unbearable mass within us, felt whether asleep or awake. Yet, we must exercise the highest courage of all, the courage to rise despite the oppressive weight and move lightly as of old. Those who have not the strength to do so are dragged down by their burden into an abyss where suffering is escaped through the surrender of all feeling.

So, knowing that after all the years of preparation and ten weeks of trial, we had at the very last moment received what was almost certain to be a mortal blow, it was necessary nevertheless to continue the argument with the same intensity as before, lest the jury detect in the flagging spirit, disheartened voice, tired movements, or unlit eyes, a discouraging turn of events.

I point to the words engraved in gold on the walnut panel behind the judge's seat, "In God We Trust," and describe the accidental receipt by Faulk of a letter not intended for him which revealed the real reason he wasn't hired.

"So we have the three letters. Exhibits 59, 60, and 61. When you go into the jury room, maybe you want to read these letters from the Don Lee Broadcasting Company. . . ."

More pleas to the jury. A furrowed brow here and there indicates the need for another recess. The court grants it. We rest for ten minutes. The weight within us is unlightened, but its gravitational pull on our spirits seems less because of the momentum of the continued argument.

We quote from the testimony of the eight experts. This only establishes loss of potential earnings.

"But the law in its wisdom says when somebody destroys your reputation, we leave it to the jury if there is malice to give another kind of damage. That is called punitive damages."

Exposition runs into argument, and argument runs into plea—and the hours are eaten up in the process.

THE COURT: Mr. Nizer . . . I want to call your attention to the fact that it is about twenty minutes after six.

MR. NIZER: I will finish in a few moments, Your Honor. I have overstepped the bounds in my zeal.

We describe the final stages of Faulk's distress, the dispossess notice by his landlord, the exhaustion of his pride in borrowing from friends, and the exhaustion of their generosity, his final trek to Austin and the pitiful advertising agency he conducts from his home.

"You cannot re-create his pain and anguish at a jury box. I have to leave it to your hearts. . . . There is no law that has ever been written that is as good as the law in your heart. . . . I will not go on with the rest of the terrible story of this man's ordeal, but now I place his life in your hands, very literally, because this man's reputation is either going to be restored by a verdict that will ring to the world, or he will be besmirched all over again.

"I leave to your hands the doing of full justice, and if you do that, ladies and gentlemen, you can sleep well because God will be awake."

Immediately after summation, the judge summoned us to his chambers, to struggle with the question of how Johnson's death would affect the proceedings. In the meantime, he concluded that the jury must not learn of the new development until joint research of counsel and the court through the night clarified the procedure to be taken the next morning. So he returned to the courtroom to make a startling announcement.

THE COURT: Members of the jury, for various reasons, and since this case has been on trial for—this is the eleventh week—I find it necessary . . . to send you to a hotel overnight. I know it is an inconvenience, but . . . I have given this consideration, and I have decided that that is the right thing to do.

Your families will be informed through the Clerk of the Court, who has your phone numbers, or if there is anyone else you want to have informed that you are not going to be home, you just let Mr. Hennigan know, and I will arrange for your families to be called.

At the hotel you will be provided with pajamas and a kit which will accommodate you, and as far as the ladies are concerned, we are providing, if you wish, a separate room for each of the ladies; and you gentlemen will be put up two in a room unless you feel strongly, any of you that you want a separate room, and that will be provided. . . .

You will not be able to have any magazines or newspapers at this point. . . .

In your rooms you will not use any radio or television; and you will abstain from talking directly or indirectly to any of the attendants about any phase of the case.

I will charge you tomorrow at two o'clock. You will be taken to the hotel by bus and you will return by bus under the supervision of the court officers. . . .

So the jury was locked up, while the litigants went home. But the lawyers and the judge voluntarily "put themselves up for the night" too. For there was no precedent for the situation in which we found ourselves, and legal research had to be completed before the next morning to deal with the novel problem.

The law is never more beautiful than when it is confronted with a new problem and it engages in the creative art of constructing a solution. The process of logical evolution is as exciting as the architecture which evolves. Like the natural law of color and prisms, which forms variable designs of unplanned, breathless beauty, the principles of logic and legal order will create an edifice combining symmetry with utility.

The following syllogistic blueprint was drawn to solve the problem of Johnson's death in the midst of trial. The Statute (Section 478 of the Civil Practice Act) provides that a verdict against a party who dies before it is rendered is void. Therefore, no verdict could be rendered against Laurence Johnson.

However, the law also provides (Section 118 of the Decedent Estate Law) that a cause of action for injury to a person (which, of course, includes a libel), may be brought against the executor or administrator of the person liable, even after he has died.

So, if Bolan's motion to sever the case against Johnson from that of Aware and Hartnett were granted, Faulk would have the right to institute a new suit against the administrator of Johnson's estate.

Why not, therefore, immediately substitute Johnson's administrator for Johnson as a defendant and permit the jury in the present case to render a verdict against the estate if it so chose? After all, the defense for Johnson had already been fully presented (though he chose not to appear), and his counsel had rested and had completed summation on his behalf. What sense would it make to put Johnson's estate and Faulk through a separate trial when all the evidence was already before the jury?

Therefore, it followed that Johnson's estate ought to be substituted for Johnson. But how? He had just died. His will had not been probated and there was no executor. An application for the appointment of an administrator to act for special purposes would ordinarily be made in the Surrogate Court in Syracuse. The jury could not be held during these delays.

However, cases were found to support the theory that the court over which Justice Geller presided was a court of general jurisdiction, which overlaps the jurisdiction of the Surrogate Court. Therefore, in his discretion he could act as a Surrogate where special circumstances required it.

Since Faulk was a claimant against the Johnson estate and a potential creditor, he could apply for the appointment of a temporary administrator to act for it.

The next morning, we submitted such a petition and a memorandum of law to support it. Justice Geller's research had led him to the same conclusion. He offered to designate Bolan or anyone he chose to act as administrator. Bolan refused, because he wished to preserve his objections to the entire procedure.

The court then signed letters of temporary administration and designated a reputable attorney, Harry G. Liese, to act as temporary administrator of Johnson's estate, to complete the trial and appeal, if necessary, but with a special provision that at any time a permanent executor was designated or administrator was appointed, Liese's authority would end. Liese was summoned immediately and accepted his duties, by signing the customary oath and filing his designation.

The court signed an order substituting the estate of Laurence Johnson in place of the deceased Laurence Johnson as a defendant.

So Johnson remained in the suit, through his estate. Even his death had not eliminated his liability or destroyed the litigation. Faulk's rights had been preserved. Although we had barely escaped disaster, and breathed with relief at the last-second reprieve, the solution was formal rather than psychological. We still faced the jeopardy of the jury's sympathy for Johnson.

Two additions were made to the structure erected by the court, one over our firm protest. The judge advised us that he would instruct the jury that no punitive damages could be granted against the Johnson estate. This was in accordance with law. Dead men cannot be deterred by punitive damages from repeating the offense.

Second, as a matter of personal discretion, the judge required us to agree not to try to collect upon any judgment which Faulk might recover, not only from the Johnson estate but from Aware Inc., and Hartnett until October 1, when the Appellate Court would be in session. The court felt that the remedy it had adopted was so unique, that the rights of all defendants to test it on appeal should be facilitated. We consented, only when it was made clear that the judge would consider such a consent favorably to us in determining whether or not to grant Bolan's motion to sever the claim against Johnson from the rest of the suit.

The jurors returned from their hotel isolation, and undoubtedly looked forward to the judge's charge which might explain why they had been forbidden to hear or see a broadcast, or communicate with their own families, except through a court clerk. Obviously, some event had intervened and they were eager to have an answer to the mystery. They received it at once. The judge opened his charge with the announcement:

"Mr. Foreman, ladies and gentlemen of the jury:

"The court and the attorneys were informed late yesterday that the defendant Laurence A. Johnson had suddenly died that same day. That was the reason the court decided to have you stay at a hotel overnight, so that this sudden development could be verified and to determine in what way the trial or the proceedings were affected."

He instructed the jurors not to speculate concerning the cause of death. No one knew the facts at the time. It was weeks later that the results of an autopsy were received. Then we learned that Johnson had taken barbiturates, and while asleep, had suffered a vomiting attack. Being unable to awake, his vomit filled his lungs and he died from asphyxiation. We never learned why Johnson had driven from Syracuse to a motel in the Bronx; nor whether the barbiturates or some other cause had irritated his achalasia condition.

The judge instructed the jury concerning the principles of law which must govern their deliberations.

"This has been an unusually long trial, but it has been evident throughout that all of you have followed the testimony with patience and attention. . . .

"If my voice should happen to crack in the course of delivering . . . this charge, you will attribute it to very little sleep that we had overnight."

One of the glories of our system of jurisprudence is the device of the judge's charge. It is not only a legal education of the principles of applicable law, but it is a model of impartiality and inspiration to do justice without fear or favor, sympathy or prejudice. The very statement of these precepts, evolved through the centuries, is a tribute to the rule of reason, man's highest achievement in the struggle against his belligerent passions. But while many charges to a jury have become standardized, such as what is an interested witness, and how his interests affect his credibility, or what the burden of proof means and how it is to be measured, the law is an artistic enterprise and each judge may mold his charge in whatever way he can best achieve lucidity. Justice Geller's charge was a brilliant dissertation of the complex law of libel. He repeatedly created a balance between an instruction on a certain point, and an unintended inference which might be drawn from it.

"Simply disregard any colloquies between counsel or between counsel and the court, and confine yourselves to the evidence presented, and of course disregard any mannerisms of the court or counsel.

"My endeavors have been constantly directed to conduct a fair and orderly trial in keeping with the tradition of a court of justice. . . ."

He advised them that they must not try to guess his view of the facts, and if they think they know, to disregard it.

"It will be your recollection of the facts . . . which is to guide you in the deliberation."

After several hours, and a brief recess, the judge continued his charge on damages. Once more, there is the exquisite precaution of fairness.

"The fact that I lay down the rules as to damages is not to be taken by you as an indication of what I think your verdict should be. I am required by law to charge you with respect to damages in the event you find there should be a verdict for the plaintiff."

He explained that the law recognizes the difficulty of proving damages with arithmetical exactness in libel actions, "from the nature of things, where a person's reputation is involved." The jury's common sense and good judgment must govern.

He explained the theory of punitive damages. They "are intended to protect the community and to indicate public decency, even though they are awarded to the plaintiff."

In view of Johnson's death, he relieved the jury of the necessity of drawing or rejecting an inference from Johnson's failure to testify.

He urged them to try by legitimate arguments to reconcile differences of opinion so as to reach a unanimous verdict, but agreement by ten out of twelve constituted a valid verdict. Finally, at 5:35 P.M., he sent them forth on the great mission.

"Members of the jury, you may now retire and deliberate. . . ."

The jurors, flanked by guards, filed out. The judge disappeared into the robing room. As if a curtain had descended on the last act, the audience in the rear of the room rose and slowly wandered out, chatting about the proceedings with recovered detachment.

Faulk, who had taken the opportunity at any recess, to express his warm sentiments to his counsel, now chose this appropriate moment to seize our hands and tell us that no matter what the outcome, he was grateful, and that we had all fought the good fight together. We, in turn, expressed our feelings for him and held out hope that the jury would vindicate him. Then, terminating the sentiments, with a jest and a pat on his shoulder, we sent him forth into the corridor, where he was engulfed by a large group of friends and well-wishers.

Hartnett had also joined his friends and family on the other side of the courtroom doors. The stenographer and court attendants had retired. The arena was left solely to the lawyers. All but a few slouched in relaxed exhaustion in the chairs which they formerly occupied with straight-up dignity.

Assistants on both sides busied themselves filing voluminous records into folders, folders into large leather briefcases, and briefcases into the hands of delivery boys waiting to cart them down to a car for their last journey away from the courthouse.

Then the vigil began. Waiting for a jury verdict is the most painful aspect of a trial. No matter how taxing the contest itself may be, one can pit his energies against the assault; no one can summon up resources and resourcefulness for the mental struggle as well. But sitting helplessly while twelve men and women in an unapproachable room decide a client's fate is throbbing frustration. For some reason all thought runs downhill. The imagination constructs pictures of disaster and the mind conjures up the reasons for it; a witness's answer which hurt, a question which should not have been asked, a witness who should not have been called, an objection which should not have been made.

Another phenomenon during the vigil is that time increases anxiety. It is as if invisible wire ran from the jury room to electrodes on one's wrists and temples and the current increased as the seconds ticked away. Tension grows. Inner tremors become more violent. The heart beats faster. The forehead and palms grow moist. The mouth goes dry. As the hours roll by, the suffering from not knowing becomes more unbearable. The physical torment only reflects the mental anguish. Inner disciplines must be strengthened to withstand the strain. Prolonged uncertainty is the devil's most ingenious instrument of torture.

The first hour is the easiest. One cannot expect a jury to determine so quickly a case which took almost three months to try. Expecting no decision eases the exasperation of inactive pause.

At 6:15 P.M., we hear the steps of a court attendant so hasty that we know his approach is purposeful. He appears and asks, "Is counsel for both sides here?" This is the customary prelude to an announcement that the jury is returning. Our hearts leap and pull us to our feet. Is it possible that a verdict has been reached so soon? If so, it is a marvelous sign. Quick verdicts usually mean good verdicts for the plaintiff. Delay usually means difference of opinion about liability or amount. Someone sounds the alarm in the corridor and there is a rush into the courtroom with stampede speed. The judge arrives hastily. Then the clerk reads a note from the jury:

"Your Honor, Judge Geller: Please submit Exhibits 35, 53, 119 and 41. Also letters from CBS re Mr. Faulk's contract agreement with CBS."

There is a noise in the room not unlike that which escapes from a punctured balloon, in this instance, a balloon of anticipation. The jury's request is complied with and shortly thereafter, an attendant advises us that the jurors have gone to dinner and will return at 8:00 P.M.

We, too, go out to eat. Our regular table at Gassner's is not large enough for the friends and wives who need no longer be excluded from our working circle. So we occupy a long table in the center of the uncrowded room.

The chief conversation revolves around the exhibits requested by the jury. We play the number game avidly. The lawyers translate the numbers into the documents they represent. Exhibit 41 is the *Bulletin*. Naturally, the jury would want that key libel document. No inference can be drawn from this demand. Exhibit 35 is the letter sent by the local American Legion Post to Faulk's sponsor, Pabst Blue Ribbon Beer, condemning him as a Communist. Exhibit 53 is the program of the United Nations Anniversary Dinner, from which plaintiff had isolated the item that Faulk appeared on "a program" with a Communist singer. Exhibit 119 is the minutes of the meeting of Aware's Board of Directors, inviting Johnson, Neuser, and Dungey to attend and speak at the next regular meeting of Aware, when the *Bulletin* attacking Faulk would be adopted. We had asked the jury to remember some of these exhibit numbers. It was not difficult for my associates and even the laymen to draw optimistic inferences from the jury's concentration upon them. Hopeful portents flowed like wine to aid the digestive juices. If anyone had any illusion about the survival of our anxiety, however, it was dispelled by everyone's eagerness to be back in the courthouse punctually at eight o'clock, even though we knew that the jury's deliberation would only resume, not conclude, at that hour.

During the day, the Criminal Courts Building is a beehive of activity. Thousands of men and women mill around its marble corridors, and the many banks of elevators are jammed full as soon as their doors are opened. It is as difficult to get out of as to get into them.

It is a symbol of our complex society that institutions designed to take care of the troubled, whether they be hospitals or courts, are inadequate in size to accommodate them.

When we return to the building at 8:00 P.M., it is deserted. There is only one elevator to take us up to the twenty-third floor where our courtroom is situated. Here, too, the corridor is empty. The building seems asleep, and the distant whirr of a cleaning machine sounds like snores.

We began our vigil again, sometimes sitting at counsel table (as if it would speed the jury back, just because we were ready), sometimes pacing outside. Night has changed everything. Only a few lights near the courtroom are shining against dark backgrounds everywhere. Bathed by shadow and light, the walls take on different colors. The flat, even, electric light of daytime (there being no windows) permitted no shadows. But now as we wander aimlessly up and down, we are multiplied by dark replicas as if to substitute for the many not there. Hundreds of differently pitched sounds from elevators and groups huddled together in conference, to which we had become so accustomed during each court day, as to be unnoticeable, now are vividly absent. Instead, new individual sounds take their place. Every footstep echoes through the corridor, as if we were tap dancers with metal strips on our shoes. We look repeatedly at our wristwatches, always surprised that only a few minutes have elapsed since the last inspection. After what seems many hours, it is only 8:30 P.M. Then after an interminable wait, it is 9:00 P.M., then 9:30, 9:45, 10:00 P.M.—and no word from the jury. Faulk and his friends sidle up to inquire about the prospects, and we give them encouragement. After all, the jury has a huge mass of evidence to discuss and evaluate.

But our senses become sharper every moment. While we chat with friends, we sift all noises to hear the call of a court attendant, and watch the courtroom doors from a corner of our eyes.

It is 10:00 P.M.—no word. Many consultations with our watch tell us it is 10:15 P.M.

Then at 10:20 P.M., the light from the courtroom door does not blink casually. It comes in quick squirts. At the same time, foot sounds, no longer leisurely, are heard in rapid succession. We look eagerly, and our senses have anticipated correctly. A blue-coated attendant appears, his face tense, and he calls out, "All counsel, inside, please. The jury is returning!"

In a moment we are all at our places. I notice Faulk's face. He is pale, and he is looking up at the bench, still empty. The jury files in. We try to read their faces for the verdict. Some are flushed, and grim. Others tired. One or two catch our eyes and smile wanly.

Then the judge, who has been waiting in his chambers, mounts the bench.

THE COURT: The court has received a note from the jury which reads as follows . . .
"Your Honor, Judge Geller: The jury would like to have a clarification on the subject of awards for punitive damages. . . . Is the jury allowed to award more than amounts requested by the plaintiff? . . ."
I give you this answer in response to your question. . . . The jury should weigh carefully the requested amounts of punitive damages stated in summation by plaintiff's counsel although you are not bound by it; but in any event, and this I emphasize, the jury may not, because of Mr. Johnson's death, increase the amount of punitive damages which they would have awarded as against Aware Inc. or Hartnett; or in other words, in awarding punitive damages, fix such an amount as represents your estimate of the proper amount according to the degree of malice, intent, or recklessness of that particular defendant only; that is, Aware Inc. and Hartnett, with a separate award for punitive damages which may be the same or a different amount as you determine.

I am going to reread because I am afraid I may have read it a little bit too fast, and I want to be sure that you understood my answer to your question.

He repeated his answer slowly and with great emphasis. Hearing his reply a second time made us certain that the question had really been asked. Could they give us more than the two million dollars punitive damages we had asked for! Faulk was gazing at us for confirmation. We all had a puzzled rather than elated look on our faces. The message had entered our ears, but had not yet penetrated our understanding. Through the happy haze, we heard the judge continue:

"I hope this answers your question fully and clearly. . . . Mr. Foreman, does that answer your question?"

MR. FOREMAN: Yes, sir.

THE COURT: You may retire and continue your deliberations.

(The jury retired to continue deliberation at 10:30 P.M.)

In a moment spectators rushed into the inner conclave where we were seated, pounding the breath out of Faulk with congratulations, or breathlessly inquiring whether the portent was what it seemed to be. Faulk worked his way to me for confirmation of a verdict not yet rendered. We were all in a sea of satisfaction, but there was enough uncertainty to prevent unconfined joy. We tried to make adverse assumptions, simply to prepare against a possible letdown, for we could not stand another emotional shock. Perhaps the question meant that the jury was not allowing compensatory damages, and, therefore, wanted to know whether punitive damages could be increased beyond our request; or perhaps a juror had simply asked an academic question of law, and the jury wished to obtain an answer for him, in order to win his consent for a unanimous verdict. None of this made much sense, and we simply had to conclude that the augury for a great triumph for Faulk was real.

The gloom on the adversary side of the table confirmed this conclusion. In tropical regions, it sometimes rains on one side of the street, while the sun continues to shine on the other side. In courtrooms, the dividing line is much narrower, just the width of a table.

Lack of certainty gave a restless quality to our excitement. We moved in groups, up and down the corridors, in and out of the courtroom, with ever-increasing speed. We lunged rather than lounged as we waited. Our talk kept pace with our pulse, and everything around us seemed to become more feverish. At 11:00 P.M., a dozen people advised us of the time. At 11:15 P.M., they told us with their eyes. At 11:30, they gestured their concern. At 11:40, an attendant chased us down the corridor, yelling, "All counsel please return to the courtroom!" The rush for the courtroom made a bottleneck at the doors, which the attendant cleared away for Faulk and his lawyers.

The jury marched in energetically and in step as if accompanied by music. They sat rigidly facing the judge, who took his seat on the edge of his high-backed chair, still buttoning his robe. All our faces were turned toward the jury.

THE COURT: Proceed, Mr. Hannigan.

THE CLERK: Members of the jury, will the Foreman please rise.

Have you agreed upon a verdict?

THE FOREMAN: We, the jury have arrived at our decision in favor of Mr. Faulk. We have awarded the plaintiff, Mr. Faulk, compensatory damages in the sum of one million dollars against Aware Inc., Mr. Vincent Hartnett, and the estate of the late Mr. Laurence Johnson.

We have also awarded the plaintiff, Mr. Faulk, punitive damages in the sum of $1,250,000 against Aware Inc. and $1,250,000 against Mr. Hartnett.

There was an incoherent chorus of joy and pain from the rear of the room, punctuated by a few involuntary individualized outcries of astonishment.

THE CLERK: I will repeat your verdict. You say you find, with respect to compensatory damages, one million dollars against all three defendants.

THE FOREMAN: Right, sir.

THE CLERK: And you find with respect to punitive damages against Aware, Inc. $1,250,000 and against Vincent Hartnett $1,250,000.

Is your verdict unanimous?

THE FOREMAN: No, sir.

THE CLERK: What is it?

THE FOREMAN: Eleven to one.

MR. BOLAN: May the jury be polled, Your Honor?

THE COURT: Mr. Hannigan, poll the jury.

(The jury having been polled voted for the verdict as recorded by a vote of eleven to one.)

MR. BOLAN: Your Honor, I have some motions, but I assume they need not be made in the presence of the jury.

THE COURT: All right, then I will hear the motions outside the presence of the jury. . . . Before I do that, go ahead, Mr. Hannigan.

THE CLERK: The jurors having been polled they affirm the verdict as rendered.

THE COURT: Let the record so indicate.

Members of the jury, the court wants to express its deep appreciation for your patience and attention to your duties and responsibilities. . . . You have served forty-seven days and I know this has been a terrific infringement and impairment of your responsibilities. . . . An order will be entered, as . . . is permitted by law, for extra compensation.

There is a bus downstairs which is available to all you jurors . . . the bus will take you right to your door.

MR. NIZER: May we thank the jury, Your Honor, as they step out? It will just take a moment.

THE COURT: Yes, I will give counsel an opportunity if you choose to.

The warm, lingering grasp of the hand was the real communication with each juror, as formal words interlaced each other in mutual interruption. A number of jurors had tears in their eyes as they expressed their deep convictions. We observed that two jurors who were most emotional had during many stretches of the trial appeared languid and almost bored. Apparently, they were then trying to hide their real feelings, which now burst into unabashed emotional display. The one juror who had dissented explained that she didn't expect our gratitude because she just couldn't go along with so huge a verdict. We told her that we were nevertheless grateful for her careful attention to the case, and respected her right to hold any opinion her conscience dictated. Our farewell to her was no less warm and sincere than to the others.

Faulk stood behind us and also thanked each juror. He was so moved by their sentiments toward him that he too shed a tear, although he struggled to prevent it.

Bolan, with traditional dedication to duty, continued to make every legal move to protect his clients. With firm voice, which belied the pain in his face and eyes, he moved to set aside the verdict on the ground that "it was contrary to the evidence and law." The court immediately denied the motion.

However, his motion to set aside the verdict on the ground that it was excessive, met with a different reception. The judge asked both counsel to submit briefs on this point, and he would decide at a future date.

MR. NIZER: Your Honor, what I am about to say is more difficult to say because we represent the victorious party . . . but I want to express very earnestly on behalf of our client and counsel, and I hope I reflect the opinion of our learned friends on the other side, . . . our admiration for Your Honor's conduct of this most difficult trial.

THE COURT: Mr. Nizer, as a matter of courtesy, I didn't want to interrupt you. I appreciate your comments. The satisfaction I get is simply out of doing my judicial duty as I see my responsibility to be, and with that, it being after midnight, I will say good night to all you gentlemen.

The moment the judge and jury departed, Faulk rushed to me. Words of mutual regard had been spoken so often, that they had lost the impact needed for this special occasion. We embraced in a Gallic gesture of deep feeling and permitted the lingering silence to emphasize that which was not said. In turn, he thanked Martinson and Berger, in varying gestures, seizing their shoulders and pumping their hands. Then, his face somewhat contorted by his effort to avoid too gross a show of sentiment, he was almost carried out of the courtroom by his friends, who had shared his suffering through the years, and were now entitled to share his triumph.

In the corridor there was a general bubbling; here a cluster around a juror who was still there, because he was not taking the bus home; there a crowd around Faulk who was holding onto his pipe as if it was his link to normalcy. Other groups formed around counsel on both sides. Of course, it was easy to distinguish the defendant's groups from our own. They huddled in quiet, solemn, reflective postures. Ours exploded with laughter and jests.

But we who were most closely involved, showed no exhilaration. The fact was that we were all numb. Nature protects us from overexhaustion by rendering us unconscious through a fainting spell, and from too much emotional excitation by dulling our feelings.

I walked toward the telephone section and Vincent Hartnett emerged, almost colliding with me. We were face to face alone, and something had to be said. Before I could think of an ameliorating word, he began to speak. In a hollow, half-whispering voice, as if a holy man were pronouncing a prophecy, he intoned very slowly and emotionally, "We will appeal. Now, Mr. Nizer, it is all in God's hands!"

"What makes you think it hasn't been there all the time," I replied.

Laymen are often confused when they read that a judge has set aside or reduced a jury's verdict, even though the jury is supposed to be the final arbiter of the facts. There is no inconsistency. It becomes a question of law, whether there were enough facts in the record to warrant a particular verdict, or whether the award of damages bore some relationship to the evidence which was supposed to support it. In other words, the law provides a final safeguard to prevent a purely emotional verdict not founded on the minimum facts required to justify it. The judge may not substitute his judgment for that of the jury, but it is his duty to decide whether on the most favorable test, there was sufficient proof to support the verdict. This test is legal, not factual. If he finds in the negative, he may either dismiss the complaint before the matter is placed in the jury's hands, or await a verdict. If it is for the defendant, the judge's test has been recognized by the jury. If it is for the plaintiff, he may set it aside. An appellate court will decide whether his ruling, as a matter of law, was correct. On the same theory, he may reduce a verdict. This is the law's way of assuring litigants that they will not be victimized by passion or prejudice, and that the jury's verdict must bear a relationship to the evidence in the case.

The unprecedentedly high verdict of three and a half million dollars, a half million more than we ourselves had requested, therefore, posed a serious question of excessiveness. We awaited Justice Geller's decision with concern. It came.

"If the court were to hold the verdict excessive the usual practice would be to direct a new trial, unless the plaintiff consented to judgment in such reduced amount as the court would fix as the maximum allowable recovery.

"The fact that the amounts awarded are very large does not necessarily render the verdict excessive as a matter of law. The question is whether there is a rational basis for the jury's awards in the evidence adduced. . . . The court should not substitute its judgment for that of the jury, unless the amounts awarded are insupportable under any fair-minded view of the facts."

He pointed out that unlike injury to a limb, where the allowable damage becomes fairly standard, an injury to reputation and public esteem may not be measured as easily.

First, he analyzed the award of one million dollars against all three defendants, for compensatory damage. While Faulk's earnings had never exceeded $35,000 a year, his future earning capacity was much greater, according to experts, and the jury had a right to consider their opinions. They had testified that Faulk, in the blossoming television field, would have earned between $150,000 and $500,000 annually.

"Defendants offered no proof in contradiction of plaintiff's experts."

For a six-year period, Faulk's earnings could well have been $900,000, and in addition the jury could take into consideration "his mental anguish and distress . . ." The court acknowledged that the estimate of an actor's earning capacity during a period when he was prevented from performing involved "probabilities, not certainties." The jury had a rational basis for its compensatory award, and the defendants' motion to set it aside as excessive was therefore denied.

Then the judge turned to punitive damages. There must be proof of malice before such an award can be made.

"There was substantial evidence from which the jury could find malice, intent to injure plaintiff pursuant to a concerted conspiracy. . . . The jury could have determined that . . . the attack upon Faulk was not an isolated instance, but was deliberately prepared to end his broadcasting career, to remove his opposition . . . to the blacklisting practices which these defendants were directly interested in having continued, and to make an example of him."

The court referred to the evidence that Hartnett had increased his earnings from his occupation as a paid "consultant," and that he had "acted dictatorially and exerted pressure in blacklisting all categories of personnel in the industry, indiscriminately and without any reason being given to persons whose livelihood was thereby placed in jeopardy."

"The jury could also have concluded . . . that Aware Inc. was an instrumentality of the group which exerted pressure on the industry to induce the blacklisting of personnel; that it had interfered in and dominated AFTRA for many years; and that its practices indicated a reckless disregard of the rights of others and an abuse of the right of free speech and press."

So the court concluded the jury was justified in awarding substantial punitive damages.

"The only question is as to the amount. Obviously, there can be no standard for measuring punitive damages. It is only when the award is clearly disproportionate to the offense that a jury's assessment is subject to review."

The jury's function in assessing punitive damages is "to vindicate public decency." In evaluating the offense to public decency, the judge stressed the importance of having closely observed the witnesses and obtained the full impact during a long trial of the defendants' designs and practices upon the radio and television industry and their effect upon the livelihoods of many persons.

Then he reached a crescendo in his opinion.

"This unprecedented award was evidently intended to express the conscience of the community, represented by this jury, composed of men and women of different walks of life, varied educational backgrounds and economic status, concerning a matter of fundamental rights deemed of great importance to the general public and to the country. On such an issue I believe that a jury's composite assessment more accurately reflects the sense of decency and moral values of the community than the estimate of an individual judge."

Citing a leading case, he expressed in a few eloquent sentences the principle which had inspired Faulk through all the years of his embattlement.

"It seems to the Court that it was the jury's purpose that this large award, even if it were not collectible, should stand as a warning to others who might otherwise be prompted, from indulging in similar conduct in the future. . . .

"In libel suits, . . . punitive damages have always been permitted in the discretion of the jury. The assessment of a penalty involves not only a consideration of the nature and degree of the offense, but the higher moral consideration that it may serve as a deterrent to antisocial practices where the public welfare is involved. The jury, representing the community, assesses such a penalty as, in its view, is adequate to stop the practices of defendants and others having similar designs."

The court refused to interfere with the assessment of punitive damages. So the judgment stood in its entirety.

The attorneys for the Johnson estate began settlement conferences. Our hopes had been high that at least this defendant was financially responsible for the one-million-dollar compensatory damages assessed against it. However, its attorneys, Lawrence Sovik and Harlow B. Ansell, demonstrated in good faith that the net assets were not worth a fraction of such a sum. All books and records were submitted to us for full inspection, and they confirmed the fact that the assets were not undervalued. Under these circumstances, a settlement of $175,000 was accepted and paid.

The gap between a man's reputed wealth and the true facts is an oft-repeated experience. As if to build a reason for envy, we are inclined to assess people as millionaires who do not approach such status. Or is it because so many live affluently, without the permanent reserves to justify it? It is strange that in other areas, such as the evaluation of talent ability or generosity, the tendency is to shrink rather than enlarge, but when it comes to guessing a man's financial worth, we are eager to exaggerate. So the shock of Johnson's estate turning out to be a small one, despite the expectation of his "many millions," was not as great to the lawyers in the case as to others. For we have too often learned that our Croesus clients leave modest estates, and sometimes to the despair of the widow and family, virtually no assets at all.

Aware Inc. and Vincent Hartnett announced that they would appeal. Having been condemned for their activities, they now sought vindication in a reversal. Cutting down the verdict, no matter how substantially, would, of course, have no practical meaning, because they were judgment proof anyhow. They were determined to justify their investigative procedures as patriotic practice.

Even the cost of printing the eight thousand pages of the record, necessary to appeal, was beyond them, and they made a special application to the appellate court *in forma pauperis*, as it is called, to permit a photostatic copy of the minutes to be used. They retained Charles E. Henry to argue the appeal. He had been the attorney for the Hearst newspapers and Westbrook Pegler in the Quentin Reynolds trial. So another echo from the past reached our ears. The defendants prepared a sixty-two-page printed brief, and we a 117-page answering brief. We argued the appeal before the five judges of the Appellate Division. So the struggle continued, purified by the absence of any money motive.

After a customary interim period to allow the judges to

study the briefs and records, they handed down a lengthy written opinion. It was unanimous. Justice Benjamin J. Rabin wrote it on behalf of the court, composed of Justices Charles D. Breitel, presiding, James B. McNally, Samuel W. Eager, and Francis Bergan.

"The proof in support of the plaintiff's case was overwhelming. He conclusively established that the defendants planned to destroy his professional career through the use of the libelous publications directed to the places where they would do him the most harm. He proved that they succeeded in doing so."

The court not only found malice, but by its legal laboratory test, characterized it as being of the most virulent nature.

"The proof established that the libelous statements were not made recklessly but rather that they were made deliberately. The acts of the defendants were proven to be as malicious as they were vicious. The defendants were not content merely with publishing the libelous statements . . . knowing that injury to the plaintiff must follow such publication. They pursued the plaintiff with the libel making sure that its poison would be injected directly into the wellsprings of his professional and economic existence. They did so with deadly effect. He was professionally destroyed, his engagements were cancelled, and he could not gain employment in his field despite every effort on his part."

Thus, the court articulated the jurors' indignation which had been expressed only in money damages. It echoed Justice Geller's findings in support of the jury verdict. The appellants had sought vindication, but they received condemnation, and what condemnation! They heard themselves described as "malicious" and "vicious," of pursuing Faulk with libel "making sure that its poison would be injected directly into the wellsprings of his professional and economic existence."

Finally, the court summed up its view of the case with a sentence whose passion must have seared the defendants:

"So, we have, as found by the jury and amply supported by the evidence, a vicious libel, deliberately and maliciously planned and executed with devastating effect upon the plaintiff, all without a semblance of justification."

When the court turned to damages, it spoke with critical asperity.

"We are greatly concerned, however, with the size of the verdict—both as to compensatory and punitive damages. True, fixing the amount of damage is primarily in the province of the jury. . . . The court, if possible, should try to avoid invading that field. However, a court may not stand by idly when it is apparent that a verdict is shockingly excessive. A jury's verdict must have some relation to reality and it is the court's duty to keep it so. We find the verdict to be grossly excessive and most unrealistic—even in the field of entertainment."

The court pointed to Faulk's previous highest annual earning of only thirty-five thousand dollars, and although it allowed for his progress, it found that the testimony of the experts "left plenty of room for speculation."

"There is hardly enough justification for the finding of compensatory damages in the amount of one million dollars, even making allowance for his mental pain and suffering. It is interesting to note that at current savings bank interest rates, his yearly income for life would exceed the best of his past earnings. We believe that the compensatory damages should be fixed at a figure no higher than four hundred thousand dollars."

The court took a similar view of the award of punitive damages, stating that there are limits beyond which a jury should not be permitted to go. It was the court's duty to keep the verdict for punitive damages "within reasonable bounds." It held that award was "grossly excessive."

"The jury awarded the sum of $1,250,000 against each of the two appellants. However, one was more culpable than the other. They should not be punished alike. While Aware was a willing participant in the publication of the libel, Hartnett was the chief actor. It was Hartnett, rather than Aware, who stood to gain or lose depending upon whether the plaintiff was to be permitted to resist his activities or be silenced. . . . The assessment of punitive damages against him should be in a much greater amount than against Aware.

"It is our considered opinion that the maximum sum that should have been awarded against Aware, by way of punitive damages, is fifty thousand dollars, and as against Hartnett, who by far was the more guilty of the two, the sum of one hundred thousand dollars."

The court concluded that if Faulk accepted these modifications of damages, the judgment would be affirmed. Otherwise, the case would be sent back for a new trial because of excessive damages. Of course, we accepted the reduced verdict. The reduction did not affect the non-collectibility from Aware and Hartnett by one cent.

But Aware Inc. and Hartnett appealed to the highest State court even from the reduced judgment. This was quite understandable. The verbal lashing they had received from the Appellate Division exceeded by far the implied contempt expressed by the jury in its huge verdict. Whatever psychological balm they might have received from the reduction of damages, was overcome by the explicit description of their venal conduct, italicized by findings of deliberate malice, and self-aggrandizement. Blacklisting was found to permeate the industry and the judicial finger doomed it to oblivion, warning others of the legal fate which awaited them if they indulged in such un-American practice. Even the apportionment of punitive damages so as to place twice as much culpability on Hartnett as on Aware Inc. was a bitter blow to the defendants, for Hartnett was fighting to vindicate his personal integrity, and the corporation remained involved through his conduct anyhow. The finding that Hartnett was twice as guilty as Aware for purposes of punitive damages did not make either of them less guilty toward society.

The defendants must have regretted making an appeal at all. Even the jury's high verdict could not have been as painful to them as the castigation by five appellate judges. So, having sought review, and having been stamped evil, they had little choice but to appeal to the Court of Appeals in Albany. This they did. Once more they moved *in forma pauperis,* to be relieved of printing expenses. They obtained this courtesy and pressed forward with a new, extended legal brief, Once more Mr. Charles Henry and I clashed in a lengthy argument, this time before the seven judges of the highest court of New York State. This Court of Appeals courtroom is the most beautiful I have seen in the nation, including the United States Supreme Court. Its delicately carved yellow-pink oak wood, with an almost golden patina, gives grace and dignity to the judges' bench, the lawyers' tables, and the lectern. Opposite a wall of ceiling-high windows looking over a lawn near the Capitol Building, is a white marble fireplace, and surrounding the entire room are shallow niches, filled not with sculpture, but with unframed oil portraits of the judges who have glorified its past history. The effect is to make one conscious of the many jurists gazing down on the scene, and silently appraising the activities of the living.

We told the court that the only truly contestable issue should have been whether the jury's verdict of $3,500,000, which was fully supported by the trial judge, who had seen and heard the witnesses, should have been tampered with at all. Even though the matter was academic from a collection viewpoint, the clash between the jury's expression of public indignation and the legal test of excessiveness by the Appellate Division was worthy of analysis and consideration. However, we conceded that under the existing law we were precluded from testing this question because we had accepted the reduced verdict rather than proceed to a retrial. Perhaps some day the statute will be changed, so that if the defendants nevertheless appeal in such an instance the plaintiff may be permitted to cross-appeal to reinstate the original verdict.

As for the issues on the merits, we pointed to the overwhelming evidence which had led the Appellate Division to reject Mr. Henry's contentions in the court below.

Several weeks later the Court of Appeals, composed of Chief Judge Charles S. Desmond, and Judges Marvin R. Dye, Stanley H. Fuld, John Van Voorhis, Adrian P. Burke, and John F. Scileppi, unanimously affirmed the judgment of the Appellate Division. Judge Francis Bergan, who had participated in the Appellate Division decision before his elevation to the Court of Appeals, disqualified himself.

The defendants were determined to take the case to the United States Supreme Court. However, there was no federal issue involved. Dauntlessly, they moved in the Court of Appeals of New York for reargument, and in the alternative to amend the remittitur (record) to state that the court had considered a constitutional question.

The court denied reargument but did amend the remittitur to state that it had considered the possible privilege of the defendants under "the First and Fourteenth Amendments to the Constitution of the United States as interpreted in New York *Times v.* Sullivan [decided by the United States Supreme Court] and held that the appellants [Aware Inc. and Hartnett] enjoyed no such privilege under the Constitution of the United States."

Now the road was clear to apply to the United States Supreme Court for *certiorari*, that is, for permission to appeal the constitutional question. The Supreme Court of the United States denied the petition for *certiorari* by a vote of 7 to 2; Justices Black and Douglas dissenting.

Still the defendants would not quit. They filed a new petition for reargument in the Supreme Court on the novel ground that the libel law had developed from the ecclesiastical law of England and, therefore, violated the First Amendment to the Constitution, providing for separation of Church and State! This petition was unanimously denied.

The defendants had done Faulk the service of testing his grievance through all the appellate courts, and thus putting the stamp of vindication upon him of eleven jurors, and nineteen judges (the trial judge, five Appellate Division judges, six Court of Appeals judges, and seven justices of the Supreme Court). Blacklisting in radio and television stood condemned by every tribunal before which Faulk's cause had been argued.

One lone man had challenged the monstrously powerful forces of vigilanteism cloaked in super patriotism, operating by duress, selfishness, callousness, or confusion.

One lone man, with virtually no resources, had dragged the defendants into the courts, and though outrageously outnumbered, had withstood starvation and disgrace and summoned enough strength to battle them into submission.

One lone man had pitted his faith in American justice against the demagoguery of flag segment of American cultural life, just as they had for a while on its political life.

One lone man was so naïve in his profound patriotism that he did not conceive of himself as fighting a heroic battle, but simply as doing what any American would do, defy the bully, spit at his pretension, and preserve his faith in his country's Constitution and principles.

That one lone man is not the first American who has earned for us all our cherished liberties. Our history is dotted with similar unknown heroes, who fought the noble fight and handed down to us a heritage which we take for granted. Too often we are unaware of the source of our great legacies.

For example, today we enjoy the privilege of settling in any one of the fifty States of our country. It wasn't always so. To prevent poor people from transferring to prosperous territories, some States enacted statutes which made it a crime to bring an indigent person to live within its borders. Fred F. Edwards defied such a California law, and brought his unemployed brother-in-law, Frank Duncan from Texas, into California. He was indicted and fought his conviction to the United States Supreme Court, which declared the State law unconstitutional and held that a United States citizen had the right to settle in any State of the Union without restriction.

Who would recognize the name of a Chinese laundryman, Yick Wo? It was he who defied a California ordinance which made it unlawful to maintain a laundry in a wooden building without securing a license from the Board of Supervisors. He was tried criminally, and proved that two hundred Chinese laundrymen had applied for licenses and all had been refused, although licenses were freely granted to non-Chinese applicants. After his conviction was upheld by the highest court of California, Yick Wo appealed to the United States Supreme Court, which freed him. It held that a State in applying its law must not discriminate against citizens of particular races, creeds, or groups. To do so was a denial of equal protection of the law guaranteed by the Fourteenth Amendment of the Constitution. This decision in 1886 gave us the legacy which in our generation has made possible the successful defense of the rights of Negroes in many States of the Union. It is the spiritual father of our Civil Rights Law.

Father John A. Cummings, a Roman Catholic priest and teacher, refused to take a loyalty oath which the State of Maryland had enacted immediately after the Civil War. He was convicted, but the United States Supreme Court reversed, because such an oath was an interference with the right of conscience of the individual, insofar as it related to beliefs held by such individual in the past.

It was Father Cummings' victory which eighty years later was a bulwark for persons who for reasons of conscience refused to take loyalty oaths during the McCarthy period.

Edward C. Tittle, a barber in a Minnesota village, incurred the enmity of the local banker, who built a competing barber shop and drove him out of business. Tittle sued, claiming that the banker was not engaging in competition for proper business purpose, but in a brutal application of force. The highest court of Minnesota upheld him and ruled that "in a civilized society, men cannot always be allowed to use their own property as their desires may dictate without reference to the fact that they have neighbors whose rights are as sacred as their own." Thus it was Edward C. Tittle who reached for the principle that use of wealth for malicious purpose may not always be justified by the doctrine of the sanctity of property rights—particularly where it offends human rights.

Grace Marsh and Arnold Tucker were members of Jehovah's Witnesses. On Saturday afternoons, she distributed magazines to her sect on the sidewalk of the only business block in an Alabama town. This street was company-owned, and she was arrested under an Alabama law for trespass.

Tucker distributed religious materials in a United States government-owned village in Texas. He too refused to leave the village on the ground of freedom of religion.

Both convictions were set aside by the United States Supreme Court, which held that "when we balance the constitutional rights of owners of property against those of the people to enjoy freedom of press and religion . . . the latter occupy a preferred position."

The genealogical line of the lone men who established the liberties we now consider "natural," traces back through the centuries. One Caious Canuleius, in 445 B.C., led the fight for the plebeians to have intermarriage rights with patricians. His victory was not even glorified in the generations which immediately succeeded him and which enjoyed the democratization of Rome, largely through his act.

In the pantheon where these lone men are honored, their names and faces are blurred. Perhaps this tradition will be abandoned. Then we will be able to discern the newest benefactor of our sacred rights.

His name is John Henry Faulk.